Adam Smith in Toulouse and Occitania

Alain Alcouffe • Philippe Massot-Bordenave

Adam Smith in Toulouse and Occitania

The Unknown Years

palgrave
macmillan

Alain Alcouffe
University Toulouse 1
Toulouse, France

Philippe Massot-Bordenave
Framespa Université Jean Jaurès
Toulouse, France

ISBN 978-3-030-46577-3 ISBN 978-3-030-46578-0 (eBook)
https://doi.org/10.1007/978-3-030-46578-0

Cover illustration: GL Archive / Alamy Stock Photo

This Palgrave Macmillan imprint is published by the registered company Springer Nature Switzerland AG.
The registered company address is: Gewerbestrasse 11, 6330 Cham, Switzerland

Foreword

The period that Adam Smith spent in Toulouse is one of the most intriguing mysteries of his uneventful life. Smith arrived in Paris in February 1764, settled in Toulouse as tutor to the young Duke of Buccleuch, visited Bordeaux and Geneva, returned to Paris in 1766, and was back in Scotland in 1767. It was his only trip outside the British Isles and the moment when he started to write *An Inquiry into the Nature and Causes of the Wealth of Nations.*

This volume is the first extended study of Smith in Toulouse. It suggests intriguing questions about Smith's life and work and leads the historian, irresistibly, into further inquiries. This is an important episode in the history of economic thought and in European history.

"The Life which I led at Glasgow was a pleasurable, dissipated life in comparison of that which I lead here at Present," Smith wrote to David Hume from Toulouse in July 1764; "I have begun writing a book in order to pass away the time." This is the celebrated first reference to *The Wealth of Nations* in Smith's correspondence (or elsewhere), and Smith's economic writings were formed, in multiple respects, by his experience in France.

The influence of the French économistes or physiocrats on Smith's thought was the subject of intense interest in the years following Smith's death in 1790. The influence of French circumstances—and of Smith's observation of the changing economic life of Toulouse and Bordeaux—is less familiar and even more intriguing. *The Wealth of Nations* is full of curious facts, and Smith was evidently an inquisitive, perceptive traveller. Jean-Baptiste Say described these "pieces of positive knowledge" as "lacking in interest for anyone other than the English". But for Smith's English critics, *The Wealth of Nations* was almost French. As the first Professor of Political Economy at the University of Cambridge wrote in his copy of an annotated edition of the work, in relation to the regulation of consumer goods, "Dr S. is speaking of Europe in general, not of Gr.Br. in particular."

The society that Smith eventually found in Toulouse—and that seems, from his subsequent correspondence, to have been even more agreeable than life in Glasgow—was profoundly European. He formed a lasting friendship with a Danish-Norwegian scholar, Andreas Holt, and Holt's two students. His closest friend, Colbert de Castle-Hill, was a French bishop, born in Scotland. There were travellers passing by en route to Spain and Italy, as Laurence Sterne recounted a few months before Smith arrived.

Toulouse was "the cosmopolitan city", in the expression of a modern historian, and it was European—and American—in its economic connections. Smith set out for France in the aftermath of the Seven Years' War, at a time when David Hume was employed at the British Embassy in Paris in the commercial negotiations that were to shape the post-war world. The Duc de Choiseul, from whom Smith anticipated letters of introduction, was minister for the navy and colonies. He was married to the heiress of the Crozat dynasty from Toulouse, who had made their fortunes in a dizzying sequence of overseas ventures, in the semi-political semi-mercantile world of regulated commerce: the expeditions of the Compagnie des Indes to the Bay of Bengal; the Asiento, or the right to supply the Spanish Empire in the Americas with African slaves; the company of Saint-Domingue (the modern Haiti); the Louisiana company; the Levantine trade.

The young Danish-Norwegian gentlemen whom Smith met in Toulouse were destined for a life in worldwide commerce; one became a director of the Danish Asiatic Company, and the other became governor of the Danish colony of Tranquebar in South India. Andreas Holt was later an official of the Danish commercial college at a time of frantic reform in Danish overseas commerce, with a new charter of the Asiatic Company, in 1772, and a period of almost entirely free trade to India, overseen by the college. It was to Holt, in 1780, that Smith sent one of the very few autobiographical letters that he ever wrote, and his most concise summary of *The Wealth of Nations*: "the very violent attack I had made upon the whole commercial system of Great Britain."

The story of Smith's time in Toulouse will inspire future inquiries (and future expeditions into the notarial acts of the *archives départementales* of the Haute-Garonne.) It shows that the years in France were of formative importance for *The Wealth of Nations*, and for Smith's own tolerant, inquiring, cosmopolitan, and European life.

Harvard University, MA, USA Emma Rothschild

Preface

In his book *Adam Smith and the Scotland of His Time*, Professor Fay begins his chapter devoted to Toulouse by reproducing the reply received from the Toulouse municipal archives on December 28, 1951:

> I unfortunately found no mention of Adam Smith's passage in Toulouse in local sources. I have fruitlessly consulted the registers of the capitular deliberations, which relate many receptions, *the history of Toulouse* of the abbé Aragon and that of Ramet. I relied more on *Toulouse in the eighteenth century*, by Lamouzèle, based on Pierre Barthès' *Heures perdues'[Lost Hours]*, but I found nothing in this work or in Barthès' manuscript either. I only learned that a group of rich English people regularly frequented our city after the peace of Paris in 1763. It was they who organised the first horse race in Toulouse on 25 June 1765. Did they receive Smith and the Duke of Buccleuch in 1764–1765? I cannot say for sure.
>
> I regret the failure of my research, and ask you, Mr Rector, to accept the expression of my devoted feelings. [in French in Fay, p. 146]

A decade later, in his history of economic theories course, Professor Cluseau, director of the Toulouse Business School, did not fail to point out to his students Adam Smith's visit two centuries earlier, without providing details, and for good reason. Since then I have often searched, without finding them in the archives and histories of Toulouse, for traces of Smith's passage on the banks of the Garonne. Apparently all the scholarship devoted to the father of modern political economy could not remedy the destruction of all his personal papers, which Smith had demanded from his most loyal friends before he died. Tracing our traveller's stay is a challenge because no travel diary has been found, despite the fact the Duke would keep one when he resumed his tour, curtailed in 1766 following the death of his brother. As for Smith, at the end of his life, he insisted to his faithful friends that all his papers be burned. Thus only 193 letters written by him and 129 addressed to him remain. The majority of them date from the latter part of his life, after the publication of the *Wealth of Nations*, and only a few date from the period of the journey. One may wonder why this destruction took place—was he afraid that the revelation of certain letters might have been embarrassing?—or did he simply agree with Voltaire's remark about Pierre Bayle that "the life of a sedentary writer is in his writings"? In any case, we find this aversion to "lives" in the letter addressed to David Hume's editor, who was preparing to publish his friend's correspondence. Smith deplored the fact that unscrupulous booksellers "would immediately set about rummaging through the cabinets of all those who had ever received a scrap of paper from him. Many things would be published not fit to see the light, to the great mortification of all those who wish his memory well" (Letter of December 2, 1776).

This destruction of Smith's papers and the absence of a travel diary from his student explain why Smith's biographies do not abound with information about his private life, such as can be found in the first, written in 1793 shortly after his death by Dugald Stewart, who had the advantage of having been close to both Smith and witnesses to his life (Smith-Stewart 1795).

With respect to the years 1764–1765, John Rae deserves praises for having identified already Abbé Colbert as Smith's guide but his biography remains very elliptical (Rae 1895), as was Edward Cannan's critical edition, published in 1904, or the biography by Francis Hirst, the publisher of *The Economist*. In the twentieth century, the second centenary of *the Wealth of Nations* saw the launch of a new edition of the *Complete Works* and multiple studies of Smith's writings. More recently two great biographies by Ian Simpson Ross (2004) 2010 and Nicholas Phillipson (2010) have synthesized two centuries of Smithian studies without bringing new insights on the great economist's only travel.

So when Philippe Massot came to suggest that I supervise his thesis devoted to Smith's stay in the continent, I warned him against the difficulty of finding sources. Otherwise, there is a risk of producing what Walter Scott in *Waverley*, his novel about eighteenth-century Scotland, noted about French literature, which, according to him, provides "an endless collection of memoirs that are hardly more truthful than novels and novels so well written that it is difficult to distinguish them from memoirs" (Scott, p. 16). In the absence of an autobiography or travel diary, Rae's approach had consisted in gleaning through the eyes of the third parties with whom Smith and his pupil had been in contact, indications of the deeds of the two travellers coming from the Scottish Enlightenment to visit the city then so despised by Voltaire, since the visit took place one year after the execution of Calas and ended shortly after his rehabilitation. Two directions were pursued: first, the path followed by Rae could be extended by further investigation into the people Smith met and expanding this network to include more people. Another way was to find in Smith's work "the things seen" during his journey. Pierre Barthès' *Lost Hours* is an inexhaustible source of daily information on what was happening in Toulouse from December 1737 to December 1780 and an obligatory point of passage when dealing with Toulouse in the eighteenth century. Certainly these are the "notable" events as seen by a poor tutor of Esquile College, whom Smith and the Duke must have met in the Rue des Lois, a street leading to both the College and the Faculty of Law. Born in 1704 into a family of craftsmen, it was probably a scholarship that allowed Barthès to study at the College run by the Jesuits, towards whom he shows great deference. In September 1763, he had lost his second wife, and with the death of many of his children, "he remained almost alone and his already rather difficult character became increasingly bitter" (Lamazouelle, p. 10). Utterly deferential to both throne and altar, his xenophobia as well as his intolerance demonstrates a virulent opposition to the ideas of the Enlightenment. This view from the other side is no less interesting in making us feel the atmosphere of Toulouse.

In the recurrent debate on the boundaries between the real and the imaginary, between history and fiction, we are well aware of their porosity, all the more so as we seek to give an account of reality (the impressions of a visit) largely through texts (letters and books) which are most often representations. The rapprochements between Smith's works and eighteenth-century Occitania are also an intellectual construction. Thus this book which intends to account for the visit of two tourists is doubly in line with Gaston Bachelard's injunction: "We can only study what we first dreamed" (Bachelard 1949, p. 32).

We will therefore first enter Adam Smith's and his student's minds by imagining from rather weak clues what a professor who has broken away from university and a young Lord leaving the family circle could expect from their Grand Tour (Chap. 1). Reaching their Toulouse residence was already no easy task, and the trip was an opportunity to confront the two European capitals of the eighteenth century, while in Toulouse there awaited their future guide, the Abbé Colbert, a Scottish compatriot (Chap. 2). Toulouse was then the centre of attention of the Europe of Enlightenment, because it unfortunately symbolized intolerance, following the punishment meted out to the unfortunate Jean Calas. This case did arouse the interest of Smith who met many of its protagonists, but the city also had other elements likely to attract attention (Chap. 3). The Parisian salons were not the only places where it was fashionable to appear, and Bagnères-de-Bigorre, a hundred miles from Toulouse, not only attracted the best company from Toulouse and Bordeaux in the summer, but also became an annex to the Parisian salons. The two tourists could not avoid going there, as well as to Bordeaux during the summer of 1764 (Chap. 4). But just as in twenty-first century Occitania, the institutions of the Languedoc were divided between Toulouse and Montpellier and Smith did not fail to show the Duke the functioning of what most resembled a deliberative assembly, the States of Languedoc, a journey which also made it possible to evaluate and view the realization of the Languedoc canal, which had impressed Europe (Chap. 5).

Toulouse, France — Alain Alcouffe

References

Bachelard, Gaston. 1949. *La psychanalyse du feu*. Paris: Gallimard.

Phillipson, Nicholas. 2010. *An enlightened life*. London: Allen Lane.

Rae, John. 1895. *Life of Adam Smith*. London: MacMillan.

Ross, Ian Simpson. 2010 [2004]. *The life of Adam Smith*. Oxford: Oxford University Press.

General Timeline of Smith's Travels in France

June 5, 1723	Baptism of Adam Smith at Kirkcaldy, Scotland.
September 2, 1746	Birth in London of Henry Scott, future Duke of Buccleuch.
February 1759	Publication in London and Edinburgh of *Theory of Moral Sentiments* by Adam Smith.
August 1759	First contact between Adam Smith, professor at the University of Glasgow and Count Townshend, Lady Dalkeith's second husband and tutor to the young aristocrat.
February 1763	Signing of the Treaty of Paris ending the Seven Years' War between France and England. David Hume arrives in Paris as embassy secretary in charge responsible for the exchange of English prisoners.
December 1763	Fast preparations for departure, Smith is in London. He has not yet resigned from his teaching post in Glasgow.
February 1764	Smith arrives in Paris for a first stay of a few days, Smith's official letter of resignation.
March 3, 1764	Arrival of Smith in Toulouse. No one is there to receive newcomers, disappointment.
Mid-March 1764	Meeting with Abbé Colbert, the travelling companion who soon became indispensable.
April–July 1764	Stay in Toulouse, the young student attends the University of Toulouse.
Mid-July	Departure for Bordeaux, stay in the capital of Guyenne and meeting with the Duke of Richelieu, encounter with Colonel Barré
Mid-August 1764	Departure for Bagnères-de-Bigorre, holiday, games, walks.
September 1764	Return to Toulouse with Colonel Barré.
October 1764	Second visit to Bordeaux to find the Duke's brother.
November 1764–January 1765	Stay in Montpellier and follow-up of the Languedoc states, note taking, meeting with John Holker.

January 1765	Second stay in Toulouse, various holidays in the Toulouse region.
October 1765	Departure for Ferney and Geneva, more than probably several meetings with Voltaire.
December 1765	Arrival in Paris, David Hume is still present for a few more days, meeting with J.-J. Rousseau.
January 1766	Rousseau and David Hume leave for England.
January–February 1766	Experience of Salon life with Horace Walpole and encounters with the principal French philosophers, Helvétius, Holbach, Morellet, Diderot, d'Alembert, Turgot, the duchess of En-ville, the duke of La Rochefoucauld.
April 1766	Departure of Horace Walpole for London, he will return only in September.
June 1766	Concert at the Conti's, in the presence of Mozart.
July 1766	Stay at Compiègne at the court of Louis XV. The young men hunt with the king.
August 1766	Sickness of the young Henry Scott, Adam Smith assiduously attends the physiocratic sect at Compiègne castle.
September 1766	Accident and illness of young Scott's brother, Adam Smith spends much time at his bedside.
October 1766	Death of the young Hew on the seventh and on the eleventh departure from Paris and return to England.
November 1766	Adam Smith stays in London, where he is commissioned by Charles Townshend as "chargé de mission".
July 1767	Death of Charles Townshend, Minister of Finance of the United Kingdom, who has just promulgated the Sugar Act, following a sudden illness.
May 1776	Publication of the *Wealth of Nations* in Glasgow and London.
July 1790	Death of Adam Smith.
January 1812	Death of Henry Scott, Third Duke of Buccleuch.

Acknowledgements

Many thanks are due to the Duke of Buccleuch and Queensbury for kindly granting the permission to use his ancestor's correspondence and family portraits. I am grateful to Marius Chevalier who convinced Philippe Massot to write a thesis and to participate to the conference Smith in Glasgow '09, where Andrew Skinner† encouraged the attempt, and to Jean-Michel Minovez who kindly enrolled him as a doctoral student and to all the members of the jury; Nick Phillipson†, Gilbert Larguier, Philippe Delvit, Michel Herland, not only for their remarks but also for having encouraged me to put the book back on the trade! Five years later, the content has been revised, pruned here, completed there, in short, considerably reworked. James S. Brennan, Edward Corp, Emmanuelle Chapron, Christine Riggle Ralph McLean, Crispin Powell have provided me with valuable information about the Abbé Colbert, Scottish genealogies, the library of the Scottish College, or Smith's library. Thanks to Christiane Alcouffe for all her help and multiple re-readings and to Marianne Lévy and Anne-Catherine Freyburger for their comments. I am thankful to Shubhangi Priya and Bhavyaa Sharma who helped me with the English version. In any event I will never be able to repay my debt to Andrew Moore who not only checked every word but also scrutinized the book for historical accuracy. Of course I remain responsible for the errors and mistakes that might remain.

Alain Alcouffe

Author's Note

Smith's two main works, *The Wealth of Nations* and *The Theory of Moral Sentiments*, have been so often cited that they are referred to by the acronyms *WN* and *TMS*. We have used throughout this book the Glasgow Bicentennial Edition of the *Works and Correspondence of Adam Smith*, sometimes referred to as the "Glasgow Edition". For Smith, we used the *Correspondence of Adam Smith* edited by E.C. Mossner and I.S. Ross in the Glasgow Edition. The letters are referred to by their number in the edition of Mossner & Ross. For Colbert's correspondence, in addition to the letters contained in the aforementioned works, we consulted the originals at the National Library of Scotland (MS 23154) and at the National Archives of Scotland (GD224/2040/62/3). As the letters from Colbert to Hume are in French they have been translated into English. The biographical information on Abbé Colbert is taken from the "Official Scottish Government website for researching government records and archives" (https://www.scotlandspeople.gov.uk/about-us). We have simplified the apparatus by giving for our references in the text only the name of the author and the page. The date appears only when we quote several works by the same author or a particular edition.

The usual disclaimer applies: the authors are solely responsible for any errors that may remain.

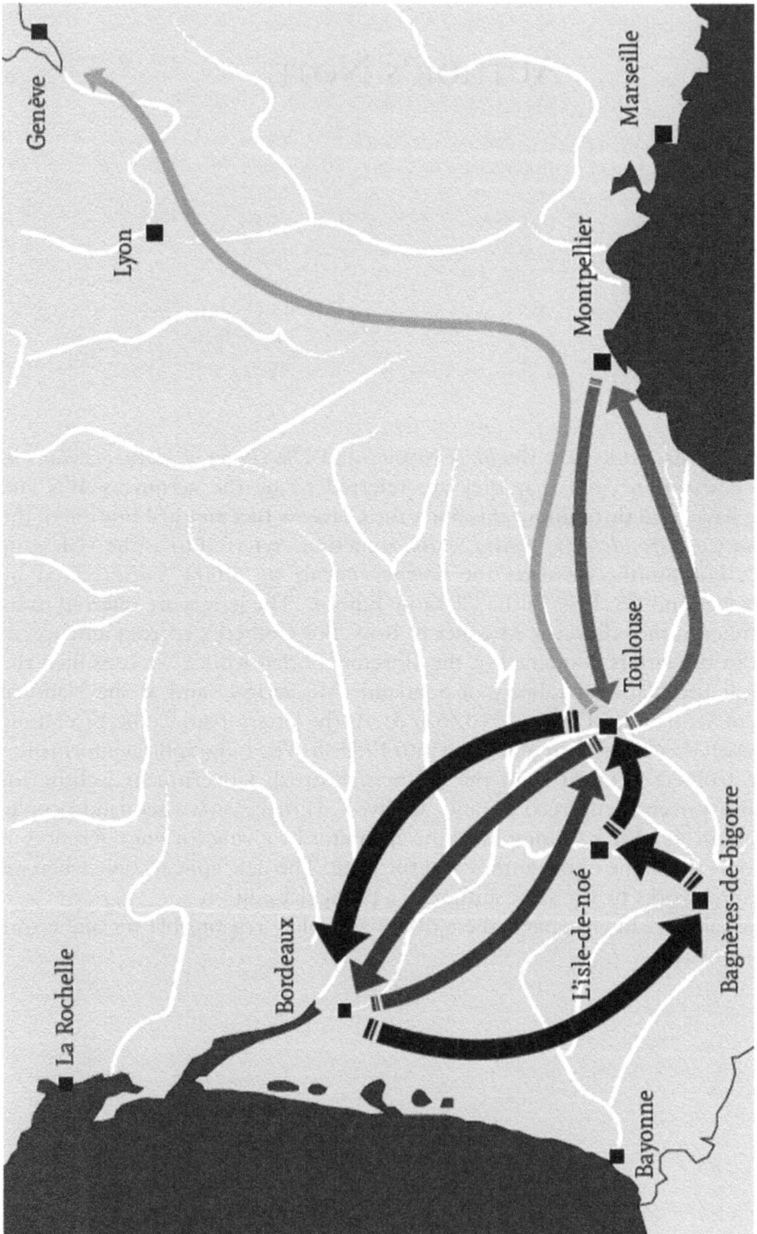
Genève
Lyon
Marseille
Montpellier
Toulouse
La Rochelle
Bordeaux
L'isle-de-noé
Bagnères-de-bigorre
Bayonne

1. Toulouse Bordeaux, July 1764
2. Bordeaux Bagnères de Bigorre, end of July 1764
3. Bagnères de Bigorre L'isle de Noé, August 1764
4. Toulouse Bordeaux round trip, September 1764
5. Toulouse Montpellier one way, November 1764
6. Montpellier Toulouse, end of December or January 1765
7. Toulouse Montpellier towards Ferney/Genève, October 1765

Contents

List of Figures

CHAPTER 1

Two Scottish Visitors

When Adam Smith arrived in Toulouse in March 1764, at the age of 40, he was not yet the "father of political economy" as he is now celebrated, following the publication in 1776 of his most famous work *The Wealth of Nations (WN)*. Yet he was already a recognized thinker of the Europe of the Enlightenment in which his native Scotland played a leading role. In 1759 he published his first book, *The Theory of Moral Sentiments* (*TMS*), which was a great success and drew attention to him, so that students from Switzerland as well as from Russia or Scandinavia benefited from his teachings at Glasgow University.

This fame was noticed by Charles Townshend (1725–1767), a British politician later to be Chancellor of the Exchequer from August 1766 to his death in September 1767. Townshend was at the time in full ascension both politically and in terms of personal success after his marriage to Caroline Campbell, eldest daughter of the second Duke of Argyll and widow of Francis, Lord Dalkeith, the eldest son of the second Duke of Buccleuch (1695–1751). Lady Dalkeith had six children. The death of her eldest son in 1749 had made her second son, Henry (1746–1812), at the age of 4, heir to the title of Duke of Buccleuch after the death of his grandfather in 1751. At the beginning of the 1760s, it was time to complete the education of the young aristocrat, and Charles Townshend envisaged a Grand Tour on the continent and in particular in France, Great Britain's principal rival power.

A. Alcouffe, P. Massot-Bordenave, *Adam Smith in Toulouse and Occitania*, https://doi.org/10.1007/978-3-030-46578-0_1

The Grand Tour, from the middle of the eighteenth century until the appearance of the railways, was considered a rite of passage to adulthood for the young people of the upper classes in Britain (as well as in Germany) in order to complete their training in the humanities and the courtly arts such as riding, fencing, music, and dance, but also to allow them to compare the political systems of Great Britain with those of the continental States. It also allowed them to forge ties with individuals of the same social background, promised similar diplomatic, military, political, or commercial future in other countries. The considerable means available to the families of young "tourists" enabled them to be provided with guides with combined duties of tutor, guardian, and chaperone. Naturally, in the case of the Duke of Buccleuch, who was of royal blood, the choice of the guide was much deliberated upon and was the subject of comments, not all of which were positive. Yet this journey would result in lasting ties between Smith and his student, which testified that both had benefited from the experience.

For Smith, whatever he might have said about the satisfaction he derived from his duties as a university professor, the Grand Tour was an opportunity to meet the French elite and particularly in Paris, the physiocrats, the first "economists". It gave him lasting financial stability and also an opportunity to establish close relations with Charles Townshend. Smith would use this visit to deepen his knowledge of economic and financial mechanisms, skills he would put at Townshend's service and which could have made him a valued adviser if Townshend's untimely death had not sent him back to his writing.

1.1 Adam Smith's Education

Adam Smith was born in June 1723 in the small town of Kirkcaldy, on the banks of the Forth estuary, a huge fjord that extends more than 30 kilometres inland, so that Scotland is shaped as an isthmus with the large cities of Glasgow and Edinburgh at either end. In the middle of the eighteenth century, the city was home to a large fleet that traded mainly with Europe and northern Scotland. But the local economy had suffered from the Anglo-Dutch wars and, after the Act of Union, from greater competition on foreign trade. According to the 1755 census made by Webster, the population of the parish had declined to 2296, despite the development of textile industries based around flax.

1.1.1 His Childhood World

In June 1723, when Adam Smith was born, his father had already been dead for five months. Born in 1679 in the port and university town of Aberdeen, 130 kilometres north of Kirkcaldy, in 1705 he became secretary to the new Secretary of State, Hugh Campbell, third Earl of Loudoun. The latter joined the Unionist side in the battle of Sheriffmuir in 1715, during the second great Jacobite rebellion. At the end of this indecisive battle, it is possible that he intervened in favour of the Jacobite prisoners. In 1707, Adam Smith Sr. became clerk to the Court Martial of Scotland, created to bring discipline to the Unionist troops through sanctions up to and including the death penalty. Smith was to refer to his father's military experience in a letter to his editor in 1760 while the *TMS* contains a reflection on capital punishment (*TMS* II. ii.3.11). In 1714 he became the customs controller at Kirkcaldy, a post which in 1723 gave him a substantial annual income of 300 pounds sterling. Curiously his son was to occupy the same positions at the end of his life.

In 1710, Adam Smith's father married Lilias Drummond, whose father, a prominent and wealthy politician, had represented Scotland during the negotiations in preparation of the Act of Union. The couple had given birth to a sickly son, Hugh, who was to die in 1749, and Adam would inherit from him. In 1720, Adam Smith's father was to remarry Margaret Douglas, again an advantageous and successful marriage. Margaret was 25 years old, and the granddaughter of Sir William Douglas of Kirkness, heir to the important family of the Earls of Morton. Margaret Smith was part of the local aristocracy in Fife County.

Adam Smith held on to documents from his father that he kept during his long years at the University of Glasgow. Amongst them is his story of a short stay in Bordeaux at the age of 19. As Adam Smith Sr. owned books written in the French language, he had obviously a certain interest in the French culture.

The childhood of the little orphan was on the whole peaceful, troubled by an incident, either real, or imagined as part of family lore. At the age of three or four, while at his maternal uncle's home in Strathendry (ten kilometres from Kirkcaldy), Adam Smith was reportedly abducted for a few hours by tinkers or gypsies, of which there was quite a large nomadic population in southern Scotland, before being recovered by his uncle. Since the same anecdote appears in the childhood of Charles Townshend, the Duke's father-in-law, it is undoubtedly representative of the prejudices regarding *gypsies* at the beginning of the eighteenth century.

Adam Smith attended Kirkcaldy School from 1731 to 1737. He had the good fortune of benefiting from the teachings of David Miller, a renowned school teacher whose teachings were based on classical authors. Adam Smith mastered them well enough to be exempted from a preparatory year when he arrived at the University of Glasgow. Smith would pay tribute to David Miller and this period of his life in Book V of the *WN*:

> The public can facilitate this acquisition by establishing in every parish or district a little school, where children may be taught for a reward so moderate that even a common labourer may afford it; the master being partly, but not wholly, paid by the public, because, if he was wholly, or even principally, paid by it, he would soon learn to neglect his business. In Scotland, the establishment of such parish schools has taught almost the whole common people to read, and a very great proportion of them to write and account. (*WN*, p. 785)

1.1.1.1 Smith, a Student in Glasgow

In 1738, at the age of 14, which was unexceptional in the eighteenth century, Smith entered the University of Glasgow. The choice of Glasgow may surprise since the University of Edinburgh was much more famous, and also geographically much closer to Kirkcaldy, but Smith did not regret this choice, and on November 16, 1787, when he had just been elected Rector of the university, he wrote in his letter of acceptance:

> No man can owe greater obligations to a Society than I do to the University of Glasgow. They educated me, they sent me to Oxford, soon after my return to Scotland they elected me one of their own members, and afterwards preferred me to another office, to which the abilities and Virtues of the never to be forgotten Dr. Hutcheson had given a superior degree of illustration. The period of thirteen years which I spent as a member of that society I remember as by far the most useful, and, therefore, as by far the happiest and most honourable period of my life; and now, after three and twenty years absence, to be remembered in so very agreeable manner by my old friends and Protectors gives me a heartfelt joy which I cannot easily express to you. (Letter Nr. 274)

Glasgow was a modest city compared to the large European cities (31,700 inhabitants in 1755). But Glasgow underwent an important transformation thanks to a growing trade, particularly in tobacco with the American colonies. It was while he was an instrument repairman at the University of Glasgow that James Watt (1736–1819) perfected the steam engine, making it a symbol of the industrial revolution. The University of Glasgow was only a small building on the high street, and Andrew Skinner counted only twelve professors in charge of teaching when Smith arrived there (Skinner 1982, pp. 17–18). Little is known about the material conditions in which Smith found himself during his three years of study at Glasgow, from 1737 to 1740; probably he boarded with a university professor as was common at the time. A few years later, when he himself became a professor, he engaged in this practice, which established a close relationship between students and professors, as is evident from the letters he exchanged with Lord Shelburne, an Irish aristocrat. On July 23, 1759, Smith detailed there, next to the registration fees, his costs for laundry and other minor expenses, traditional in the case of both just accommodation and full board.

A decisive encounter for Smith quickly occurred when he met Francis Hutcheson (1694–1746), one of the figures of the "Scottish Enlightenment" (Abitboul 2003, pp. 5–15). In December 1729 he had been chosen to fill the vacant chair of philosophy at the University of Glasgow by a majority vote, proof that the University was divided between conservatives and supporters of new ideas. Hutcheson had been prosecuted in 1728 by religious authorities:

> for teaching to his students in contravention to Westminster confession the following two erroneous and dangerous doctrines, first that the standard of moral goodness was the promotion of the happiness of others, and second that we could have knowledge of good and evil, without and before knowledge of God. (W.R. Scott 1900, p. 84)

Hutcheson's students mobilized and wrote a piece defending their master, who mocked this "grotesque buffoonery concerning his heresy". He counter-attacked during the subsequent years to drive out the supporters of traditional Presbyterianism in favour of the "New Light" (ibidem., p. 85 et seq.). Smith may have participated in these struggles while he was a student. Hutcheson also broke with tradition by teaching in English instead of Latin, and walking around the classroom instead of standing still at the lectern. He did not confine his teaching to the university but to disseminate his ideas he also taught free outside the institution, attracting important audiences. But it was above all the changes made by Hutcheson to the subjects taught and to the way they were articulated that proved to be the most important for Smith's career development and for the development of economics as a discipline.

In his works and teachings, Hutcheson made himself known through a critique of the conception of human nature as it is present in Hobbes (1588–1679), Bayle (1647–1706), and Mandeville (1670–1733), and to which he linked the *Maximes* of François de La Rochefoucauld (1613–1680). He rejected their conception of a human nature dominated by selfishness, solely directed towards the individual's own satisfaction and incapable of acts of benevolence towards others. Among the examples he mentions in his writings, is parents' love for their children. Aware that considerations of interest may be involved in such cases, he imagines an extreme situation:

> To make this yet clearer, suppose that the Deity should declare to a good Man that he should be suddenly annihilated, but at the Instant of his Exit it should be left to his Choice whether his Friend, his Children, or his Country should be made happy or miserable for the Future, when he himself could have no Sense of either Pleasure or Pain from their State. Pray would he be any more indifferent about their State now that he neither hoped nor feared any thing to himself from it, than he was in any prior Period of his Life? (Hutcheson (1752 [1726]), p. 147)

In his reflections, Hutcheson comes to formulate a judgement that would be taken up by economists in the following centuries: "The best action is that which brings greater happiness to a greater number of people, just as conversely that one is the worst which causes the most misery" (Hutcheson (1752 [1726]), Part II, p. 155).

His influence on David Hume, as on Adam Smith, is quite notable, as the latter was to acknowledge in a famous formula which appears in his aforementioned letter of thanks dated November 16, 1787:

> Glasgow University appointed me for another job, where the abilities and virtues of the one who must never be forgotten, Dr. Hutcheson, had given an example of the highest degree. [...]

1.1.2 Smith, Student at Oxford

After three years in Glasgow, Smith received the *Snell Exhibition* scholarship as a poor but brilliant student. These scholarships were intended to enable students from the University of Glasgow to continue their studies at Balliol College in Oxford (Addison 1901). They were financed through a bequest from John Snell who, at the end of the seventeenth century, had wished to provide for the education of the Scottish clergy of the Episcopalian Church. The Episcopalian Church had lost its official character at the end of the seventeenth century. Moreover, in the mid-eighteenth century, the commitment to take orders in Scotland as stipulated in John Snell's will was not binding and there was no sanction for those who did not respect it. Smith's family and close friends strongly encouraged him to choose a more secure career. It seems that his cousin William Smith, who was the Duke of Argyll's secretary, played a leading role in this affair (Skinner 1982, p. 24). The Dukes of Argyll are a very important Scottish family. The first Duke Archibald Campbell (1658–1703) had received his title in 1701 for joining William of Orange. The second Duke, John Campbell (1678–1743), helped the King to persuade the Scottish Parliament to accept the Act of Union in 1705 and became commander in chief for Scotland in 1712. Critical of the government, he rallied to the Whigs in 1713. One of the daughters of the Duke of Argyll, Caroline Campbell, married the Earl of Dalkeith, son of the Second Duke of Buccleuch, and was none other than the mother of Henry Scott, Smith's travelling companion during his stay in France.

His years at Oxford were always considered by Smith as the worst period of his life. The amount of his grant was £40 per year. Smith joined the college on July 7, 1740, after returning from Kirkcaldy, where he had gone to greet his mother during the university holidays (Skinner 1982, p. 26).

The scholarship was insufficient given the costs involved in studying at Oxford and Smith had to seek relief from his family, as the following letter to his cousin William Smith (August 24, 1740) tells us:

> Sir
>
> I yesterday receiv'd your letter with a bill of sixteen pounds inclos'd, for which I humbly thank you, but more for the good advice you were pleased to give me: I am indeed affraid that my expences at college must necessarily amount to a much greater sum this year than at any time hereafter; because of the extraordinary and most extravagant fees we are obligd to pay the

> College and University on our admittance;3 it will be his own fault if anyone should endanger his health at Oxford by excessive Study, our only business here being to go to prayers twice a day, and to lecture twice a week.
> I am, dear Sir, Your most Oblig'd Servant
> Adam Smith (Letter # 1)[1]

The town of Oxford, its university, and especially Balliol College, was at that time the centre of an episode which was to enflame the United Kingdom for the last time during the year 1745: the expedition of the Jacobite pretender to the throne of Scotland, the famous Bonnie Prince Charlie. Balliol College was an important Jacobite centre. The Jacobites were the followers of King James VII (of Scotland) and II (of England) and his heirs. James VII and II had ruled from 1685 to 1689, but as he was Catholic, he had been ousted by his daughter Mary and her husband, the Dutch Prince William of Orange, who were Protestant. Those who continued to support King James (*Jacobus* in Latin) in exile were called "Jacobites". The last pretender lived in Saint-Germain-en-Laye, maintaining a small court there under the benevolent protection of King Louis XV of France. The Jacobites were attached to the monarchy by divine right and opposed the Whigs who were supporters of the constitutional monarchy, hostile to the Stuarts. The Whigs won elections to the English Parliament in 1715 and remained in government until 1760.

Keeping himself out of contemporary political debates, Smith turned to the study of ancient languages such as Latin, and also Greek, of which he became a fine connoisseur. He also practised French and Italian, acquiring a great knowledge of the main literary works in these languages.

According to Dugald Stewart, Smith practised translating French to English to improve his style. He thus studied those important French authors of the eighteenth century whose works were then taught at Oxford: Pierre Bayle, Descartes, Malebranche, and Pascal. He also translated François de La Rochefoucauld and his *Maximes*, against whom his mentor Hutcheson had inveighed. Smith, for his part, would bracket La Rochefoucauld and Mandeville together, in order to criticize them as authors of "licentious systems" in the *Theory of Moral Sentiments*, published in 1759. During his stay in Paris, Smith's judgement of the author

[1] Smith's correspondence is quoted from Smith (1977) as numbered by the editors, E. Campbell Mossner and Ian Simpson Ross. Generally the date is added when it is useful for the argument.

of the *Maximes* earned him the reproaches of the latter's descendant who was anxious to defend his grandfather's ideas; Smith agreed to withdraw the disputed passage in the sixth edition of the *TMS* published in 1790, shortly before his death.

He was also introduced to French plays at this time, notably to the works of Racine and Marivaux. One can guess the affinities between Marivaux, who wrote *Les effets surprenants de la Sympathie* or *Les Aventures de* *** in 1713, and Smith, whose *TMS* accorded sympathy a very important role.

An anecdote from the years at Oxford may help explain Smith's departure in 1746 (Smith-Stewart, pp. 45–50). The 21-year-old was reportedly surprised in his college room reading a book by David Hume. The book was probably the *Treatise on Human Nature*, in which Hume presents his philosophy of religion (Hume 2002 [1739]). The debate continues to this day as to whether Hume was an atheist or an agnostic, but it is certain that such a work was not recommended in the eighteenth century as a reading for a young man destined for the priesthood (Shane 1993).

This anecdote, noted by Stewart, shows that the relationship between the two men began very early. Intellectual admiration at first, due to the age difference, (Hume was born in 1711) followed by real friendship developing through encounters, and a complicity that would further blossom during the simultaneous sojourns of the two philosophers in France, one in Paris, the other in Toulouse.

Even if the Snell scholarship allowed him to continue his studies for ten or eleven years at Oxford, the stay there was not a sinecure, since Smith felt isolated in an environment whose ideas he did not agree with. He also experienced health problems, probably related to a lack of exercise and a poor diet, or a hypochondriac temperament.

1.2 Smith, the Teacher

1.2.1 Smith Back Home, August 1746–1748

Smith left Oxford at the end of August 1746, shortly after Francis Hutcheson's death on August 8 in Dublin. Hutcheson had recommended Smith for the Snell Fellowship and Smith, still extremely cautious in religious matters, might have feared that the breach of his commitment to the Church of Scotland could be blamed on Hutcheson. As there was no longer a reason for this fear, it may have precipitated Smith's departure

(Gavin Kennedy 2005, p. 20). His return took place at a time when the wounds inflicted by the second Jacobite rebellion had not yet healed in Scotland and northern England. This uprising began when the Stuart pretender to the throne took advantage of a favourable combination of circumstances: during the War of the Austrian Succession, the King of England had forged an alliance with Queen Maria Theresa of Austria, while the King of France took sides with the King of Bavaria and the King of Prussia. George II had sent the bulk of his troops to the continent to defend the Austrian Netherlands against France. In May 1745 the Battle of Fontenoy took place. Despite the losses suffered by both armies, the French forced the British, Hanoverian, and Austrian forces to withdraw and seized part of Flanders. Charles Edward Stuart considered that the period was favourable for relaunching the Jacobite insurrection. Having rallied some Scottish clans, he succeeded in raising an army of 2000 Scots who marched on Edinburgh. The Battle of Prestonpans, also known as the Battle of Gladsmuir, is the first significant battle of the second Jacobite rebellion. On September 21, 1745, the Jacobite army commanded by Charles Edward Stuart defeated George II's Hanoverian army under Sir John Cope at Prestonpans in East Lothian, 17 kilometres from Edinburgh. The rebellion, after some initial successes, was finally defeated at the Battle of Culloden on April 16, 1746, by the Duke of Cumberland's army, which was highly disciplined and experienced, with a high proportion of regiments having served with him in Flanders. The heavy defeat of the Jacobites, who lost half their numbers, marked the end of the Scottish rebellions (Daiches 1973, pp. 193–218). Among the survivors, many men who fought on the Jacobite side were later to enlist in or be pressed into the British army and serve in the Seven Years' War, where their suitability to the rough terrain and skill in battle was not lost on their commanders. The British army went on to defeat the French during the Seven Years' War with numerous personalities related to Culloden, including James Wolfe, the Hero of Quebec, playing prominent roles.

In fact, we know little about the period between Smith's departure from Oxford and the start of his classes in Edinburgh. According to the most probable hypothesis, he taught in two ways during this period, that is, as a tutor for one or more young pupils, and in public and paid readings organized in Edinburgh by private clubs or lodges. The year 1749 marked an important turning point in Adam Smith's life: on the one hand, in a letter dated February 4 to the Dean of Balliol College, Smith renounced all the advantages he might still have gained from the Snell scholarship.

This also marked the official end of his involvement with the Church of Scotland. On the other hand, he embarked on a series of courses in October or November when intellectual life resumed in Edinburgh.

1.2.2 Smith as a Lecturer in Edinburgh

Back in Scotland, Smith met Edinburgh's most prominent figure, Henry Home, who became Lord Kames in the second half of his life. Intellectual life was in effervescence within clubs where literature, politics, and history were discussed while enjoying good company. Lord Kames was the founder of the *Select Society* in 1754: James Boswell, David Hume, and Adam Smith were among its celebrities. The *Select Society* was to give birth to the *Edinburgh Society for the Encouragement of Arts, Science, Manufacturing, and Agriculture* in Scotland, whose name emphasizes its ambitions. In the late 1750s, the presence of French privateers off the English coast during the Seven Years' War led the British Parliament to set up a militia to fight a possible invasion. Since Scotland had been in rebellion as late as 1745, it was not forced to raise such a potentially dangerous reserve force. Wounded by the persistence of anti-Scottish sentiments reflected in this stricture, *literati*, often from the *Select Society*, decided to found the *Poker Club*, in which Smith participated. Its intention, as the name suggests, was to stir up the embers of the militia project.

This concern to promote Scotland in Great Britain would have pleased Lord Kames, who, by his leadership, played a predominant role in the establishment of the "Enlightenment" in Scotland (Ross 1972, p. 131). A determined opponent of the Jacobites, he urged his compatriots to develop their nation within the new configuration offered by the Act of Union. He contributed to the introduction of new agricultural techniques which led to a transformation in Scottish society, while through his reflections on history, he can be considered one of the fathers of anthropology (Kames 1728, 1734, 1751, 1760). Lacking a classical education himself and no doubt impressed by Adam Smith's talents, he entrusted him with public lectures. In 1778, in a letter noting Lord Kames' reservations about his theories, Smith was to show his respect for "such a good friend of so long ago" (letter # 195). It was also in Kames' entourage that Smith approached David Hume (1711–1776) who played an essential role in the journey to Europe. Smith also met the family of James Boswell (1740–1795), and thus some of the town's lawyers. Boswell was among Smith's first students in Glasgow. A great traveller, he journeyed to Corsica from 1763 to 1767 and wrote a book that met with some success in the United Kingdom and contributed to the English commitment to the people of the island (cf. Boswell 1769). Edinburgh's intellectual life was very lively and Smith had to prove the quality of his teaching for it to be lucrative.

1.2.3 *Adam Smith Back in Glasgow*

Smith's recruitment as a university professor gave him a more stable position and opened a long period of thirteen years—from 1751 to 1764—which he celebrated in a vibrant manner at the end of his life in his letter dated November 16, 1787:

> The period of thirteen years which I spent as a member of that society I remember as by far the most useful, and, therefore, as by far the happiest and most honourable period of my life; and now, after three and twenty years absence, to be remembered in so very agreeable manner by my old friends and Protectors gives me a heartfelt joy which I cannot easily express to you. (Letter #274)

Although we have already briefly described the University of Glasgow and the city itself, it is appropriate to return to the environment in which Smith would live during those thirteen years.

The city of Glasgow, due to the rapprochement with England and new customs regulations, experienced rapid development driven by trade with the American colonies. The city benefited twice because in addition to the profits from this important commerce and from the rich merchants, the shipyards of the Clyde River, which provided the ships needed to transport men and goods, developed rapidly. This in itself led to the growth of the steel industry, followed a few years later by the development of steam engines, improved by James Watt, the famous engineer from the local university.

Smith, a renowned university professor, had many opportunities to build relationships with big businesses and the early industrialists, whose children constituted the bulk of the battalions of students in his classes (Skinner, pp. 59–65).

The three "exotic" products that the Port of Glasgow treated as a priority were sugar, tobacco, and cotton. Sugar came from the English West Indies, mainly Jamaica, and Glasgow became the main import destination in Great Britain, with the port's traffic accounting for over 50% of total imports of this product. Cotton and tobacco came from colonies in Virginia, North Carolina, and South Carolina. The economic elite of the city were essentially traders who set up long-distance operations and who, once the goods were introduced into the kingdom, also distributed them throughout the territory, including to southern regions.

1.2.4 Smith as a Pedagogue

The university that welcomed Smith in 1751 was founded in 1451, the same year as Aberdeen's, while St. Andrews, the eldest of the Scottish universities, was founded in 1413. The most prestigious university in the middle of the seventeenth century and also the most recent, that of the capital Edinburgh, only appeared in 1583 (Skinner, p. 45).

He now occupied an official and paid position with a modest but fixed salary. At 28, the Chair of Logic in the Philosophy department represented an enviable position to many young intellectuals. John Millar (1735–1801), who had attended Smith's first logic classes in 1746 at a very young age before befriending him, informed Dugald Stewart not only of the course content but also of Smith's pedagogical qualities (Scott, ASSP, pp. 70 and 115). Millar himself became an important figure in the Scottish Enlightenment. His *Observations on the Distinction of Ranks in Society* constitute a highly innovative treatise on economic sociology (Millar 1771). He was Smith's successor at the University of Glasgow when the latter gave up teaching. He describes his master in the first lessons he attended thus:

> There was no situation in which the abilities of Mr. Smith appeared to greater advantage than as a Professor. In delivering his lectures, he trusted almost entirely to extemporaneous elocution. His manner, though not graceful, was plain and unaffected; and, as he seemed to be always interested in the subject, he never failed to interest his hearers. Each discourse consisted commonly of several distinct propositions, which he successively endeavoured to prove and illustrated these propositions, when announced in general terms, had, from their extent, not unfrequently something of the air of a paradox. In his attempts to explain them, he often appeared, at first, not to be sufficiently possessed of the subject, and spoke with some hesitation. As he advanced, however, the matter seemed to crowd upon him, his manner became warm and animated, and his expression easy and fluent. In points susceptible of controversy, you could easily discern, that he secretly conceived an opposition to his opinions, and that he was led upon this

> account to support them with greater energy and vehemence. By the fulness and variety of his illustrations, the subject gradually swelled in his hands, and acquired a dimension which, without a tedious repetition of the same views, was calculated to seize the attention of his audience, and to afford them pleasure, as well as instruction, in following the same object, through all the diversity of shades and aspects in which it was presented, and afterwards in tracing it backwards to that original proposition or general truth from which this beautiful train of speculation had proceeded. His reputation as a Professor was accordingly raised very high, and a multitude of students from a great distance resorted to the University, merely upon his account. (Smith Steward, I.22, p. 276)

Smith's teaching ability, celebrated by John Millar, "one of his closest and most valuable friends", according to Stewart, did not seem to have convinced all his contemporaries. Smith himself had a much more mixed view of the effects he was having on his audience. There is also a serious caveat in the correspondence of James Wodrow, librarian and ninth son of historian Robert Wodrow. In a letter to Kenrick dated January 21, 1752, he wrote:

> Smiths Reputation in his Rhetorical Lectures is sinking every day[.] As I am not a scholar of his I don't pretend to assign the cause. He begins next week to give lectures on Jurisprudentia which I design to attend. I hear he has thrown out some contemptuous Expressions of Mr. Hutchison. Let the young man take care to guard his Censures by the Lines[,] Palisades and counterscarps of his science Rhetoric[.] For there are some of Mr. H[utcheso]—fragment ns scholars still about the Coll[ege] who perhaps will try to turn the mouths of the Cannon against himself. (London, Dr. Williams' Lib., MS 24.157, 14, 16) (quoted by Ross 2010, p. 111)

An even harsher judgement can be found in the biographical note published shortly after his death in the *Times*, on July 24, 1790,[2] which reports that Smith attacked those students who took notes and said he hated "scribblers". Perhaps it is simply one of those petty disputes traditional in teaching. The innovations brought by Smith in his teaching of logic, his emphasis on rhetoric, might have appeared as a criticism of Hutcheson's teaching. Moreover, there was probably a gap between the expectations of those who heard him lecture in Edinburgh and those of his students in

[2] http://en.wikisource.org/wiki/The_Times/1790/Obituary/Adam_Smith.

Glasgow. The former audience was seduced by Smith's new ideas, did not have to take exams, and thus did not care about taking notes. In Glasgow, on the other hand, the students had more utilitarian concerns so that the accuracy with which they could note the teacher's words worried them more than the content itself. Although opinions were not unanimous, Smith's reputation was gaining him students. So James Boswell, who enrolled in Glasgow in 1759, was to write:

> My greatest reason for coming hither was to hear Mr. Smith's lectures (which are truly excellent.) His sentiments are striking, profound and beautiful, the method in which they are arranged clear, accurate, and orderly, his language correct, perspicuous, and elegantly phrased. His private character is really amiable. He has nothing of that formal stiffness and Pedantry which is too often found in Professors. So far from that, he is a most polite, well-bred man, is extremely fond of having his Students with him and treats them with all the easiness and affability imaginable. (The correspondence of James Boswell and John Johnston of Grange, quoted by Phillipson 2012, p. 135)

Among these students from diverse backgrounds, Smith soon welcomed into his apartments the children of aristocrats. Skinner (pp. 55–56) talks about payments of about £100. This relationship allowed the teacher to frequent those aristocratic circles from which the young students always came. Thus in 1758, Adam Smith received Thomas Fitzmaurice (1742–1793), the youngest son of the Earl of Shelburne. This family played an important role in the development of political economy: Anne Petty, the mother, was the daughter of Sir William Petty (1620–1687). Petty had been very famous in the seventeenth century for his scientific work and indeed for his political role since he had been Cromwell's representative in Ireland. Karl Marx considered him the founder of political economy. William, the eldest son of the Earl of Shelburne (1737–1805) distinguished himself during the Seven Years' War and became George III's aide de camp. When his father died in 1761, he took over his titles and was henceforth known as Lord Shelburne. Both brothers had a brilliant political career. The elder became the first Home Secretary in 1782 and then the Prime Minister from 1782 to 1783 at the end of the war with the United States. He negotiated the Treaty of Paris. A staunch Francophile, he maintained a lengthy correspondence with Voltaire and his friend Morellet. Thus although Glasgow did not have the prestige of Edinburgh, a university town whose close-by port of Leith was very much turned towards Europe, Adam Smith's reputation as an educator had already brought him considerably closer to the British elite.

Smith was appointed to the Chair of Logic and Metaphysics in January 1751. His teaching loads were soon modified. Indeed, the holder of the chair of moral philosophy who had succeeded Francis Hutcheson, Thomas Craigie, fell ill and was allowed to take a leave of absence in Portugal. His teaching load was divided between the Glasgow professors, and Smith was allotted courses in natural and political jurisprudence. Craigie's death rendered the chair of moral philosophy vacant. Smith was elected to it in April 1752 and therefore found himself within less than two years responsible for a chair to which Hutcheson's teachings had given great prestige.

1.3 Smith's Work from 1749 to 1759

John Millar, Smith's first disciple, described for his first biographer Smith's teachings in this post:

> His course of lectures on this subject was divided into four parts. The first contained Natural Theology; in which he considered the proofs of the being and attributes of God, and those principles of the human mind upon which religion is founded. The second comprehended Ethics, strictly so called, and consisted chiefly of the doctrines which he afterwards published in his Theory of Moral Sentiments. In the third part, he treated at more length of that branch of morality which relates to justice, and which, being susceptible of precise and accurate rules, is for that reason capable of a full and particular explanation. Upon this subject he followed the plan that seems to be suggested by Montesquieu; endeavouring to trace the gradual progress of jurisprudence, both public and private, from the rudest to the most refined ages, and to point out the effects of those arts which contribute to subsistence, and to the accumulation of property, in producing correspondent improvements or alterations in law and government? This important branch of his labours he also intended to give to the public; but this intention, which is mentioned in the conclusion of the *Theory of Moral Sentiments*, he did not live to fulfill. In the last part of his lectures, he examined those political regulations which are founded, not upon the principle of justice, but that of expediency, and which are calculated to increase the riches, the power, and the prosperity of a State. Under this view, he considered the political institutions relating to commerce, to finances, to ecclesiastical and military establishments. What he delivered on these subjects contained the substance of the work he afterwards published under the title of *An Inquiry into the*

> Nature and Causes of the Wealth of Nations. (Stewart 1980 [1795], pp. 274–275)

His lectures centred increasingly on the philosophical themes of the period. It was in this way that Smith approached the relationship between natural philosophy and moral philosophy. The reason for moral feelings and themes relating to the conduct of the individual in the public sphere were the subjects of his lessons. He also dealt more and more frequently with the organization of the State or the organization of legal systems, which is not surprising since Scottish law claimed a specific tradition of "written law" (Scott 1965 [1937], pp. 113–117).

In summary, Smith's courses corresponded to the subjects found today in faculties of social science or political science.

1.3.1 First Essays

Very quickly, Smith felt cramped in Glasgow in his straightforward role as a teacher. In 1755 he took part in the launch of an ephemeral magazine, which only produced two issues. This project was initiated by members of the *Select Society*, one of the associations dedicated to disseminating the Enlightenment as it appeared throughout eighteenth-century Europe. Smith had been one of its founding members in 1754, perhaps even one of its initiators. Its preface had been written by Alexander Wedderburn, a friend of Smith's, who stated the journal's purpose in contributing to the advancement of knowledge and announced that it would report on books published in England and other countries in the previous semester. In fact, only English books were mentioned, except for the letter Smith published in the second and last issue. In the first issue of August 1755, he published a review of Johnson's dictionary. Though this contribution appeared in anonymous form, in the limited society of Scottish *literati*, the informed reader could certainly identify Smith as the author. Moreover, in his biography, Dugald Stewart confirms that Smith did not make a mystery of it, even if, prudently, he had abstained at the time from signing the article. This caution was justified, for criticism was levelled at the journal, particularly because of the authors' links with the sulphurous David Hume. In order to avoid any further confrontation with the Presbyterian Church, the journal thus disappeared after the second issue.

If Johnson's dictionary review is proof of Smith's interest in rhetoric and language, the *Letter to the Editors* published in the second and last issue demonstrates his profound knowledge of the European intellectual landscape of the early 1750s (Lomonaco 2002, pp. 659–676). The purpose of the "letter" is to encourage Scots to broaden their horizons by drawing their attention to the intellectual "productions" of France and England.

Smith is also interested in the organization of knowledge and argues that countries with powerful academies allow scholars to produce works jointly. But according to him, the distinct genius of France and England renders them capable of producing thinkers who think for themselves and are thus capable of pure thought, free from any financial or institutional contingency. Smith would apply these considerations to himself and put in place a personal strategy to ensure complete financial autonomy.

This review of knowledge in different countries is not accompanied, for Smith, by any nostalgia for an independent Scotland. He is openly in the camp of the Unionists, whereas a David Hume or even more an Adam Ferguson had opinions far from being so clear-cut (Ferguson and Mossner 1960). This rally to the English cause is also an opportunity to point out the possibilities for Scotland to contribute its stone to the construction of Great Britain:

> As, since the union, we are apt to regard ourselves in some measure as the countrymen of those great men,[3] it flattered my vanity, as a Briton, to observe the superiority of the English philosophy thus acknowledged by their rival nation [France].
>
> It seems to be the peculiar talent of the French nation, to arrange every subject in that natural and simple order, which carries the attention, without any effort, along with it. [...] There is not only no tolerable system of natural philosophy in the English language, but there is not even any tolerable system of any part of it. (Smith, Letter to the Edinburgh Review, p. 245)

Smith of course refers to the *Encyclopédie* project launched by Diderot and d'Alembert (Diderot et al. 1765), whose first volumes appeared in 1751, a project that was close to his heart and for which he was full of praise, quoting "*MM d'Alembert, Diderot, D'Aubenton, Rousseau de Genève, Ferney, secretary of the Berlin Academy and several others" (ibidem, p. 258). The* idea of this encyclopedia seduced him, particularly by the nature of its elaboration and by the long articles which allowed a clear

[3] It's Bacon, Boyle, Newton. But Smith also mentions the names of d'Alembert, Diderot, D'Aubenton, Rousseau, but also Maurepas, Buffon for his gigantic *Natural History*, Réaumur for his *History of Insects*.

presentation of the selected notions. By 1755, five volumes had appeared and Smith made sure they were purchased by the University of Glasgow (Scott 1965 [1937], p. 179). Smith notes that:

> This work, which has several times been disagreeably interrupted by some jealousy either of the civil or of the ecclesiastical government of France, to neither of which however the authors seem to have given any just occasion of suspicion, is not yet finished. The volumes of it which are yet to be published, will deserve, as they successively appear, to be particularly taken notice of in your future periodical reviews. You will observe, that tho' none of the authors of this collection appear to be mean or contemptible, yet they are not all equal. (Smith, ibidem., p. 247)

We see that Smith closely followed the French literary news, interested not only in publications, but in the conditions with which French authors struggled. In the face of such admiration, one can speculate that a curious man like Smith would wish for an opportunity to meet and establish close links with the people he admired most in the world. Smith would be in Paris in 1765 and early 1766 when the last volumes of the *Encyclopédie* were published.

His admiration is not completely uncritical and he is unhesitatingly severe on a subject that he himself would treat at length shortly afterwards:

> The article of Amour, for example, will tend little to the edification either of the learned or unlearned reader, and might, one should think, have been omitted even in an Encyclopedia of all arts, sciences and trades. These censures however fall but upon a few articles, and those of no great importance. (ibidem., p. 248)

There is no doubt that this is a reaction from the future theorist of "sympathy". One can understand this, since his text is already under gestation, particularly through the elaboration of the system of moral philosophy largely inherited from Francis Hutcheson (Scott, op. cit., pp. 51–71).

It may be noted in passing that Smith read French perfectly since all these works were only available in French and no translation was envisaged. This Francophilia can be related to his acquaintance with French authors at Oxford and his long experience in translating their publications.

He was nonetheless critical of Descartes' successors and of the French School of Philosophy and, in particular, of Father Malebranche

(1638–1715), whose thinking would influence Quesnay, the founder of the Physiocratic school which he would eventually come to confront, once in France. In his review of French philosophy, Smith mentions Pierre Sylvain Régis (1632–1707), a now forgotten philosopher. After having pursued most of his studies in Cahors, then a city and a study centre of some importance, Régis completed his education at the Sorbonne where he became familiar with the theories of Descartes. In 1665, he travelled to Toulouse where he gave very popular lectures and took part in the meetings of the "Lanternists", who will be returned to when later presenting the intellectual life of Toulouse. He diverged from Descartes on several points and maintains that "the body knows itself as well as the soul, innate ideas depend on the senses (born with us, they are constantly present in the soul only by sensations), the objects of reason and faith are so disproportionate that it is impossible to explain one by the other".[4] Having briefly identified various English contributions in the field of moral philosophy, the limits of which he underlines, Smith returns to the French authors.

> This branch of the English philosophy, which seems now to be intirely neglected by the English themselves, has of late been transported into France. I observe some traces of it, not only in the Encyclopedia, but in the Theory of agreeable sentiments by Mr. De Pouilly is a work that is in many respects original; and above all, in the late Discourse upon the origin and foundation of the inequality amongst mankind by Mr. Rousseau of Geneva. (ibidem., p. 250)

Since Smith was always fascinated by new ideas, the appearance here of Rousseau's philosophical essay is not surprising. Begun in 1753 and published in 1755, in response to a subject proposed by the Dijon Academy, it was entitled: "What is the origin of unequal conditions among men?" For Rousseau, this origin is not to be found in nature but in the society that shapes the individual. This position is largely contrary to the great principles of Smith's philosophy but also and mainly to that of Hume and can constitute the first moment of the rupture between Hume and Rousseau which would occur during Smith's stay in France.

Adam Smith called Jean-Jacques Rousseau "Rousseau de Genève" to distinguish him from another Rousseau, the publisher of the *Journal*

[4] http://dictionnaire-journalistes.gazettes18e.fr/journaliste/668-pierre-sylvain-regis.

encyclopédique published in Liège. Pierre Rousseau is also called "Rousseau de Toulouse" because he was born in that city. Indeed, as will be seen the influence of the *Journal encyclopédique* would be decisive in the way the *Theory of Moral Sentiments* was received.

For the moment Smith continued his review of all the philosophical doctrines of the early Enlightenment period by introducing the various conceptions of humanity:

> Dr. Mandeville represents the primitive state of mankind as the most wretched and miserable that can be imagined: Mr. Rousseau, on the contrary, paints it as the happiest and most suitable to his nature. (ibidem., p. 250)

For Smith, Mandeville, in the *Fable of the Bees* in 1714, made human selfishness (and the interplay of their passions and vices) the sole and unique foundation of a society. For him, altruism or the collective interest was absent from social life.

These are themes that Smith would take up again at great length in both the *TMS* and the *WN*, which are often wrongly considered to be contradictory to each other, whereas Smith put them on an equal footing, insisting that the titles of his works be engraved on his tomb with characters of the same size (Dixon and William 2006).

1.3.2 A Turning Point for Smith: The Publication of the TMS

This book, published by Smith in 1759, anchored his material security and allowed him to leave his teaching post; he could henceforth devote himself fully to his research. He developed arguments in line with those of the French moralists of the eighteenth century as well as with the English philosophy of Hobbes, Locke, Mandeville, and, of course, his master Francis Hutcheson. The title of the book echoes Levesque de Pouilly's (1691–1750), *Théorie des sentiments agréables.* Levesque de Pouilly had introduced Newton's ideas to France at a very young age. He published a *Dissertation on the uncertainty of the history of the first centuries of Rome* (1723) provoking a debate on skepticism with regards to history. He had spent a year in England where Newton called him "his friend". He was familiar with English philosophical circles and he would have received the young David Hume in his town of Reims. In his *Theory* (originally published in 1736), he proposed "the rules that Nature follows in the distribution of pleasure, to establish the principles of natural theology and those of moral philosophy". Levesque de Pouilly indicated in Chap. 1 that "there is a science of sentiments as certain and more important than any natural science". After celebrating Newton and his law of "the distribution of movements", he added:

> It is true that matter, space, and time have the advantage of lending themselves easily to geometrical calculations, and of providing them with a vast career: but, although secret modifications of body and soul are not susceptible to precise measurement; they are nonetheless objects of reliable knowledge. (Levesque de Pouilly, pp. 1–3)

Perceptible here is the argument that Max Weber developed a century and a half later, that the social scientist has the advantage over the scientist of hard disciplines in that he can *understand* his subject of study. For his part, Smith would develop an understanding of these famous "moral sentiments". Is man a wolf to man as Hobbes claims? What about the opposition between private vices and public virtues praised by Bernard de Mandeville? What about the virtue on which La Rochefoucauld casts doubt? Is God the indispensable regulator of human society? An in-depth analysis of the *TMS* has no place here, but it is useful to present some elements that help to understand Smith's intellectual journey as well as the reception of his book in England and in France, which he was about to visit. The *TMS* provides nuanced answers to questions that have been raised in Western philosophy since antiquity. To achieve this, Smith uses three new or reinterpreted concepts. Sympathy first of all, which he defines as man's ability to experience the sorrows and joys of his fellow men in varying degrees. This "sympathy" is in human nature, as he affirms in the opening pages of the book, where he maintains that "the most brutal, hardest robber, those who violate the laws of society, is not totally devoid of them" (*TMS*, Chap. 1. Of Sympathy).

From sympathy, he gives rise to a capacity for judgement in the shape of the "impartial spectator". This represents our ability to abstract ourselves from our self to evaluate our actions and compare them to those of others in order to construct a scale of good and evil (*TMS*, p. 197).

It is in this work that Smith introduces a concept, some would say by sleight of hand, when he tackles the question of the distribution of wealth, a theme that he will naturally take up in his economic analyses in the *WN*: how to justify the monopolization of wealth by a small number of "rich people" whose [...] "sole end which they propose from the labours of all the thousands whom they employ, be the gratification of their own vain and insatiable desires" (TMS, p. 165). According to Smith, this remains acceptable because "they [the rich] are led by an invisible hand to accomplish almost the same distribution of the necessities of life that would have taken place if the earth had been divided equally among all its inhabitants" (TMS, ibidem).

The book follows lectures attended by young men. It is well-structured, which explains its accessibility to a broad public little versed in philosophy.

1.3.3 Dissemination and Reception of the TMS

The book's success, according to Hume and his publisher Andrew Millar, was immediate, first in England and subsequently spreading very quickly across Europe. The book would be published in several editions. The second, responding to comments from the first readers, appeared in 1761. In total, no fewer than six versions were published, the last of which was greatly enriched and published only a few weeks before his death. Smith learned of his good fortune shortly after the book was printed, thanks to a letter dated April 12, 1759, from David Hume, who was then in London where he stayed more and more, following his many bestsellers. Hume, after various considerations on the distribution of the book, gives a humorous account of the great success Smith had achieved:

> Supposing, therefore, that you have duely prepard yourself for the worst by all these Reflections; I proceed to tell you the melancholy News, that your Book has been very unfortunate: For the Public seem disposd to applaud it extremely. It was lookd for by the foolish People with some Impatience; and the Mob of Literati are beginning already to be very loud in its Praises. Three Bishops calld yesterday at Millar's Shop in order to buy Copies, and to ask Questions about the Author: The Bishop of Peterborough said he had passd the Evening in a Company, where he heard it extolld above all Books in the World• You may conclude what Opinion true Philosophers will entertain of it, when these Retainers to Superstition praise it so highly. (Letter #31)

This must have reassured Smith: his first attempt was a masterstroke. It is true that Hume chose with great care the addressees of the book, among whom three draw particular attention. The first was Archibald Campbell, third Duke of Argyll—founder of the Royal Bank of Scotland, he was then described as the most powerful man in Scotland, controlling the vote of the sixteen Scottish peers in the Westminster Parliament. Leader of the Whigs, he was the grandfather of Smith's future student. Horace Walpole (1717–1797) was also among them, the prototype, so to speak, of the dilettante aristocrat, historian, and Whig parliamentarian in London. He is famous for having done a Grand Tour of Europe. In 1764, he published *The Castle of Otranto* which, beyond the pre-romantic vision of its subject, launched the style of the fantastic and Gothick novel (Gwynn 1971, pp. 29–50). But the recipient who would later have the most importance in Smith's life was none other than Charles Townshend. Hume probably already had a project in mind for Smith when he sent the book to Townshend, then looking for a tutor for his son-in-law. He wrote on April 12, 1759:

> Charles Townsend, who passes for the cleverest fellow in England, is so taken with the Performance, that he said to Oswald he wou'd put the Duke of Buccleuch under the Authors Care, and woud endeavour to make it worth his while to accept of that Charge: As soon as I heard this, I calld on him twice with a View of talking with him about the Matter, and of convincing him of the Propriety of sending that young Nobleman to Glasgow: For I coud not hope, that he coud offer you any Terms, which woud tempt you to renounce your Professorship: But I missd him. Mr Townsend passes for being a little uncertain in his Resolutions; so perhaps you need not build much on this Sally. (Letter # 31)

That establishes a direct link between the *TMS* and Smith's later career as the presentation of the voyage will make clear.

1.3.4 The First Reception in France

While waiting for the Grand Tour to take shape, success quickly crossed the English Channel and the book benefited from a very comprehensive review in the *Journal encyclopédique* that Pierre Rousseau had been publishing abroad since 1756 to escape French censorship, first in Liège and then five kilometres from the French border in Bouillon, when he was threatened by ecclesiastical wrath. The very title *Journal encyclopédique* emphasizes its link with the *Encyclopédie*, of which it wanted to be the propagator. In his prospectus of 1755, he set himself as "the object [...]

of gathering, every fortnight, all that is happening in Europe that is of great interest in the Sciences and Arts [...]. France, Germany, England, Italy, Spain, Holland, the Netherlands, in a word the learned world will be the object of our research, our care and our work".

Faithful to this commitment and despite the growing prevalence of French as a language of international communication, it made room for works published in other European languages, underlining the appearance of a European readership that translated into subscriptions throughout Europe. Voltaire, who supported him, wrote in 1758 in the preface to *L'Écossaise* that the *Journal encyclopédique* was "the first of the one hundred and seventy-three newspapers which appeared every month in Europe".

Even if its print run did not exceed 2000 copies, there is no doubt that the Scots of the Enlightenment were very attentive and Hume or Smith had undoubtedly sent a copy of the book to Pierre Rousseau. Whatever the case may be, the review in the *Journal encyclopédique* of October 15, 1759, is extensive (no less than seventeen pages) and concludes on a very complimentary note:

> This work seemed recommendable to us by the strength and warmth of its style, by the beauty and nobility of its feelings, by the novelty and accuracy of its reflections by the imposing tone of its reasoning; but what makes it even more precious is that everything breathes the purest virtue, and that religion is respected everywhere.

This last phrase may come as a surprise and we will come back to it. For now, let us note two characteristics of the *Journal* of interest. The principal mover behind this project, Pierre Rousseau, was born in Toulouse in 1716 and to avoid confusion with his illustrious contemporary namesake, he was sometimes called Rousseau de Toulouse. After his studies, he gave up a career in the church, tried surgery, then went to Paris to work for a lawyer and a notary, where his accurate spelling and his beautiful penmanship were much admired. He wrote a few plays, trying to adapt burlesque theatre to Paris, and a salacious novel that might have put him in prison, so he opted for another equally dangerous profession, journalism. The publication of the *Encyclopédie* had begun in 1751, and Rousseau had come into contact with its authors, making friends notably with Diderot, Voltaire, and d'Alembert. According to Desbarreaux-Bernard, he then conceived the idea of a newspaper able to extol the publications of the

Encyclopedia and at the same time to do battle with the enemies of this enterprise. Thus was born the *Journal Encyclopédique*. But despite the newspaper's wide-ranging aim of giving a large place to travel stories, there is hardly any edition which did not include at least one article devoted to Toulouse, as his Toulousain biographer notes:

> It is the annual analysis of the collections of the Floral Games; it is the translation of a dramatic Languedoc pastoral work, it is the examination of the historical works of which Toulouse is the subject, it is a reasoned eulogy of the works of the Academy of Sciences, Inscriptions and Belles-Lettres of Toulouse which was beginning to publish..; it is a study on Fermat on the subject of a thesis crowned by this Academy; it is an account of Darquié's astronomical observations; it is an appreciation of the theatre of Cailhava de L'estandoux, and so on. In a word, nothing that could interest Toulouse from near or far, and Toulousains did not escape his solicitude, always alert to that city. (Desbarreaux-Bernard 1854, p. 397)

This concern for Toulouse may have played a role in the atypical Grand Tour to come, especially since the *Journal encyclopédique*, while reporting on travel accounts, evaluated them according to criteria highlighting the quality of travellers' concerns. The February 1781 edition makes the following remark:

> To travel is not to travel with brilliance through states, provinces, cities, to spread one's riches through the universe, and perhaps one's vices or one's absurdities. It is to walk the globe, to subject it to research and reflect; to question man, art, and nature everywhere, to bring eras closer together to compare them, and finally to have fun and learn. That is the Philosopher's task.

By the middle of the eighteenth century, stories of the Grand Tour were only appreciated if travellers had particular literary qualities. To capture and hold the reader's attention, it was necessary to have prepared for the trip by accumulating information, starting with knowledge of the language.

1.3.5 The French Translation of the TMS

The success of the first edition of the book in English led, at the beginning of 1764, to the publication of a translated edition under a more catchy title: *Métaphysique de l'âme, or Théorie des sentiments moraux*. It was written by Marc-Antoine Eidous (1724–1790). Born in Marseille, he is a near contemporary of Smith, to within a few months. Before devoting himself to translation, he served the Spanish crown as an army engineer. When he moved to Paris, he made friends with Diderot and became his *amanuensis*. He collaborated on two articles in the *Encyclopédie*. These translations were criticized by contemporaries, notably Grimm in the *Correspondance* in 1767, but this did not lessen the demand for his services. In total, he was responsible for more than seventy translations from English, Latin, and Spanish. He was well prepared for translating Smith because he had translated Francis Hutcheson as early as 1749 and Horace Walpole's *Castle of Otranto*. It is possible that he met Smith. Indeed, Eidous added a note of his own in the most exotic part of the book, which detailed, with a certain complacency, the torture inflicted in America by the natives on their prisoners of war. The footnote on page 180 of the second volume reads:

> (a) Examples of the firmness and courage of the Indians can be seen in the *Orinoco History of* Fr. Gumilla, Jesuit, which was translated into French by Mr. Eidous.

Smith owned a copy of this work which he quoted in the *WN* as evidence about El Dorado (*WN*, IV.vii.a, p. 583).

The translation of the *TMS* was published by the Parisian publisher Briasson, based in the rue Saint-Jacques. The book is briefly mentioned—quite neutrally—in the *Journal encyclopédique*. *L'Année littéraire*, which was its conservative counterpart, provided a review as complimentary as that of the 1759 *Journal*, celebrating an author who refuted moral utilitarianism (1764, VI, p. 145). A more critical mention can be found in December 1764, but it refers to the quality of the translation. It needs to be qualified by Grimm's permanent obsession: denouncing in the *Correspondance littéraire* the defects of Eidous' translations: exceptionally, instead of invective, this presents an interesting reflection on translation:

> For some time now, the *Theory of Moral Sentiments*, a work by Mr. Adam Smith, professor of moral philosophy at the University of Glasgow, has been translated in two volumes in-8°. The translator or the bookseller, to give it a more spicy title, named it wittily *Metaphysics of the Soul* [1764 a vol. in-12. The translator was Eidous, who put so many English books into our language.] This work has a great reputation in England, and had no success in

> Paris; this is not a comment on its merit. After poetry, metaphysical works are the most difficult to translate; perhaps one would have more success in rendering the images of a poet rather than the precise ideas of a metaphysicist. In order to succeed at this task, one would still have to find exactly equivalent terms in both languages to express in as many French words the idea that the original author would have said in so many English words. Now, each people arranges its abstract and scientific ideas in its own way and assigns in its own way words for which it is impossible to find terms always exactly equivalent in another language. For any expression where this conformity between two languages occurs, there are a hundred, there are a thousand where it does not exist. Now, take away from a metaphysical book its precision, and there remains only an obscure and vague jargon, which is that of the translator of the *Theory of moral sentiments*.

Finally, we can say that the reception of the book was uniformly positive and any imprecations aimed at the translator could only arouse curiosity about the author.

1.4 The Duke of Buccleuch

The trip to the continent was for Smith's pupil the culmination of his education. It would be a pivotal period in his education before he became the head of one of Scotland's most important aristocratic families; it was also important for Adam Smith who, from 1759 onwards, would go from being a professor at a distant university to being in contact with great minds not only in Scotland but also in England and France. The publication of the *Theory of Moral Sentiments* radically changed the philosopher's life. It was his reputation that led to him being chosen to accompany the Duke of Buccleuch on his Grand Tour, and he thereafter entered the circle of a family watched over by Charles Townshend, then Chancellor of the Exchequer (Scott 1965 [1935]).

1.4.1 The Childhood of an Aristocrat of Royal Blood

Smith's student did not yet officially bear the title of Duke, and during his voyage, he would simply be Henry Scott. The title of Duke of Buccleuch had been created for James Scott (1649–1685), the eldest of the illegitimate (though recognized) children of Charles II, King of England, Scotland, and Ireland (1630–1685). James Scott, asserting his Protestantism, had led a rebellion to depose his uncle James II of England

(James VI in Scotland), who was a Catholic. After this rebellion failed, he was beheaded. The title was then taken by his grandson, Francis Scott (1695–1751), who had studied at Eton and dedicated his life to research. Freemason, member of the Grand Lodge at a time when science figured prominently within its objectives, he was its Grand Master from June 1723 to June 1724. He became a Fellow of the Royal Society in March 1724 and in April 1745 received an honorary doctorate in civil law from Oxford University. His son, Francis Scott (1721–1751), was given the title of Earl of Dalkeith. Since he died before the second Duke, he never bore the title, so Henry became the third Duke when he came of age (Figs. 1.1 and 1.2).

Francis Scott, Earl of Dalkeith, married Caroline Campbell in 1742, the eldest daughter of John Campbell, fourth Duke of Argyll (1693–1770). The Duke of Argyll had a dual political and military career. In 1745, he defended Western Scotland against the Jacobite forces of Bonnie Prince Charlie. In 1746, he was promoted to military commander for Scotland. His eldest son John Campbell (1723–1806) distinguished himself during

Fig. 1.1 The Gainsborough portrait of Henry Scott, third Duke of Buccleuch. (Source: Buccleuch Living Heritage Trust)

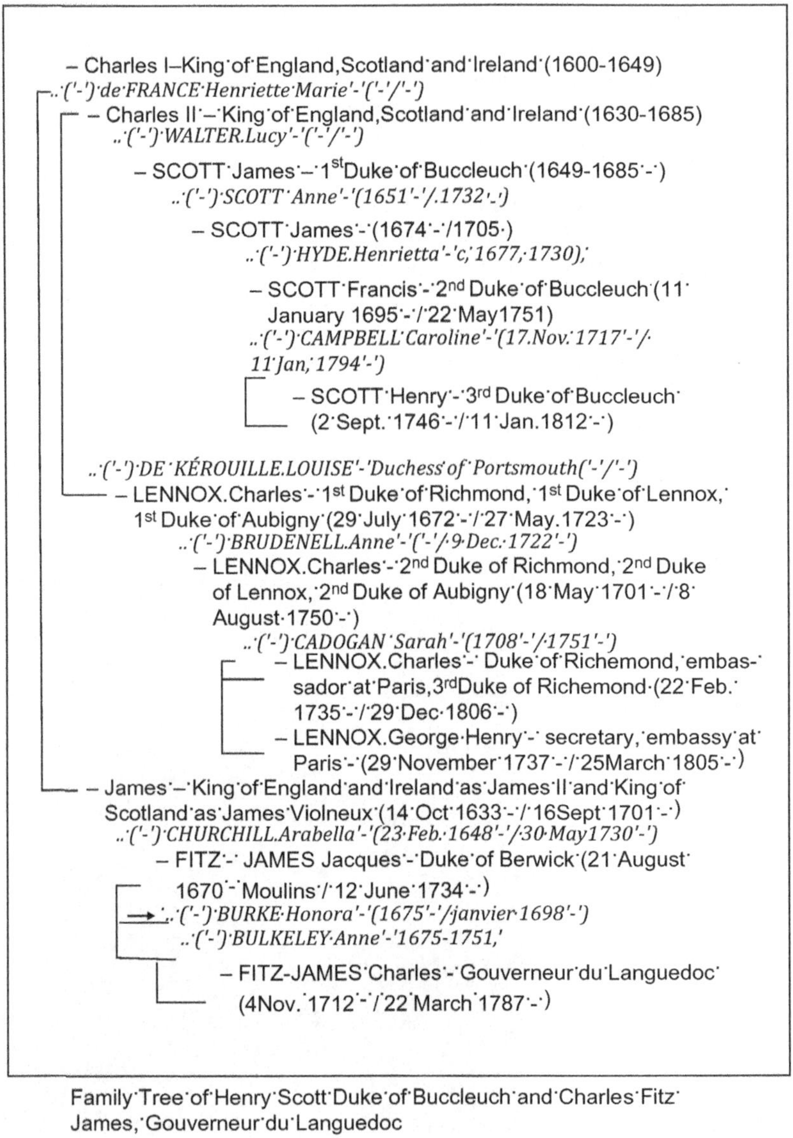

Fig. 1.2 Ascendency tree of Henry Scott, third Duke of Buccleuch

the repression of 1745 and in particular, during the final battle of Culloden by his ferocity towards the Jacobite rebels, which made him very unpopular for many Scots who considered the repression too cruel.

The royal origin of the Buccleuch family reinforced its prestige. The succession of Charles II was at the heart of the great rivalry between the Tories and the Whigs. Charles II, who took the throne of England at the restoration, had promised Louis XIV to return to Catholicism. It was a reaction to this impulse that led to the passing of the exclusion law intended to prohibit the future James II, a Catholic who was to reign only two years before being dethroned, from acceding to the throne. The Tories had opposed this law of exclusion, while it was supported by the Whigs who were persecuted during the short reign of James II.

The close family ties between the French and Scottish crowns are also noteworthy. King Charles I, grandfather of the first Duke of Buccleuch, had married Henriette-Marie de France (1625–1649), the youngest daughter of Henri IV and Marie de Médicis. Thus the young Duke was directly related to King Louis XV. At Drumlanrig Castle, the Dumfriesshire home of the Duke and Duchess of Buccleuch and Queensberry, one can still find furniture bearing the seals of Versailles and Louis XIV. These pieces of furniture, as well as some paintings by Leonardo da Vinci, continue to be noteworthy evidence even today of the close links between the two families (Montegu Douglas Scott 2009, pp. 10–26). The letters exchanged with the house of France indicate that the first Dukes of Buccleuch were designated under the desirable term for that time of—"dear cousin".[5] However, despite the good relations maintained with the family of France and perhaps because of any absence of a claim to the throne of England or Scotland, the family as a whole played a quite different yet specific role in the history of the new union. This behaviour is probably due to the third and main origin of the family, namely the Douglas clan. Clans are based on family. The term derives from the Gaelic word *clann*, which means children. But it is not necessary to belong to the biological descent of an ancestor to be part of the group. The sense of belonging or community of interest could lead farmers or inhabitants of territories on which the clan was well represented to declare their belonging to it, often by adding the name of the clan to theirs. Thus, a clan included a group of families more or less related to each other but recognizing the authority of the clan chief, who was at the same time their

[5] National Archives of Scotland, GD 224/31/15, GD224/925, GD224/935/22.

protector. It has been possible to identify about 150 clans. Of course, marriages have blurred the boundaries between clans over the centuries. This structure had largely become anachronistic following the Act of Union of 1707, and the solicitation of clan solidarity during the Jacobite rebellions was less and less effective. The defeat of the Jacobites at the battle of Culloden led, among the reprisals inflicted by the victors, to a ban on the wearing of the colours of the clans that had supported the Jacobites. A few decades later, Walter Scott presented a romantic image of the clans as the hostility of the authorities towards them had declined, partly for the sake of reconciliation but also because their importance had greatly diminished. In Scotland, where genealogies and peer relationships retained a considerable weight, it was significant that Henry Scott was the great-grandson of William Douglas, Duke of Queensberry and head of the Douglas clan. It was the most important clan in Scotland (Maclean 1995, p. 234) in both area, of influence and number. At the clan's apex was a Duchy, Queensberry, which the young Duke would also inherit. He became the fifth Duke of Queensberry as well as the third Duke of Buccleuch.

The castle of Drumlanrig and the county of Dumfries, which is the territorial fiefdom of the Douglas family, are in the Borders region, that is, the part of Scotland which serves as a somewhat artificial border with England. The family has thus always suffered both influences and has often served as a police force to maintain the separation between the two nations. The rapprochement of the two nations from the middle of the eighteenth century and increases in trade led the family to become more and more interested in regulations, the economy, and customs exchanges, which the clan regulated, probably the source of its immense fortune. In the late eighteenth century, the Douglas clan played a significant part in the Battle of Dunkeld (1689) and victory over the Jacobite troops. They continued to support the British government during the eighteenth century, while the political manoeuvring of the Second Duke of Queensberry contributed to the vote on the Act of Union in 1707.

The young Duke Henry was born in London, which is symptomatic of a family strongly integrated into the new configuration resulting from the Treaty of Union. If both his father and mother belonged to the very first circle of the Scottish aristocracy, he was only the third child and one of six siblings. The two eldest were Caroline (1743–1753) and John (1745–1749) while Henry was followed by Hew Campbell (1747–1766), who had joined the Grand Tour but tragically deceased in Paris on October 19, 1766, James (1748–1758), and the youngest girl, Frances (1750–1817).

Francis Scott, the father, died in 1751 at the age of 30 of one of those diseases that the medicine of the time could not remedy: probably small-pox, a dreadful disease whose treatment by inoculation in low doses would be the subject of a scientific and philosophical quarrel in France as in England, and which was particularly heated during Smith's voyage. The young widow was then responsible for five young children. As in many aristocratic families, it seems that love and attention towards children were not at the centre of her concerns, and Henry and even more so his sister complained of their mother's lack of affection. In letters, addressed much later to Henry Dundas, a Scottish politician who was pejoratively nick-named "the uncrowned King of Scotland", the Duke also lamented that his education had been somewhat neglected and entrusted to mere servants. But in 1755, Lady Caroline remarried Charles Townshend with whom she would have three more children, and as a step-father who was sympathetic to the Enlightenment's ideas on education, he became interested in his stepchildren. In 1757, the young Duke entered Eton College, near the royal castle of Windsor. This college, founded in 1440, was the alma mater of many young aristocrats and provided a high quality of basic education in classical subjects. The young aristocrat, who showed great love for his mother, sent her odes written in Latin,[6] in a style that was certainly clumsy but full of charm and love. As the years went by, the young nobleman's verse would turn to more bucolic subjects showing increasing interest in the theme of love. The subjects taught at the school also included dance and fencing, essential pursuits in order to enjoy a full social life in Europe, which was quite homogeneous in these matters. Young Henry would be joined at Eton by his brother Hew and both would benefit from a private tutor, who would supplement their education in the fields of history, philosophy, and mathematics. Having a private tutor to complement the classes taught by college or university professors was a fairly common practice in such an environment in the eighteenth century. The first contacts between Professor Smith and young Henry occurred as early as the summer of 1759 through a series of books that Smith recommended that his future student should study. The list of books which included the Latin classics indicated a concern with broadening the cultural horizons of the young aristocrat. It was obviously a

[6] NAS GD 224/31/15/3-8.

question of opening this young mind to a knowledge of the world. Thus any preparation for a possible "Grand Tour" was oriented towards the Mediterranean world and those civilizations directly stemming from classical Latin thought. The young Scott, who was 13 at the time of these initial interactions, would remain at the school for another four years. He would leave it finally at the age of 17 for his journey through Europe. Given the role played by Charles Townshend, his step-father, in the association between Smith and the young traveller, in the preparation of the voyage, and later in Smith's career, it is relevant to examine more broadly both the personality of this man and his role in the history of England.

1.4.2 *Charles Townshend, a Caring Step-Father*

Charles Townshend played a key role in organizing the future Duke of Buccleuch's trip to France and more specifically to Toulouse. It was also he who directed Smith towards political economy, a subject which occupied most of the second part of his life. The effervescent Townshend is not an easy character to describe. Because of his role in the American Revolution, historians often make very harsh judgements about him (Namier and Brooke 1964, pp. 150–171). He was difficult to approach, ill-tempered, and famous for fits of anger which often turned into epileptic seizures, a disease which probably worsened towards the end of his short life and of which he finally died. Born on August 27, 1725, the youngest son of Charles Townshend, the third Viscount, he belonged to a notable English family that had been providing Whig politicians for years, notably during the reign of George II, who reigned from 1727 until his death in 1760.

The Townshends were close to the Walpole family, who distinguished themselves in the eighteenth century both politically—Robert Walpole was Prime Minister—and as writers—his son Horace, a politician himself, is known as the creator of the Gothick novel, prefiguration of nineteenth-century romantic novels. The Walpoles were quite Francophile, and Horace Walpole made frequent visits to France from 1739 onwards.

Charles Townshend's childhood was a sad one: he lived in a family where his parents were quite distant from each other. They eventually divorced, as the Anglican religion allowed. The young Charles then lived with his father from the age of 15. His first epileptic seizures struck him during childhood. Some blamed the young man's sensitive nature, and the very bad family atmosphere during his early years, as well as a certain lack of maternal love, as all attention was focused on the elder of the dynasty, Charles went to Eton, like his brother George (1724–1807), then on to Clare College, Cambridge. George joined the British army in 1743, fighting in Germany during the War of the Austrian Succession, while the young Charles continued his studies and, as was the custom at the time, planned to complete his education with a stay on the continent. George enjoyed a brilliant military career and was a brigade commander under General Wolfe, the commander in chief of the British expedition that captured Quebec in 1759. George Townshend would replace General Wolfe, who was killed during the Battle of the Plains of Abraham. He also distinguished himself during the siege of Quebec alongside another character, Colonel Barré, a descendant of Huguenots who had emigrated to Ireland after the revocation of the Edict of Nantes: Smith and the Duke would meet him in Bordeaux and Toulouse. Charles Townshend would indeed travel to the continent, not for a Grand Tour, but to study in Leiden in the United Provinces, an industrial and commercial city well known even as far as the Languedoc for the quality of its sheets. Leiden University was the only university in the Netherlands that had escaped Spanish control. The quality of teaching there was renowned. It gave young English jurists the opportunity to improve their skills in Roman law, whereas in their own country Common law prevailed, derived from both Norman law and Northern European law (Otterspeer 2001, 2008). His residence there was planned to last one academic year, but the young Charles Townshend experienced multiple money problems. In spring, he planned a tour of the United Provinces and perhaps northern France, including a possible visit to Paris. However, his poor health seemed to have got the better of this project. He returned to England in some haste.

It seems that at this time conflicts with a very authoritarian father played a decisive role in shaping his character, leading him to prefer negotiation and the art of politics rather than direct confrontation with power (Namier and Brooke 1964, pp. 20–26).

To this somewhat chaotic education can be attributed the about-faces and sudden changes of opinion that earned him a bad reputation. In 1747, he became a member of the British Parliament after a long and costly election campaign, even though his electorate was very small. Thus began his long career as a parliamentarian during which he became interested mainly in trade with the colonies.

However, during his first term, he made a name for himself in the debates that led to the first marriage legislation in Britain. Two camps opposed each other: some parliamentarians wanted to surround marriage with great publicity and ensure that parents gave their agreement to avoid misalliances; another camp, of which Charles was a member, wanted to preserve freedom of choice and refused to allow State interference in the private lives of individuals. Despite his plea for the freedom of the spouses, the marriage law was passed, but it did not prevent Charles from marrying an heiress far richer than he was eight years later.

In order to ensure his re-election until 1754, while he did not have a personal fortune and could hardly count on that of his father, he often called on somewhat obscure financing and involved himself in speculative ventures on the borders of legality, involving trade with the East India Company. Perhaps it was this monetary and financial need that led him to set his heart on a young Scottish widow, Lady Caroline, the mother of the future Duke. She was eight years older than he was and already had five living children, so contemporaries imagined that financial considerations played at least as important a role as sentiment in this union. This interpretation can be based on his interventions in Parliament, in which he was closely interested in the administration of family fortunes in the event of a marriage and particularly dowries, as well as in the laws of guardianship, which were different in Scotland and England. This is also what emerges from his exchanges with his father in July 1755, who wrote:

> You inform me by your letter [wrote Lord Townshend] that the lady you have contracted with is Lady Dalkeith. She is certainly I acknowledge lady of high rank and fortune and that an alliance with a family of such great rank is what must be very desirable.
>
> You further inform me that her present jointure and income is £3000 net receipt, which will be increased to £5000 net receipt at the death of the Duchess of Argyll now 78 years of age, and that she has besides to dispose of in money and personal estate about £46,000, £30,000 of which you are empowered by her to say she will settle on you if the marriage takes place, and that she has besides very large and probable expectations from the Duchess of Argyll ... You write that the Duchess of Argyll and the Duke of Argyll[2] gave their consent to you last week and desired you to wait on me, and at the same time that you expressed their consent to inform yourself of my opinion and disposition upon this matter. (Namier and Brooke, p. 34)

Charles had to obtain his father's consent and put forward the material advantages of this marriage. Though the mismatch in fortunes provoked much gossip at the time, this union was also of interest to Lady Caroline since it allowed her to escape the situation of a widow responsible for children.

To conclude the episode of Charles Townshend's marriage, this is how Horace Walpole, so representative of this Anglo-Scottish aristocracy fond of both culture and convention, presented it with some irony in a letter to a friend on July 17, 1755:

> Charles Townshend marries the great dowager Dalkeith; his parts and presumption are prodigious. He wanted nothing but independence to let him loose: I propose great entertainment from him; and now, perhaps, the times will admit it. (Walpole 1840, t.3, p. 131)

Given the degree of calculation surrounding this union, one would have expected the husband to have shown little interest in the children of his wife's first marriage. Yet Townshend, who gave Lady Caroline three more children, was very concerned about his stepchildren's education. He only went to Scotland in 1758 where he stayed for a few months in his wife's castle, not far from Edinburgh. He then tried to become a Member of Parliament for Edinburgh, against the rules of Scottish society which required a Scot to represent their city, thus provoking hostility, including that of his wife. He at least succeeded in being elected a member of the *Select Society*, to whom he had the pleasure of speaking. It is therefore only natural that Smith sent his book to this powerful and inescapable man, who was trying to establish roots in Scotland. Smith, for his part, could see from his very first meetings with the ambitious politician the advantages he could derive from proximity to a powerful statesman. Indeed Townshend was already well known on the political scene. He was a member of the Board of Trade from June 1749 to April 1754, then a member of the Board of the Admiralty from April 1754 to December 1755, before becoming Treasurer of the House (November 1756 to March 1761), Secretary at War (March 1761 to December 1762), First Lord of Trade (February to April 1763), and Paymaster-general from May 1765 to July 1766. He reached the peak of his career, which death interrupted prematurely, as Chancellor of the Exchequer in July 1766.

This brief review of the stages of his career as a statesman shows that from the late 1750s onwards, Townshend held positions in which economic concerns, and international economic relations in particular, played a major role. This sequence of positions relates not just to an appetite for honours but also to Townshend's character, which oscillated between majority and opposition on several occasions. Despite this, he achieved the feat of staying constantly in positions of responsibility in the economic field. It should be noted that the brevity of his time at the Secretariat during the war was due to his opposition to the Prime Minister who wished to put an end to the conflict. Townshend thus bore the responsibility for the prolongation of hostilities and thus for the public debt used to finance them. With the success of the *TMS*, which placed Smith at the forefront of intellectual life, this man of thought and spirit seemed perfectly capable of playing the role of advisor to a politician at the heart of power in London.

1.5 The Long Gestation of an Atypical Grand Tour

It was shortly after the publication of the *TMS* that the first contacts were established between Charles Townshend and Professor Smith, aimed at perfecting the education of his step-son (Letter # 39). At this time Smith was not free to devote himself to this task since he was the special tutor of the young Fitzmaurice, Lord Shelburne's second son. But he began the process by drawing up a list of books for the future Duke to study. The fifty-three books prescribed by Smith consisted mainly of Latin literature. This emphasis on the authors of antiquity is entirely consistent with the educational principles of an era when Latin remained the language of culture, and indeed in which Newton published his great work *Philosophiae naturalis principia mathematica* in 1687.

The emphasis on Latin is also consistent with the project, perhaps nurtured from the outset, of a Grand Tour which would lead to the countries of southern Europe, countries where Latin has remained the language of the law and the Catholic liturgy. It should also be noted that in the list of recommended works is *De Reditu Suo* by Rutilius Namatianus (see Collombet 1842). The author was probably born around 370 AD in a city in the Narbonensis which is not explicitly named, except that it is called *Palladian*, from which we can deduce that it is Toulouse (*Palladia Tolosa* in the words of the poet Ausonius). Rutilius was the son of a landowner who followed a career as a Roman civil servant and who returned to his country as Rome collapsed under the blows of the barbarian invasions. The sack of Rome by the Visigoths of Alaric I, which marks the end of antiquity, took place in 410 AD. These Visigoths made Toulouse the capital of a kingdom that they would eventually extend into Spain. The difficult return to Rome described by Rutilius is one of the rare testimonies we have of this dark era of the Roman Empire. The author evokes the religious conflicts as well as the confrontation between the pagans (among whom he probably ranks himself) who were tempted by Egyptian religions, Judaism, and Christianity.

These reflections on the fate of empires and religious struggles that may have inspired the writing of a poem in Toulouse in the fourth century were sufficient for attracting attention, and it can be surmised the route he described is indeed the one Smith intended to follow with his student a few years later. In the immediate future, a trip to the continent was not appropriate because France and England were once again at war in 1759. Since 1756, a new conflict had again torn Europe apart, after the War of the Austrian Succession (1740–1748). Historians would later call it the Seven Years' War since it ended definitively with negotiations that began at Fontainebleau in November 1762 and ended with the signing of the Treaty of Paris in January 1763.

During the negotiations, France was represented by the Duc de Choiseul and England by the Duke of Bedford. There is no doubt that Ambassador Hertford and the new Secretary of the British Embassy David Hume were involved, if not in the discussions preceding the treaty, since it was signed in January, at least in its implementation and in the monitoring of the various articles which provided for the restitution and exchange of certain territories. David Hume's main task would be the exchange of the many prisoners and hostages. He presented these tasks in a pleasant way in a letter to Adam Smith dated August 9, 1763:

> Address: To Mr. Professor Smith at Glasgow Edinburgh, 9 Aug. I763
>
> My dear Friend
>
> I have got an Invitation, accompany'd with great Prospects and Expectations, from Lord Hartford, I if I woud accompany him, tho' at first without any Character, in his Embassy to Paris. I hesitated much on the Acceptance of this Offer, tho' in Appearance very inviting; and I thought it ridiculous, at my Years, to be entering on a new Scene, and to put myself in

> the Lists as a Candidate of Fortune. But I reflected, that I had in a manner abjur'd all literary Occupations, that I resolvd to give up my future Life entirely to Amusements, that there coud not be a better Pastime than such a Journey, especially with a Man of Lord Hertford's Character, and that it wou'd be easy to prevent my Acceptance from having the least Appearance of Dependance: For these Reasons, and by the Advice of every Friend, whom I consulted, I at last agreed to accompany his Lordship, and I set out to morrow for London. I am a little hurry'd in my Preparations: But I coud not depart without bidding you Adieu, my good Friend, and without acquainting you with the Reasons of so sudden a Movement. I have not great Expectations of revisiting this Country soon; but I hope it will not be impossible but we may meet abroad, which will be a great Satisfaction to me. I am dear Smith Yours most sincerely David Hume (Letter # 73)

Having almost entirely concentrated on war on land, the position of France on the European continent had not changed vis-à-vis its neighbours. France, in particular, was given back the small possession of Belle-Île-en-Mer that the English had taken, but had to give up Minorca to the English. France withdrew from the positions it occupied in Germany and in particular in the Duchy of Hanover, which remained the private domain of the British Crown and King George II.

France was more affected with regard to its colonies. It was forced to abandon many overseas possessions. In particular, the loss of Canada and the lands of the American Central Plain in the subsequent years would affect the outlets of its businesses, particularly the firms belonging to the low-end textile industry of which these countries were major consumers.

If in the rest of the world, France's possessions were preserved, English competition became more significant, particularly in India and Africa. France retained the island of Gorée but lost Saint-Louis du Sénégal, its main land base in Senegal (Frewen 1897), for a period of time. The treaty also provided for a period of six months to verify that both parties complied with its various clauses. This ended in November 1763, three months before the start of the Grand Tour.

1.5.1 *The End of the Seven Years' War and the Green Light for the Grand Tour*

While Townshend and Smith were pondering a journey, the Seven Years' War reached a turning point (Dull 2009, pp. 200–212). In August 1759, plans to conquer the Gulf of St. Lawrence were fulfilled and Quebec City fell at the end of a battle in which Georges, Charles Townshend's brother, took part (Townshend 1901). France, for its part, was planning an invasion of Scotland from the north and of Ireland from the south—landings which, if all went well, would lead to the invasion and fall of England.

In this war, Choiseul did not intend to rely on Scottish nationalism and did not want Bonnie Prince Charlie to take the lead. It must be said that the latter had lost his lustre. Preparations for the landing lasted the whole of spring of 1759, but the shortage of barges and, more generally, the inferiority of the French navy led to the abandonment of this new attempt at an expedition, not for the last time (Corp 2005).

In any case, the period was too uncertain for Smith to envisage a departure for France since this was the most tormented and decisive year of the whole war. He probably wouldn't have been well received in France. The quality of his student, his great proximity to power, and the presence of Townshend's brother at the head of the army besieging Quebec City made it risky.

Moreover, Smith, although in contact with Townshend, did not forget his particular student of the time. He was also an aristocrat of great renown since he was the son of Lord Shelburne, brother of Horace Walpole. He was then stationed in Dublin. A letter dated April 26, 1759, from Lord Shelburne to Smith presents what is expected of a tutor charged with the education of young English aristocrats. Lord Shelburne did not just praise Smith for his "academic" teaching but emphasized character formation: a stay in a small town where distractions are rare promotes a certain community of life between the tutor and his disciple. This type of education encourages the establishment of links for the rest of their lives between aristocrat and teacher, who becomes to some extent the adviser or confidant of a young man about to become eminent in his country.

32. From Lord Shelburne

MR., GUL Gen. xo35/t38; Scott 245–8.

Dublin, 26 Apr. 1759

Sir I have lately received your letter of the 4th inst; your former of the 10th of March, came also to my hands in due time. I can not sufficiently express my Satisfaction at the account you give me of my Son, now under your care; the description you make of him, convinces me of your power of looking into him, so does the Scheme you chalk out for the prosecution of his Studies, convince me of your judgment;

> Every thing confirms that you merit that Character which made me wish so much that you should take the Charge of him upon you, and, if I mistake you not, I shall make you much amends by assuring you, that the more I reflect on the Situation he is in, the more I am happy; so much so, and so satisfied both of your Ability and Inclination to do him Service, that I must refuse the request you make, that I shou'd point out what I wish to have done, I can point out nothing, I can only approve of what you mean to do. The great fault I find with Oxford and Cambridge, is that Boys sent thither instead of being the Governed, become the Governors of the Colleges, and that Birth and Fortune there are more respected than Literary Merit;
>
> [...]
>
> Oeconomy seems likewise to have a just place in your attention; No fortune is able to do without it, nor can any man be Charitable, Generous or Just who neglects it, it will make a man happy under Slender Circumstances, and make him Shine if his Income be Affluent. Your Pupil comes into the World a sort of an Adventurer, intitl'd to nothing, and will, if I may venture to prophesy concerning him, have more in proportion as his own wants are few. (Letter # 32)

Lord Shelburne, although there is undoubtedly some confusion due to the polysemy of the term economy, notes Smith's evolution towards the themes developed in the *Lectures on Jurisprudence*, which are known to date from this period.

Smith devoted the years 1759–1763, devoid of salient events, to his studies and teaching, oriented towards economic themes (Scott 1965, pp. 94–102). He would later find that these years of study and strong investment in organizing university life comprised the most positive period of his life.

At the beginning of 1763, the Treaty of Paris marked the end of hostilities and new perspectives were opened up, as the news sent to him by David Hume suggested:

> Lisle Street, Leicester Fields, 13 Sept. 1763
>
> Lord Shelburne resignd because he found himself obnoxious on account of his Share in the Negotiation. I see you are much displeasd with that Nobleman but he always speaks of you with regard. I hear that your Pupil, Mr Fitzmaurice, makes a very good figure at Paris. (Letter #75)

David Hume refers to the negotiations that followed the signing of the Treaty of Paris, in which Lord Shelburne took part as an adviser. Lord

Shelburne's son, a former student of Smith's, began a long career as a diplomat in Paris, which soon led him as an ambassador to the four corners of Europe and then the world.

With a clear horizon ahead, Charles Townshend returned to his project to entrust the Duke of Buccleuch to Smith:

> Adderbury, 25 Oct. 1763
>
> Dear Sir The time is now drawing near when the Duke of Buccleugh intends to go abroad, I take the liberty of renewing the subject to you: that if you should still have the same disposition to travel with him I may have the satisfaction of informing Lady Dalkeith and His Grace of it, and of congratulating them upon an event which I know that they, as well as myself, have so much at heart. The Duke is now at Eton: He will remain there until Christmass. He will then spend some short time in London, that he may be presented at Court, and not pass instantaneously from school to a foreign country; but it were to be wished He should not be long in Town, exposed to the habits and companions of London, before his mind has been more formed and better guarded by education and experience.
>
> I do not enter at this moment upon the subject of establishment, because if you have no objection to the situation, I know we cannot differ about the terms. On the contrary, you will find me more solicitous than yourself to make the connection with Buccleugh as satisfactory and advantageous to you as I am persuaded it will be essentially beneficial to him.
>
> The Duke of Buccleugh has lately made great progress both in his knowledge of ancient languages and in his general taste for composition. With these improvements, his amusement from reading and his love of instruction have naturally increased. He has sufficient talents: a very manly temper, and an integrity of heart and reverence for truth, which in a person of his rank and fortune are the firmest foundation of weight in life and uniform greatness. If it should be agreeable to you to finish his education, and mould these excellent materials into a settled character, I make no doubt but he will return to his family and country the very man our fondest hopes have fancied him.
>
> I go to Town next Friday, and should be obliged to you for your answer to this letter.—I am, with sincere affection and esteem, dear sir, your most faithful and most obedient humble servant,
>
> C. Townshend.
>
> Lady Dalkeith presents her compliments to you. (Letter # 76)

This letter provides us with much information on the state of mind of the putative travellers. Townshend does not hide his concerns surrounding the moral ambiguity and the corruption of *sentiments*, themes that are often found in J.-J. Rousseau. Beyond London, Townshend considers Paris to be the great city that corrupts minds and morals. From this point of view, size gave Toulouse an advantage over Paris.

The date of the letter is also important. The Treaty of Paris provided for a transitional period of six months for the exchange of territories. Yet in the desire for lasting peace, countries fulfilled the most important part of their obligations as early as July (Dull 2009, p. 370). As far as France was concerned, no ship had gone to the rescue of New France and indeed a squadron had just arrived off the coast of France, aboard which were the last leaders of the colony, abandoning to their fate the French settlers who had become, in spite of themselves, subjects of the Crown of England. Charles Townshend was well aware of all these important facts and for him, the way was clear for a departure to France.

The letter also confirms that the trip had been planned for a few years and Townshend believed that the time had come to focus more explicitly on Smith's services. The war ended in an undeniable victory for the British-led coalition. The United Kingdom had taken over many territories, forming the basis of its immense future empire, but this had come at a high cost which worried the Chancellor of the Exchequer. This war had been very expensive, both for the French side where the State finances would quickly be perceived as a major problem and for the victorious side. France's financial difficulties at the end of the eighteenth century are well known. They have their origins in the exceptional deficit that burdened the economy following the Seven Years' War. All the efforts of many ministers—Choiseul, Necker, Turgot, and Loménie de Brienne—failed to restore equilibrium, curb the phenomenon, or even take stock of its dimension, since the appropriate tools were lacking (Roche 1993, pp. 404–424 and pp. 551–571).

The situation for the victorious side was not much better. The financial situation worsened and the measures taken to involve the colonies led to the great American Revolution and the independence of the United States in 1776 (Belissa et al. 2007). Charles Townshend would furthermore be the originator of the "*Sugar* Act" of 1764, an attempt to subject the American colonies to new taxes for the benefit of the crown on the importation of sugar, mainly from the Caribbean islands (Chaffin 1970).

During these years, Townshend was not only looking for innovative solutions but also for an understanding of the financial systems. He was particularly interested in a form of deficit financing by setting up "Sinking Funds". The specific study he asked Smith to do on the subject will be examined later (see also Scott 1965).

1.5.2 The First Development of Smith's Economic Thinking

A chronological reading of Smith's lectures shows that in the years preceding the voyage, Smith became increasingly interested in the production of wealth. Long passages on labour show that Smith definitively adopted it not only as a tool for measuring wealth but also as the main factor of production. Smith's focus was on the division of labour which would open the *Wealth of Nations* in 1776, ten years after his return from France, but also thirteen years after the first lessons that addressed this theme.

Other economic issues were also dealt with, such as the value of goods, the notion of natural and market prices, along with currency and the balance of trade with foreign countries. The very last lessons focused on the opulence of nations or how nations can be classified according to their level of development in agriculture, in the arts, or in trade, many subjects that he probably intended to study further during his stay in Europe.

If young John Milard is to be believed, the last lesson was about war and the best ways to end it, very much a direct allusion to the Seven Years' War.

It is remarkable that Smith, preparing to travel to Toulouse, had almost become more of an "economist" than a philosopher. It was not the meeting with the[7] French physiocrats, during his stay in Paris in 1766, that made him change course. On the contrary, we now know, thanks to Professor Scott in particular, that during the last weeks of his stay in Glasgow, Smith prepared a brief addressed to Charles Townshend entitled "Opulence of the nations". The manuscript, which had been dictated, was found in the 1930s in the Buccleuch family archives.[8] It is an important document because it can be considered a preliminary sketch for the *Wealth of Nations*. This short 42-page document shows Smith's preoccupation with writing a treatise on economics. Townshend also annotated the document, which demonstrates his involvement and cooperation with Smith.

[7] Currently held as MS 23 254 at the National Library of Scotland.
[8] Currently held as MS 23 254 at the National Library of Scotland.

As has been seen, the question of debt was very important for the Chancellor not only because the British deficits had increased following the Seven Years' War but also because of disorders in colonial trade. Smith and Townshend were concerned about debt amortization and searched for the best way to organize Sinking Funds (Ross 1892). It is possible Townshend hoped to take advantage of Smith's trip to gather information on the way France was proceeding to clean up its finances. As will be seen, the documents reported by Smith tend to prove that this hope was justified. Nevertheless, shortly before Christmas 1763, Smith made his decision, as he informed his long-time friend David Hume, who had held the very official post of Secretary of the English Embassy in Paris for several months. As was also reflected in the article in the *Edinburgh Review*, he was attracted to Paris and France; the situation was now ideal, with Hume having official duties in Paris. The latter, who would make Smith the executor of his will, had spared no effort to ease his journey. Obviously, Hume had not held Smith responsible for his lack of support a few years earlier when he had been a candidate to succeed Craigie, Hutcheson's successor at the University of Glasgow. Smith had then formulated a somewhat ambiguous and not very courageous justification: "I should prefer David Hume to any man for a colleague; but I am afraid the public would not be of my opinion; and the interest of the society will oblige us to have some regard to the opinion of the public" (Letter #10 November 15, 1751). It is true that the same cabals that had prevented Hume's recruitment to Edinburgh University were at work in Glasgow within the university senate.

1.5.3 A Hasty Departure

More than four years after the first contacts between Townshend and Smith, it was by a letter of December 12, 1763, that Smith announced the imminence of his departure to Hume:

> To David Hume
>
> My Dear Hume,
>
> Glasgow, 12 Dec. 1763
>
> The day before I received your last letter I had the honour of a letter from Charles Townshend, renewing in the most obliging manner his former proposal that I should travel with the Duke of Buccleugh, and informing me that his Grace was to leave Eton at Christmas, and would go abroad very soon after that. I accepted the proposal, but at the same time expressed to

Mr Townshend the difficulties I should have in leaving the University before the beginning of April, and begged to know if my attendance upon his Grace would be necessary before that time. I have yet received no answer to that letter, which, I suppose, is owing to this, that his Grace is not yet come from Eton, and that nothing is yet settled with regard to the time of his going abroad. I delayed answering your letter till I should be able to inform you at what time I should have the pleasure of seeing you …

I ever am, my dearest friend, most faithfully yours,

Adam Smith (Letter # 78)

It was Smith himself who had to solve the problem of his leaving with his university because Townshend refused any delay, and so the departure for London took place, with considerable haste, around Christmas 1763, to the point that Smith's resignation would only be announced to the Rector of his university once the journey had begun and the travellers had arrived in Paris.

To Thomas Miller

Address: To the Right Honourable Thomas Miller Esqr. His Majesty's Advocate for Scotland

University; Scott.

My Lord

I take this first opportunity, after my arrival in this Place, which was not till yesterday to resign my Office into the hands of Your Lordship, of the Dean of Faculty, of the Principal of the College and of all my other most respectable and worthy colleagues. Into Your and their hands therefore I do hereby resign from my Office of Professor of Moral Philosophy in the University of Glasgow and in the College thereof, with all the emoluments Privileges and advantages which belong to it. I reserve however my Right to the Salary for the current half year which commenced at the 10th of October for one part of my salary and at Martinmass last for another; and I desire that this Salary may be paid to the Gentleman who does that part of my Duty which I was obliged to leave undone, in the manner agreed on between my very worthy colleagues and me before we parted. I never was more anxious for the Good of the College than at this moment and I sincerely wish that whoever is my Successor may not only do Credit to the Office by his Abilities but be a comfort to the very excellent Men with whom he is likely to spend his life, by the Probity of his heart and the Goodness of his Temper.

I have the Honour to be my Lord, your Lordship's most obedient and most faithful Servant

Adam Smith (Letter #81)

Between the announcement of the voyage on December 12, 1763, and the letter from Paris of Saturday, February 14, 1764, we have only indirect testimonies concerning Smith's stay in London as well as of his voyage. An attempt at a reconstruction starts from the few clues which are available.

His departure from Glasgow took place in the early days of 1764 or the very last days of 1763, and he arrived in London in mid-January. Testimony of Smith's passage through London is provided in the biography of Joshua Reynolds, then the fashionable painter of the English aristocracy and founding member of the *Dining Club*, to which Smith was admitted in 1775.

> I find one note of a dinner in Dartmouth Street, Westminster, on Sunday, March the 11th, when his host, I have little doubt, was Dr. Adam Smith, then in London, preparing to start for the Continent as travelling tutor to the young Duke of Buccleuch. He had been selected for the post by Charles Townshend, who had married the Duke's mother. (Leslie and Taylor 1865, p. 238)

The author of the biography places the dinner with Smith in March 1764, but there is some confusion about this date. The same book notes that a small business card found a few years later in Reynolds' diary indicates Smith's address in London: "*At Mrs. Hill's Dartmouth Street, Westminster.*"

This meeting between Reynolds and Smith was perhaps the occasion to evoke other Grand Tours, those of Laurence Sterne, the novelist, or the celebrated Shakespearean actor David Garrick, most well-known for being responsible for putting Stratford upon Avon on the map with his *Shakespeare* Jubilee. Reynolds had painted a magnificent portrait of Laurence Sterne a few years earlier. In January 1764, Sterne was about to leave Toulouse, where he had spent a year, for Montpellier. For his part, David Garrick, with his Viennese wife, had undertaken in September 1763 a tour of Europe which included a stay in Paris where he would be the darling of the salons—and in particular of Mrs Riccoboni who was also enamoured with Smith during his stay in Paris in 1766, to the point of giving him a letter of introduction addressed to Garrick.

It is also conceivable that the famous portrait of the Duke by Thomas Gainsborough, the other great painter of the English aristocracy at the end of the eighteenth century, was part of the preparations for the long and uncertain journey. It was safer to acquire one last picture before embarking on an adventure full of dangers and possibly diseases in a continent where there were still cases of cholera, a terrible malady whose epidemics were as sudden and deadly as they were ignorant of the social classes. This portrait of great artistic quality shows us a young aristocrat with fine features and in excellent health, who seems somewhat fragile but possessed, as he should be, of a determined gaze. He is carrying a small dog which gives the viewer essential information about the character of the young Duke, who would be a great animal lover all his life. He even prohibited hunting on his land, preferring to see wild animals in his parks.

The travellers left London in the first days of February, arriving in Paris on February 13, 1764, if Smith's letter of resignation is to be believed.

The two travellers probably crossed the English Channel towards Calais or Boulogne, which for the English and Scots were the two easiest ports of entry into the Bourbon kingdom. The archives of the city of Calais and also the departmental archives cannot provide a possible list of travellers for the year 1764, however grand and prestigious they may have been. The traffic, for a while interrupted, had become very important for a crossing that only took a short time (at most one day, if the weather was kind).

The two travellers were accompanied by one or two servants, as was customary at the time, including a Mr. Cook. Mr. Cook is described simply as a servant by Smith's many English biographers, but the duties assigned to him suggest that he was a butler attached to the young Duke. Before reaching Toulouse, their final destination for a few months, they would make a very short stop in Paris. This is a Grand Tour which, from its beginning, promised to be atypical—unusual, in particular, because this Grand Tour would be centred around a city of the South of France. More than a tour, it was, in a way, a long period of residential study. It was also atypical in its choice of a final destination. If Paris was the "City of Lights", Venice was certainly the show city of Europe. As for Rome, the "Eternal City", it represented for all Latinists and lovers of classical literature the culmination of every journey and every intellectual quest for a man of culture. Was not seeing the ruins of ancient Rome to discover the truth underlying the history of our civilization? Instead of these usual destinations for the Grand Tour, the pair of travellers would take the direction of Toulouse for a long stay of almost two years.

References

Abitboul, Olivier. 2003. Préface à Francis Hutcheson. *Essai sur la nature et la conduite des passions et affections avec illustrations sur le sens moral* (1726). Paris: L'harmattan, pp. 5–15.

Addison William Innes. 1901. *The Snell Exhibitions: From the University of Glasgow to Balliol College*, Oxford, Glasgow: MacLehose.

Belissa, Marc, Edmond Dziembowski, Jean-Yves, Guiomar. 2007. De la Guerre de Sept Ans aux révolutions: Regards sur les relations internationales. *Annales historiques de la révolution française*, N°349 juillet–septembre.

Boswell, James. 1769. *An account of Corsica the journal of a tour to that island, and memoirs of Pascal Paoli.* London: Printed for Edward and Charles Dilly in the Poultry.

Chaffin, Robert J. 1970. The Townshend Acts of 1767. *The William and Mary Quarterly Series*, Vol. 27, No. 1, pp. 90–121.

Collombet, François. 1842. *L'Itinéraire de Rutilius Claudius Namatianus, ou son retour de Rome dans les Gaules*, Poème en deux livres, Paris: Éditions Jules Delalain.

Corp, Edward T. 2005. The Jacobite Presence in Toulouse during the Eighteenth Century, in *Revue Diaspora Framespa*; No. 5 *Généalogie rêvées*, pp. 224–246.

Daiches, David. 1973. *Bonnie Prince Charlie, the life and times of the Charles Edward Stuart*, London: Thames and Hudson, pp. 193–218.

Desbarreaux-Bernard, Tibulle. 1854. Notice biographique de Pierre Rousseau, *Mémoires de l'Académie impériale des sciences inscriptions et belles-lettres de Toulouse*, pp. 368–397.

Diderot, Denis et al. 1765. *Encyclopédie, ou Dictionnaire raisonné des sciences, des arts et des métiers, par une société de gens de lettres, Tome neuvieme, JU-MAM*, Neufchâtel, Faulche.

Dixon, William & Wilson David. 2006. Das Adam Smith Problem, a critical realist perspective, *Journal of Critical Realism*, Vol. 5, No. 2, pp. 251–272.

Dull, Jonathan R. 2009. *La Guerre de Sept Ans, Histoire Navale, Politique et Diplomatique*, Éditions les Perséïdes, pp. 197–208.

Ferguson, Adam & Ernest Campbell Mossner. 1960. "Of the Principle of Moral Estimation: A Discourse between David Hume, Robert Clerk, and Adam Smith": An Unpublished MS. *Journal of the History of Ideas* Vol. 21, No. 2 (Apr.–June), pp. 222–232.

Frewen, Lord Walter. 1897. Goree: A Lost Possession of England, *Transactions of the Royal Historical Society.* New Series, Vol. 11, pp. 139–152.

Gwynn, Stephen. 1971. *The Life of Horace Walpole.* London: Edition Ayers Publisher.

Hume, David. 1739. *A treatise of human nature.* London: John Noon.

Hutcheson, Francis. 1752 [1726]. *An Inquiry into the Original of our Ideas of Beauty and Virtue. In Two Treatises. L Concerning Beauty, Order, Harmony, Design. II. Concerning Moral Good and Evil*, London: R. Ware.
Kames, Henry Home Lord. 1728. *Remarkable decisions of the Court of Session, from 1716 to 1728*, Edinburgh: T. Ruddiman.
Kames, Henry Home, Lord. 1751. *Essays on the principles of morality & natural religion*. Edinburgh: Printed by R. Fleming, for A. Kincaid and A. Donaldson.
Kames, Henry Home, Lord. 1760. Principles of Equity. Edinburgh: Millar.
Kames, Henry Home, Lord. 1774 [1734]. Sketches of the history of man: Book II. Edinburgh: W. Creech.
Kennedy, Gavin. 2005. *Adam Smith's Lost Legacy*. London: Palgrave Macmillan.
Leslie, Charles Robert & Tom Taylor. 1865. *Life and Times of Sir Joshua Reynolds*, Volume 1: With Notices of Some of his Contemporaries. London: J. Murray.
Lomonaco, Jeffrey. 2002. Adam Smith's Letter to the Authors of the Edinburgh Review. *Journal of the History of Ideas*, Vol. 63, No 4, pp. 659–676.
Maclean, Fitzroy. 1995. *Highlanders: a history of the clans of Scotland*. London: Adelphi.
Millar, John. 1771. *Origin of the distinction of ranks, on an inquiry into the circumstances which give rise to influence and authority in the different members of society*. Edinburgh: William Blackwood.
Montagu Douglas Scott, John. 2009. *Drumlanrig, The Castle, its people and its paintings*. Hawick: Caïque Publishing.
Namier, Lewis (Sir) & John Brooke. 1964. *Charles Townshend*. New York: Mac Millan & Co Ltd, pp 150–171.
Necker, Jacques. 1821 [1784]. *Œuvres complètes*. t. IV: *De l'administration des finances de la France*. Paris: Treuttel & Würtz.
Otterspeer, William. 2001. The University of Leiden: An Eclectic Institution, in Early Science and medicine, Vol. 6, No. 4, *Science and Universities of Early Modern Europe*, pp. 324–333.
Otterspeer, William. 2008. Bastion of Liberty: Leiden University Today and Yesterday. Leiden: Leiden University Press. pp. 138–230.
Phillipson, Nicholas. 2012. *Adam Smith: an enlightened life*. New Haven: Yale University Press.
Roche, Daniel. 1993. *La France des Lumières*. Paris: Librairie Arthène Fayard.
Ross, Edward A. 1892. Sinking funds, *Publications of the American Economic Association*, Vol. 7 N°4/5 July–September, pp. 9–106.
Ross, Ian Simpson. 1972. *Lord Kames and The Scotland of His Day*. Oxford. Clarendon Press.
Ross, Ian Simpson. 2010 [2004]. *The life of Adam Smith*. Oxford: OUP.
Scott, William R. 1900. *Francis Hutcheson, his life, teaching and position in the history of philosophy*. Cambridge: Cambridge University Press.

Scott, William R. 1935. Adam Smith at Downing Street, 1766–7. *The Economic History Review*, Vol. 6, No. 1 Oct., pp. 79–89.

Scott, William R. 1965 [1937]. *Adam Smith as student and professor*. New York: Augustus M. Kelley.

Shane Andre. 1993. Was Hume an Atheist? *Hume Studies* 19 (1):141–166.

Skinner, Andrew S. 1982. *Adam Smith*. London: Routledge.

Sterne, Laurence. 1794. *Letters of the late Laurence Sterne to his most intimate friends*. With a fragment in the manner of Rabelais. London [i.e. York?]: Printed for A. Millar, W. Law, and R. Cater.

Smith, Adam. 1980 [1755–6], A Letter to the Authors of the Edinburgh Review, quoted from Smith 1980.

Smith, Adam. 1977. *The correspondence*. Oxford: Clarendon Press.

Smith, Adam et al. 1980. *Essays on philosophical subjects*. Oxford: Clarendon Press.

Stewart, Dugald. 1980 [1795]. *Account of the life and writings of Adam Smith LLD*. In Smith 1980.

Townshend, Charles. 1901. *The military life of Field-Marshal George first marquess Townshend, 1724–1807: who took part in the battles of Dettingen 1743, Fontenoy 1745, Culloden 1746, Laffeldt 1747, & in the capture of Quebec 1759; from family documents not hitherto published*. London: J. Murray.

Walpole, Horace. 1765. *The castle of Otranto: a Gothic story*. London: Printed for William Bathoe and Thomas Lownds.

Walpole, Horace. 1840. *The Letters of Horace Walpole, earl of Orford, including numerous letters now first published from the original manuscripts*. London: R. Bentley.

CHAPTER 2

Two Scots in Toulouse

> Cross one of the finest plains of wheat that is anywhere to be seen; the storm, therefore, was fortunately partial. Pass St. Jorry; a noble road, but not better than in Limosin. It is a desert to the very gates; meet not more persons than if it were 100 miles from any town.—31 miles. 14*th*.
>
> View the city, which is very ancient and very large, but not peopled in proportion to its size: the buildings are a mixture of brick and wood, and have consequently a melancholy appearance. This place has always prided itself on its taste for literature and the fine arts. It has had a university since 1215; and it pretends that its famous academy of Jeux Floraux is as old as 1323. It has also a royal academy of sciences, another of painting, sculpture, and architecture. The church of the Cordeliers has vaults, into which we descended, that have the property of preserving dead bodies from corruption; we saw many that they assert to be 500 years old. (Arthur Young *Travels in France* On the road to Toulouse (1909 [1789]), p. 31)

At Dover, the two Scots were to be joined by a third, Sir James Macdonald of Sleat, a young baronet who had been the Duke of Buccleuch's classmate at Eton. He led the highland MacDonald of Sleat clan. Mac Donald had lived in France since the restoration of peace and had conquered the Parisian salons if one is to believe the note Grimm dedicated to him when he died prematurely in Italy in 1766. According to this obituary, "He surprised everyone by the variety and extent of his knowledge, by the soundness of his judgment, by the accuracy and maturity of his mind" (Grimm, p. 144). James Macdonald was related to the son of the British ambassador in Paris and had also come into contact with

A. Alcouffe, P. Massot-Bordenave, *Adam Smith in Toulouse and Occitania*, https://doi.org/10.1007/978-3-030-46578-0_2

David Hume. Unfortunately, health problems led to the baronet's rather quick departure for Italy, where he died in 1766 before he could leave traces other than his correspondence with the writers of the Enlightenment. These Scottish encounters on French soil were to continue both in Paris and in Toulouse, where they met and got to know another young Highlander. The three forged links that would remain constant throughout their lives.

2.1 From Paris to Toulouse

According to Adam Smith's correspondence and various exchanges of letters, the first Parisian stay was brief. If the difficulties of travel and the fatigue it causes are taken into consideration, the stay can thus be summarized as a simple stopover, a period of rest with no notable activities.

Adam Smith states in his letter of resignation to the Dean of the University of Glasgow that he arrived in Paris on Monday, February 13, 1764. Abbé Colbert, who will play an important role in the daily life of Smith and his pupil and who will be discussed later at greater length, wrote from Toulouse a letter dated Saturday, March 3, in which he indicated that the travellers had just arrived there.

According to *L'Indicateur fidèle*, the mail service for Toulouse left Paris on Wednesday morning and the journey took fifteen and a half days. Smith is known to have arrived in Toulouse on Thursday, March 1st, 1764, implying that the stop in Paris was very brief.

Charles Townshend took care to follow the journey closely, according to his letter dated April 10, 1764, which he sent *poste restante* to Toulouse, and he asked for a rapid reply.

The two travellers did not know France and even less Paris; Smith's only contact was David Hume (1711–1776), his great philosopher friend who was known and appreciated in Parisian intellectual circles, where his works were a great success. Hume, at 23, had left Scotland to pursue studies in France, which led him to the collège de La Flèche in Anjou, where Descartes and Mersenne had also studied in the previous century. During a stop in Reims, it is possible that he had met Levesque de Pouilly, the author of the *Théorie des sentiments agréables*, about whom more later. It was there that Hume prepared his *Treatise of Human Nature* from 1734 to 1737, which he published on his return to Scotland in 1739–1740 in three volumes. The first two were published anonymously, while the third, published under his name, contained an anonymous abstract of the first two. Experts have long debated the identity of the author of this summary, which is often attributed to Adam Smith, although it seems today that Hume's authorship is less controversial. According to Michel Malherbe, the *Treatise*, despite some reviews, remained unknown during the 1740s, and in 1765, the translator of a historical work by Hume wrote to him again to ask if he was the author of the *Treatise* so that Hume's notoriety in France grew only with the translation of the *Political Discourse* and even more with that of the *History of England* whose various volumes he published in 1754, 1756, 1759, and 1761. In the middle of the eighteenth century, history was no longer limited to a pure chronicle of the succession of royal families, battles, wars, betrayals, and treaties, but was more a matter of reflecting on monarchical regimes (divine law) and their origin. Hume's *Histoire d'Angleterre* was a true bestseller in Paris because of its literary character, quality of research, and ease of reading, along with Voltaire's historical works *L'histoire de Charles XII*, which dates from 1731, and the very famous *Siècle de Louis XIV*, published in 1751. The philosopher's presence in Paris is explained by the fact that in 1763, at the end of the Seven Years' War, Hume accepted with great enthusiasm an appointment as embassy secretary. His mission was initially relatively technical and discreet since he was more particularly responsible for the exchange of aristocratic prisoners, as opposed to ordinary soldiers whose fate was of little importance to the belligerents. As time passed and the issue of prisoners was resolved, he took charge of legal matters that his compatriots might encounter in France. His reputation, presence, good elocution, ferocious appetite, and a taste for the good wines of France as well as for the ladies of the capital made Hume a man of the salons that hosts loved to receive. As soon as he arrived in Paris, he attended Madame de Boufflers' very Anglophile salon. In 1763, she had gone to London for the peace negotiations and had established a relationship with Horace Walpole, whom she welcomed in Paris. Her salon was thus a place where the Scottish and French Enlightenment could converse.

Like the rest of the trip, the brief stop in Paris has not left much of a trace. Adam Smith and his young pupil had to confine themselves to a few visits to the English embassy to meet their long-time companion and friend David Hume, who was the instigator of the trip. This is what emerges from a letter addressed to David Hume dated March 4, 1764, at the arrival of the travellers in Toulouse, by the young Abbé Colbert, one of the vicars general of the diocese of Toulouse:

> I am flattered and grateful, Mr. and dear cousin, for the honour you give me to address your friend, Mr. Smith. It seems to me everything you say in your letter, a man of spirit and an honest man.

We can thus reconstruct Smith's short stopover in Paris. He visited Hume who gave him a letter addressed to his "cousin", the vicar general of the archdiocese of Toulouse who bore a famous name and who will be a presence throughout Smith's stay on the continent.

During his short stay in Paris, it is more than likely that Smith and his student stayed at the Hôtel du Parc Royal in the Faubourg Saint-Germain, very close to the English Embassy, in an aristocratic district where the hôtels of the great families during the end of the reign of Louis XV were located: Hôtel de Conti,[1] Hôtel de Maurepas, Hôtel de Bonneval, Hôtel de Seignelay,[2] Hôtel de Condé, Hôtel de Riquet-Caraman, Hôtel de Maupeou, and hôtel de Brienne. The last three have links with Toulouse since the Riquet-Caramans were the descendants of the builders of the Canal du Languedoc, or Canal de jonction des Deux-Mers, and were linked to the Maupeou family while Étienne-Charles de Loménie de Brienne was the Archbishop of Toulouse. We have some insights on the travel conditions that awaited travellers, thanks to a letter addressed from Abbé Colbert to the Young Duke in the autumn of 1766:

> I was six weeks between Paris and Toulouse [...] I stayed in the various places along my route; I didn't travel like you, My Lord, in a good coach or in an English post-chaise, at your ease, eating good food and enjoying the girls; but I either trotted along on hired horses which fell at every step, or I rode at full speed along the post roads, my buttocks bleeding, my bones dislocated and my whole body bruised [..] Letter from Colbert to Henry Scott-Douglas, 09/18/1766[3]

Thus Abbé Colbert did not follow the most direct route through Orléans and Limoges. This route could be problematic in winter, and travel guides still recommended a comfortable and safe trip down the Rhône valley. The river was easily navigable even if, as our letter-writer

[1] It was in this hôtel that the young Mozart lived at the same time (Mozart, Paradis 2005).

[2] Although bearing this name, the young Abbé Colbert did not own this mansion. He had no rights on this property despite a distant real or imaginary relationship with the Colbert family.

[3] National Archives of Scotland, GD 224/2040/62/3.

tells us, it remained dangerous without the many dams that now regulate its course. At the foot of the famous bridge in Avignon, travellers landed and reached Montpellier by road via Nîmes.

From Montpellier, the journey continued either by land, by post chaise, or along the canal, thanks to a water coach service. The canal boat was certainly more comfortable, but much slower than the horse-drawn coach. Given the speed of their two-week journey from Paris to Toulouse, we can deduce that Smith took the direct land route, which was probably more expensive. This was confirmed by Abbé Colbert's letter since he deplored the bad horses he had to settle for, while the Duke and his professor travelled in luxury sedans.

Individual transport, in addition to the speed it offered, avoided the kind of inconveniences that give a journey some spice, such as the picaresque meeting with a Capuchin friar described by the Abbé.

Colbert's short half-phrase "eating good food and enjoying the girls"[4] also seems to indicate that travellers had stayed in the best inns on the road, which may have offered more than just a good night's sleep. Though not unlimited, the means of the young Scottish aristocrat were considerable, especially in rural and country France where travellers of such high rank were rare.

The travellers probably looked for the best possible experience in terms of hotels, inns, and means of transportation, while wishing to preserve the greatest possible anonymity in order to avoid troublemakers or criminals.

Anecdotes about hostelries in travel literature are numerous and often humorous. However, British Grand Tour travellers generally reported that the services and quality of French inns were the best of all the countries visited. Thus the two passengers lived it up in style on the roads of France despite the risk of being assailed by highway robbers! The second part of the half-phrase is more difficult to interpret. Was this a lewd joke alluding to the sulphurous reputation of the Grand Tours? Jeremy Black confirms that these trips abroad provided multiple opportunities for sexual adventures for tourists, young, healthy, rich, with little or no supervision. These adventures were generally frowned upon, in particular due to the fear of venereal diseases, the prevalence of which, particularly in the southern regions of Europe, was the subject of numerous warnings. It is therefore not surprising that there are few clues concerning the behaviour of the

[4] Colbert wrote "baisant les filles". In the eighteenth century, the verb "baiser" already had the double meaning "to kiss" and "to have sexual intercourse".

Duke, over whom Adam Smith and Cook, the Maître d'Hôtel, were nevertheless watching. Yet one of the aims or functions of the Grand Tour, which took place during the transition period between adolescence and adulthood, was also to give the young aristocrat a knowledge of the arts of love in the very physical sense of the term, far from the oversight of family or ancestral castles where rumours could spread rapidly. But the Abbé's letter probably refers more to the Duke's return to Paris and his stay in that great city where, even more than elsewhere in late eighteenth-century France, women had the reputation of showing great "flexibility".

Although this aspect was little explored in travel literature, the Grand Tour also allowed a sentimental or sexual education in quasi-anonymity. In the case of the Duke and his guardian, it reveals to us a completely new and unexpected face of Smith that nothing suggested previously. Indeed, on the whole, Smith's biographers have always presented him as a serious, rigorous character, amiable but little inclined towards female conquests. The only "lady of the heart" mentioned is the famous "Lady of Fife". A letter from Abbé Colbert in the summer of 1766 mentions her existence while listing the many female relationships formed in Toulouse.

Back to the last month of winter 1764: after at most two weeks of travel, on Saturday, March 3, 1764, the two travellers crossed the ramparts of the city of Toulouse through the Arnaud-Bernard gate. At this point, the stay in Languedoc really begins.

2.2 Arrival in Toulouse

Arriving in Toulouse at the end of winter on a chilly day, Smith and his companion did not meet the Cardinal of Brienne, as they would have hoped following David Hume's recommendation, since he was still in Montpellier. Smith and his pupil probably settled down on their arrival at the Hôtel des Princes, located on the present Place Saint-Georges (Fig. 2.1).

There existed in Toulouse in 1764 many places to spend a night or to tarry in the city. However, the nature of these institutions was quite variable. The difference between an establishment named *Auberge chez Baptiste*, located in the Minimes suburb, and the *Hôtel de France*, in the city centre, seems to have been quite notable. The names of the visitors and their quality, which are indicated on the police book, also give good information about the various categories of hotels. In view of this information and the lifestyle that seemed to be that of the travellers, the only place likely to have accommodated them is the *Hôtel des Princes*, which is located in close proximity to the spot where the Toulouse merchant Jean Calas had recently been tortured.

The hotel was also the privileged place of residence for all English travellers who, following the end of hostilities with France, again followed the paths of adventure. Some even complained of certain promiscuity with their fellow travellers; these existed in a closed microcosm which was not conducive to immersion into French.

Smith was rather disappointed by this arrival and was very dissatisfied, especially with his student whom he was supposed to protect from the hectic life of a hotel, even one in the provinces.

Smith, a man of networks, who took good care at every moment of his life to resort to letters of recommendation, found himself in a city whose spoken language he did not handle perfectly and where he was completely unknown. Smith was undoubtedly well equipped to overcome this setback, a recurrent problem at a time when the means of direct contact between people were relatively slow. Indeed, he dealt in the *Theory of Moral Sentiments* (*TMS*) with anonymity in the crowd:

> The poor man goes out and comes in unheeded, and when in the midst of a crowd is in the same obscurity as if shut up in his own hovel. Those humble cares and painful attentions which occupy those in his situation, afford no amusement to the dissipated and the gay. They turn away their eyes from him, or if the extremity of his distress forces them to look at him, it is only to spurn so disagreeable an object from among them. The fortunate and the proud wonder at the insolence of human wretchedness, that it should dare to present itself before them, and with the loathsome aspect of its misery presume to disturb the serenity of their happiness.
>
> The man of rank and distinction, on the contrary, is observed by all the world. Every body is eager to look at him, and to conceive, at least by sympathy, that joy and exultation with which his circumstances naturally inspire him. (Smith, *TMS*, p. 93)

But with regard to this situation, Smith could rejoice in owning clothes which should have distinguished him, and in particular, he had the good fortune to be able to rely on a man, a quasi-compatriot, to open for him the merely glimpsed doors of private mansions and castles. The young Abbé Seignelay Colbert de Castle-Hill possessed many qualities, the first of which will be very useful in reconstructing Smith's journey: he was a fluent and frequent writer, with a mind turned towards the practical

Fig. 2.1 Fonds Ancely—A ESTAMPES 2—Toulouse, and the road from Paris to this city by Montauban, taken from above the bridge, on the Canal de Languedoc (August 21, 1818). (Source: Bibliothèque municipale de Toulouse)

aspects of life. This is his letter dated March 3, 1764, to David Hume describing the arrival of the *voyageurs*:

> He has only just arrived and I only saw him for a moment, I hope that we will get to know him more particularly in the future. I am annoyed that he did not find the Archbishop here. He has been in Montpellier for about two weeks, from whence he will go to Paris soon. He spoke to me of his great desire to get to know you, I am sure you will appreciate each other very much. I fear that my long black cassock will frighten the Duke of Buccleugh, but apart from that, I will do everything to make his stay in this city as pleasant and useful as it will be profitable.
>
> A recommendation like yours is a powerful and respectable reason for me to do whatever I can to respond to it.
>
> I do not know if you sometimes see the Countess de Gacé, she must have told you many things, at least I so asked her in a letter I wrote to her.
>
> Here I am, dear cousin less pleasantly occupied than when I interacted with the beautiful ladies of Paris, but those times could still return, for now it will be necessary to get through this one.

Please believe me, with high esteem and true attachment, my dear cousin, your very humble and obedient servant and loving cousin.

The letter demonstrates the helpfulness of the Abbé Colbert, always ready to assist others, and the importance he attaches to David Hume. While David Hume was Scottish, like the Abbé Colbert, to the point of calling each other "cousins", they corresponded in French even though Colbert was fluent in English. It is likely that, as with Adam Smith, the Abbé Colbert would also express himself in French, using English only in exceptional cases, the mastery of French being a sign of distinction.

In the second paragraph of his letter, he refers to the archbishop. This was the Archbishop of Toulouse, Charles Loménie de Brienne, who became Louis XVI's finance minister and was engulfed by the French Revolution. Abbé Colbert always took a back seat in all matters involving his protector. This modesty serves also as a reminder that Hume's recommendation was addressed not only to the Abbé but also, and mainly, to the archbishop.

It must be said that Loménie de Brienne resided as often as possible in Paris in his beautiful hôtel on rue Saint-Dominique, as close as possible to royal power, and in his family château in Champagne.

Of course, the allusion to the Abbé's cassock provides evidence that Colbert was able to joke with religious themes and during his life long friendship with the Duke, he never failed to tease him, belonging to the the Scottish Episcopalian Church with the Catholic decorum.

The last paragraph of the letter tells us that despite his lack of means, Abbé Colbert was nonetheless anxious to appear in the Parisian salons or at least not to be forgotten. In Paris, he frequented the Countess of Gacé, a member of the upper ranks of the French nobility close to the Matignon family. She was born in 1733, Diane de Clermont d'Amboise, into one of the oldest noble French families. She had married Marie-François Auguste Goyon de Matignon, Comte de Gacé (1731–1763), whose father, Maréchal de France, had commanded the expeditionary force in Scotland with the Jacobite pretender in 1707. Diane's mother was Henriette de Fitz-James, the sister of the Duke of Fitz-James, who had made a name for himself in Toulouse. He was also assiduous in attending Madame du Deffand's salon, and many years later, he helped edit her correspondence with Walpole. Colbert's political orientation and religion did not affect the warmth of his relationship with Hume or the good disposition he showed his visitors.

Arriving in Toulouse, without a large reception committee, the two travellers probably settled, after a few days in a hotel, in a house whose exact location remains the subject of speculation, and will be examined later.

2.3 That Strange Abbé Colbert

But who was this character that the travellers encountered in Toulouse? His surname suggests that he belonged to a family that included a great line of ministers of the Kings of France and in particular the greatest of them, Jean-Baptiste Colbert. Born on August 29, 1619, in Reims, he was one of Louis XIV's principal ministers, and he died on September 6, 1683, in Paris. He held the posts of Comptroller General of Finance from 1665 to 1683, Secretary of State for the King's House, and Secretary of State for the Navy from 1669 to 1683. His eldest son (Jean-Baptiste Antoine, 1651–1690) had been made Marquis de Seignelay by Louis XIV and had succeeded his father as Secretary of State for the Navy. The brother of the Grand Colbert, Charles (1625–1696), followed a career in administration and then in diplomacy, which led him to play an important role as an intermediary between France and England where he was the ambassador in London from 1668 to 1674.

Abbé Colbert also included in his surname the name Castlehill which links him to the great Scottish families. It is, therefore, appropriate to get to know better the person who will become the cicerone of the two travellers—a travel companion, guide, and a source of logistical support, if we express ourselves in modern terms.

In fact, Abbé Colbert descended from one of the branches of the Scottish family of Cuthbert and had been baptized under the name of "Seignelai",[5] rather incongruous in Scotland, to recall the links between the Cuthberts of Scotland and the Colberts of France. The similarity of the surnames Cuthbert and Colbert is not very obvious, yet the Grand Colbert, anxious to claim a relationship with the "nobility of the sword", since his father was a simple merchant draper, had been convinced by genealogists that he came from this noble family of Scotland. The evidence for this claim relied on the presence of a snake in the arms of both families to fill in any gaps in the documents. However, on April 29, 1686, the Scottish Parliament agreed that the origin of the Colberts of France lay in the noble Cuthbert family. The Parliament was thus responding to the

[5] Seignelai (later Seignelay) was baptized by Presbyterian Minister Alexander M'Bean, nicknamed the John Knox of the North.

requests it had received when Charles Colbert de Croissy was ambassador to London. For the Parliament, it was an opportunity to consolidate the Auld Alliance between France and Scotland, then still independent for a few decades yet, and it was perhaps not insensitive to a few subsidies provided in return.

Seignelay was baptized at Castlehill on August 13, 1735 by Presbyterian Minister Alexander M'Bean, nicknamed the John Knox of the North, on the lands of an old Scottish family located in the far north of the country, near the small town of Inverness (Scott & Murray, 1866). This town was not far from the sad site of Culloden where the last Jacobite rebellion was to be crushed, about ten kilometres from Loch Ness, famous to tourists from all over the world. Inverness is one of the most extreme ports in Scotland: the climate is harsh and life must have been particularly austere and difficult in a country with very low agricultural potential.

His father, George Cuthbert, the twelfth Lord of Castle-Hill, was a sheriff-deputy of Inverness and a witch hunter. In 1748 he suffered a fall from a horse, from which he did not recover, at the very place where he had caused the witches to be executed. Legend had it that these women had taken revenge. He left his domain in a very bad financial condition. Two of his brothers, taking advantage of the good relations with the Colbert family of France, had already emigrated there. The first was known as the Abbé Alexandre Colbert (1702–1782). He became the thirteenth Lord of Castlehill and tried to save the family estate from creditors. The second was Lachlan (born 1710) who was married in Calais to the heiress of an English family from that town and served in the "Royal-Ecossois" (Scottish Royal Regiment in the French army) as Major General. He was taken prisoner at the Battle of Culloden in 1746 and spent a few months in prison in Inverness before being exchanged. Thus Seignelay's relatives sought to escape a compromised economic situation by taking orders, joining the army, or moving to the colonies. Some of Seignelai's siblings left for Jamaica or Canada, while the youngest, Lachlan, (born in 1743) was trained at the British artillery school in Woolwich. A promising young officer, he covered himself with glory during the British expedition which led to the occupation of Belle Isle (1761–1763) in Brittany during the Seven Years' War. At the end of the war, during which he had been seriously wounded, Lachlan returned to France for treatment, perhaps with his uncles or brother, but he died in 1764.

When Seignelay became Bishop of Rodez, the *Scots Magazine* presented his career as follows:

> This gentleman is the eldest son of the late Mr Colbert of Castlehill; in Invernes-shire. He came over to France at the age of fourteen years, and was placed by his uncle, a Roman·Catholic clergyman, in the Scotch college at Paris, where he remained some years: He was afterwards in the college of Harcourt. He returned to the Scotch college, received priestly orders, was made Vicar-general in the diocese of Tolouse.

The "Collège d'Harcourt", founded in the thirteenth century and linked to the University of Paris, enjoyed a great reputation and could boast of illustrious former students (Boileau, Racine, Montesquieu, among others). Colbert distinguished himself there, particularly by winning prizes which proved his great application to his studies and his good integration in the Parisian university world. Above all, he made his college proud by being nominated two years in a row, in 1753 and 1754, to the "Concours Général", organized every year since 1747 between the students of the Parisian colleges. In 1754, Colbert, designated as *Scotus*, even won the "prix d'honneur", a feat that had not been achieved by any student of the Collège d'Harcourt since 1750 (Bouquet, p. 384). This virtuosity in French and Latin discourse opened the doors to Parisian salons.

During this period, the young man met a young tutor or teacher, Loménie de Brienne, who would change the course of his life. Étienne-Charles de Loménie de Brienne (1727–1794) made him one of his vicars general when he was appointed Archbishop of Toulouse, alongside the younger members of famous French families (Fig. 2.2).

Loménie often ensured that they, in turn, became bishops. This was the case for Abbé Colbert, who became Bishop-Count of Rodez, as well as for Chaumont de la Galaizière, later Bishop of Saint-Dié, suffragan of Trèves, and the Abbé Osmond de Médavi, future Bishop of Comminges. Loménie dreamt of restoring the prestige of his family and saw Toulouse as a stage to reach the heights of both church and State. He thus nurtured his relations in the capital where he stayed regularly. A follower of Turgot (1727–1781), who did not take clerical orders, and Morellet (1727–1819), who undertook the translation of the *Wealth of Nations (WN)* in his residence, where he also welcomed Colbert, Loménie was also close to d'Alembert.

Thus the young Abbé Colbert, through his mentor, Loménie de Brienne, was in contact with the French intellectual elite, while his origin allowed him to remain in contact with the Scottish aristocracy, especially those who had nursed Jacobite sympathies. Indeed he was involved in the stormy debates around the legacy of the Duke of Douglas. This was a court case that would be heard in Edinburgh, but also in France, and finally decided in London. As shall be seen, Smith's last-known activity in Toulouse in early autumn 1765 consisted precisely in gathering the testimony of Abbé Colbert who had been involved in the case. This will be returned to in more detail when presenting Smith's last days in Toulouse.

Like for many at that time, Abbé Colbert's entry into orders was not exclusively due to a religious vocation. His parents belonged to the Presbyterian Church (being possibly underground Catholics) and his two uncles abjured when they arrived in France and converted to Catholicism. As attested to in part by his correspondence with Mr. Boudard, the director general of the treasury of the diocese of Lisieux, by becoming a clergyman he intended to obtain a rank in France in conformity with that which he thought should be his in Scotland. To have a prestigious name and to have an income that would allow him to shine in society were the criteria that would allow him to be part of the elite during the last decades of the modern period. Unfortunately, for Colbert, financial comfort would be a long time coming. He could not expect anything from Scotland because the family estate was riddled with debts and indeed went into judicial liquidation a few years later. Moreover, there was no specific remuneration for vicars general, who could only expect to receive the income from an

Fig. 2.2 Seignelay Colbert, deputy of the clergy for Sénechaussée de Rodez, Estates General, 1789. (Source: Assemblée Nationale)

abbey bestowed by the bishop who nominated them (John McManners 1998, p. 192). The visit of the Duke and his guardian was, therefore, an excellent opportunity for him to shine in the provincial world where he displayed his cassock in churches, Episcopal jurisdictions, and ecclesiastical assemblies. For those lacking income, intellectual work also conferred a notable reputation in the eighteenth century, which saw the invention of the impassioned intellectual, specifically around the Calas affair. But Catholic Enlightenment, if it was not non-existent, had difficulty emerging, and the two books that Colbert would publish under the pseudonym of Baron de C**, in 1770 (*Les Eléments du droit de la nature et de la morale naturelle*) and in 1782 (*Projet d'un traité de paix générale et perpétuelle entre les différentes puissances chrétiennes de l'Europe précédé d'explications préliminaires*) would go largely unnoticed. He achieved glory only fleetingly by bringing his vote to the Third Estate during the Estates General in 1789, before deciding to emigrate to London in 1792 (see Alcouffe and Moore 2020).

The travellers arrived in Toulouse in March 1764. Now that their main guide has been introduced, it is appropriate to present the conditions of their stay in the city as well as the places and institutions they visited.

2.4 Settling in and First Impressions of Toulouse

After a few days spent at the Hôtel des Princes, the travellers began to settle in. To date, the place chosen is not known, but Smith is clear in the letter he addressed to Hume on July 5, 1764: he has a place which he shares with his pupil and the few servants essential to keep a house in order. Fortunately, other British travellers have reported on trips to southern France in the 1760s, for example, Tobias Smollett (1721–1771) and Laurence Sterne (1713–1768). The first was a Scottish writer who travelled to France and Italy from April 1763 to June 1765. Tobias Smollett had studied medicine at the University of Glasgow, but he turned to literature, publishing translations from French (*The adventures of Gil Blas de Santillane*) and Spanish (*Don Quixote*), works which inspired his most famous novel, *The Adventures of Roderick Random*, published in 1748. In the account of his travels across France and Italy, Smollett speaks little of Toulouse, having established his quarters in Montpellier, except to mention the transport of his luggage by sea to Bordeaux, then on the Garonne to Toulouse and, of course, by the Canal du Languedoc (now called Canal du Midi) to Sète (Smollett 1766). Comparatively, Sterne's accounts are much more interesting at this stage of Smith's journey. Laurence Sterne had published *Tristram Shandy's Life and Views* starting in 1759. The book was an immediate success, in England as on the continent and particularly in France, where Diderot was inspired to write *Jacques le Fataliste* while Crébillon suggested that Sterne and he should write a book jointly. Sterne was a close friend of Charles Townshend's, to the point that he had been able to tell one of his correspondents, Stephen Croft, in March 1761, that Townshend was to be appointed Secretary at War, one month before the official announcement.

In Paris, Sterne was received in the best salons, notably at the home of the Baron d'Holbach, whom Hume also frequented. He enjoyed the affection that people showed him and he confided to a friend that "the French love an absurd man like me". Thus it was an author already famous in Paris who arrived in Toulouse. In a letter dated August 14, 1763, to a friend who had remained in Paris, he gives us abundant details of his residence in Toulouse. Already in poor health at 50, he stayed in a house he describes as follows:

> Well! here we are, after all, my dear friend, and most deliciously placed at the extremity of the town, in an excellent house, well furnish'd, and elegant beyond any thing I look'd for.—'Tis built in the form of a hotel, with a pretty court towards the town—and behind, the best garden in Toulouse, laid out in serpentine walks, and so large that the company in our quarter usually come to walk there in the evenings, for which they have mr consent—"the more the merrier."
>
> The house consists of a good *Salle a manger* above stairs, joining to the Very great *salle à compagnie* as large as the Baron d'Holbach's; three handsome bedchambers with dressing-rooms to them—below stairs two very good rooms for myself, one to study in, the other to see company.—I have, moreover, cellars round the court, and all other offices.—Of the same landlord I have bargained to have the use of a country house which he has two miles out of town, so that myself and all my family have nothing more to do than to take our hats and remove from the one to the other.—My landlord is, moreover, to keep the gardens in order—and what do you think I am to pay for all this? neither more nor less than thirty pounds a year—all things are cheap in proportion—so we shall live for very little. (Sterne, pp. 216)

He had been even more specific in another letter two days earlier, stating that "the garden measures two acres, he has a very good cook, his wife has a decent maid and a nice looking lackey and he owes it all to the Abbé McCarthy". Smith would be reminded of this Abbé McCarthy in a letter from Abbé Colbert dated June 17, 1770, so he probably provided Smith's accommodation as he had done for Sterne.

The description provided by Sterne corresponds to the indications found in the letters of Smith or Townshend. The site is close to Abbé Colbert's residence and is not more than twenty minutes' walk from the University of Toulouse, located in the Basilique Saint-Sernin district. There is thus a cluster of presumptions which suggests that Smith could have occupied the same house as Sterne had. The house would then be situated near the present "Jardin des Plantes", planned in the *Projet pour le commerce et les embellissements de Toulouse (Project for trade and the beautification of Toulouse)* published in 1754 by Louis de Mondran.

Finally we have other indications about Smith's probable lifestyle by looking at the Earl of Morton's during his stay in Toulouse a few years later. Lord Morton was a Scottish aristocrat whose social status was similar to that of the Buccleuchs. In the eighteenth century, their two destinies crossed, not only in Toulouse but also because the Buccleuch family bought the castle of Dalkeith in the suburbs of Edinburgh from the Morton family. Unlike the Duke, the Earl, who may have had limited financial resources, maintained a house "daybook" during his stay in which he recorded the expenses of his household very accurately.

Older than the young Henry Scott, he travelled alone and remained in Toulouse from 1772 to 1774 from whence he left for Naples. It was not exactly a Grand Tour, as he, like many others, travelled for health reasons. It seems that a lung disease led him to seek the sun. He would not return from his trip to Naples, and his diary is one of the few memories he would leave.[6]

Here are the expenses that he noted for early March 1772 (eight years after Smith's passage):

[6]NAS, GD150/2720—Household Book in French during Earl of Morton's Stay in Toulouse and Naples 1772–1774.

March 5, 1773:		
Gardening		19 d
½ lamb, head, sweetbreads, feet	2 £	4 d
Olives		24 s
March 6, 1773:		
18 oranges	2 £	14 d
March 7, 1773:		
Gardening	1 £	5 d
1 poularde	1 £	4 d
1 lamb wedge and sweetbreads	1 £	7 d
1 dozen eggs	1 £	5 d
Olives and watermelons	1 £	17 d
4 quarters tea sugar	2 £	17 d
Sweetbreads and almonds		18 d
March 8, 1773:		
Gardening		17 d
1 half lamb and sweetbread	2 £	30 d
2 poulardes and 2 chickens	3 £	28 d
2 pigeons	1 £ 40	d
2 woodcocks	1 £ 18	d
1 yeast	1 £ 4	d

This short excerpt from the diary allows some deductions. The Count rented a house with a garden, like Sterne and probably Smith. The document as a whole appears to be principally a record of accounts between the servants and the master of the house. It seems that it is the Count himself who wrote it because it is penned in the same hand whether in Toulouse, Naples, or when he went to Bagnères-de-Bigorre in the summer of 1772 to take the water and possibly follow some treatment.

The prices also seem relatively high; perhaps the Count could not bargain or meat was very expensive during this lent period when it should not be consumed. Based on the quantities, it seems he was having lunch or dinner. It must be said that he had been present in Toulouse for a few months and that the Count of Morton had a large network of acquaintances since he was an influential member of Scottish Freemasonry, which was booming in Toulouse during this period.

The Earl of Morton had several servants, at least two according to the account book, but he also used either sedan chairs or carriages to get around. He also hired additional servants for a single day or evening, probably for receptions, for whom he paid little.

Smith and the Duke also had their own staff. The butler (Mr Cook) accompanied the young aristocrat throughout his stay. He played a protective role when the travellers ventured onto the roads. He was in charge of other servants recruited locally, as happened during the stay in Toulouse. It is he who would welcome Hew, the Duke's young brother, in Caen. He would even vie with Smith over the supervision of his young masters when they were bedridden to the point that Smith would complain to Hume about his "jealousy". His presence bears witness to Charles Townshend's concern to protect his step-sons.

During the sixteen months they were to spend in Toulouse, it is likely that the voyagers were permanently served by one or two servants if Earl Morton's household is anything to go by.

During his stay in Paris, during the second part of the journey, he took another servant, a certain Jean Garneaux, known as Saint Jean, a servant that David Hume recommended to him (letter from Hume, January 1766).

The material conditions of the visitors thus seem quite pleasant. Despite the disappointment of not having found Loménie de Brienne when they arrived, everything quickly returned to normal and Smith never complained about the material conditions of his stay.

The quality of one's stay, however, is mainly due to the circle in which one moves, and for Adam Smith, the first periods in Toulouse were not the easiest.

2.5 A Studious Stay

Beyond the material and purely functional side of his visit, it would be interesting to know how Smith felt about this period in residence. Although not very focused on writing, he nevertheless left a few words about his first impressions. Without solving much of the mystery, since these impressions are well known, it appears they may often have been misinterpreted by his British biographers.

It is in a letter dated July 5, 1764, almost four months after his arrival, that Smith presents his first feelings about Toulouse. As he will remain there for another fourteen months, one should not judge his stay on the basis of simple remarks which, evidently, are intended to be humorous.

> We have heard nothing, however, of these recommendations and have had our way to make as well as we could by the help of the Abbé who is a Stranger here almost as much as we. The Progress, indeed, we have made is not very great. The Duke is acquainted with no french man whatever. I cannot cultivate the acquaintance of the few with whom I am acquainted, as I

> cannot bring them to our house and am not always at liberty to go to theirs. The Life which I led at Glasgow was a pleasurable, dissipated life in comparison of that which I lead here at Present. I have begun to write a book in order to pass away the time. You may believe I have very little to do. If Sir James would come and spend a month with us in his travels it would not only be a great Satisfaction to me but he might by his influence and example be of great service to the Duke. Mention these matters, however, to nobody but to him. (Letter #82)

This "boredom" has earned Toulouse a poor reputation; however, it can be explained quite simply and through multiple causes. The first is, of course, the relative lack of preparation for the journey. Indeed, as has been mentioned, after a long waiting period the trip was only decided on in a few weeks, making it difficult to set up a network of acquaintances. Moreover, even if the Seven Years' War was over, the enemy, as Pierre Barthès often reminds us, were the English, which did not help facilitate contacts even if the notion of nationality was not to be confused with that of patriotism.

To this, we must add that Smith had retained his Scottish accent, despite his years in Oxford. It is also necessary to take into account that nearly 80% of the population of Toulouse, the circles of the craftsmen and petty tradesmen, the people of the street, spoke only the local variety of Occitan, a long way from academic French, which a university professor might use and study through classical works such as the theatre of Marivaux.

As everywhere in Europe at the end of the eighteenth century, Latin was still widely used. Smith read it fluently and used it in the homework he set his pupil. However, Latin was a language spoken less and less outside university or religious circles. This spoken Latin was often a translation of a national language, thus losing its character as a language for international communication. Furthermore, Smith was not necessarily immersed in foreign languages since there were many English people in Toulouse. With the stages of the Grand Tours coinciding once again, Smith even found Scandinavians in Toulouse, the brothers Peter and Karsten Anker and their guide Andreas Holt, who had previously stopped in Glasgow to listen to his lectures. A diary of this Grand Tour was kept and on March 16, shortly after the arrival of Smith and the Duke in Toulouse, Smith wrote in their diary:

> Having had the pleasure of meeting Messrs Anchers and Holt in Toulouse. It is with the greatest pleasure that I count myself among their relations. (Quoted in Banke, p. 54)

Smith himself wrote to Peter Anker and Andreas Holt regarding the Danish translation of the *Wealth of Nations* and recalled warmly his memory of their meeting in Toulouse (ibidem.). However, events to be mentioned later concerning the political and judicial situation in Toulouse, marked by the Calas affair on the one hand and the conflict between the Parlement and the governor on the other, may explain a mixed reception in Toulouse where, however, far from the fanaticism of which it would be accused by Voltaire, the spirit of the Enlightenment was beginning to appear.

Michel Taillefer, the great Toulouse historian, describes the change that took place in the city at the beginning of the 1760s despite the contradictory impression the persecutions of the Protestants and the fate meted out to Calas could give:

> Around 1760, the political and religious conformism that traditionally prevailed at the Académie des Jeux Floraux gave way to a growing commitment to "enlightened" ideas, and more particularly to the idea of tolerance. It guided the choice of several subjects proposed for the eloquence prize: in 1770 the eulogy of Jean-Pierre Duranti, first president of the Parliament of Toulouse in 1771 and 1772 the eulogy of Raymond VII, Count of Toulouse in 1776, (Raymond 7 was not comte de toulouse in 1776 I think there is a punctuation error in the book) the eulogy of Michel de l'Hospital, Chancellor of France; in 1773 the eulogy of Pierre Bayle was forbidden by the government.

This is all the more remarkable as it is expressed in a city where the memory of the wars of religion remains very vivid within an institution still controlled by the Parlement, the condemnation of persecutions and fanaticism is part of a wider movement of adherence to new ideas which led the Academy to put in the contests of 1786 and 1787, a eulogy of Jean-Jacques Rousseau, the first consecrated to him in France by a literary society.

Thus Toulouse's awakening corresponded well with Smith's years there, which explains why, despite his initial disappointment, he did not seek to shorten his stay.

2.6 In Pursuit of Loménie de Brienne

Smith and his pupil had acquired a cicerone, the very devoted Abbé Seignelai Colbert de Castle-Hill who stated in a letter to Hume: "I will forget nothing to make his stay in this town as pleasant and as useful as it will be profitable."

Colbert in his letter to his "cousin" Hume recounts Smith's arrival and regrets the absence of Loménie de Brienne, in whose wake he operates:

> I am angry that he did not find the Archbishop (or 'Monseigneur the archbishop) here; he has been in Montpellier for about two weeks from where he will go to Paris soon. He spoke to me of his great desire to get to know you, I'm sure you would be get on very well. (Letter from Abbé Colbert to Hume dated March 4, 1764)

One may wonder whether Hume thought of sending Smith to meet Loménie de Brienne, whose reputation was growing since his homily at the General Assembly of Bishops in 1763. The archbishop spent some time in Rome before going to Toulouse where he needed to get to know his large diocese and take part in the meeting of the Languedoc Estates of 1763. In fact, the archbishop's absence would continue. He was in Montpellier when Smith arrived, after which he would travel up the Rhône valley to Paris. He would return to Toulouse only around July 1764, if Pierre Barthès' chronicle is to be believed. His presence is recorded during the laying of the first stone of the building site of the Church of La Daurade. If he had hoped to meet him soon, Smith's disappointment was understandable. The Archbishop of Toulouse was, during Smith's passage, the "great man" of Toulouse. He would later go on to the national stage when he became Louis XVI's principal minister of State from May 1787 to August 1788. The reforms he proposed (tax reform, free trade within the country, and provincial assemblies) pitted the Paris Parlement against him and led to the convening of the Etats Généraux. Loménie de Brienne took the oath to the civil constitution of the clergy in 1790 and became constitutional bishop of the Yonne département in 1791. But arrested during the Terror, he died, perhaps poisoned, on February 19, 1794.

Charles Loménie de Brienne has a famous name. His distant family originated from the Limousin marches and experienced a slow rise to prominence during the sixteenth and seventeenth centuries until an ancestor became Secretary of State for Foreign Affairs in the service of Anne of

Austria. His great-grandfather, Louis Henri de Loménie de Brienne (1635–1698), was a childhood friend of the young future King of France Louis XIV, younger than him by three years. At the instigation of his father, Louis Henri de Loménie de Brienne undertook a Grand Tour in northern Europe, as far as Lapland, from which he brought back a travel diary that earned him fashionable consideration among the curious. He was also a great collector of works of art, but the King's favours were unreliable and Louis XIV dismissed him in 1662 when he decided to rule alone after Mazarin's death. Henri de Loménie de Brienne fell into disgrace. A compulsive writer, alternating debauchery with religious concerns, he was interned in 1674 for 17 years in Saint-Lazare asylum, described by Michel Foucault as a "maison de force" where libertine, profane, debauched, prodigal, and "mentally ill" people rubbed shoulders within a disciplinary regime (Foucault 1972, p. 176).

The path followed by Henri Loménie de Brienne impressed Voltaire as well as Saint-Simon. His great-grandson, the future Archbishop of Toulouse, was the classmate of Turgot and the Abbé Morellet at the Sorbonne. Morellet wrote in his memoirs that "still a schoolboy, he was already thinking of becoming a minister, and seemed certain of the future. He had great application; studying theology like an Hibernois [Irishman], to become a bishop, and the *Memoires* of the Cardinal of Retz, to be a statesman" (Morellet & Lemontey 1822, p. 18).

The youngest of the family, he was educated at the Collège d'Harcourt as he was destined for an ecclesiastical career in which he persisted even when his older brother died, abandoning his birthright to a younger brother, attracted as he was by the prospects of enrichment in "a well endowed church".

His ambition was matched only by his intelligence. The future Archbishop of Toulouse became a doctor of theology in 1751, although the orthodoxy of his theses was suspect. A formal critique was propounded in a small 29-page booklet by the Abbé Mey, a supporter of Jansenism. He questioned Loménie's references to Locke's theory of knowledge, which maintains that all our ideas actually derive from the experience of our senses and our thinking. Abbé Mey also spoke out against the view presented by Loménie, for whom the role of God was limited to creation while the world subsequently obeyed laws which did not require permanent intervention by the Creator. This offended against the traditional conception of miracles. But it was above all Loménie's political philosophy that was criticized. According to Mey, Loménie sought the source of the authority of princes "both in the consensus of peoples and in the authority of God. God and the people join together to communicate to the Princes the authority with which they are clothed." Abbé Mey rebuked this notion, invoking the authority of Saint-Paul and that of Pierre Nicole that "authority comes entirely from God". In the negative portrait drawn up by Abbé Mey can be clearly distinguished a young intellectual who is trying to meld several features of the philosophy of the Enlightenment, from the theory of natural law to that of the social contract, which was enough to unleash the hostility of people on the fringes of Jansenism, particularly attached to the monarchy of divine law. But Loménie's ideas were not so unique, even within the church and at the Sorbonne. Two years later, he published *Le Conciliateur* (a piece often attributed to Turgot), dated May 1, 1753, in which he advocated a compromise with the Protestants that he would eventually manage to implement when he became Louis XVI's minister.

His career developed brilliantly, since in 1760 he obtained the bishopric of Condom, at the time an important post, endowed according to the *Royal Almanac* with an income of 60,000 Livres, or approximately 3000 English pounds. On February 2, 1763, he succeeded the Archbishop of Toulouse Arthur Dillon (1721–1806), after a stay in Rome of which Vatican archives do not seem to have kept any trace. It is useful to dwell for a moment on this predecessor at the archiepiscopal see. Born in Saint-Germain-en-Laye, he was the eighth child of the Honourable Arthur Dillon, colonel and owner of the regiment of the same name, and Catherine Sheldon. He was, therefore, a younger child destined to serve the church. Admitted to the Sorbonne to pursue his studies, he obtained his degree in 1746 with a thesis on the sacrament of ordination and the validity of Anglican sacraments. In 1748, he was ordained as a priest and assigned as Grand Vicar to the Archbishop of Rouen. On August 18, 1753, he became Bishop of Évreux and doctor at the Sorbonne at the end of the same year. Five years later, in 1758, he was appointed Archbishop of Toulouse, then according to the custom of the time, Archbishop of Narbonne in 1763. The Most Reverend Arthur Richard Dillon was the very type of great lord bishop of the eighteenth century. If one refers to the traditional distinction between administrator bishops and evangelical bishops, he belonged, without question, to the first category.

It is important here to understand the functioning of the Languedoc Estates, after a long evolution. Here is how Georges Fournier presents the institutions of the Languedoc:

> At the top the Estates [latin: Comitia Occitaniæ] continued to perfect their administration, to widen their field of intervention. Apart from their annual session, their president, the Archbishop of Narbonne, and their three syndics-general seemed to play a role at least as important as the king's representative, who was also attentive to the privileges of the province. Below, in each civil diocese the assemblée de l'assiette (civil diocesan assembly) and the diocesan administration reflected the decisions of the Estates and assumed increasing responsibilities in the field of public works. Perhaps more than the subdelegate of the 'intendant', the diocesan trustee exercised concrete supervision over the communities. At the base of the structure, each of these had its consuls, in charge of enforcing the decisions of the higher administrations, but also of exercising "law enforcement" and managing collective interests. Their action was placed under the control of councils of residents who listened to the presentation of any matter of any importance, deliberated and voted. (Fournier 1989, p. 51)

Thus Judge Albisson in his monumental work on institutions could speak of a true "political constitution" whose origin he traced back to the administration imposed by Caesar and perfected by Augustus (Albisson 1780–1787, p. 7). The bishop played a central role in this system, as Massol recalls by demonstrating the continuity of the institutions of the Languedoc: "It was in a diocesan assembly, which was called 'l'assiette', that the interests of the people were discussed, that the requests to be made to the Estates for the good of the diocese were deliberated on, and that the contributions themselves were shared out under the presidency of the bishop" (Massol 1818, p. 26). The bishop, at the head of the first order, played an eminent role in the administration of the territory of his bishopric, in addition to his spiritual role.

In Toulouse, during his short passage, Dillon undertook to control the flow of the Garonne whose torrentuous course endangered economic activities. The "aygat" (flood) of September 12, 1727, had destroyed the Bazacle causeway whose position in the middle of the city made it possible not only to bring supplies to the renowned mills but also to create a body of water allowing port activities. Dillon undertook the raising of a dyke to contain the waters of the Garonne. These developments were continued by his successor at a time when the industrial revolution in England constructively combined waterway transport with economic progress. The Bridgewater Canal, which was the first canal in Britain to be built without following a river, was inaugurated on July 17, 1761. Its digging had been organized by the very young Duke of Bridgewater who had conceived the idea during a Grand Tour which had led him to the Canal du Languedoc. It was very characteristic of the first industrial revolution since it was mainly intended to transport coal from the Duke's mines, located in Worsley, to Manchester.

Loménie de Brienne, during his twenty-five years in Toulouse, showed exceptional qualities in the administration of his bishopric. When he arrived in Toulouse, he was only 36 years old and his move from Condom to Toulouse earned him an income estimated at between 100,000 and 200,000 pounds, more than twice that of Condom, depending on the year and on his progression within the institution. Thanks to this archbishop, the King could hope to have a man of both thought and action in a city which was experiencing at that time some very important events. The Abbé Morellet remembers that tolerance had been the subject of exchanges between Turgot, Loménie, and himself long before the *Conciliateur* was drafted.

> Another more important question at that time was the same question [of religious and civil tolerance]. Protestants were accused of stirring events up in the Languedoc to obtain freedom for their religion. In the meantime, they married clandestinely; they had their children baptized by priests, from whom they obtained that the religion of fathers and mothers would not be mentioned: they complained bitterly about being excluded from public employment; they asked to become fellow citizens of their brothers once again.
>
> We were strongly concerned with all this and driven by the philosophical spirit, which had begun to arise freely in the great work of Montesquieu[7] and in the Encyclopédie, those of us who had the most verve did not balance between the two opinions and braving the prejudices of school and false politics declared themselves for civil tolerance by striving to distinguish it from ecclesiastical tolerance. (Morellet & Lemontey 1822, pp. 32–33)

This was a very useful state of mind for an archbishop who arrived in a city where capitouls and Parlement were being accused by all Europe of condemning with no other evidence than membership of the Reformed religion. During his years at the head of the diocese of Toulouse, he showed a pronounced taste for long stays in Paris in his Brienne hotel, and he always mingled with influential circles of power. Thus he was elected in

[7] He refers here to *De l'esprit des lois*, a major work by Montesquieu published between 1748 and 1750.

1770, at the age of 43, to the Académie Française. He owed his election less to his activity in Toulouse than to his attendance of the Parisian salons, especially that of Madame du Deffand and the very Anglophile Madame de Boufflers.

Regarding Brienne's arrival in Toulouse, Pierre Barthès, through his chronicle, observes directly a popular and particularly religious and ceremonial Toulouse at the end of this modern period. The new archbishop arrived in Toulouse with Abbé Colbert in his suite on August 19, 1763, according to Barthès' description:

> Monsieur de Dillon, the last Archbishop of this city, having been appointed by His Majesty to the Archbishopric of Narbonne, we saw with great satisfaction on the 19th of this month[8] at four o'clock in the afternoon, Charles Etienne de Brienne, the former Bishop of Condom, coming from Paris, arrive in this city to fill the See of Toulouse to which he was appointed by the King to be Archbishop.
>
> The following day, 20th, he was received by the chapter in the usual manner, as I had previously reported to the reception of Mr. de la Roche Aimon after he was harangued by all those who are obliged to do so by the duty of their office; he answered all with great politeness and affability which gained him in that moment the general affection and friendship along with the respect of all hearts.
>
> On the 22nd after the visits were made, he was received as a councillor in the Parlement of Toulouse as is customary when receiving prelates in the councils of the sovereign courts, to the great satisfaction of all the members who make up the body of this august and respectable Senate which congratulates itself daily at counting among its councillors such a worthy subject.
>
> This prelate of an illustrious house and of a very old family in the kingdom, who seems not yet to have reached the age of 40, of a solid piety and of a very distinguished merit among the princes of the Church seems to promise much by the good dispositions in which he finds himself towards the people subject to his rule and in particular towards the poor whom he loves very much and whom he can indeed support for the condition of his virtues and the abundant alms which he is in a good condition to make, being extremely rich.

Rich, Loménie certainly was because he had "the resources of several abbeys, Saint-Michel, Fontfroide, Saint-Orens, Bonne-fontaine, Moissac,

[8] It is August 1763, only a few months before Smith and his student arrived.

Saint-Wandrille, Moreille, Corbie which ensured for him, with a crowd of canonicates and priories, a princely income" (Cormary 1935, p. 3).

During these twenty-five years at the head of the archbishopric of Toulouse, this prince of the church carried out considerable religious and civil works, far removed from the clichés that depict him as an unbelieving, debauched "salonnard" who ultimately led the monarchy to its ruin. It is true that his attempt to reform the religious orders earned him a tenacious hatred from many "charitable abbots" who poured torrents of slander on him that obscured his achievements. Of his religious work, it can simply be said that it was an attempt to adapt Catholicism to the Enlightenment by insisting on the sacred books of the Old and New Testaments, based on the Gallican tradition. Concerned to bridge the gap between science and faith, he created a small seminary in the former convent of the Abbés of Merci, where he wanted young ecclesiastics to be initiated into all sciences. A century later, the Abbé Salvan, when writing a book devoted to the historical study of the liturgy, could only celebrate the liturgical reform carried out by Loménie (Salvan 1850). His trajectory, very similar to that of Abbé Colbert, is incomprehensible if one only sees him as a worldly unbeliever. Loménie took the oath to the civil constitution, but he never wanted to consummate the schism by consecrating constitutional bishops. In the end, "his veiled and cautious adherence to the party of philosophers" is quite similar to that of Adam Smith's, and the warmth detected in the exchanges between Smith, Colbert, and the Duke are thus better understood.

But even more than the place of religions in society, it was Loménie's civil work that might have interested Smith. Loménie was particularly concerned about the development of primary education, including in the countryside. He involved municipalities in a way very similar to what had been done in Scotland previously and promoted the education of young girls. As early as 1765 he showed his concern for the economic problems of "manufacturers", but it was especially in public works that Loménie was to show the same concern for transport systems (especially waterways) found in the *Wealth of Nations.*

The founding book of economics contains an analysis of public works which draws on Smith's observations and conversations in Toulouse. Indeed, as soon as he arrived there, Loménie continued the development of the banks of the Garonne, and above all, he undertook the digging of a canal which would allow the junction of the Languedoc canal with the port of La Daurade (upstream of the Bazacle causeway) in order to avoid the trans-shipment of goods destined for or coming from Toulouse. The Brienne canal, named in homage to its promoter, connects the Garonne to the Languedoc canal over a mile, the junction taking place at the *Port de l'Embouchure*, equipped with Ponts Jumeaux (twin bridges), which are actually triplets since the Brienne canal continues downstream towards the Canal Parallel to the Garonne which really establishes the link between the Mediterranean and the Atlantic (Canal des Deux-Mers).

The public works launched by Loménie de Brienne raise interesting economic questions of financing and management. First of all, the containment of the Garonne is a case in which it is not so easy to apply the principle that public works are the sole responsibility of the beneficiaries, simply because it is difficult to identify the beneficiaries. For example, the dikes that protect against floods!

In the *Wealth of Nations* there are early attempts at cost/benefit calculations and considerations on the limitations of private initiative in such matters. Thus Smith could only support Loménie's initiatives in public works:

> PART III
>
> Of the Expence of publick Works and publick Institutions
>
> The third and last duty of the sovereign or commonwealth is that of erecting and maintaining those publick institutions and those publick works, which, though they may be in the highest degree advantageous to a great society, are, however, of such a nature, that the profit could never repay the expence to any individual or small number of individuals, and which it, therefore, cannot be expected that any individual or small number of individuals should erect or maintain. The performance of this duty requires too very different degrees of expence in the different periods of society. (WN, V.i.c, p.723)

For his part, the Duke on his return to Great Britain was to show the same enthusiasm for water transport as Smith or Loménie de Brienne. Thus in 1768, he financed lengths of roads, and he subscribed to the company created to dig a canal along the Forth & Clyde Rivers.

2.7 The Jacobites of Toulouse

Even if Abbé Colbert was almost "a stranger to the city of Toulouse", he was certainly of greater help to the travellers than Smith is willing to admit, and a perfectly devoted and pleasant companion. Proof of this is the continuation of the letter he sent to his "cousin", Hume.

> Mr. Smith is a sublime man, his heart and his mind are also esteemed, I congratulate myself every day that he has had the desire to come to Toulouse, send us many like him and we will be most obliged to you. The Duke his pupil is a very elegant subject. He does his exercises very well and makes progress in French. My friends Malcolm and Urquhart from Cromastie who are here entrust me with a thousand kind words on their behalf. If some English or Scottish people ask you where they should go for their exercises: you can safely recommend Toulouse to them. There is a very good academy and a lot of very honest people to see here.

This letter is valuable because it tells us about Smith's and his student's occupations during the initial months spent in Toulouse. It should be noted here that the Abbé highlights the intellectual life of Toulouse and not the monuments or the mummified bodies that were displayed as an attraction at the Cordeliers and Jacobins monasteries, often highlighted in the descriptions of visiting travellers. Thus Father Labat mentions that while making a brief stop in Toulouse, he deplores not being able to visit the "mass grave of the Cordeliers"; the Prior of the Jacobins had replied that he would "see as many here as in the Cordeliers", and Labat explained that "according to the arrangement of time [these very light bodies] are straight or curved; moisture relaxes the tension of the skin and makes them bend, [whereas] dryness straightens them up" (Labat 1730, Vol. II, p. 15).

This proximity to corpses, if it was pushed to excess in Toulouse, was common in the Christian West where many wished to be buried near the relics of saints preserved in churches and convents and failing that, "under the gutters". In the eighteenth century hygiene and health considerations took precedence. The Languedoc Estates were concerned about this problem and paid close attention to a report presented to them by Haguenot, professor at the Montpellier Faculty of Medicine, during the public meeting of the Royal Society of Sciences held in the large chamber of the town hall of Montpellier, in the presence of the members of the

Languedoc Estates, on December 27, 1746. The newspaper reproduced the conclusion of the report:

> Mr. Haguenot ends his Memoir by recalling the imperial constitutions and the decrees of the councils which proscribe this abuse, against which his own humanity protests; and he hopes that the magistrates' zeal for the preservation of the citizens and from that of the clergymen to restore the old discipline of the Church, that the two powers will come together to destroy an abuse so indecent, so intolerable and at the same time so pernicious.

Persuasion having not been enough, Loménie de Brienne, as an archbishop of the Enlightenment, had undertaken to prohibit burials in churches and curb this fascination for corpses. His "mandement" of March 23, 1775, ordered that churches no longer be used for such purposes, a practice which he attributed to "the mad vanity of the great who always want to be distinguished and that of the little people who never cease to want to be equal to the great" (Lassère 1994). However, ten years later, Mrs. Cradock reported in her diary her visit to the Carmelite Church and how her husband bribed the sacristan so that she could see one of these mummies, a viewing in principle forbidden to women (Cradock, p. 175). Still on the eve of the Revolution, Arthur Young visited the crypt of the Cordeliers and observed that:

> If I had a vault well lighted that would preserve the countenance and physiognomy as well as the flesh and bones, I should like to have it peopled with all my ancestors; and this desire would, I suppose, be proportioned to their merit and celebrity; but to one like this, that preserves cadaverous deformity, and gives perpetuity to death, the voracity of a common grave is preferable. But Toulouse is not without objects more interesting than churches and academies; these are the new quay, the corn mills, and the canal de Brien. (Young, p. 31)

It was not these somewhat barbaric usages, that the Revolution would later get rid of (Martinazzo Duhem), that Abbé Colbert promotes, but an environment conducive to the experience of true culture rather than the sensational.

Beyond the hyperboles (sublime, delicious) which are typical of the eighteenth century, Abbé Colbert's letter to Hume suggests that Smith in his own behaviour applies the precepts he developed in the *Theory of Moral*

Sentiments. It demonstrates the four cardinal virtues that emerge from it: prudence, justice, beneficence, and above all self-control.

As the Abbé's letter points out, the main purpose of this journey was indeed the studies and education of the young Duke and it made a good deal of sense that the Abbé should speak of exercises. Beyond intellectual exercises, Toulouse also offered training opportunities for young aristocrats such as the "Académie de manège et d'équitation" which benefited—is this a coincidence or an indication of the archdiocese's relations with our two travellers?—from a first largesse of Loménie de Brienne worth 1200 livres on January 7, 1765 (Cormary 1935, p. 118).

Colbert also refers to two other Scots present in Toulouse at that time, Mr. Malcolm and Mr. Urquhart de Cromartie. Though we have no information about the first gentleman, we know that the second was a Scottish veteran of the 1746 expedition and of the Battle of Culloden. Thus, beyond the political differences that were beginning to fade, it was shared nationality that mattered, particularly during encounters abroad. It should be remembered that in Toulouse there was an "Irish college" which gathered together any Jacobites passing through or having settled in Toulouse. The Cromartie (or Cromarty) clan was famously represented by Sir Thomas Urquhart of Cromarty (1611–1160), a writer and translator whose best-known work is a translation of Rabelais, still today among the best for the harmony it maintains between the original language and English. The Urquhart of Cromartie clan was located near Inverness, the birthplace of Abbé Colbert.

To conclude the analysis of this letter, it can be related to information provided by Pierre Barthès. He indeed reported that:

> English lords, the richest of their country, accustomed to Toulouse since the freedom offered by the last peace, wanting to entertain themselves and brighten others' lives by experiencing an entertainment unheard of before today in this city; it was declared two or three days before the last Saint John's day, by a town cryer with his drum in all the squares of the city, and by posters applied at all the crossroads, that "on the 25th of last month we could go on horseback to the Sept-Deniers to run there with other competitors, in order to win money prizes, for those who will precede the others in this competition". So on the day, marked by a blazing sun, there went beyond the Embouchure, in carriages, in sedans, in cabriolets, nearly 30,000 people of all conditions, of all sexes and ages, to be spectators of a game which, as new as it was, and highly recreational in appearance, caused a great

deal of inconvenience to many who, exposed in this new circus to the heat of a burning sun, brought home only extreme weariness. (Barthès, p. 260)

Barthès continues his narration of June 1765 by pointing out that one could see a rowboat race on the Garonne, which underlines the influence of the British on the lifestyle in Toulouse. There is no doubt that the Duke took part in these demonstrations.

By mentioning other Englishmen or Scotsmen present in Toulouse, Colbert demonstrates his role as an adviser in diplomatic matters, an important matter for an ambitious young man seeking support for an emerging career.

Thus the South of France was still of great interest to travellers, as Tobias Smollett's excellent travel account demonstrates.

2.8 The Duke's Curriculum

Thus Smith and his pupil, if they were perfectly settled materially, thanks to the sums of money at their disposal and access to the circle, albeit limited, that Abbé Colbert could offer, were preparing to begin a life of study in Toulouse. We must not lose sight here of the fact that Charles Townshend only authorized the trip on the condition that it was not a Grand Tour aimed merely at visiting various holiday resorts but an opportunity to improve the Duke's training, as he reminds him in a letter dated June 10, 1765:

My very Dear Lord,

I grew uneasy upon not hearing from you, but your letter soon removed all anxiety, both for your health and your situation, as it assures me you enjoy the one perfectly and are pleased with the other. I have often told you that almost every young man's mind and, indeed, his life takes its colour from his manner of passing and employing the few important years between his leaving school and entering into the world, and I have therefore never thought of this part of your education without much solicitude.

My love for you could not have been more sincere or more hearty if I had been your father. My own experience in business convinces me that, in this age, any person of your rank and fortune may with tolerable discretion, competent knowledge and integrity be as great as even this country can make him and therefore I wished to see you placed with your own approbation, in a foreign country for some time, where you might give to the necessary exercises of the body, to the improvement of your mind, and to the amusements of your youth. (Ross 1974, p. 185)

Townshend was a very serious man. At the time of writing this letter he was Chancellor of the Exchequer to King George III. While a minister's job is probably in normal circumstances a very demanding one, Townshend's task seems to have been even more so since he was at the centre of two important situations.

On the one hand, he had to deal with the Kingdom's finances, which were in a very bad state following the end of the Seven Years' War, and on the other hand, he sought to tax the colonies, the beginning of a long episode which would lead to the American Revolution. However, beyond his professional life, which he himself considered very busy, he took the time to write to his son-in-law. The tone of the letter is interesting: not exactly that of a father to his son, nor that of two friends, but that of a person who has great moral authority over another, showing true consideration for the young Duke. This concern underpinned his reasons for choosing the city of Toulouse, for its calm environment and the absence of dangerous nightlife, resembling life in the Scotland of his birth more than the hectic and insecure life of London or Paris.

The purpose of the trip is also clearly stated. It is a question of discovering the lives of good men and women, particularly those of means, before embarking on one's own life, one's own career, or even making the first experiences of life in a setting where it would not leave any traces. Going into life for Townshend meant starting a political career, being a Member of Parliament, and having a social and cultural life. It also meant, on one hand, reading between the lines, having a sex life, and therefore finding a wife in Britain, but on the other hand, have varied experiences away from a society where every action can have an important consequence.

The programme of the stay thus seemed to be articulated around two axes, if we believe the letter: the study of the political and social structures of the city of Toulouse and its province, the Languedoc, then in a second period of France itself, and the other, immersing oneself in a social network. It is a question of learning to associate with people who needed to be of his own rank and level of fortune.

To achieve these objectives, and among others, manage the transition period between studying and entering business and politics, Townshend did not choose a travelling tutor specialized in journeying in Europe. He chose a person for whom he seemed to have a real and deep admiration, even if he reproached him for his lack of ambition and for not being a man of action.

> [...] Mr Smith, among many other advantages, possesses that of being deeply read in the constitution & law of your own country: he is ingenious without being refined, he is general without being superficial and he is learned without being too systematical or singular in his notions of our government and from him you will grow to be a grounded politician in a short course of study. When I say a Politician, I do not use the word in the common acceptance, but rather as a phrase less severe, and for that reason more proper to your age, than statesman, who the one is the beginning of the other and they differ chiefly as this is the work of study and that the same work finished by experience and a course of ethics. (Adderbury, June 10, 1765)[9]

Here then is the programme of the stay. It is about giving his step-son a culture of public affairs so that with experience he can become a true statesman. Without going into a psychoanalytical analysis of the relationship between the two characters, it can be noted that Lord Townshend had a problematic relationship with his parents, as he had had difficulty justifying his marriage to a relatively old widow with children. The couple had three children, two boys born in 1758 and 1761 and a daughter Anne born in 1756. Perhaps he felt that he would not have time to see his own children grow up, so he projected onto his wife's children his affection, and as he stated in his letter to the Duke dated June 10, 1765, "[his] love for [the Duke] could not have been more sincere or hearty, if [he] had been [his] Father" (Ross 1974, p. 185).

Thus the stay in Toulouse, far from being a holiday aimed at tourism or establishing contacts, must be a period of study. Young Henry was required to take advantage of this period to complement and enhance the knowledge acquired during his studies at Eton, and especially to be initiated into developing relations in the best society. Classical studies, for example, as illustrated by the study library supplied by Smith in 1759, presented the political world of antiquity. Under Smith's direction, the young Duke would have to produce real analyses extending beyond simple descriptions on the organization of local authorities in the province of Languedoc, as well as on the role of the Toulouse Parlement.

[9] Source: National Archives of Scotland—reference: RH4/99 Townshend Papers (quoted by Ross, p. 185).

To his good fortune, he would witness history, since during his stay in Toulouse, the political life of the city was particularly active, thanks, if this can be said, to the Calas affair provoked by the town's Capitouls, and the Fitz-James affair, in which the Parlement, also involved in the Calas affair, opposed the King's representative. Finally the travellers would go on to observe the third place of power in the Languedoc, the provincial Estates in Montpellier, which they would visit in November 1764. It is certain that the work carried out by the young Duke under Smith's guidance had been sent in the form of letters and reports and had reached Lord Townshend, since he refers to them in his letters, commenting favourably. Unfortunately, research, notably in Scotland in the archives of the Dukes of Buccleuch, could not find them.

Fortunately, still available are four letters from Charles Townshend sent to the Duke during his stay in Toulouse. He rarely wrote about family life and elaborated much more on the problems he encountered in Parliament.

His letters thus often go beyond a focus on the stay in Toulouse and are more descriptive of London society than of life in Toulouse. However, based on what Smith and his student sought to know, it is possible to determine what the prime interests of the two visitors were, beyond studying.

A few months after their arrival, Smith still notes, with a rather disillusioned tone, that he:

> cannot cultivate the acquaintance of the few with whom I am acquainted, as I cannot bring them to our house and am not always at liberty to go to theirs. (Toulouse, July 5, 1764, Letter #143)

Hence, it was necessary for Smith and his pupil to bide their time since the city of Toulouse and its elite were not to be easily convinced without letters of recommendation, as Smith also willingly recognized.

The city of Toulouse had three main centres of interest for those wishing to study the social structures of the country. The first of them was, as in all the big cities of the kingdom, its local government, here represented by the *capitouls* who sat in the town hall and who administered the city economically and judicially.

Secondly, the "Parlement" of Toulouse, which served as a relay of the laws, edicts, and decrees adopted in Versailles. Finally, and this is specific to certain provinces, the "Pays d'Etats", a relatively democratic assembly, in this case the Languedoc Estates, that met every two years.

However, they did not meet in Toulouse during these years, for practical reasons, but in Montpellier.

Beyond these three institutions, which, by their elective and collective nature, can be seen as an embryo of democracy or public representation limited by royal power or the seed of future democracy, according to the point of view of the historian, there were administrative positions directly dependent on the King. These were represented mainly by the "Intendant", whose role of control and organization seems, in Languedoc, to have been exercised on the whole successfully, in agreement with the local institutions.

Moreover, the whole organization of finances and tax collection should also be mentioned although the purchase of charges led to a multitude of local particularities that were very difficult for a visitor to understand.

This complex organization was sure to puzzle Smith. His many questions concerning the competencies of each level of authority would often remain unanswered. Thus he wrote in the *Wealth of Nations* as follows:

> In France the stamp-duties are not much complained of. Those of registration, which they call the Contrôle, are. They give occasion, it is pretended, to much extortion in the officers of the farmers general who collect the tax, which is in a great measure arbitrary and uncertain. In the greater part of the libels which have been written against the present system of finances in France, the abuses of the Contrôle make a principal article. Uncertainty however, does not seem to be necessarily inherent in the nature of such taxes. If the popular complaints are well founded, the abuse must arise, not so much from the nature of the tax, as from the want of precision. (*WN*, V.ii.h, p. 863)

From this observation, we can reconstitute what Smith's concerns were: first, to understand the mode of operation of the various authorities present in Toulouse, then, more broadly, of the Languedoc Estates. In the second phase, Smith, always with the intention of studying fully the French system of government, not only in all its complexity but also in its diversity, wished to go to a province not administered by democratically elected Estates, even if it was a rather limited form in this case, but in a "Pays d'élection", that is to say where the intendant was, with the governor, a true viceroy, the principal administrator of the province. Perhaps by chance, or by calculation, the neighbouring province of Guyenne was precisely, due to the evolution of its governance over time and since the English conquest, centuries before, a so-called Pays d'élection.

Thus, logically, Smith's programme in the first weeks of his stay in Toulouse included an examination of these various powers. If the institution of the capitouls was easy for him to understand since it resembled, with some variations, that which could be observed not only in the big cities of Scotland and in particular in Glasgow or Edinburgh, but also cities of less importance such as Dundee or Aberdeen, the Parlement of Toulouse and the Languedoc Estates were completely different institutions from those Scotland had known since the Act of Union of 1707 and its administrative and legal attachment to England.

The Parlement of Toulouse and the Estates of Languedoc perpetuate the memory of the County of Toulouse and its attachment to the Kingdom of France in 1229; they were vigilant on the matter of respect for the rights and freedoms of the province. Thus it is fiction that the contribution of the Estates to France's budget was a "don gratuit", a "free gift" defined as follows:

> The deliberation which is undertaken each year before granting the 'free gift', states that the Estates deliberating on the subject of the request made to them by the king, of a free gift of three million Livres granted liberally and free of charge to His Majesty, and without consequence, this sum of three million, under the conditions which were expressed during the deliberation, and whose principal stipulation is that no taxation nor raising of funds can be made on the general of the province, nor on the cities and communities in particular nor on the inhabitants, by virtue of any 'édits bursaux' (money edits), declarations, 'jussions' (orders) and other provisions contrary to its rights and freedoms, even if they have been made on the generality of the kingdom. (Guyot 1784–1785, vol. 10, p. 23)

Smith would be able to observe the endless debates within the local institutions, as well as those between them and the central power, whether through its local representatives or even directly with the ministers and the court or the services of the royal administration which sat in Versailles. This was a powerful source of information for the envoy of a British minister who was looking for the best solution that the central government in London could adopt towards a Scotland newly integrated into Britain.

References

Albisson, Jean. 1780–1787. *Lois municipales et économiques de Languedoc.* A Montpellier: Chez Rigaud et Pons.

Alcouffe, Alain, & Andrew Moore. 2020, Smith's Networks in Occitania - March 1764-October 1765, retrieved from https://hal.archives-ouvertes.fr/hal-02614246.

Banke, Niels. 2003. On Adam Smith's Connections to Norway and Denmark, 1955, in Lai, Cheung-Cheung, *Adam Smith across nations: translations and receptions of The Wealth of Nations*. Oxford: Oxford University Press, pp. 52–64.

Barthès, Pierre and Edmond Lamouzèle. 1914. *Toulouse au XVIIIe siècle d'après les "Heures perdues" de P. Barthès.* Toulouse: Marqueste.

Cormary, Abbé Gentil. 1935. *Loménie de Brienne à Toulouse: (1763–1788)*. Préface de Émile Appolis. Albi: Librairie Ginestet.

Cradock, Anna Francesca, & O. Delphin-Balleyguier. 1896. *Journal de Mme Cradock: voyage en France (1783–1786)*. Paris: Perrin.

Diderot Denis, et al. 1765. *Encyclopédie, ou Dictionnaire raisonné des sciences, des arts et des métiers, par une société de gens de lettres, Tome neuvieme, JU-MAM*, Neufchâtel, Faulche.

Foucault, Michel. 1972. *Histoire de la Folie à l'âge classique.* Paris: Gallimard.

Fournier, Georges. 1989. Les institutions municipales, de l'Ancien Régime aux expériences révolutionnaires (1750–1800), *Études héraultaises*, pp. 51–60.

Graham, Henry Grey. 1901. *The Social Life of Scotland in the eighteenth century.* London: Adam & Charles Black.

Guyot, J.-N. 1784–1785. *Répertoire universel et raisonné de jurisprudence civile, criminelle, canonique et béneficiale*. Paris: Visse.

Labat, Jean-Baptiste. 1730. V*oyages du P. Labat, ... en Espagne et en Italie*. Paris: Delespine.

Lassère, Madeleine. 1994. La création du cimetière de Terre-Cabade à Toulouse au XIXe siècle: une opération de prestige, *Annales du Midi*, Tome 106, No. 205. pp. 79–96.

Loménie de Brienne, Charles-Étienne. 1751. *Quaestio theologica: quis in principio creavit coelum et terram ? Genes. cap. I, V. 1... Has theses... praeside... Nicolao Buret,... tueri conabitur Stephanus-Carolus de Loménie de Brienne,... die... trigesima mensis octobris, anno...* (S. l. n. d.).

Martinazzo, Estelle & Sophie Duhem. 2013. Étude des corps momifiés de Toulouse sous l'Ancien Régime, *Cahiers d'études du religieux. Recherches interdisciplinaires.* Accessed August 2017. http://cerri.revues.org/1306.

Massol, Jean-François. 1818. *Description du département du Tarn.* Albi: Baurens.

Mey, Abbé Claude. 1752. Remarques sur une thèse soutenue en Sorbonne, le samedi 30 octobre 1751, par l'abbé Loménie de Brienne, présidée par M. Buret.

McManners, John. 1998, *Church and society in eighteenth century France.* Oxford: Clarendon.

Morellet, André & Lemontey, Pierre-Edouard. 1822. *Mémoires (inédits). de l'abbé Morellet*: suivis de sa correspondance avec M. le comte R***, ministre des finances & Naples: précédés d'un éloge historique de l'abbé Morellet. Paris: Baudouin.

Mozart, Wolfgang Amadeus. 2005. Annie Paradis & Bernard Lortholary. *Lettres des jours ordinaires, 1756–1791.* Paris: Fayard.

Roche, Daniel. 1993. *La France des Lumières,* Paris: Librairie Arthène Fayard.

Ross, Ian Simpson. 1974. Educating an Eighteenth-Century Duke, in Cant, Ronald Gordon & Barrow, Geoffrey Wallis Steuart, *The Scottish tradition essays in honour of Ronald Gordon Cant.* Edinburgh: Scottish Academic Press, 2001. pp. 178–197.

Salvan, Adrien. 1850. *Recherches historiques sur la liturgie en général et celle du diocèse de Toulouse en particulier, par M. l'abbé A. Salvan.* Paris: Sagnier et Bray.

Scott, Hew, and John Murray. 1866. *Fasti ecclesiae Scoticanae: the succession of ministers in the parish churches of Scotland, from the reformation, A.D. 1560, to the present time.* Edinburgh: William Paterson; London, John Russell Smith.

Smith, Adam, et al. 1976 [1776]. *An Inquiry into the Nature and Causes of the Wealth of Nations.* Oxford: Clarendon Press.

Smollett, Tobias. 1766. *Travels through France and Italy.* London: Printed for R. Baldwin.

Sterne, Laurence. 1794. *Letters of the late Laurence Sterne to his most intimate friends.* With a fragment in the manner of Rabelais. London [i.e. York?], Printed for A. Millar, W. Law, and R. Cater.

Taillefer, Michel. 2014. *Vivre à Toulouse sous l'Ancien régime.* Toulouse: Ombres blanches.

Young, Arthur, and Matilda Betham-Edwards. 1909. *Arthur Young's Travels in France during the years 1787, 1788, 1789.* London: Bell.

CHAPTER 3

Smith and the Calas Affair

> I am more Languedochian[1] than ever, but my affection does not extend to the Parliament of Toulouse. Many philosophers are formed in the southern provinces; yet there are fewer than white, blue and grey penitents. The number of fools and madmen is always the greatest. (Voltaire, Ferney, May 2, 1766, Letter CXCIV. to M. the Marquis of Florian)

The city in which the travellers settled for eighteen months was at the time the centre of attention of Europe's Enlightenment, ever since Voltaire seized on the Calas case to campaign against fanaticism and for a reform of judicial procedures. This campaign, which took place during the Seven Years' War, had a great impact across the channel where many of Calas' co-religionists had taken refuge. Anne-Rose Cabibel, Jean Calas' wife, was born in 1710 in London; she was the daughter of Pierre Cabibel, from Mazamet, and through her mother, she was "allied to a great number of noble families: the de Marsillac, de Saint-Amans, de Riols-Desmaziers, d'Escalibert, several of whom were senior officers and Knights of Saint-Louis; the Marquis de Montesquieu, as well as the Polastron-Lahillère were her second degree cousins" (Tournier 1901).

Voltaire had been interested in the Languedoc for several decades, and he had also devoted a chapter to his final days in the County of Toulouse.

[1] Voltaire follows the usage advocated by Trévoux's dictionary and systematically writes "Languedochien", perhaps there is a hint of irony when he attacks parliamentarians as the end of Languedochian sounds very much alike "Languedoc-chien" (chien = dog).

A. Alcouffe, P. Massot-Bordenave, *Adam Smith in Toulouse and Occitania*, https://doi.org/10.1007/978-3-030-46578-0_3

Voltaire denounced, "these crusades against the Languedoc [which] lasted twenty years. The desire alone to seize the belongings of others gave rise to them, and at the same time produced the Inquisition" (Voltaire 1877b [1756]). This was a good opportunity for him to question and attack the Catholic Church and the monarchy. This "affection" for the Languedoc did not include the Toulouse Parlement, several of whose members would become Smith's interlocutors in the following months. It is thus important to revisit the history and institutions of the city chosen to improve the education of the Duke and Theatre of the Calas affair, which will find a place in the last edition of the *Theory of Moral Sentiments (TMS)*.

3.1 Toulouse and the Languedoc

The province of Languedoc was earlier limited to the south by the natural border formed by the Pyrenees, which separated it from the kingdom of Spain. For more than a century, owing to the Treaty of the Pyrenees concluded between the Bourbon kings of France and the great family of the Habsburgs of Spain in 1659, peace had reigned between the two nations. They allied in conflicts which had occurred in the regions of the north of Europe during the entire reign of Louis XV. An example of these conflicts is the Seven Years' War which has just ended, during which Spain, while playing its own cards in the colonies, allied itself with France against England.

The result for the Languedoc was a long period of peace and tranquility. The troops that criss-crossed the province were either on their way to combat areas along the Mediterranean or the Atlantic coast and its islands, often under English occupancy, or regiments undergoing exercises—in training or at rest.

> When the king's troops—his noblemen or officers—passed through any part of the country, the yeomanry were bound to provide them with horses, carriages, and provisions, at a price regulated by the purveyor. Great Britain is, I believe, the only monarchy in Europe where the oppression of purveyance has been entirely abolished. It still subsists in France and Germany. (*WN*, III.ii, p. 394)

To the west and north lies the Guyenne, a "Pays d'Election" which encompassed the Basse-Guyenne, strongly oriented towards an Atlantic trade—then in full development, and the Haute-Guyenne, stretching over the Quercy and the Rouergue. Abbé Colbert, after becoming Bishop of

Rodez, would preside over the Assembly of Haute-Guyenne, an institution created by Necker.

The Seven Years' War had confirmed France in its possessions in the Caribbean. The port of Bordeaux then experienced a prodigious new boom, mirroring that of the growth of Glasgow in the same period.

To the northeast, the Vivarais was the northernmost limit. The limit there was the Rhône, which was considered the principal shipping route to Paris, due to its safe and comfortable means of transport. Power was divided between two large cities, Toulouse and Montpellier. While Montpellier was the city where the Estates had their headquarters and where the intendant usually resided to make use of better communication facilities, Toulouse was the most populous city, benefiting from the trade of the rich Lauragais plain as well as the abundant resources of the Pyrenean foothills. The economy of the province was clearly inclined towards the south, that is to say the Mediterranean and its trade potential with the Levant, but also with Italy or Venice.

Toulouse, by its size and by its history, was considered as the capital of the province. A legacy of the 1229 treaty, Toulouse was the seat of an important Parlement whose jurisdiction extended even beyond the boundaries of the province. More generally, based on the chronology of the connections to the crown rather than on simple demography, Toulouse considered itself the second city of the kingdom, just after Paris.

Around 1765, Toulouse counted about 50,000 inhabitants, making it the eighth city of the kingdom by its population. As an illustration, according to the same sources, Paris had a population of around 600,000 and Lyon, the second city of the kingdom by population, could boast 114,000, but the third, Marseille, had a population of only 68,000, followed very closely by Lille (63,000) and three ports on the Atlantic, Rouen (66,000), Bordeaux (62,000), and Nantes (60,000), a classification which evolved little over the centuries.

The province of Languedoc had about 1.5 million inhabitants. The share of the rural population was predominant, occupying many small towns and villages. It should be noted that the population of the Languedoc was greater than that of Scotland.

The history of the Languedoc was marked in the thirteenth century by the development of Catharism and the Albigensian Crusade, used by the French monarchy to destroy the dream of the Counts of Toulouse of an Occitan-Catalan State straddling the Pyrenees, a dream that was shattered during the battle of Muret:

> At the end of the thirteenth century, everything is over and a page is turned: there may not have been destruction through Occitan territory as was once thought. It has shifted into the orbit of the North: it is the beginning of the break with the Mediterranean universe, connected with the increasingly important weight of northern Europe. It is also the unexpected extension a century earlier of the Capetian domain: France is no longer a province between the Loire and the Seine, it is now a State. (Martel 1979, p. 344)

This subjection of Languedoc lands was reflected in the subsidies the Estates of the Province had to pay, for the benefit of the French monarchy. It is precisely the determination and distribution of this tax that would give a first semblance of administrative existence to the former lands of the Count of Toulouse. These were first consultative assemblies in the thirteenth century which evolved into more formal bodies in the fourteenth and fifteenth centuries. Their institutionalization in the sixteenth century made the Estates of Languedoc one of the most original assemblies of the Ancien Régime, up until their disappearance in 1789.

In modern times, the Toulouse region experienced a period of splendour linked to the pastel shades produced by the local dyers. Pastel is a plant, *Isatis tinctoria*, also called dyer's woad, or glastum, whose beautiful yellow flowers one can still observe in spring in the meadows of Languedoc. In the medieval world, the Christian Church allowed three colours for clothing: the white of purity, the red of Christ's blood, and black as a symbol of mourning and penance, except for the Virgin Mary. Profound in his faith, King Louis IX, later called Saint-Louis, renouncing the colour purple and inclined to the simplicity of blue. This colour was mostly used in his coats of arms. Long despised, blue became the colour of the sky and of the spirit. It would gradually become the emblem of nobility. Drapers and dyers demanded a dye of value. The East had indigo, but its importation was too expensive and too uncertain. In the West, in the thirteenth century, pastel was cultivated throughout Europe. Perhaps as a consequence of the Hundred Years' War (1337–1453) or for climatic reasons, the Albigeois, the area around the city of Albi, became the land of choice for this culture as early as the fourteenth century. It was the Bearnese who opened the pastel routes to Spain and England and Flanders from the ports of Bayonne and Bordeaux. Competition was fierce with Italy, Germany, and England, but this trade was very lucrative.

In the fifteenth century, even though Albi still dominated this trade in Occitania, Toulouse took advantage of its geographical position between the pastel areas and the ocean ports. The Garonne's navigability had been improved and flat-bottomed boats, the gabarres, could proceed as far as Bordeaux without scraping against the river's shoals. Rich Toulousains took their place in this market. They generalized the culture of the plant in their domains, creating pastel mills. They also began to loan money while a cultural triangle, between Toulouse, Albi, and Carcassonne, emerged.

In the sixteenth century, the great merchants entered the system. The centre of their activity was Toulouse. Not all of them were Basque, Rouergat, or Spanish, but they all endorsed the spirit of trade, of foreign markets and success. The city became a cosmopolitan financial capital. The region acquired the nickname of "Pays de Cocagne", a land of plenty, which referred to the prosperity brought by pastel.[2]

Poor harvests, dubious practices, religious wars, and especially "the financial measures that ended the Hapsburg Charles the Fifth's reign and inaugurated that of his son, seriously shook Antwerp, which had become the main destination and outlet for the precious dye" (Gilbert Larguier). This undermined the trade of the valuable dye in the Atlantic, already hit by competition from indigo from India and the West Indies. However, export to the Mediterranean via Narbonne was more resilient. Yet, everything suddenly collapsed from 1561 onwards. The 1560 harvest was abundant, but of poor quality. Even so, the Toulouse merchants tried to maintain the usual prices. The 1561 harvest, following heavy rains, was even more abundant than the previous ones, but of even poorer quality. The market was collapsing. Some traders tried not to sell the crops, but the Albigensians did not follow suit and flooded an already saturated market. Although it was not completely ousted on the Atlantic side, since "Toulouse" pastel entered England until 1638, Languedoc pastel was forced to reorient itself towards the Mediterranean at a time when the world economy was shifting towards the Atlantic and America (Fig. 3.1).

[2] The "cocagne" was the ball of leaves crushed and compacted by hand by pastel growers. It was then dried and sold to dye manufacturers at such a high price that the entire pastel industry became extremely rich. This cultivation area was located in the Albi-Carcassonne-Toulouse triangle, which became the land of cocagne.

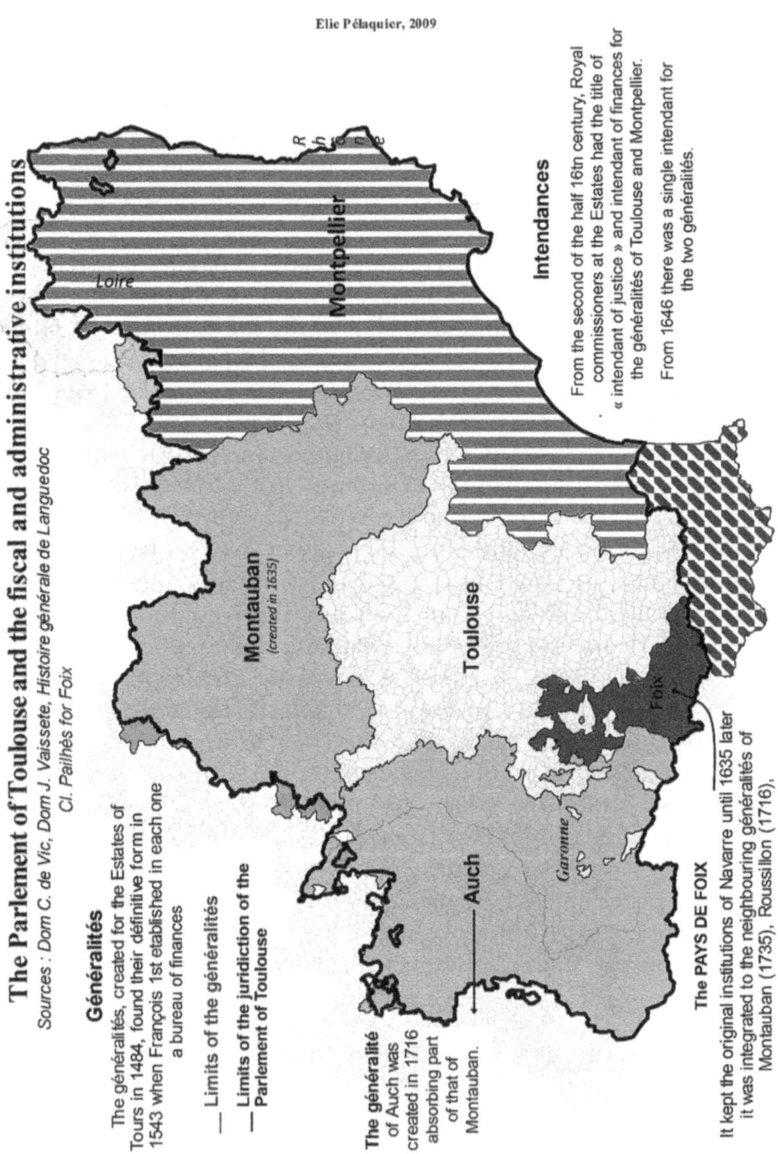

Fig. 3.1 The Parlement de Toulouse and the fiscal and administrative institutions. (Adapted from Élie Pélaquier 2009)

3.2 The Parlement of Toulouse

The wealth of the city disappeared, rapidly leaving only beautiful buildings, in particular mansions of red brick (some of which are still visible nowadays). The city was then controlled by the Parlement, according to the monumental history of this institution written by Dubédat:

> In Toulouse, which was above all a city guarded and defended by the judgments of the courts, the Parlement was not only a power, but it formed a whole society embracing legions of magistrates, lawyers, prosecutors, clerks, of bailiffs, clerics of the Basoche,[3] officers in long robes and short robes, a whole valiant and brave crowd, in love with the tumult of war and with the clash of argument, proud of the glory of the Parlement and having deep roots in the various classes of this great city. (Dubédat 1885, p. VII)

Dubédat traced Toulouse's institutions back to Roman antiquity in a historical fresco of uncertain accuracy, bolstering the Toulousains' shared conviction of the importance of institutions which had ancient origins. Thus, Dubédat linked the capitouls to the curia,[4] the members of the municipal senates of the empire, while insisting on the seniority of the Parlement of Toulouse, an ancient city honoured by the poet Ausonius. Passing rapidly over the judicial institutions of the Visigothic capital, Dubédat traced their evolution since Charlemagne, observing in the "placits",[5] the ancestor of the Parlement. Dubédat highlighted, "the city of Toulouse, which became the capital of the kingdom of Aquitaine, founded by Charlemagne for Louis le Débonnaire, was both the throne of royal power and the seat of justice." However, these reminders are only an echo of the claims made by the Parlement in the eighteenth century. Thus the Parlement of Toulouse, in its "remonstrances"[6] of September 27, 1756, harangues the King, "You are, Sire, the King of the Franks and not

[3] The Basoche was the guild of legal clerks.

[4] The Capitole de Toulouse proudly displays the letters C. P. Q. T. M. D. L. V., which means: *Capitolium Populusque Tolosanus 1555*, celebrating the date of its reconstruction and modelled on the famous SPQR (*Senātus Populusque* Rōmānus) of the Roman Republic.

[5] Charlemagne had or would have restored the Germanic practice of assemblies of representatives of the people, and these were the general "placits", gatherings during which the general affairs of the kingdom were discussed.

[6] The right of remonstrance, during the Ancien Régime, is the right of Parlements to contest a royal edict before its registration if they consider that the edict is contrary to the interests of the people or the fundamental laws of the kingdom.

of the serfs", and on December 22, 1763, when Smith began his journey, the Parlement played its part in the "philosophical whirlwind of the century" (Slimani, p. 184):

> To shape men free to be enslaved, all duties must be concentrated in one, that of forcing obedience through fear, encouraging the abasing of the soul; to make them forget the ever so sweet ideas of freedom, property, laws, homeland. (Dufey 1826, vol. 2, p. 129)

The purpose of the reconstruction of the origin of the Parlements was to emphasize their role in the mechanisms of the monarchy through a shift from the control of the legal framework to the co-production of laws. Thus the insistence of the Parlement of Toulouse on its historical origin aimed to strengthen its place in the monarchy of the kingdom. It is a question of affirming that the Parlement (*curia regis*) was the counterpart of Royalty while the Parlement of Toulouse considered itself as a simple emanation of the Parlement of Paris, created because the distance prevented the inhabitants of Languedoc to defend their interests in the Parlement of Paris. The local specificities (civil law) and the date of its association with the monarchy made it possible to maintain that the Parlement of Toulouse was the second Parlement, retaining the precedence of the Parlement of Paris as purely formal (*primus inter pares*). But in this claim to share the power of the sovereign in the name of a certain representation of society, the Parlement of Toulouse competed with the Estates General, which explicitly constituted a representation of the three orders. In Languedoc, the Estates, which gathered annually, were much more representative of the population than of a closed cenacle of councillors whose wealth and revenues were so far removed from those of the common people.

It is pertinent to describe more eloquently this Parlement of Toulouse at the time of Smith's arrival. It had existed permanently since 1442. At the end of the eighteenth century, it consisted of 111 members: a first president; five "présidents aux mortiers"[7]; two honorary advisers, who were high dignitaries of the clergy; eight clerics; twenty-eight advisers to the Grand'Chambre, fifty-two advisers on investigations; two presidents and ten advisers for petitions; and finally, the representatives of the King: the public prosecutor and the two advocates general. To become a "parlementaire", one had to, on the one hand, hold an office by inheritance or

[7] Principal magistrates of the Parlement. The mortier was their special hat (mortar).

purchase and, on the other, satisfy certain conditions in order to exercise the office and be approved by the Parlement. The first condition was financial, while the other was legal. This system of offices was organized by the law of 1604, which instituted the venality of offices: against payment of an annual fee calculated on the basis of the value of the office—a "parlementaire" could transfer his office to his heir or sell it. Values ranged from 15,000 livres at the bottom of the judicial pyramid (counsellor for motions) to 300,000 livres for a first president. In other words, parliamentarians were among the wealthiest people in Toulouse (Paulhet, pp. 189–204).

In Toulouse, the post of "parlementaire" was all the more significant in local society as it was reinforced through the conjunction of two entirely different phenomena: the decline of trade and the absence of a traditional nobility. Indeed, since the end of the period of speculation on pastel, one could no longer become rich by practicing the trade in Toulouse. Additionally, those who had made a fortune in this business hastened to use their money to buy an office, resulting in the decline of merchant wealth. The second element that helped to increase the importance of the "parlementaires" was the decadence of the nobility of the sword, whose roots went back to the Middle Ages. In the Languedoc, there was no high-ranking nobility, since it had been decimated during the Albigensian Crusade and had never recovered. The "hobereaux", the minor nobles who survived, vegetated in their manors and did not come to live in Toulouse. The "intendant" Lamoignon de Basville, who was in office in the last years of the eighteenth century, wrote in his *Mémoire* of the nobility of Languedoc, "All these houses perished in the Albigensian war. All their property was confiscated or fell into disrepair" (Lamoignon de Basville, p. 102).

The "parlementaires" of Toulouse undoubtedly formed the richest and most influential group in the city, dominating all cultural institutions. Despite the convergence between the economic policies defended by the Toulouse Parlement during the 1760s and Smith's relations with several "parlementaires", Smith's assessments of the Parlement's role were mixed. He appeared to deplore the fact that the offices were sought for the prestige they offered, more than for the income they generated: thus the wealth which was necessary to acquire them was in a way diverted from investments which would have been more useful to the local economy; the only exceptions that Smith noted were the ports of Bordeaux and Rouen. The paradox for Toulouse was that the revenues from the offices themselves were very limited. Smith nevertheless praised the probity of the "parlementaires" (Fig. 3.2).

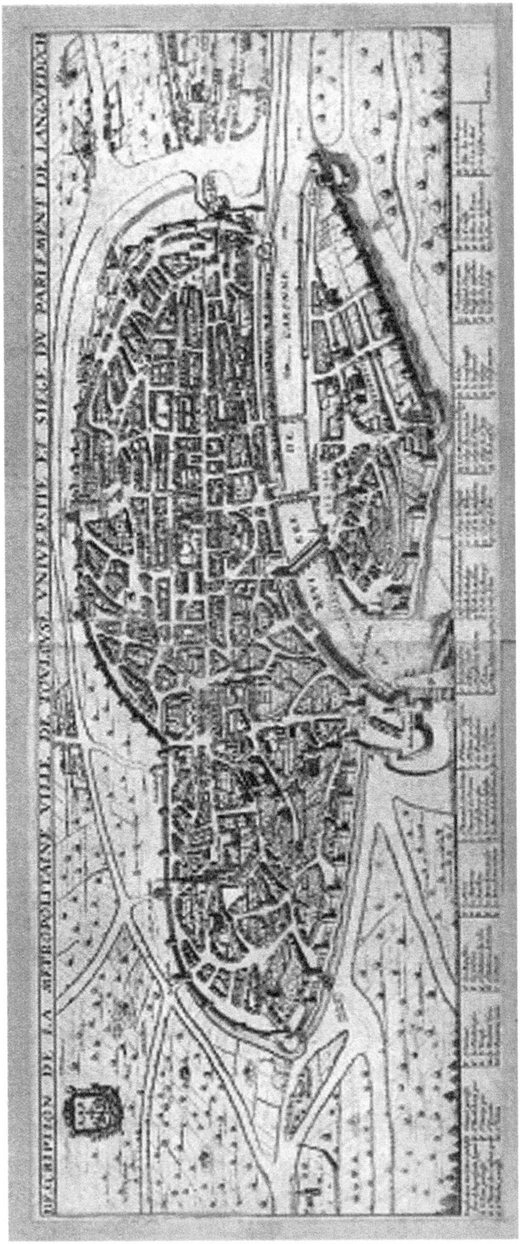

Fig. 3.2 Musée du Vieux-Toulouse Plan gravé. (1645) "Description de la Métropolitaine ville de Toulouse, université et siège du parlement du Languedoc"

> In the different parliaments of France, the fees of court (called Epices and vacations) constitute the far greater part of the emoluments of the judges. After all deductions are made, the neat salary paid by the crown to a counsellor or judge in the parliament of Toulouse, in rank and dignity the second parliament of the kingdom, amounts only to a hundred and fifty livres, about [88] six pounds eleven shillings sterling a year. About seven years ago that sum was in the same place the ordinary yearly wages of a common footman. The distribution of those Epices too is according to the diligence of the judges. A diligent judge gains a comfortable, though moderate, revenue by his office: An idle one gets little more than his salary. Those parliaments are perhaps, in many respects, not very convenient courts of justice; but they have never been accused; they seem never even to have been suspected of corruption. (*WN*, V.i.b, p. 720)

3.3 The City of the Three Letters S

Smith arrived in Toulouse, a city deemed the "city of the three Ss", one corresponding to "Soiled", the second to "Saint", and the third to "Scholarly". Like all shortcuts, this may include a dose of truth, but also exaggeration.

3.3.1 Hygiene and Urban Planning

With regard to the first S, there is no question here of going back over the characteristics of hygiene during this period which have often been portrayed. But it must be noted that Toulouse was a city with a strong craft tradition and a very dynamic proto-industry, located at the very heart of its dense urban development.

Born from water and the civilization of water, on the eve of the birth of industry, the city suffered the inconveniences of a craft industry which was earlier a major user of a resource that was considered abundant.

The most convincing evidence of this civilization based on water was the massive roadways which confined the upstream and downstream end of the Garonne as one entered the city of Toulouse.

The great mills of the Bazacle were one of the prides of the city in their gigantism and the quality of their production. The completely original organization of the management of the mills made it one of the very first joint-stock companies and certainly one whose share price is known over the longest period since the series began in the Middle Ages.[8] Smith must have known of their existence and perhaps considered them when he accepted some exceptions to his condemnation as a matter of principle of joint-stock corporations. Smith noted that they are "always run by a body of directors", but since most owners rarely claimed to understand anything about business and were only interested in dividends, this left a wide margin of discretion for the directors:

> The directors of such companies, however, being the managers of other people's money rather than of their own, it cannot well be expected, that they should watch over it with the same anxious vigilance with which the partners in a private copartnery frequently watch over their own. Like the stewards of a rich man, they were quick in paying attention to small matters as not for their master's honour, and very easily rewarded themselves a dispensation from having it. Negligence and profusion, therefore, must always prevail, more or less, in the management of the affairs of such a company. It is upon this account that joint stock companies for foreign trade have seldom been able to maintain the competition against private adventurers. (*WN*, V.i.e, p.741)

But Smith makes four exceptions to this condemnation of the corporation:

> 1. the bank's business 2. that of insuring against fire, sea and capture risks in time of war 3. the undertaking of building and maintaining a navigable canal 4. a similar undertaking, that of bringing water for the supply of a large city.

His argument that it was either routine operations (banking, canal maintenance, water supply) or ones that appeared to be uncertain may seem surprising, but perhaps he included the Bazacle company in these exceptions.

To return to considerations of hygiene, a good example of the filthiness of Toulouse can be perceived through the description of the island of Tounis between two channels of the Garonne. The drying of the Garonnette in 1954 removed this insularity. During Smith's stay, it was a neighbourhood composed of artisans and small industries that was certainly dynamic, but it also produced much polluting waste. The

[8] https://corpgov.law.harvard.edu/2015/09/17/development-of-corporate-governance-in-toulouse-from-1372-to-1946/.

transformations of the right bank of the Garonne done by Loménie de Brienne impressed Arthur Young, who noted that "The quay is in all respects a noble work" and the "magnificence" of the Canal de Brienne despite there is "more magnificence than trade" (Young 1909, p. 32).

The Abbé Julien describes his own parish:

> Masons, carpenters, plasterers, laundresses, seamstresses, would meet on this spit of earth and in the morning at the crack of dawn, it was in noisy and rushing gangs that one could see them moving towards their workshops carrying their bread for lunch or dinner under their arms. (Arrouy 2005, p. 45)

Still enclosed in 1764 behind hypothetical protective military walls which restricted urban development, but also more prosaically the evacuation of waste, the scarcity of rain and the fervour of the sun often present in the summer months gave the city this reputation of being "dirty". Thus, "Soiled" provided the first of our three letters S.

3.3.2 Toulouse and Religion

The second S that describes the city of Toulouse is that of "Saint". Toulouse was evangelized very early and boasted the largest Romanesque building in the Basilica of Saint-Sernin, where the relics of Saint-Saturnin rested; he had been martyred in the middle of the third century, his relics sheltered since the fourth century in a primitive church on the current site, at the very time the Catholic Church saw its existence made legal by Constantine's Edict of Milan (313); however, paganism remained the religion of the majority of the people in Toulouse. Under the Visigothic kingdom, the position of the church was strengthened at the end of the sixth century by the conversion of the Visigoths. In the centuries that followed, the religious history of the Languedoc was marked by Catharism and its repression through the Albigensian Crusade, both of which established royal power and strengthened the power of the church. It may be argued that the crusade led to the gradual unification of the Kingdom of France, leading to the decline of *Occitan* literature. The second consequence, following the founding of the Inquisition, was the imposition of a religious orthodoxy which would however be later shaken by the Reformation. While the development of Protestantism in the cities of the Languedoc was remarkable and linked by some to Catharism, the memory of the glorious literature of the troubadour era had greatly faded, and it was only at the end of the eighteenth century that it was rediscovered by Rochegude and Raynouard. The seventeenth century witnessed the triumph of absolute monarchy in France, which certainly awoke opposition in the Languedoc, where its "high point is the Adventure of Montmorency". The Governor of the province from 1614, Duke Henri II of Montmorency, "took the head of his revolted province, fought like a lion in Castelnaudary against the King's troops; he was beheaded in the Henri IV courtyard of the Capitole of Toulouse" in 1632 (Lafont 1970, p. 304). The Duke, protector of "esprits forts", could not prevent the execution of Lucilio Vanini in 1619, prosecuted for atheism and for his "vice against nature". A century and a half later, the last manifestation of this Catholic intolerance would occur through the very symbolic Calas affair, the conclusion of which would take place during Smith's passage in Toulouse.

Toulouse remained, in the eighteenth century, a city marked by strong church presence. Historians speak of 200 representatives for the secular clergy, to which must be added "about 1100 persons (nearly 400 men and 700 women) in twenty monasteries, beggars, regular clerics, brothers of societies embracing communal life for men, or in twenty-four communities of nuns or congregations for women" (Castan 1983).

One only has to read Jean Aymar Piganiol's description of the city to be convinced:

> Toulouse is home to the Carmelites, Augustinians, Dominicans, Oratorians, Cordeliers, Franciscans, and of course, many Jesuit schools. There is no mention in the description of the minor orders of the Minimes and the Récollets who owned monasteries in the immediate periphery of the city. (Piganiol 1750, p. 27)

But Piganiol also mentions:

> The Compagnie des Pénitents bleus de Toulouse is the most notable in the whole kingdom. It has in its registers the names of many kings, of many princes of the blood, and of all that is most distinguished in the clergy, in those of the sword and of the robe. Their chapel is one of the most regular in Europe. It was King Louis XIII who laid the first stone. (Piganiol 1740, t. 2, p. 30)

Indeed, what underpinned the "holiness" of Toulouse were the societies which brought together lay people, clerics, and those in regular orders within companies formed by fervent Christians who, through frequent processions throughout the city, practised an ostentatious religion. This ostentation was the result of the eventful history of Languedocian Protestantism. In the middle of the sixteenth century, the progress of Calvinism worried Catholics, who saw rich merchants like Jacques de Bernuy and several capitouls converted. Even though Catherine de Médicis, through the edict of Saint-Germain-en-Laye, recognized Protestantism as a religion, her efforts however failed to bring about peace between the two confessions. On the contrary, each party intended to assert itself and the incidents multiplied until the days of May 1562. The Protestants attempted to seize Toulouse by a coup de force, which called upon Monluc, commanding the royal forces of Guyenne. From May 12 to 17, violence erupted in the city. Finally, the Protestants were forced to flee after having suffered heavy losses. Monluc wrote, “it very nearly occurred that this opulent city, the second in France, should have been destroyed and ruined forever” (Montluc 1872, vol. 3, p. 57). For six months, the Parlement reigned in Terror and, in memory of the “deliverance”, ordered an annual memorial procession on May 17. Although forbidden by the King in 1563, the procession would take place until 1791. Toulouse then entered a period of unrest embedded with wars of religion during which a great distrust of the royal power was also evident. Suspected of Calvinism, Bernuy’s family had to sell their hotel in 1565 to three rich bourgeois, who donated it to the capitouls on the condition that they set up a college of the Society of Jesus. Jean-Étienne Duranti, the Speaker of the Parlement, was simply suspected of being soft on the Reformed faith and was put to death by the “Ligueurs” in February 1589. The Edict of Nantes was poorly received in 1598 and ascribed a rather restrictive interpretation, as the Parliament intended to stifle Protestantism “one small swallow at a time” by prohibiting everything that the letter of the edict did not specifically allow. On the contrary, the revocation of the edict by Louis XIV in 1685 was welcomed “with favor and relief by the Toulouse elites of the robe and the cassock” (Garrisson 2004, p. 45).

But in the eighteenth century, the fronts were many and despite the sympathy of the city and Parlement towards the revolt of the Duke of Montmorency, royal power finally imposed itself in Toulouse, which appeared as a stronghold of Catholic counter-reform for another long century, as witnessed by the ceremonies of the bicentenary of the “Deliverance” organized in May 1762, a few months after the execution of Calas. As Barthès wrote:

> The capitouls of this year, convinced that the time of their administration could not be marked by a greater event more dear to the citizens of this city and more glorious for them; eager to renew the vows of their predecessors and to thank the Lord for the marked favor he did to our ancestors by delivering Toulouse from heresy; resolved to celebrate the secular year of this deliverance in an extraordinary way and with extraordinary pomp, in order to remember the grave events that the Almighty vouchsafed our fathers and to renew in all hearts piety and gratitude. For this purpose they were made known to all manner of people, by their order of the 29th of previous month, posted in the accustomed places, that on the 17th of that month, the general and secular procession celebrating the deliverance of the city would be organised. To make it more solemn, it was agreed that all the relics which rested in the church of Saint-Sernin would be displayed for eight days to engage public veneration in this august temple. This was carried out and confirmed by a bull of His Holiness, who, in renewing the bull of Pope Pius IV dated 1564, wished to grant to the piety of the most zealous magistrates the bull of indulgence in the form of a jubilee for all the faithful who would devoutly visit once only the churches of St. Sernin and St. Stephen and pray as instructed by the aforementioned bull.
>
> The procession having thus been earmarked for the 17th and this news having been answered in the distance, an account was made of his arrival in this city. In the six days that preceded this feast, 30 000 people from the outside arrived who are usually 'called cousins'. To place these people many people of the city were obliged to send for beds from the countryside; others to make camp beds, many to rent beds elsewhere, and others to embarrass themselves in any way to give their parents or friends the most gracious and favorable welcome. Finally, these people of all ages, all sexes and all conditions always seemed to find a place, hoping to recover through the sweetness of their stay and the good grace of their parents.
>
> The feasts were spoiled by incessant rains which prevented the planned fireworks, yet the solemn procession of the constituted bodies, of the congregations, of the troops were possible on the morning of May 17, by taking advantage of the temporary clearing of the weather.

After the revocation of the Edict of Nantes, the Protestants who were left had to have their children baptized by Catholic priests. They also had to deceive to escape from extreme unction, but for marriage, recourse to a priest was also necessary; hence in the 1760s, the "Protestants" were the second or third generation of "new converts" forced to practise the official religion, at least on the surface. Jeanne Garrisson makes a very enlightening parallel:

> Similar to the 'conversos', the converted Jews of Portugal and Spain, they were stained in a way that time and the advent of new ideas on tolerance do not succeed in erasing. In the neighborhood, in the city, the memory of Catholics is faithful, it never forgets that such or such is a new convert, therefore a suspect. (Garrisson 2004, p. 47)

The rapprochement is striking here because the Bernuy family, which was persecuted in the 1560s, was a family of "conversos" who had hoped to escape stigmatization by settling in Toulouse at the end of the fifteenth century and was still suspected of heresy almost a century later.

This religious climate certainly bathed the city at the time of Smith's arrival, as Pierre Barthès' chronicles testify in their own way. His only ambition was to reproduce certain scenes from life in Toulouse in a handwritten notebook. One can be surprised by the subjects he chooses to treat in his chronicles and in particular by the application he puts into the description of many torments, thanks to which the hold of the church on souls and bodies was still very visible, as confessors were present until the last breath of the condemned. There is no doubt that a large part of public opinion at the time related positively to these "death rites", even if another approach was beginning to emerge, since it was the very moment when Beccaria published his *Treaty on Crimes and Sanctions* in 1764.

In reality, the supremacy of Catholicism was less unshakeable than supporters like Barthès would have liked it to be. It was itself traversed by conflicts that opposed Jansenists, Gallicans, and Jesuits. Thus in 1762, an unlikely alliance between the first two factions led to the expulsion of the Jesuits. These represented the intellectual framework of the Catholicism of Toulouse through their colleges and seminaries. However, in the early 1760s, the Duke of Choiseul faced strong hostility from the people of the robe and the Parlements. To appease these high magistrates, strong gallicans, and French anti-Roman nationalists, Choiseul agreed to feed them, as if giving a dog a bone, the Jesuit order (Leroy Ladurie 1998). In France, the case began with the bankruptcy of the Reverend Father La Valette in Martinique: brought before a tribunal by his creditors, the person in charge of the Jesuit missions made the mistake of appealing to the Paris Parlement, where the Jansenist magistrates seized the opportunity to demand an examination of the statutes of the order in 1761. The Parlement of Toulouse, for once, followed in the footsteps of Paris and the Prosecutor General Riquet de Bonrepos (whom Smith would soon meet) claimed to examine all the company's constitutions to ensure their conformity with the laws of the kingdom. He underlined "the disadvantages that the absolute, excessive obedience of the Jesuits to their general, who himself depended entirely on the Pope, could have for the State" (see Du Mège, p. 590). The doctrine of tyrannicide provided the ideological backbone for the elimination of the Jesuits and for removing the support they received from the King. Until the end of the eighteenth century, any study on the variety of political regimes necessarily included some considerations on tyranny, the right to resist the tyrant, and even to put him to death. This tradition went back to classical antiquity; Aristotle, like Cicero, looked into this question, and the Bible itself contained at least one example of tyrannicide. It did not seem that the Jesuits were particularly quick to justify tyrannicide, but Riquet reproached them for their complacency towards this doctrine. It must be recognized that the approval awarded by Voltaire to prosecutor Riquet, the same person who had accused Calas, did not lack irony because it was nothing but a relentless defence of the monarchy of divine right.

The Parlement of Toulouse was eventually to pronounce a judgement:

> forbidding the so-called Jesuits, and all others, from wearing the habit of the said society; from living under the laws of the institution of said society; from maintaining any direct or indirect correspondence with the General and superiors of said society, or others presupposed by them enjoining the so-called Jesuits to clear out the houses of said society within fifteen days. (From February 26, 1763)

This led to the closure of their colleges and their ban from the kingdom in 1764.

In any case, whether it was Arthur Dillon, archbishop from 1758 to 1762, or Loménie de Brienne thereafter, the Catholic hierarchy was careful not to get involved in theological conflicts. Loménie de Brienne endeavoured to channel this ostentatious piety, and the reform of the breviary which he had adopted was in keeping with the Gallican tradition. In 1765 he even tried to repair relations between the monarchy, Parlements, and the church at the General Assembly of Bishops in June 1765. For a century, bishops, Parlements, and ministers had been hesitant about the policy to enact vis-à-vis the Jansenists. To force them to obey Rome, a formulary of submission to the Pope, had been prepared by Jesuits shortly before Mazarin's death in 1661. Mazarin was wary of them because of their support for the Fronde (a series of civil wars in France between 1648 and 1653 opposing King Louis XIV to the princes, the nobility, and the Parlements) and their distrust of the Pope. He persuaded the latter to force them to sign the formulary of submission, the Assembly of the Clergy going even further by wanting to force all clerics (and school teachers) to sign this formulary. Pascal, in one of his last texts, argued against it, acknowledging the condemnation of Jansen and that of Saint Augustine. In 1661, the convent of Port-Royal was closed, but the spread of Jansenist ideas did not halt. The royal power and the Parlements were hesitant about the application of the law to the notice. Each of the parties involved was embarrassed: for royal power, was it necessary to oppose the Jansenists at the same time as the Protestants to strengthen Catholicism as a State religion? For Parlements, the notice reinforced the power of a Pope they distrusted. For the church, appealing to royal power to decide religious questions was just as dangerous. In the early 1760s, the question of whether or not to apply the formulary's legal strictures continued to increase tension and was on the agenda of the 1765 Assembly of the Clergy. A sign of the influence acquired by the young Archbishop of Toulouse , it was he who was in charge of leading the commission charged with writing the articles, establishing the position of the church. In other words, his talents as conciliator were put to test: how to ensure broad support within the church without displeasing the monarch while at the same time neutralizing the encroachments of the Parlements?

The ideas of tolerance were progressing, however, especially in Toulouse, where the Parlement was trying to create space for Protestants, some of whom were welcomed into its midst under cover of false certificates of Catholicity. The development of Masonic lodges was another indication that religion was losing its monopoly on the organization of social and intellectual life.

In this evolution, the vicars general, with whom Loménie of Brienne surrounded himself, played an important role if one is to believe the *History of Toulouse* written by Aldéguier:

> The abbés of Saint-Phar [natural son of Philippe d'Orléans], of Osmont [future bishop of Comminges], of Aulichamp, of Jarante, of Colbert, of Chauvigny [future bishop of Saint-Dié], etc., were the vicars general of M. de Brienne. They were court abbés, almost all of whose names had a historical bearing. Their education was very distinguished; they were younger sons of families, destined for the episcopate. They were widespread in the high society of Toulouse, where they introduced a tone of urbanity,

> an ease, a freedom, a spirit of affability and tolerance, which the stiffness of the parlementaires and the pretentiousness of the nobles very often removed from good company. All were handsome men; the women appreciated their tone, their manners, as they were very different from those of their husbands. The husbands, for the most part, received them at home without taking umbrage, and with some exceptions with pleasure. We have already had an occasion to say it; mores were suffering somewhat, yet without scandal however. (Aldéguier 1830, p. 364)

Concerning the first two letters S, the comparisons that Smith draws between different French cities underline the negative regard in which he holds the first S (soiled). As for the second letter relative to sanctity, the manifestations of Catholicism could only confirm his conviction that the religious fragmentation which promotes:

> that candour and moderation which is so seldom to be found among them, whose tenets being supported by the civil magistrate, are held in veneration by almost all the inhabitants of extensive kingdoms and empires, and who therefore see nothing round them but followers, disciples, and humble admirers. (Smith, *WN*, V.i.g, p. 793)

3.3.3 The University

The third S is bound to attract the attention of the academic or the intellectual, standing as it does for "Scholarly". It is therefore necessary to examine comprehensively its significance in Toulouse.

First of all two dates can link this S to the previous one, by delving very far back into the history of Toulouse—proof that the third S, "Scholarly", has deep roots and is not circumscribed to a century which put forward human reasoning as one of its principal themes. The University of Toulouse was formally founded in 1229. This date, largely arbitrary since the teaching of law had not ceased since Roman times, corresponds to that of the Treaty of Paris which was imposed on the Count of Toulouse, Raymond VII, by the King of France Louis IX. One of the clauses of this treaty directed the Count to reserve a sum of 4000 marcs in order to sustain fourteen masters for ten years: four in theology, two in canon law, six in the liberal arts, and two in grammar (University of Toulouse 1931, p. 42). The will of the church and the King of France to set the County of Toulouse straight and the new university was deemed "a foreign colony, composed of teachers and students from far away and particularly from

Paris" (ibidem., p. 43). Among the first masters, it can be noted that the most famous was Jean de Garlande. He was English and had studied at Oxford prior to teaching in Paris. He held one of the two chairs of grammar. Yet, the Toulousains' welcome was not very warm. Jean de Garlande thus had to flee and return to Paris "when a violent storm" soon took shape and burst against this nascent university. It was not until 1271, the day after the final attachment of the County of Toulouse to the Kingdom of France, that the university took root in its own territory.

Throughout the long period of the Middle Ages, the University of Toulouse set up a novel method of teaching, particularly in the major field of law, borrowing its teaching staff not only from the faculties of northern France (Paris, Orléans) but also from the universities of northern Italy, thus producing a diverse teaching methodology whose reputation quickly extended well beyond the borders of the kingdom. This reputation reached Scotland, a country whose law and teaching borrowed much more from Roman law than was the case in England.

In the second half of the eighteenth century, the situation of universities in France was turbulent in maintaining corporate traditions, as by not welcoming scientific innovations, universities had gradually isolated themselves from contemporary culture (Julia, p. 194). The King tried to remedy this situation and saw hope for the weakest in mergers. Thus, in May 1751, he decreed:

> The decadence into which we learned that the University of Cahors had been falling more and more for several years, having committed to receiving a full account from there very particularly, we judged that it was all the more difficult to remedy it, as professors and students were not under the eyes of the principal magistrates of our Parlement of Toulouse, in the reinforcement of which this university was established. It also seemed useless and inappropriate to allow two universities in two cities as close as Toulouse and Cahors to continue any longer. So, we combined the latter with that of Toulouse. (Baudel and Malinovski 1876, p. 168)

The argument must have seemed curious to Smith when there were no less than four universities in Scotland in the eighteenth century: St Andrews (founded 1413), Glasgow (founded 1451), Aberdeen (founded 1495), and Edinburgh (founded 1583). The two most remote universities (Aberdeen and Glasgow) were 220 kilometres apart, while Edinburgh was only 80 kilometres from both Glasgow and St Andrews.

As far as the Toulouse law faculty in particular was concerned, it led "a modest existence, stripped of the authority and prestige that had surrounded it in previous centuries" (University, p. 121). This was because the links between the faculty and the Parlement had been loosened: professors were forbidden from being advisers to the Parlement, and the venality of the offices contributed to the creation of a caste that looked down on the faculty. The Faculty of Medicine, closed in on itself, also had difficulty keeping up with the progress of knowledge. It was outside its aegis that the teaching of pharmacy, botany, and chemistry (which became the Society of Sciences in 1729) developed within the Society of Lanternists or that a Royal School of Surgery was founded in 1762.

It should also be noted that, thanks to its partnership with other university institutions, Toulouse had libraries open to the public towards the end of the eighteenth century. Most libraries did not lend books; they could only be consulted in the reading room. When Smith arrived in Toulouse, the only prominent and well-constituted library was that of the Jesuits, which was entrusted to the Royal College.

His companion, the young Henry Scott, was, according to the letters of his step-father, enrolled at the Toulouse Faculty of Law. It is impossible today to find a record of his enrolment because the university unfortunately only kept track of students who had graduated. However, there is no reason to doubt his registration as it was part of the young aristocrat's obligations during his journey.

The buildings were located in the western part of the city, close to the present Rue des Lois, thus named for this reason. One can still fortunately see nowadays well-restored buildings belonging to the University of Toulouse. The law faculty, whose teaching took place in the Middle Ages in colleges, was equipped with amphitheatres in the sixteenth century. Two centuries later, the professors strove to obtain the support of the city for the maintenance of the premises. The situation seemed rather contrasted, since, according to a 1779 memoir, "the law faculty of Toulouse aspires to the same magnificence as that of Paris, which is decorated in a similar way to Sainte-Geneviève church". However, a few years later a deliberation of the professors drew the attention of the capitouls to the buildings which threatened ruin. In any case, before Smith arrived, the town had a well built and the latrines renovated.

The courses undertaken by the Duke are not known, but the teaching was marked by the influence of François de Boutaric (1672–1733), whose works were still, in those years, the subject of new editions by printers in

Toulouse. Brief presentations showed topics such as tolls, leases, emphyteutic leases, rent law, hunting rights, as well as numerous developments on property rights. These were subjects that can be read about at length in Smith's *Wealth of Nations (WN)*, but also, and more surprisingly, in the handwritten instructions that the young Duke wrote upon his return to Scotland to ensure the management of his many lands. There is no doubt that the teaching in Toulouse, in its diversity and precision of its arguments, played a pivotal role in his training.

3.4 Academies and Learned Societies

However impactful the university institutions may have been in the perception of the inhabitants of Toulouse, a learned city, other organizations were also present and contributed to its influence. Among them were the learned societies, especially those which became real institutions, but also those that were more democratic and widespread, including the multitude of Masonic lodges, in full expansion during this period, when liberalism was benefiting from the effects of fashion.

3.4.1 The Floral Games Academy and Literary Societies

Toulouse is still proud today to have the oldest European Academy. The Compagnie des Jeux floraux was founded at the latest in 1323 by seven troubadours with the aim of perpetuating in Toulouse the traditions of courteous lyricism. In 1694, the Compagnie des Jeux floraux was transformed by Louis XIV into a forty-member Academy by the decree of Fontainebleau, following certain approaches taken by Simon de La Loubère. He was quite representative of the trajectories of so many Occitans who had "gone up to Paris". After studying at the Jesuit College, he went to Paris where he made a name for himself through poetry, but also through mathematical works that introduced him to Leibniz. He, therefore, made a career for himself in French diplomacy and was the extraordinary envoy of Louis XIV to Siam, bringing back the first description of that country to the west. Elected to the French Academy in 1693, he was shocked by the debasement of the Floral Games competition during a visit to Toulouse, so much so that he intervened with Louis XIV's decision and finally obtained the letters patent for establishing the Academy, which, it was agreed, would offer him the first vacant seat available. This royal recognition and the reorganization it implied made it an imitation of the French Academy, instituted by Cardinal Richelieu, King Louis XIII's chief minister, in 1638. In return, the Oc language competitions were abandoned for the next two and a half centuries. This only confirmed the forgetfulness or timidity with regard to the language of the institution, which, in contempt of its original goals, had granted only a minor reward to the Toulouse poet Godolin for a play in French.

At the same time as the reformation of the Floral Games Academy, the end of the eighteenth century saw the creation of new learned societies. It was as early as 1640, shortly after the foundation of the French Academy, that academic conferences were created in Toulouse, later transformed into the "Société des gens de lettres" in 1688. In 1729, a Society for Sciences was constituted, which, from 1734, proposed to provide the city with an observatory, a concern to which Adam Smith, who was trained in the Newtonian method and was the author of a *History of Astronomy*, must have been sensitive. The convergence of the efforts of the two societies was crowned by the creation of a Royal Academy of Sciences, Inscriptions and Belles-Lettres in 1746.

To complete this picture of an intellectual activity, a Fine Arts Society was formed in 1746 and its achievements enabled it to obtain by letters patent its transformation into the Royal Academy of Painting, Sculpture and Architecture on December 15, 1750. This budding Academy was interested not only in the figurative arts but also in music. As Smith was a lover of music, and the author of several treatises on comparison of the various arts, our Scottish traveller had enough to satisfy his interests in Toulouse.

When Smith arrived in Toulouse, the Académie des Sciences et Belles-Lettres was at the pinnacle of its glory and power. Indeed, the Archbishop of Toulouse, Charles Loménie de Brienne, who was perhaps one of Smith's motivations to visit Toulouse, had for some months been the protector of this institution.

Scientific problems, including the composition of the waters of the Pyrenees and their curative virtues, but also astronomy or medicine, were readily discussed within this Academy. The frequent debates about vaccination against smallpox were a very good example of the individual interests that contributed to the creation of collective interest.

The Belles-Lettres side, on the other hand, cut across not only literature but also philosophy. Its latest development reached out towards the thinking of the physiocrats and beyond the still somewhat embryonic and very agricultural speeches of the sect of economists under the leadership of Dr. Quesnay.

3.4.2 *Masonic Lodges*

Even more than in other French cities, the eighteenth century witnessed the development of a large number of Masonic lodges in Toulouse. The lodges in Toulouse, and also in Bordeaux, were the consequence of the immigration of Jacobites from Scotland or Ireland. Thus the Barnewal family, father and son, were the promoters of the lodges on Toulouse.

Now recognized by the King of France as his "true and natural subjects and regnicoles", (that is to say inhabitants of the realm) the Counts of Barnewall of Trimlestown, as they called themselves, quickly adapted to their new homeland. Their settlement in Toulouse was undoubtedly facilitated by the presence of a small colony of compatriots, mainly Irish Jacobites, but also some Scots, gathered around a seminary founded in 1660 to train Irish missionaries, the Irish College, which disappeared during the Revolution. In this institution, the monks, without denying their British origin, tried to integrate themselves into local society while preserving their modern ideas on the conception of the role of man in his social environment. Thus, they participated in the creation and animation of the Masonic network in Toulouse, of which the most important lodges were around 1760, "Saint Jean de l'Harmonie" or "La Parfaite Harmonie" (1750), "Saint Jean fille de Clermont" (1745), "La Française Saint Jean des Arts" (1745), "La Sagesse" (1757), "Saint Jean de la Parfaite Union, Montmorency" (1762), and "La Parfaite Amitié" (1765).

There also existed in Toulouse a Masonic movement of lodges based on the "Scottish Rite", which were also experiencing considerable growth, such as the lodge "Les Écossais fidèles" and "La Vieille Bru" (1747).

3.4.3 *"Arts Martiaux"*

The overview of the sites for social activities focused on knowledge and a desire to learn, which reinforced Toulouse's reputation as a city of knowledge, would be incomplete if the part played by Townshend's "exercises of the body" was absent from the discussion. It is probable that horse riding and fencing had been taught in Toulouse since time immemorial. Young people from the nobility could not neglect this training if they wished to hold their rank in society. In France, riding academies came up during the sixteenth century. The academies, which developed in the years 1590–1650, would take part in this renewal. The first of them was founded in 1594 by Antoine de Pluvinel, the first French riding masters. The

Toulouse riding school was founded in 1598 or 1616. It was, it seems, the first Academy created in outside Paris. Positioned against the city walls, between the Montgaillard and Montoulieu gates, it included both open-air and covered carousels. In January 1617, to teach young people how to ride horses, the capitouls granted Mr. Du-Jardin, the squire and director of the Academy, a vacant room between the Montgaillard gate and the Hauts-Murats prison. This would become the "covered manège". The Academy, in addition to riding, taught how to "shoot weapons" and offered lessons in dance, good manners, and other necessary teachings for the education of young people.

A century later, the same objectives were pursued by the Academy, and in 1726, Villeneuve, who had just been appointed riding master of the Toulouse Academy, claimed that he would "teach young people to ride horses, provide dancing masters, teach how to use weapons, trick ride, play the lute, read mathematics and other exercises that one has become accustomed to teaching nobility. All in accordance with the previous deliberations of 11 January 1640, 10 September 1663, 15 September 1674" (Roux 2001).

This institution, although torn between the city, the Estates, and the King, and despite many vagaries, succeeded in crossing the centuries and even regimes since its existence was attested under the Second Empire (de Chanal). Its durability seemed to have been sustained by the continuous investment of the riding masters who kept their posts for four or five decades and often transmitted them to their sons or sons-in-law.

In the second part of the eighteenth century, riding master Fraîche was particularly appreciated by the Capitouls, who asked for a fivefold increase in the funds allocated to him, while also expatiating on the quality of his establishment which is

> so decent in a rich province that it would be almost indecent to stop supporting it. As for the quality of the young students who trained there he can say with truth that he had all the best in the province, both of the Nobility and of the Law, as Mr. de Mirepoix, Messrs. de Thézan, M. de Bernis, Messrs. Dapché father and son, Mr de Valance, Mr de Chalvet, Mr Le Comte, Mr de Pivert [Roux de Puivert], as well as everything that makes up our parliament, both presidents and councillors, not to mention several English, Spanish and Italian lords. (Chanal 1872)

Of course, the aforementioned English lords may have been the descendants of the Jacobites, but it is very likely that the Duke attended this establishment, near the site where the house rented by our travellers was situated. Riding was not the only martial training offered, but fencing was also practised with passion in Toulouse by a large part of the student population and by all young people from good families, thus justifying the existence of these fencing schools since the sixteenth century at least. Three schools were opened in 1751 and in the 1780s. The fencing halls were located along the Rue des Cordeliers and Rue des Jacobins, near the university and schools (Roux 2001).

3.5 The Conflict Between the Governor and the Parlement, and the Ensuing Crisis (1763–1764)

Smith was also served by local and contemporary political events; as the always vigilant Pierre Barthès analysed, the city of Toulouse was then shaken by events which were only one of the episodes of a long confrontation between judicial power and royal power, which would continue up to the Revolution and the overhaul of France's political and administrative system. Once again Pierre Barthès, as the city chronicler, informs us as follows:

> Registration of the King's letters:
>
> On the 26th of that month (April, 1764) the feelings of the King appeared on the orders given by His Majesty to the deputies with injunction to register his letters patent given at Versailles last February 25. They order the execution of the declaration of 21 November last and impose absolute silence on what had happened so far with regard to the objects that gave rise to the declaration. The letters patent signed by Louis and countersigned by Philipeaux were posted everywhere with the decree of registration of the 24th of the same month following the report from M. Bastard, which had ordered that the court would resume without delay and in a manner that would be uniform., The ordinary functions of justice that had been suspended in all courts since last August to the prejudice of an infinity of clerks, as lawyers, bailiffs, secretaries (?) and litigants who by this cessation, were reduced to an appalling misery in a time when food was extraordinarily expensive, with wheat at the price of 6 deniers the hundredweight, wine at 10 and 12 livres. As money was already extremely scarce, trade was lost and the arts were consequently degraded. As a result of this decision, the court has resumed its functions and the justice system is now in force, to everyone's great satisfaction today 30th of the current.

So, as Pierre Barthès described it with his usual candour, the city of Toulouse and its Parlement had just experienced a crisis, a crisis of justice which led, without Barthès seeing the link of cause and effect, to a real economic crisis limited to the city of Toulouse. What was happening in Toulouse that year? After persistent interventions due to protests at the court of the city of Toulouse, the Parlement ceased its activity. As Barthès rightly pointed out, this situation led to a decrease in the circulation of money. According to the columnist, this also led to an increase in the prices of raw materials as well as basic foodstuffs among which he considered bread and wine to be most representative. This increase in price was general and was not due to lack of a raw materials, but because of a sudden change in the behaviour of the people who most represented local economic life. The phenomenon may have been rapid, a few weeks, a few months at most, because when money tended to flee the city, it could not be contained as there was no regulator to restore trade and confidence.

Was Smith aware of the phenomenon? In any case, he was the victim of a ramification of this crisis since, as Barthès tells us, "the arts are degraded". Smith, who thought that he would arrive in a city fond of spectacle, found himself in a city that was experiencing a crisis, that had led to the driving out of the travelling theatrical players who preferred to avoid Toulouse and instead concentrated on Montpellier or Bordeaux. These troupes had the opportunity to travel and present their shows wherever they could attract an audience. This was not the case in Toulouse, while Bordeaux was in full expansion following the resumption of colonial trade at the end of the Seven Years' War as well as the presence of the governor of the province of Guyenne, a very influential man of spirit and culture, Richelieu.

So Smith, a man who appreciated shows and the way feelings were represented, found himself in a city where there was a total absence of entertainment. During these few months following Smith's arrival, the town was all the duller, as the religious ceremonies that filled Fr. Barthès' diary seemed to multiply. Thus, based on Barthès' views, Schneider made religious ceremonies a characteristic mark of Toulouse from 1738 to 1780 (Schneider 1995).

Pierre Barthès brought together in his commentary the economic stagnation caused by the absence of lawyers, bailiffs, clerks, and litigants. However, this contrasted with the conception of the physiocrats, then trending in France, for whom wealth was produced solely by agriculture, while the secondary function of the population was simply to help it circulate. Smith, who opposed this view, was to some extent sustained in his analysis.

Thus, beyond the purely legal and institutional role he observed in Charles Townshend's more or less direct injunctions, Smith discovered that the Parlement also played a major economic role. Agriculture and the emerging industry were not the only areas that contributed to wealth creation in the provincial capital city.

Pierre Barthès also provides us with information on the outcome of the quarrel that opposed the Parlement of Toulouse to the King for several months. This quarrel was resolved by an injunction of Louis XV, who, from Versailles, put a temporary end to the question by an authoritative decision that could not be contested by anyone.

While Britain, since its Revolution at the end of the eighteenth century, had had a central Parliament in which all the subjects of the British Crown were represented with an element of variety, the French-style Parlement was merely a judicial institution whose role was not to draft laws like its British counterpart, but only to register them while also rendering justice.

In the United Kingdom, since the revolutionary period at the end of the seventeenth century, Parliament had become the place where members met, more or less democratically elected by members of the English and Scottish "gentry" (suffrage remained selective). However, according to Charles Townshend, as noted by Lewis Namier, electoral campaigns were very expensive and required a great fortune, especially to break into the political world, in addition to the qualities of oratory which were of course the basis of the profession.

Towards the end of the modern period, this type of institution ceased to exist in France. There was indeed a push towards survival from the past, constituted by the Estates General of the kingdom, but these suffered from several handicaps. First of all these were assemblies which were not permanent and convened only at the express request of the King. The second aspect that hindered their functioning was that the agenda was set strictly in advance and there could be no discussion of other items, leaving no room for flexibility. Finally, these particular Estates had not taken place at the national level for over 150 years, and their last meeting had ended without any decision. Smith could therefore only note a lack of democratic discourse at the national level.

The Toulouse Parlement therefore did not have the same powers as its homonymous institution in England. In Scotland, the situation after the Act of Union was even simpler as the Scottish Parliament, which functioned in the same way as the English Parliament, was dissolved by this Act and only a small number of members were integrated into the Westminster Parliament.

Smith became interested in the Toulouse Parlement, which, through its judgements, produced original case law, combining a strong legacy of Roman law, as was the case in Scotland, with the custom of Toulouse, adapting French law accordingly.

Some historians have claimed that there was no apparent interruption in legal matters between the end of the Roman period and that of the Middle Ages. For a specialist of the Parlement of Toulouse, this institution enjoyed an important prestige by its origin since it remained the only guarantee of a certain amount of autonomy that had been extinguished over the centuries.

> It should not be believed that the cradle of the Parlement of Toulouse was sheltered under the banner of its Counts; this would take away the glory of its royal origin. The city of Toulouse became the capital of the kingdom of Aquitaine, founded by Charlemagne for Louis le Débonnaire, and was both the throne of royal power and the seat of justice. In the years 790–798, the king held a plenary court or a parliament. He administered justice in person and sometimes delegated his authority to his chancellors and counts palatine. The counts and envoys of Emperor Charlemagne did not cross the borders of the kingdom of Aquitaine; they stopped at the borders of Gallia Narbonnensis. Toulouse had its own independent judiciary and reported only to the King of Aquitaine. (Dubédat 1885, p. 5)

The Parlement, as Smith observed, had been created in 1420 at the express request of the Languedoc Estates. It was a sovereign court, autonomous with regard to its colleague from Paris, while representing the monarchy in the south. One of the reasons for its creation was to ensure that the trial of the litigants in the Languedoc would be carried out at home, by judges who were better educated in the Roman legal background of the southern courts than could be expected from Parisian magistrates working in an environment of customary law.

> For many historians of French institutions, the Toulouse court appeared to be “a factor of unity in the service of the monarchy”, as well as a tetchy yet determined defender of provincial privileges. Of course, the Parlement represented the king, but it was neither flexible nor docile; in fact, one could estimate that at least eighty ordinances put into force in the jurisdiction of the Parlement of Paris were not recognized in the Languedoc, because the Parlement had decided not to register them. It is quite true that the Toulouse Parlement was able to control almost all legislations, and this often worked

> to the Languedoc's advantage. This control reflected the court's affinity with the Estates, with respect to the privileges of the province. Both jealously guarded the privileges of the province, and both appointed special officers to coordinate information on royal legislation and policy that they felt was inconsistent with the interests of the province. As far as the local authorities were concerned, the Parlement was jealous of their prerogatives; on the other hand, they were ready to show solidarity with these local authorities when defending provincial privileges was concerned: with the provincial Estates and municipalities, effective resistance was thus organized against the King's agents. (Brink 1976, pp. 288–289)

Thus, the Parlement of Toulouse was, since the Middle Ages, the second Parlement of France by its date of creation as by the extent of its jurisdiction, which went beyond the province of the Languedoc proper. Hence, the importance of the city's legal professions disturbed the functioning of the economy when the Parlement ceased its activities.[9] It seemed that spices[10] represented significant sums in this operation and acted as an injection of capital coming from all the provinces and beyond, into Toulouse's own economy.

This unique situation of the Parlement of Toulouse between the King and the province was certainly of interest to a professor of Scottish jurisprudence, who was concerned with the articulation of the rights of the subjects of the British Crown.

In the middle of the eighteenth century, the Parlement had three main functions, and Smith had the opportunity, as we shall see, to rub shoulders with the various activities that the institution undertook.

The first function was the one that resulted in the crisis described by Pierre Barthès. This was the registration of royal edicts, which if they were to apply in the jurisdiction of the Parlement, must have been registered by the latter to examine its compatibility with local law. This was undoubtedly the origin of the conflict.

[9] At the time of Smith's arrival, there was also a Parlement in Bordeaux which was a Pays d'Election. However, the creation of the Bordeaux Parlement was much more recent than that of the Toulouse Parlement. The foundation of the Bordeaux Parlement dated back to the fifteenth century and corresponded to the end of the English occupation of the province. However, the Bordeaux Parlement enjoyed a better reputation than the Toulouse Parlement, mainly due to the high quality of its magistrates (Montaigne, La Boétie, Montesquieu).

[10] Spices referred to the royalties that litigants had to pay to judges (a term that had become synonymous with "bribery" in the modern sense). This is disputable, as the spices were paid into a fund and redistributed by the first president as judges' remuneration or to pay his staff.

The second function was the publication of judgements. The judgements of the Toulouse Parlement, in the form of memoranda, were regularly published. As such, they constituted a true jurisprudence of the national law and its adaptation to the local customs and circumstances of the whole province of the Languedoc.

The third function of the Parlement of Toulouse was that of a court of justice, a court of appeal, with the first level of justice being ensured by the Capitouls of Toulouse or any other seigneurial jurisdiction within the framework of the organization, which further had a right to administer justice. Such was the case, for example, of the Canal du Languedoc, where Riquet de Bonrepos had a right of justice over the whole area of the canal, a right granted to the family from Toulouse to Sète.

However, the arrival of Smith and his student corresponded with the end of a long period of institutional crisis concerning the Parlement, disrupting the life of the city and thus colouring Smith's first impressions. This crisis was quite emblematic of the tensions that were emerging between a central and absolute power on the one hand and more collective powers representing local interests on the other. The Parlement of Toulouse, the second oldest in France, would not be the only one to enter into dissent in 1763, but was probably the one whose protest would go the farthest. The crisis went so far as to provoke armed confrontations that would have taken on the appearance of a veritable civil war, at the scale of the province, a conflict of legitimacy brought to its paroxysm.

It all began with the arrival of the Duke of Fitz-James in the autumn of 1763. Barthès immerses us in the unique atmosphere of the time:

> On Friday the 9th of this month, the Duke of Fitz-James arrived in this town through the Saint-Étienne Gate, commanding for the King in the province of the Languedoc, coming from Paris to register in the Parlement the edicts which pleased His Majesty to give for the establishment of the new subsidies; he went down to the gate of the town and emerged on foot surrounded by his guards without further pomp and circumstance to the Archbishop's palace where he took accommodation. (Barthès, September 1763)

Thus began a period of rebellion that would last nine months. In this short text, nothing seemed to suggest that things would go wrong. The very respectful chronicler went so far as to write that the edicts must have been fair because they came from the King. Barthès was always very approving and respectful of established powers.

It is thus advisable to comprehend the subject of these edicts, as they touch directly on the economy and on subjects on which Adam Smith would comment extensively in the last book of the *Wealth of Nations*.

The War of the Austrian Succession (1741–1748), which itself followed the War of the Spanish Succession (1702–1714), ended for France in an absence of territorial gains and losses, but as Voltaire deplored, France worked for the King of Prussia and, in the end, the country put itself into a delicate situation not only with Austria but also with England and finally with Prussia itself. France was weakened—economically, diplomatically, and militarily, would be drawn irresistibly towards the Seven Years' War, whose fatal consequences began to be felt at the time when Smith travelled to Toulouse.

These recurring wars that the kingdom endured deepened irremediably and periodically, the deficits of the royal finances. Even though statistical tools were rather primitive at that time, the conclusion was absolute. It was thus necessary to impose new taxes. The lack of the efficiency of statistical tools ran the risk of underestimating the debt, and also of delaying observation of its imminence, especially as the likelihood of a default approached.

As economics was still in its infancy, the idea was to find a tax that was remunerative, easy to collect, and as fair as possible, or the least unfair as was possible. It should be recalled that France mainly imposed indirect taxation, that is, taxes and duties that were sometimes complex and often poorly distributed. While indirect taxes were by definition the easiest to collect, their regressive nature was strongly felt: taxes on basic necessities weighed on the poorest, and ultimately the rate of effort decreased as income increased.

This led to the emergence of a new type of tax called "le vingtième" or "twentieth", which broke with the logic of constantly increasing indirect taxes. It was a matter of filling the State coffers quickly and permanently. This tax, considered a direct tax, had to be paid by all, provided that the payers were property owners, and was based on great transparency, since the taxpayer had to declare his property and possessions himself, which were subject to taxation at a rate of 5%, justifying the name of the tax.

From the outset, it raised a profound opposition from the most powerful members of society who were directly targeted. The Parlement of Paris in 1759 claimed, "It is necessary to preserve the secrecy of all shops and the state of the fortune of all traders in order to preserve their credit" (Flammermont and Tourneux, p. 229), while for the "Cour des Aides" of

Aix-en-Provence, "What the trader hides, what he must hide from the public, the vile clerk will come to search for, and discover" (Aix Court, p. 21).

Willingness to pay taxes was uncommon in a monarchy that excluded most of the population from the decision-making process. The affair thus followed its course, and in 1763, the rebellion of the Parlements throughout France was at its height, particularly in Toulouse, where the Parlement refused the registration of the edict that aimed to bring into force this new form of taxation. However, in Toulouse, this affair was coupled with a dispute over legitimacy between the governor and the Parlement. Thus for nearly nine months, from September 1763 to April 1764, the date of the return of the delegates from Versailles, or more precisely from the neighbouring Château of Choisy-le-Roi where the councillors were received, quarrels escalated between the Duke of Fitz-James and the Parlement. The Duke wisely withdrew to the Château de Mont-Blanc located a few minutes from Toulouse, in the present Croix-Daurade district, but outside the walls. The city did not seem safe for him and he also wished to use diplomacy. The links between the capitouls and the Parlement of Toulouse were close, and even if they were often in competition, capitouls and parlementaires knew how to unite to oppose the central power. It must be said that the two environments were porous and that very often a capitoul, once his function was fulfilled, dreamt of becoming a parlementaire and thus reach the peak of his career, which he could crown by acceding to the nobility.

After a few weeks of vain palaver, the Duke of Fitz-James, Governor of Languedoc, sought to have the parliamentarians arrested. But the members of the Parlement, in the name of their own authority, sought on their side to seize the person of the Duke, an incredible ambition, the Duke being a peer of France. From then on, each party would try to convince the royal power of the righteousness of its cause. The ecclesiastical authorities also got involved and tried to mediate, which worried and irritated the Duke even more, if we are to believe the account of the Duchess who, during the most acute period, from December 6, 1763, to January 12, 1764, sent no fewer than fifteen letters soliciting the Duke's sister in Paris to defend their cause. Her letters describe the power relations in Toulouse, seen from the other side: thus on December 7, the Duchess indicates that the president of the Parlement having been deposed, and it was henceforth by the intermediary of the prosecutor Riquet de Bonrepos that the

Duke tried to address the Parlement. But it is above all the portrait of the archbishop that is interesting:

> Sunday afternoon Mr. de Loménie and the Abbé of La Galaizière, Grand Vicar, arrived here. I was waiting for them, because someone always come to this shop to fish for information when there was something new. The abbé pulled Mr. de Fitz-James aside and handed him a letter without telling him from whom it was coming. Mr. de Fitz-James took it, and having recognized the Prosecutor General's handwriting and suspecting the fact, he returned the letter to the abbé without unsealing it, telling him to take it back to where he had got it from. Then the abbé assured him that there was nothing in this letter which could displease him and which was not honest, with an air of truth which committed him to take it back and to open it. I'll include it here and you can judge for yourself. After reading it, Mr. de Fitz-James said as an answer to the abbé: "Monsieur the Prosecutor General is taking you for a fool. "The abbé seemed surprised by the compliment, and wanted to reply. Mr. de Fitz-James repeated the same words and turned his arse (in English) towards him. A few minutes later, the abbé came to him and said, "Sir, I will tell the Attorney General that you do not want to answer him. "Sir," said the Duke of Fitz-James, "I didn't tell you this, but the Prosecutor General thinks you're a fool. "The abbé and his companion went out a few minutes later than the people who were at my house and who thus knew the story. [...]
>
> The archbishop came on Monday. Mr. de Fitz-James took him to his office and asked him if he had had any advance knowledge of the foolish and impertinent approach of his Grand Vicar. He said yes and wanted to start explaining this. Mr de Fitz-James replied that it did not need any comment, that he only wanted to know if he knew about it and that it was enough for him. The archbishop then wanted to talk about all the pains he had given himself in all this on the King's service. Mr. de Fitz-James replied that he was well paid for it and that he wanted to believe it. They went out of the office and he left shortly after. As for the Archbishop, he only said what he perceived. But for me, I would like to be rid of him for this meeting of the Estates and that he be ordered not to go. I even believe it necessary for the good of business. This man wants to play the role of Cardinal Retz here. He's not that witty, but he's also mean and prone to confusion. It would be unfortunate if he came to disturb the Estates again. And there is a great probability that he will. What I'm telling you is known here to everyone. The confabulations of the Procurator General and those of his party are held at his home and the judgments are made there. (Duchess of Fitz-James, pp. 143–145)

These episodes of disorder, the most epic, but also the least flattering and rather damaging to the city of Toulouse, are abundantly described, with much delight, by the chronicler Pierre Barthès.

To conclude the relation of this quarrel's events, let Pierre Barthès describe the Duke of Fitz-James in terms and with precautions that suggest that the Scottish Jacobites were not necessarily the most beloved characters of the city of Toulouse:

> Many people who will read these memoirs will be surprised to read so many times the name of a man who has given so many opportunities to the troubles that have agitated the Parlement in the various circumstances I have written about above, and will not be angered, as I think, to learn of his origin, and will stop looking at him as a foreigner, untitled, even though he really is a peer of France. We will thus learn that this lord is the son of the late Jacques de Fitz-James, Duke of Berlin, peer and Marshal of France and one of the greatest generals of his century who was the natural son of James the second King of England[11] and of Arabelle Churchill, sister of the Duke of Marlborough. He was born in 1671 in Moulins en Bourbonnais where his mother gave birth to him while returning from the waters at Bourbon. He gave in his youth brilliant proofs of his value and military talents. He moved to France with the King his father in 1689 because of the troubles in England; he then commanded in Ireland and had a horse killed under him at the battle of the Boyne in 1690.
>
> This marshal stood out in a great number of sieges and battles, he won on 23 April 1707 the famous battle of Almansa in Spain, stormed Barcelona on 12 September 1714 and was killed by a cannon shot on 12 September 1734 at the siege of Philisburg after having rendered the most important services to France. These are the ancestors of the Duke who as commander of the province came to Toulouse for the reasons written above. His origin could not be more noble, as one can see and so one will not be annoyed at being informed.

The very Catholic and royalist Barthès was shocked by the fact that the Duke's legitimacy could be called into question. At least that is what this long plea tends to prove, in which he recalls in detail the feats of arms of the ancestors of the commander of the province. One is struck, first of all, by the accuracy of the biographical information. Pierre Barthès, if he did

[11] James II of England is also James VII of Scotland, the last King of Scotland to have ruled.

not get the information directly from the Duke himself (he would not have failed to tell us about this meeting), obtained it either from his Secretariat or from an article published in the *Affiches de Toulouse* or the *Courrier d'Avignon* that the Duke had published to legitimize his presence in Toulouse through his origins.

It should also be noted that the Duke of Fitz-James and the Duke of Buccleuch were both descendants of Charles I of England (1600–1649), who was beheaded during the Revolution. But this cousinhood did not allow Smith to establish relations because when he arrived in Toulouse, Fitz-James had already taken, since the very beginning of 1764, the road back to Paris. The quarrel between Parlement and governor was closed by the decision that Louis XV communicated to the delegates who had come to him.

Fitz-James' departure in January 1764 seemed to be a victory for the Parlement and the capitouls, but when the representatives who had gone to seek the King's arbitration returned and arrived in Toulouse three days before Smith, they announced a defeat: the King had decided and ordered the registration of the edict. One consequence of the quarrel was that "Louis XV abhorred these companies of judges, who claimed, by buying their offices, also to buy the right to disobey him and to excite his subjects to revolt" (Aldéguier 1830, p. 325).

As we have already pointed out on several occasions, we are missing Smith's direct comments on the events that have just taken place in Toulouse. However, one finds in the book V of the *WN* the following passage which can be applied to the situation which agitated the city in which he had just arrived:

> Fear is in almost all cases a wretched instrument of government, and ought in particular never to be employed against any order of men who have the smallest pretensions to independency. To attempt to terrify them, serves only to irritate their bad humour, and to confirm them in an opposition which more gentle usage perhaps might easily induce them, either to soften, or to lay aside altogether. The violence which the French government usually employed in order to oblige all their parliaments, or sovereign courts of justice, to enregister any unpopular edict, very seldom succeeded. (*WN*, V.i.g, p.799)

3.6 The Calas Affair

The second case which had troubled the capitouls and the Parlement of Toulouse since September 1761 had repercussions throughout Europe and gave a deplorable image of the Parlement and the city. In the Calas affair, the Age of Enlightenment had found an illustration of the darkness of past centuries with which it was eager to make a break. This case was exemplary in two respects. First of all, it was one of the last cases in which a man was atrociously put to death on the wheel without his guilt for the crime he was accused of having been formally established. Further, the way in which Voltaire took hold of the case and obtained a review of the trial, brought about reforms of the justice of his time which underpinned in Europe a decisive stage in the role that public opinion would later play on the French and European stage. The Calas affair, by its scale and because of the protagonists involved, will be as singularly significant in our history as the trial of Captain Dreyfus at the turn of the nineteenth century. Regular references to these cases reflect their long-term impact on public life. They are a reminder that a judicial system does not necessarily conform to the sense of justice perceived by contemporaries. Pierre Barthès writes:

> By judgment of the court of yesterday 9th of this month and executed today 10th at 4.30 p.m., Sieur Jean Calas trading in this city for over 40 years, linen merchant, rue des Filatiers, in the house of Sieur Rambaut, a man of great stature and complexion, a native of La Cabaré near Castres, aged 67, following five months minus three days of detention in the prisons of the town hall where he had been taken on the 13th day of October with his wife, a younger son, his servant and the younger Sieur Lavaïsse; having been accused and convicted of having strangled in his house Marc Antoine Calas, his beloved son, as I reported in his place, was condemned to be broken alive and placed on the wheel for two hours, then strangled, then thrown into the fire to be consumed; his ashes then thrown into the wind. This will be executed to the letter today 10th of this month at St. George's Square at the time marked above.
>
> This man of Huguenot origin and obstinate Protestant, if ever there was one, as well as all his family suffered his torture with prodigious constancy and never wanted to surrender to the holy admonitions of the Dominican preacher Bourges and another father his deputy…; who from 4 o'clock in the morning until 6 o'clock in the evening never stopped trying to persuade him to save his soul by opening his eyes to the light of the truth, which can

> only be found in the bosom of the Catholic Church, by a sincere conversion, by abjuring the errors with which he was (imbued) from childhood; but they could not shake him in any way, he died as a reprobate as we must believe and nevertheless suffered the torture to which he was condemned, in the sight of countless people, even people from the countryside who came to this city on purpose to see die a father who was doing unworthy violence to nature, as he did not abhor strangling his own son. "Nemo Parricidae supplicio misericordia commovetur."[12] (Barthès, March 10, 1762)

To the purely circumstantial exposition that Pierre Barthès the chronicler can relate on the evening of Calas' torment has been opposed to Smith's thoughtful view. He wrote between 1780 and 1790, long after his return to his native land, a commentary inserted in a new edition of the *TMS*:

> The innocent man, on the contrary, over and above the uneasiness which this fear may occasion, is tormented by his own indignation at the injustice which has been done to him. He is struck with horror at the thoughts of the infamy which the punishment may shed upon his memory, and foresees, with the most exquisite anguish, that he is hereafter to be remembered by his dearest friends and relations, not with regret and affection, but with shame, and even with horror for his supposed disgraceful conduct: and the shades of death appear to close round him with a darker and more melancholy gloom than naturally belongs to them. Such fatal accidents, for the tranquillity of mankind, it is to be hoped, happen very rarely in any country; but they happen sometimes in all countries, even in those where justice is in general very well administered. The unfortunate Calas, a man of much more than ordinary constancy (broke upon the wheel and burnt at Tholouse for the supposed murder of his own son, of which he was perfectly innocent), seemed, with his last breath, to deprecate, not so much the cruelty of the punishment, as the disgrace which the imputation might bring upon his memory. After he had been broke, and was just going to be thrown into the fire, the monk, who attended the execution, exhorted him to confess the

[12] Barthès refers here to Cicero, "Misericordia est aegritudo ex miseria alterius, injuria laborantis: nemo enim parricidae aut proditoris supplicio misericordia commovetur" (Pity is a sadness given to us by the misery of others, when they suffer without having deserved it, because no one feels pity at the ordeal of a parricide or a traitor.) (Tusculans, IV:18). Cicero, Marcus Tullius. 1834. Complete works /[books II–V]/short story by M. Matter. Paris: C.L.F. Panckoucke.

crime for which he had been condemned. My Father, said Calas, can you yourself bring yourself to believe that I am guilty?[13] (Smith, *TMS*, III.2. 1 2, p. 120)

Put side by side, the two texts clearly show the relationship between Calas' trial and torture, and reflections on the "moral feelings" involved in the Calas affair. Pierre Barthès acts as a journalist from the point of view of immediate history. His vision of the present moment is an exciting testimony. It contains all the passion that the case aroused from the start. On the contrary, Smith's step back is marked by a certain detachment as he coldly dissects the human soul. The emotion that the reader experiences in Barthès' sad tale, which this time does not repeat his conviction of Calas' guilt, is more contained in Smith even as he asserts the innocence of Calas, who appears as a simple icon of absolute intolerance.

If Smith sought to raise the level of his considerations and to propose shared human feelings, he was the victim of his own demonstration, for Calas was reduced to the role of simple spectator (which is horrible to write, given the circumstances), and all emotion and passion tend to disappear as the reader is forced to proceed to an experiment of thought in order to be able to imagine the State of mind of the tortured man—overwhelmed by what he can imagine of the thought processes of the spectators of his torture.

In Barthès, who is often open to criticism for his stances, we perceive a doubt that he expresses through the description of the condemned: "he is rich, but not a proprietor, he is old, but still robust, he dies holding on to his convictions with great dignity, but in error." So many oxymorons immediately instil confusion in the mind of the spectator, as a direct witness of the events.

Such perceptible doubts are rather rare in Barthès' commentaries, and it shows from the beginning that Calas' trial and torture were not

[13] According to a note in the edition of the *TMS*, "the last words of Calas addressed to the monk as reported by Smith probably come from conversations he had while he was in Toulouse" (note 1, p. 120). Smith certainly researched the Calas affair while in Toulouse, but the exchanges between Father Bourges and Calas were already included in the bilingual edition of the original pieces on Jean Calas' trial and execution published in England in 1762 (cf. "Further Account of the Death of Mr. John Calas, Merchant, at", °who was executed there for the supposed Murder of his own Son. From the Original Pieces on that Subject, by the celebrated Mr. de Voltaire in *The London Magazine, or, Gentleman's Monthly Intelligencer*, Volume 31, pp. 518–9).

ordinary. In its support, he adds that the influx of spectators is larger than usual, because to the regulars of this type of execution which occurred at least once a month in Toulouse, was added here a whole crowd of ordinary people. While emotion is detectable in Barthès' account of Calas' execution, written in the hours that followed the event, Smith's account several decades later was placed rather coldly in a chapter entitled "The love of praise, and the desire to be worthy of it; the fear of blame, and the fear of being worthy of it". (*TMS*, Part III, Chap. 2)

The extreme sobriety in recalling the tortures suffered by Calas, ultimately rather insensitive, certainly relates to what Smith wrote in the *Theory of Moral Sentiments*, when he dealt with "passions that have the body as their origin".

> Pain never calls forth any very lively sympathy unless it is accompanied with danger. [...] The little sympathy which we feel with bodily pain is the foundation of the propriety of constancy and patience in enduring it. The man, who under the severest tortures allows no weakness to escape him, vents no groan, gives way to no passion which we do not entirely enter into, commands our highest admiration. His firmness enables him to keep time with our indifference and insensibility. We admire and entirely go along with the magnanimous effort which he makes for this purpose. We approve of his behaviour, and from our experience of the common weakness of human nature, we are surprised, and wonder how he should be able to act so as to deserve approbation. (Smith, *TMS*, I.ii. 1.9–12, pp. 30–31)

These lines which apply so well to Calas, appear in the first edition of 1759. This insensitivity of Smith's was denounced by his contemporaries such as John Horner Tooke,[14] but it is important to underline also that the place ascribed to the judgement of posterity is found in the arrangements which he planned to make prior to his death; to make his personal papers disappear and thus to control the image which posterity would later preserve of him.

With Calas being executed on March 10, 1762, and Adam Smith arriving in Toulouse in March 1764, approximately two years later, one could have expected the case to be closed, with the trial and execution only being a moment in the collective memory of a city that was accustomed to ruthless, severe, and expeditious legal institutions. However, that was not the case. The torture of Calas as described in detail by Barthès evolved, in

[14] Smith would meet him in Montpellier.

the months which followed, into the Calas affair which would inflame not only all of France but also Europe, and symbolize all the perversions of religious fanaticism. Smith arrived in a city that had judged and condemned an innocent man, as the English press argued very early, and at a time when Voltaire's obstinate desire to obtain a review of the judgement of those he called the "Languedochiens", "dogs of the Languedoc", was about to come to fruition. Voltaire pointed out recent contentious religious cases in France and more particularly in the Languedoc. In the whole kingdom since the revocation of the Edict of Nantes in 1685, only one religion, the Catholic religion, was supposed to prevail. But it was very difficult to eliminate practically the Reformed religion, which was the official religion in several European states. Further, a declaration of May 14, 1724, specified and aggravated the methods of the revocation of the Edict of Nantes, as the abstract summarizes it:

> The King's declaration of 14 May 1724 against the so-called Reformed religion contains important provisions. His Majesty recalls that as soon as he came of age, his first duty was to be represented by the edicts, declarations and judgments of the Council on the subject, in order to renew their provisions, and to enjoin all his officers to have them observed with total accuracy; but that having been informed that the execution had been slowed down for several years, especially in the provinces which had been afflicted by contagion, and in which there are a greater number of his subjects who have previously professed the supposedly reformed religion by false and dangerous convictions, that some of them have not sincerely reunited in the Church, and stimulated by foreign agencies that have wanted to insinuate themselves secretly during his minority, he finds himself committed to giving new attention to such an important object …; that it has been recognized that the main abuses which have crept in, and which call for a more prompt remedy, concern mainly illicit assemblies and preaching, the education of children, the obligation for all those who exercise some public functions to profess the Catholic religion, the sentences ordered against relapses, and the celebration of marriages. (Du Saulzet and Lemerre. 1764, p. 1363)

It was indeed the "extinction of heresy" that was targeted, and in this policy, the emphasis placed on the role of the foreigner and on the provinces in which Protestantism had been particularly well established, and thus the Languedoc, is highlighted.

As far as the Languedoc was concerned, where the remembrance of the war with the Camisards was still fresh, one character, the intendant of the province, the Vicomte de Saint-Priest (1714–1785), who was in office from 1751 until his death, stood out particularly for his zeal: the repression was severe and seemed to target particularly the ministers of the Protestant cult, many of whom were put to death.

On September 13, 1761, one month before the discovery of the corpse of the eldest son of Jean Calas, quite by chance, it seemed that a certain François Rochette was arrested in Caussade in the generality of Montauban. For his misfortune, he had in his bag a pastor's outfit and records. During his imprisonment, peasants armed with sticks tried to free him, which alarmed the authorities, who multiplied patrols. One of them came across Protestant gentlemen who were probably on their way to a meeting over which Rochette was to preside. All four of them were then taken to Toulouse and were executed on the Place du Salin on February 19, 1762, during the Calas trial. Barthès points out that the beheading, which had not been practised in Toulouse for 84 years, offered a very popular "spectacle" and after having noted the "constancy and the prodigious firmness" of the tormented, he welcomed the work of the executioner.

> This time the executioner did his apprenticeship in cutting off heads with a new knife, and did it well, accurately and firmly. We had never seen such a bloody execution in Toulouse of at least three people taking place on the same day. (Barthès and Lamouzèle 1914, p. 215)

There is no doubt that the authorities and, first and foremost, the Intendant Saint-Priest, by punishing gentlemen, therefore members of the same social class as themselves, sent a message to the entire population on their determination to maintain royal absolutism. But in the last months of the Seven Years' War, a new affair involving the Reformed church was still in the news. On January 4, 1762, the body of a young girl, Elisabeth Sirven, aged 24, was found in a well near the town of Mazamet. This was the beginning of a third case in less than four months, proof if need be that suspicions against Protestants had reached their apogee.

The Sirven case was indicative of the persecution suffered by Protestants. Pierre-Paul Sirven, the young girl's father, suspected that his confession would lead to the accusation of his having thrown the child into the well, especially since, like Calas' son, who was said to want to convert, the young girl wanted to enter a convent. He then fled to avoid Calas' fate and hid in the Cevennes, among a population who kept alive memories of the repression of the Camisards. Scattering, the Sirven family fled to

Switzerland and turned to Voltaire. This new case could only confirm him in his determination to attack the justice of the Languedoc in his fight against obscurantism.

Voltaire had made Ferney into a place of convergence for everything that happened in Europe. Thus, on March 20, 1762, he received at his property of Ferney Dominique Audibert, a rich merchant from Marseilles who arrived from Toulouse after a stay of a few days to deal with business in the city; the following is how the hermit, who communicated with the whole world, reacted in the moment by addressing on March 22, 1762, a letter to the councillor le Bault, the closest person, who sat in the Parlement of Burgundy:

> You may have heard of a good Huguenot who was tricked by the Toulouse Parliament for hanging his son. However, this Reformed saint believed that he had done a good deed because his son wanted to become a Catholic, and that this was to prevent apostasy. He sacrificed his son to God and thought he was superior to Abraham because Abraham had only obeyed, but our Calvinist had hanged his son from his own movement and for the gain of his conscience. We are not much but the Huguenots are worse than us and moreover they declaim against comedy. (Voltaire 1877b, volume XLII, pp. 69–70)

The least we can say is that beyond the philosopher's normal tone of persiflage, his interlocutor from Marseilles had not presented him with a version of the crime and the trial that was very different from the version that Pierre Barthès related. One can note in particular that he did not reject the accusation of patricide on religious grounds that Catholics lent to Calvinists, and Voltaire displayed all his mistrust towards Protestants. But three days later, he already reproached himself for his lightness and began to doubt the guilt; he then sent various letters to share his doubts. Thus, on March 25, he asked Cardinal de Bernis, Ambassador of France to the Holy See, what really happened in Toulouse. For him there was no doubt: "We must look at the Parlement of Toulouse, or the Protestants, with horrified eyes" (Voltaire, ibidem., p. 75). From then on, he attempted to put together an argument by mobilizing all the resources that his correspondents (the Duke of Richelieu, de Bernis, d'Alembert, Choiseul) could bring him, but above all, by meeting the Calas children. In June 1762, his opinion solidified and he saw the potential for this case to become a fight against intolerance. Voltaire's founding act was the publication in 1763 of his memoir on the Calas affair, *Traité sur l'intolérance*. This treaty comprised two parts: one was a true study of the trial, the other part a long reflection on the analysis of religious tolerance in France. This second part was not without some passages reminiscent of Turgot's work but more in fact of Loménie de Brienne's work, *The Conciliator*.

The Treaty on Tolerance was written and published rapidly by Voltaire in January 1763. To say that its success was immediate is a euphemism: it is one of the greatest literary achievements of all time. Voltaire produced successive editions and print runs that would give details on the progress of the procedure as it unfolded; it is almost the chronicle of an exceptional judicial process.

For this reason, the late 1763 edition that is commented on here is surely the most useful for the reader, for it contained the developments still in progress at the arrival of Smith. The case took a new turn since the Parlement of Toulouse was no longer solicited and it was in Paris that the case was pleaded.

> On the 7th of March, 1763, a council of state being held at Versailles, at which all the great ministers assisted and the chancellor sat as president, M. de Crosne, one of the masters of requests, made a report of the affair of the Calas family with all the impartiality of a judge, and the precision of one perfectly well acquainted with the case, and with the plain truth and inspired eloquence of an orator and a statesman, which is alone suitable to such an assembly. The gallery was filled with a prodigious number of persons of all ranks, who impatiently waited the decision of the council. In a short time a deputation was sent to the king to acquaint him that the council had come to a unanimous resolution: that the parliament of Toulouse should transmit to them the whole account of its proceedings, together with the reasons on which it had framed the sentence condemning John Calas to be broken on the wheel; when his majesty was pleased to concur in the decree of the council.
>
> Justice and humanity then still continue to reside amongst mankind! and principally in the council of a king beloved, and deserving so to be; who, with his ministers, his chancellor and all the members of his council, have not disdained to employ their time in weighing all the circumstances relating to the sufferings of a private family with as much attention as if it had been the most interesting affair of war or peace; whilst the judges have shown themselves inspired by a love of equity and a tender regard to the interests of their fellow-subjects. All praise be given therefore to that

> Merciful Being, the only giver of integrity and every other virtue. (Voltaire, *Treatise on Tolerance*, 1765, Chap. 1, p. 8)

Thanks to Voltaire's campaign, the trial finally became political, but it nonetheless remained a judicial case from which even absolute power could not be totally freed. However, in the second half of the eighteenth century, conflicts multiplied between the provincial parliaments and the central government. These disputes mainly concerned fiscal and economic problems, with the need for fairer and better distributed taxes, which constantly offended local conservatisms. Yet the case continued to run its course. While it was being investigated in Paris, Smith however stayed in Toulouse. The victory of March 9, 1765, would be experienced in various ways when it became known in Toulouse.

> The day arrived (March 9, 1765) when innocence fully triumphed. Mr. de Baquencourt, having reported on the entire procedure, and having investigated the case down to the smallest circumstances, all the judges, in an unanimous vote, declared the family innocent, tortured and abusively judged by the Parlement of Toulouse. They rehabilitated the father's memory. They allowed the family to appeal to whom it might concern in order to take its judges to task, and to obtain costs, damages and interest that the Toulouse magistrates should have offered themselves. It was universal joy in Paris: people gathered in public places, on walks; they ran to see the family, so unhappy and so completely vindicated; they clapped their hands when they saw the judges pass by and showered them with blessings. What made this spectacle even more heart-warming was that that day, the ninth of March, was the very day Calas had perished in the most cruel torture (three years earlier). The 'Maîtres des Requêtes' had rendered complete justice to the Calas family, and in this they had only done their duty. There was another duty, that of charity, more rarely fulfilled by the courts, who seemed to believe their role is only to be fair. The 'Maîtres des Requêtes' decreed that they would write as a body to His Majesty to beg him to repair by his gifts the ruin of the family. The letter was drafted. The King answered by delivering thirty-six thousand livres to the mother and the children; and of these thirty-six thousand pounds, there were three thousand for the virtuous servant who had constantly defended the truth by defending his masters. (Ibidem., pp. 12–14)

It is therefore from Paris and from the royal power that came the legal conclusion of the Calas affair. The Parlement of Toulouse and the capitouls—in particular the capitoul David de Beaudrigue who acted as commissioner—could only note that they were totally disavowed by the Hôtel des Requêtes.

> The King, by this kindness, deserved, as by so many other actions, the nickname that the love of the nation gave him. May this example serve to inspire tolerance in men, without which fanaticism would desolate the earth, or at least always sadden it! We know that there is only one family here, and that the rage of sects has destroyed thousands of them; but today that a shadow of peace lets all Christian societies rest, after centuries of carnage, it is in this time of tranquility that the misfortune of the Calas family must make a greater impression, much like the thunder that falls into the serenity of a beautiful day. These cases are rare, but they happen, and they are the effect of that dark superstition that leads weak souls to blame crimes on anyone who does not think like them.

Voltaire thus concluded his Chapter 2 of the *Treaty on Intolerance*. He thus confirmed that victory was total in the Calas affair, a victory which he concluded was his victory, pertinently that of the Enlightenment over darkness.

3.7 Smith, His Network, and the Calas Affair

So what was Adam Smith's link to the Calas case? Was this case the reason he came to Toulouse? It is clear that Smith and his young pupil could not have attended the killing of the trader of the rue des Filatiers, as some of his biographers, annoyed by the timings, have asserted. When Smith arrived in Toulouse on March 4, 1764, poor Calas had been reduced to ashes for almost two years, since exactly March 10, 1762.

Nonetheless the memory of his torture and the trial which had caused such a furore was reverberating in many memories, less in that of the spectators accustomed to attending on average one execution per month than with the various protagonists involved in the legal procedure, because the ashes of Calas had hardly been scattered when his family and the Protestant networks began agitating in order to obtain a revision of the trial.

Observation of the relations between the British Isles and France in the second half of the eighteenth century shows that we can be sure that Smith was aware of the case before he left Scotland. In the years 1761–1763, the two countries were at war and each scrutinized the treatment of religious questions in the other: did France not welcome the mainly Catholic or

Episcopal Scots Jacobites, while the Protestants driven out of France by the revocation of the Edict of Nantes found refuge in the mainly Protestant countries like Great Britain? Thus, one can read in *The Gentleman's Magazine* of March 1762 a very complete relation of the martyrdom of François Rochette and the three gentlemen of the region of Foix with precise details of the events which one does not find commonly at this date in France. The same diary reports the following month on Calas' ordeal while recalling the English origin of Anne Rose Cabibel, Calas' wife. It should also be pointed out that this English origin was only the consequence of emigration after the revocation of the Edict of Nantes. Her father was a Protestant merchant himself from Bordeaux. Her mother was born De Roux and her grandmother was called La Garde Montesquieu, a name that is clearly of an Occitan origin.

The speed with which the torment of Pastor Rochette and the gentlemen from Foix spread in England showed that the information circulated quickly, and Voltaire's outburst would certainly only focus more attention on the case. But there was a risk that the support of their foreign co-religionists made the French Protestants appear as traitors in the middle of the war. In any case, documents addressed to Lord Hertford, the future negotiator of the Treaty of Paris, showed that the future ambassador was personally interested, on behalf of the interests he was about to represent, in the Calas affair and Voltaire's involvement. And from Lord Hertford to Charles Townshend, there were only a few benches in the Westminster Parliament. It also seemed that Charles Townshend himself spoke in the English Chamber of Deputies on the subject of Calas. It is not surprising either that Hume, secretary to Ambassador Hertford, declared in December 1763 his dismay at not having succeeded in obtaining a copy of Voltaire's *Treaty on Tolerance*.

Is it possible to go further and imagine that Smith, on his way to Toulouse, was commissioned to gather information for Hume, or even Townshend? As far as Townshend was concerned, he was probably not inclined to run the risk of making the trip suspicious out of inappropriate curiosity, but it is clear that Hume kept abreast of the actions of the protagonists in the Calas affair and unhesitatingly asked Abbé Colbert for information. This emerged very clearly in a letter from Abbé Colbert to Hume in which he evoked the capitoul David de Baudrigue, the capitoul who certified the death of Marc-Antoine Calas. He then monitored the entire procedure, reporting directly to the minister, the Comte de

Saint-Florentin.[15] He questioned Jean Calas again before he was put to death. He crystallized all the hatred of Calas' followers. As always when an institution has experienced a fiasco, it tends to look for a leader to throw to the wolves and the Calas affair was no exception to this: the review of the trial was accompanied by the disgrace of capitoul David de Baudrigue: his particular status (a "perpetual capitoul" having bought his office and thus not elected) and his commitment to ensuring order reigned had attracted many enemies among the elected capitouls and in the Parlement. When the review of Calas' trial was approaching, a letter from the minister to the Capitouls on February 14, 1765, "blamed David de Baudrigue's conduct during the burial of the English" and added "The king judged it appropriate to withdraw from this capitoul the powers he had granted him in order to avoid the return of such scenes" (Dutil 1944, p. 104). In reality, the decisions attributed to David de Baudrigue vis-à-vis the English had caused an intervention by the British ambassador and the minister would oppose an intervention in his favour by the prosecutor Riquet de Bonrepos. According to Saint-Florentin:

> What happened recently because of the burial of the two Englishmen was not the only reason why the King ordered his removal. Many other very serious complaints against this capitoul had been forwarded to H.M. They had been studied in depth and since it was only in full knowledge of the facts that H.M. pronounced against him, there would be no point in proposing that he should rescind his decision. (Dutil 1944, pp. 42–43)

Another of Smith's acquaintances would appear in the story of Calas' accuser; it is in any case what emerged from a long embarrassed answer that Abbé Colbert addressed to Hume, who must have questioned him on it. The letter (in French) was in two parts with the signature in the middle and a copious post-scriptum. Given its interest, we reproduce it in extenso:

> I believe with you, my dear cousin, that Capitoul David deserves all the indignation with which he is charged, and that the first perpetrator of the murder of an unfortunate father must be an object of horror for all honest people who have not been warned. But it is possible that a very bad man is

[15] Louis Phélypeaux, known as the Count of Saint-Florentin, was born in 1705. In 1725, continuing a family tradition, he succeeded his father as Secretary of State in charge of the so-called Reformed religion. He was received into Freemasonry in 1735. Louis XV made him a minister of State in 1751.

nevertheless innocent of a particular crime attributed to him and for which he is punished. So I believe that if someone, out of ignorance of the facts, has attributed to this wicked man a crime he did not commit and had him punished for it, he must repair this wrong and do justice in this particular event. David had no part in the vexation of Messrs. Forester and de Roure, however Mr. de Florentin in the letter in which he announces his disgrace says it is to punish him for this conception. It was believed here that this punishment was as a consequence of the representations made to the court by the Ambassador of England.

In this assumption, I believed, as the only one in a position to give an account of this affair, I ought to write to Milord Hertford and to give David, although I abhor him, the testimony due to innocence. At the same time, I deprived his Excellency of interceding for him, assuming that he had accepted that he was the author of this vexation.

Here is my request and the principle underlying my request, my dear cousin; I take no interest in this capitoul, I have never spoken to him, I have seen him only once and that by chance in the street, I hate the author of an event that dishonors this city and I rejoice at his disgrace. At the same time I must testify to his good conduct towards some Englishmen who are in Toulouse, but these particular actions will never blind me to the other side of his life. I couldn't deny him a testimony I thought was due to him, he has a son worthy of a better father, he has parents here who are good people.

These are the reasons for my conduct, by which you are surprised; I would have wished that the real culprits (and they are even meaner people than David) should have been punished for the case of Mr. Forrester and that the capitoul was accused for a real crime: the murder of Calas.

If you think I should have denied him my testimony in a particular case, I would submit to your decision, but I hope you will be willing to distinguish an act (which I thought I had to do) of justice from an interest (which you might suppose me to have) in a man I hate. Looking at Calas' death, the common opinion here is the most horrible effect of an outrageous fanaticism, I would be unworthy of your regard, my dear cousin, if I did not question myself on the subject and if I did not join with the cry of humanity to avenge the memory of an unhappy father on the author of his misfortune; but what I did on that occasion had a pure motive; perhaps I was wrong in form. I am always ready to retract anything I have done for a man I hate and despise as much as I love and respect you, my dear cousin.

S. Colbert V. G.

Toulouse, 10 April 1765,

There are many English people here and the place is very suitable for them. The people here are of a fanaticism that would astonish you; despite what has just happened, everyone believes Calas the father guilty, and it is useless to talk to them on this subject or even remind them of wisdom and moderation, as it will destroy many institutions that are concerned with religion and this reform can only come little by little but we will finally come to the end of it.

We hope to have Mr. Smith for another month or two.[16]

This letter, while informing us of the end of Smith's stay, confirmed the interest which the English embassy brought to the Calas affair and to the fate of the English residing in Toulouse. It must be noted that the rehabilitation of Calas aroused bitterness and resentment towards the English in Toulouse, as evidenced by the notes slipped into his diary by Pierre Barthès:

The widow Calas and her family.—At the beginning of this month [April 1765], the journalist of Avignon learned that Anne Rose Cabibel, widow of the sieur Calas, this obstinate heretic whom we saw on Saint-Georges' square, exposed on a wheel and consumed by flames, as I reported above, pursuing in Paris the restoration of his family's reputation, had obtained a decree from the Hôtel des Requêtes, which breaks the decree issued by the Parlement of Toulouse rendered against her husband, and that the king on certain representations, had granted to his family a gratuity of 36 000 livres. By letter of the 26th of the same month, it was also learned that the judgment of the Hôtel's applications in favour of Calas had been received enthusiastically in England and that a subscription had been opened in London for this family, which it was hoped would produce 40,000 or 50,000 écus in their favour. So great is the eagerness of the subscribers, so great is the blindness and fanaticism of these islanders, who, leaving a prodigious quantity of excellent workers in all kinds of arts to starve, as we have learned from the same news, hasten to raise up and congratulate a proscribed and patricidal family, convinced of the most dreadful monstrosity, a prior example of which we have not seen in centuries of history.

Colbert's letter to Hume also indicated that had the Abbé shared the Enlightenment's hostility towards the role of Capitoul Beaudrigue in the Calas affair, he testified in the name of truth and justice in his favour in another affair, at the risk of displeasing Hume. But it was above all the

[16] National Library of Scotland Call Number MS 23154/67.

prosecutor Riquet whom Smith met, as the amiable Abbé again indicated in a letter of October 18, 1766, to Henry Scott (the future Duke of Buccleuch), in which he reported on Smith's relations in Toulouse. The public prosecutor Riquet de Bonrepos belonged to the Toulouse branch of the family, which owned a third of the shares in the Canal du Languedoc, with the Caraman branch holding the majority of the shares. This was a family that he seemed to know very well, since in another letter, Colbert gives news of the Caraman family but also of the Bonrepos branch. As will be seen, Smith would be effusive in his praise of the management of the canal.

Jean-Gabriel-Amable-Alexandre de Riquet de Bonrepos (1712–1791) was the grandson of the creator of the canal, and as such he was co-owner with the other heirs, among whom stand out two branches (Bonrepos and Caraman). But he was also the King's attorney general in Toulouse at the time of the Calas affair, and he could undoubtedly had provided Smith with any information he wished.

> Mr. Caraman is anxious to be reminded of Mr. Smith. He is going to Paris this winter, if you are there I will give him a letter of recommendation for you.
>
> The Toulouse Parliament is as you left it, except that a new first President has come to replace M. Bastard.
>
> He is tormented as was his predecessor although a perfectly honest man and very eloquent. Mr Rafin is his antagonist, Mr de Bonrepos his friend. The others are divided each according to his taste or interests; but all believe they have an interest in having no leader and that business goes according to their whim and not according to fixed and invariable principles.
>
> (Colbert to Henry Scott-Douglas, National Archives of Scotland: GD 224/2040/62/3)

His role was thus quite eminent since he would be the person to prosecute Calas, but it was also he who, in the name of the same King, would read out a few years later the decree of rehabilitation. If he did have doubts about Calas' guilt, he never expressed them publicly, which did not prevent the rich aristocrat from Toulouse—manager of an important collective utility—and the economist from developing relations based on common concerns.

Although Smith was very close to Calas' accusers during his stay, he nevertheless closely followed the arguments in favour of Calas, as the fact that he brought back to England the defence's principal documents collected during his stay in Toulouse proves.

The sovereign judgement of the "Requêtes Ordinaires" of the "Hôtel du Roi": this annuls the charges against Anne-Rose Cabibel, widow of Jean Calas, merchant in Toulouse; Jean-Pierre Calas, his son; Jeanne Viguiere, maid in the Calas household; Alexandre-François-Gualbert Lavaysse; and the memory of the said deceased Jean Calas, from the accusation against them: on March 9, 1765. Paris: Imprimerie royale.

But before closing the chapter devoted to Calas, it is appropriate to dwell on the religious policy of the Parlement so despised by Voltaire and contemporarily rehabilitated by the legal historian Ludovic Azéma, who studied the archives of the Parlement, reading in extenso 400 civil registers of the Grand'Chambre of the Parlement of Toulouse. He showed that any judgement made concerning the Parlement and the parlementaires may change if one stops being fixated on the Calas affair and instead analyses more globally its significance in religious matters. Several capital events exercised people throughout the century around the Protestant question, the Jansenist question, and the great Jesuit affair. The court participated in the secularization movement, which was characteristic of the century. Many parlementaires adhered to the new activities that were developing along with the spread of the Enlightenment. They participated in academies, and many were members of Freemasonry. The court's Protestant jurisprudence was moderate towards Protestants very early. It was even ahead of the other courts in its recognition of the State's oversight of Protestant children. The Calas affair itself must be understood within the context of criminal law in the eighteenth century. As for the problems caused by the Jansenist and Jesuit struggles, the divisions within the court were numerous, testifying to a lack of unanimity, and reflecting the attitude of all Parlements. However, here again, by its attitude during the affairs of the refusals of sacraments and by the suppression of the Society of Jesus, the court participated in a movement that tended to consider the missions of the church as "public service" missions. Thus, on many points, the Toulouse Parlement anticipated the work of the Revolution (Azéma 2010).

It undoubtedly took time to discover these developments in depth, obscured as they were by the storm raised by the Calas affair. By reading again the July 5, 1764, letter addressed to Hume, as well as taking these details into account, it is easier to understand why the beginning of the stay was frustrating. The Toulouse Parlement was no longer active and was the cause of a deep consumer crisis in the city. Activities were reduced, life was mundane and expensive, aristocrats preferring, in the absence of activities, to holiday in their country homes rather than undertake a boring stay in town.

Hence, very quickly Smith and his pupil, as soon as the free courses of the faculty of law had been completed, without the constraint of the examinations which the young Scott would not sit, considered going to visit another city, other countries, thus approaching the requirements of the Grand Tour. Hume is again called upon by Smith:

> Toulouse, 5 July 1764
> My Dearest Friend
> The Duke of Buccleugh proposes soon to set out for Bordeaux where he intends to stay a fortnight or more. I should be much obliged to you if you could send us recommendations to the Duke of Richelieu, I the Marquis de Lorges and Intendant of the Province) Mr Townshend assured me that the Duke de Choiseul was to recommend us to all the people of fashion here and everywhere else in France. (Letter #81)

It should be noted that the Duke of Richelieu, about whom more later, is the person to whom Voltaire turned before engaging in the defence of Calas.

Concluding on the very first months of the stay, it should be remarked that in Adam Smith's library, probably from his purchases in Toulouse, there is a book by a dramatic author, Jean Galbret de Campistron (1656–1723), who was born and died in Toulouse in a family of parlementaires. This author was very successful in Paris and at the court of Versailles, thanks to classical tragedies. The names of these plays and opera libretti evoked the great Jean Racine (1639–1699), his eldest son, to whom he is often compared. *Acis et Galatée*, set to Lully's music, was one of his successes at court, but the pieces that survived, him before sinking into total oblivion, were *Arminius, Virginia, Andronic, Alcibiade, Phocion*, and *Tiridate*. After his success and without waiting for his disgrace, he returned to live in Toulouse and became a legend of the city, thanks to his lifestyle:

> In Toulouse, he led a very active life shared between his duties as master of his household, his activities as supporter of the Floral Games, member of the Brotherhood of Black Penitents, director of the Saint-Joseph de la Grave Hospital; obligations which caused him to participate in numerous banquets

and libations: the thin horseman of the battle of Steinkerque,[17] gradually acquired a notable stoutness! Several trips to Paris, and an abundant correspondence linked him to his past life. But happiness he found at the castle of Cayras, as lord of Saint-Orens-de-Gameville. (Soubeille 2006, pp. 129–137)

Such a successful life in the eyes of the Toulouse population gave rise to a proverb or rather a saying that some old Toulousains, by oral tradition, in its Occitan version, still know: "Uros como Campistrou!" or "Happy as Campistron!". So we have to invent one for Smith that could take the form of "Malastros como Smith!" (Unhappy as Smith).

References

Aldéguier, J. B. Auguste d' 1830. *Histoire de la ville de Toulouse: depuis la conquête des Romains jusqu'au règne de Charles X*. Toulouse: Dagalier.

Arrouy, Jean Marie. 2005. *L'île de Tounis, Histoire d'un quartier au cœur de Toulouse du XVIIe au XXe siècle*. Toulouse: Éditions Loubatières.

Azéma, Ludovic. 2010. *La politique religieuse du Parlement de Toulouse sous le règne de Louis XV*. Aix-en-Provence: Presses universitaires d'Aix-Marseille.

Barthès, Pierre, Les Heures perdues de Pierre Barthes repetiteur en Toulouse, ou recueil des choses dignes d'être transmises a la posterité, arrivées en cette ville, ou prés d'icy, Bibliothèque municipale de Toulouse, Manuscripts 699 à 706. http://rosalis.bibliotheque.toulouse.fr/.

Barthès, Pierre and Edmond Lamouzèle. 1914. *Toulouse au XVIIIe siècle d'après les "Heures perdues" de P. Barthès*. Toulouse: Marqueste.

Baudel, Joseph et Jacques Malinowski. *Histoire de l'université de Cahors*, Cahors, Laytou, 1876.

Brink, James E. 1976. Les États de Languedoc de 1515 à 1560: une autonomie en question. In: *Annales du Midi*, Vol. 88, No. 128, pp. 287–305.

Castan, Yves. 1983. Le temps des Lumières, in Wolff, Philippe, et alii. *Le Diocèse de Toulouse*. Paris: Beauchesne.

Chanal (de) Adolphe. 1872. Notice historique sur l'académie d'équitation de Toulouse, *Mémoires de la société archéologique du Midi de la France. 1866–1871*, L IX, pp. 192–210.

[17] The battle of Steinkerque is a battle that saw the capture of Namur by the Marshal of Luxembourg who led the French armies at the expense of William III of Orange, who would become King of England a few years later. It took place on August 3, 1692, and the young soldier Campistron took part.

Cour des comptes, aydes et finances de Provence, *Remontrances au Roi sur les déclarations du 7 juillet 1756.*

Du Mège, Alexandre. 1846. *Histoire générale de Languedoc: avec des notes et les pièces justificatives, composée sur les auteurs et les titres originaux*, T. 10, Toulouse: J.-B. Paya.

Dubédat, Jean-Baptiste. 1885. *Histoire du Parlement de Toulouse.* Paris: A. Rousseau.

Du Saulzet, Marc, & Pierre Lemerre. 1764. *Abrégé du recueil des actes, titres et mémoires concernant les affaires du clergé de France ou, Table raisonnée en forme de précis des matières contenues dans ce recueil.* Paris: G. Desprez.

Dufey, Pierre-Joseph-Spiridion. 1826. *Histoire, actes et remontrances des parlements de France, chambres des comptes, cours des aides et autres cours souveraines, depuis 1461 jusqu'à leur suppression.* Paris: Galliot.

Dutil, Léon. 1944. Un capitoul perpétuel, David de Beaudrigue, *Mémoires de l'Académie des Sciences, Inscriptions et Belles-lettres de Toulouse*, 13e série, T. VI., pp. 63–112.

Élie, Pélaquier. 2009. *Atlas historique de la province de Languedoc*, Montpellier: Centre de Recherches Interdisciplinaires en Sciences humaines et Sociales, Université Paul-Valéry Montpellier III. Retrieved from https://pierresvives.herault.fr/ressource/atlas-historique-de-la-province-de-languedoc-0.

Fitz-James, Victoire Louise Josèphe Goyon de Matignon (duchess of) & Simon Surreaux. 2013. *Aimez-moi autant que je vous aime: correspondances de la duchesse de Fitz-James, 1757–1771.* Paris: Vendémiaire.

Flammermont, Jules & Maurice Tourneux. 1895. *Remontrances du Parlement de Paris au XVIIIe siècle.* Tome deuxième. Paris: Imprimerie nationale.

Garrisson, Janine. 2004. *L'affaire Calas: miroir des passions françaises.* Paris: Fayard.

Gatien-Arnoult, Adolphe-Félix. 1865. *De l'Université de Toulouse à l'époque de sa fondation en 1229.* Toulouse: Impr. de P. Savy.

Gatien-Arnoult, Adolphe-Félix. 1866. *Jean de Garlande, docteur régent de grammaire en l'Université de Toulouse de 1229 à 1232.* Toulouse: Impr. de Bonnal et Gibrac.

Julia, Dominique. 1986. Les institutions et les hommes, in Jacques Verger (Dir.), *Histoire des universités en France*, Toulouse: Privat.

Lafont, Robert, *Renaissance du Sud.* Paris: Gallimard. 1970.

Lamoignon de Basville, Nicolas de. 1736. *Mémoires pour servir à l'histoire de Languedoc*, Par feu Mr. de Basville, intendant de cette province. Amsterdam: Chez J. Ryckhoff le fils, libraire.

Larguier, Gilbert. 1998. Narbonne et la voie méditerranéenne du pastel (XVe-XVIIe siècles). In: *Annales du Midi.* Tome 110, No. 222. *Le commerce du pastel du XVe au XVIIe siècle*, pp. 149–167.

Martel, Philippe. 1979. Le XIIIe siècle: Ordre Chrétien et ordre monarchique, pp. 291–344, in *Histoire d'Occitanie*, sous la direction d'A. Armengaud, et R. Lafont, Paris: Hachette.

Montluc, Blaise de. 1872. *Commentaires de Montluc*. Paris: Hachette.
Namier, Lewis (Sir) & John Brooke. 1964. *Charles Townshend*. Macmillan & Co. Ltd, New York, pp. 150–171.
Paulhet, Jean-Claude. 1964. Les parlementaires toulousains à la fin du dix-septième siècle. In: *Annales du Midi*, Tome 76, No.°67, pp. 189–204.
Piganiol de la Force, Jean-Aymar. 1740. *Nouveau voyage de France*. Paris: T. Legras.
Riquet de Bonrepos, Jean-Gabriel-Aimable-Alexandre. 1763. *Plaidoyer de monsieur le procureur général du roi au parlement de Toulouse, dans les audiences des 8, 11 & 17 février 1763, sur l'appel comme d'abus par lui relevé de l'institut & constitutions des soi-disans jésuites*. A Toulouse: De l'imprimerie de la veuve de Me Bernard Pijon.
Roux, Pascal. 2001. Éducation et formation des officiers militaires à Toulouse dans la deuxième moitié du XVIIIe siècle. In: *Histoire, économie et société*, 20 année, no. 3. Les miroirs de la santé, pp. 371–383.
Saint-Priest, François-Emmanuel Guignard de Barante. 1929. *Mémoires publiés par le baron de Barante*. Paris: Calmann-Lévy.
Schneider, Robert A. 1995. *The Ceremonial City. Toulouse observed 1737–1780*. Princeton: Princeton UP.
Slimani, Ahmed. 2004. *La modernité du concept de nation au XVIIIème siècle (1715–1789)*: apports des thèses parlementaires et des idées politiques du temps. Aix-en-Provence: Presses univ. d'Aix-Marseille.
Soubeille, Georges. 2006. *Humanistes en Pays d'Oc, Campistron, Après Racine et malgré Hugo*. Toulouse: Éditions Universitaires du Sud, pp. 129–137.
Tooke, John Horne. 1813. *Memoirs of John Horne Tooke, interspersed with original documents 1.1*. London: Johnson.
Tournier, Gaston. 1901. *Souvenirs de famille: notices biographiques accompagnées de généalogies*. [S.l.]: [s.n.])
Université de Toulouse. 1931. VIIe Centenaire de la fondation de l'Université de Toulouse. 1229–1929. Livre d'or. Toulouse, Impr. d'E. Privat.
Voltaire. 1765. *Traité sur la tolérance*.
Voltaire. 1877a [1756]. Croisade contre les Languedochiens, in *Œuvres complètes*, tome XI. Paris: Éditions Garnier.
Voltaire. 1877b. *Œuvres complètes*, tome XLII. Paris: Éditions Garnier.
Young Arthur. 1909. *Travels in France during the Years 1787, 1788, 1789*, London: George Bell and Sons.

CHAPTER 4

Smith's Journeys in the Southwest

The travellers' connections and those of their relations indicate numerous trips between Toulouse and Bordeaux, Toulouse and the Pyrenees, Toulouse and the Mediterranean. The stationary Grand Tour finally came to life and encounters multiplied. The difficulty in tracing their peregrinations comes from the fact that their agenda was so full that it is difficult to reconstruct it given the travel times. If none of the clues discovered is excluded, the only hypothesis that gives coherence to this eventful summer implies a lot of time spent on the roads; tourism however was in its infancy and the pleasure of travelling repaid voyagers who endured hours spent in stagecoaches and other post chaises. Without guaranteeing the accuracy of the exact journeys undertaken to get to the various stages of their trip that have been identified, it is likely that the travellers went to Bordeaux in July, that they then travelled to Bagnères-de-Bigorre where a good part of the high society used to meet up, coming not only from Bordeaux and Toulouse but also from Paris, and even from other European capitals. The trips then included a stop in L'Isle-de-Noé then another in Toulouse before a second visit to Bordeaux, just before a trip to Montpellier.

4.1 On the Way to Bordeaux

Around mid-July 1764, Adam Smith decided, in agreement with the young Duke, to leave Toulouse for a few weeks in Bordeaux. Although they were more accustomed to life in France by then thanks to the four

A. Alcouffe, P. Massot-Bordenave, *Adam Smith in Toulouse and Occitania*, https://doi.org/10.1007/978-3-030-46578-0_4

months they had already spent in the first city of the Languedoc, becoming familiar with the customs and the language of the French, they nevertheless took care to assure themselves for the trip of the services of Abbé Colbert, their cicerone. If Pierre Barthès in his chronicle is to be believed, Archbishop Loménie de Brienne has just returned to Toulouse. After one of his habitual long sojourns in his Parisian hôtel and on his lands in Champagne, he allowed Abbé Colbert to join up with Smith and the Duke, which is a sure sign that communications between Smith and Loménie de Brienne were well established. Abbé Colbert was one of those people who loves to travel. In his past and future existence there are countless stays he made in Paris, possibly to Normandy, where he was abbot 'in commendam' of the abbey of Val-Richer that he strove to improve, to England, but also to Scotland. The trip to Bordeaux thus seemed a good opportunity for a young abbé, full of ambition and who according to the archives consulted did not yet know the capital of neighbouring Guyenne. The archbishop of Bordeaux was Jean Audibert de Lussan, a descendant of one of the great families of the Vivarais which was at that time part of the Languedoc and which had been shaken by the strange affair of the beast of the Gévaudan.

Abbé Colbert himself became Bishop of Rodez, succeeding Bishop Champion de Cicé who had been nominated to become the last archbishop of Bordeaux before the French Revolution. This serves to demonstrate the closeness of relations between the two regions and the multiplicity of exchanges between them.

Smith and his young pupil, after a rather difficult debut in Toulouse, due to circumstances which they probably did not fully grasp, sought to find in Bordeaux a city less crushed than was Toulouse by its Parlement.

Firstly, Bordeaux and generally Guyenne as a whole had been possessions of the British Crown for over a hundred years. English domination ended only with the Battle of Castillon (7–8 July 1453) which ensured the final departure of the English. It is however useful to specify that for many Bordelais, it represented the conquest of a new territory by the King of France rather than a territorial liberation following a long period of occupation.

A long period of political, economic, and even physical reconstruction then began, and was continuing during the period when our travellers were journeying to Bordeaux. In terms of buildings, for example, the city was occupied in its centre by a vast citadel built at the end of fifteenth century by the English in fear of a return of the French troops. In

Bordeaux, the Château Trompette impressed our visitors by its antique aspect because it threatens ruin after three centuries of redundancy. It consisted of a large complex of buildings that housed, among others, the seat of political authority, the governorship of the province. The city of Bordeaux had a Parlement restored, by the royal authority the day after the departure of the English, but on the other hand Guyenne did not have estates. It was a 'Pays d'élection' and was thus more subject to the centralizing power of the monarchy. As the various territorial divisions (ecclesiastical, military, fiscal) did not coincide, it can be noted that the provinces of Bigorre and Béarn preserved their estates.

This was all the more the case since to ensure a rapid reconstruction following the departure of the English and in order to revive the economy of the city, the inhabitants of Bordeaux obtained privileges which, of course, manifested themselves as tax exemptions. These privileges were the subject of numerous quarrels between the "jurats" of Bordeaux, the Parlement, and the governors, thus making the province of Aquitaine more and more dependent on royal power. However, from a strictly economic point of view, leaving aside the religious conflicts that remained there too, the Bordeaux region and its port experienced an important initial period of growth during the Renaissance period. Relations with the English, beyond political oppositions, remained excellent; it was the case in particular for the Bordeaux families who launched themselves into foreign trade. By its unique situation on the Atlantic, the port of Bordeaux was a great beneficiary of the colonial policy of the Kings of France but also of the triangular trade with the slave colonies. It must be said that at a time when the Atlantic trade was taking off, the port of Bordeaux, in the centre of a city on the banks of a river, was perfectly situated to ensure a multiplicity of trading links. Bordeaux thus became a hub which traded with England, Scotland but also Northern Europe, the ports of Antwerp and Hamburg, and as far as the cities of the Baltic. This was the first expansion of the port of Bordeaux and was followed by another wave during the period of colonial trade. Furthermore, Bordeaux was known to be the favourite destination, for nearly two centuries by then, of Jacobite refugees fleeing the multiple religious repressions in England, Scotland, or Ireland, as well as one of the favourite places of transit for the British who were undertaking a Grand Tour in Europe. Smith and his pupil were thus sure to find in that city an important population of compatriots along with places of conviviality, making it possible to create a network of acquaintances which the two men certainly had been missing during their stay in Toulouse.

Many Jacobite families had well-known names that and already held important positions in the various branches of the bourgeoisie or the Bordeaux nobility. These families could be found engaged in commerce and small industry, sensible areas for migrants to integrate themselves in, as well as in the ecclesiastical professions, the career of arms and military trades, and in more surprising fields, as John Holker's career as an important royal clerk illustrates.

The occupation of these professions proves that integration was fairly easy in a region that recognized only duties but no citizenship rights for its subjects. Titles of nobility were easily transposable from one country to another as long as the immigrant and his family were able to maintain their standard of living. Was Colbert, the little Abbé who accompanied Smith, not the extreme illustration of this: a man born in the north of Scotland into a ruined family but who, through the play of circumstances and his own obstinacy, became, through his surname, linked to one of the greatest ministers of the great-grandfather of the current King Louis XV?

The great Jacobite families were, depending on the date on which they obtained letters of naturalization, the Walsh (1709), Quin (1710), Clarke (1718), Mitchell (1721), Shee (1735), Meade (1758), the Kirkvan family (1763), Mac Carthy (1765), Sandlands (1762), O'Byrne (1771), O'Rourke (1773), to name only the best known. They would bring a new dynamism to the city. Originating from the British world, and despite the risk of losing rank, newcomers, to great extent, when they did not choose the profession of arms, turned to business, finance, and banking, but also to nascent industry. All these activities had too often been neglected by the original population, while these new businesses would rapidly grow and expand.

The port of Bordeaux is also located on a deep and long estuary, that of the Gironde, a link between land and sea whose geographical and economic situation is reminiscent of the city of Glasgow and its estuary the Clyde. That town was dear to Smith's heart, and he probably liked to draw comparisons with the life he had lived there for over fifteen years, "the happiest moments of my life", he wrote. Perhaps he was looking for a few moments of greater animation and activity after a long winter and a dull spring. Final important point, Bordeaux was the French city that his father, who died before Smith was born, had visited at the beginning of his life during a journey, more than sixty years previously. Smith could also thus have considered this stay as a kind of pilgrimage; he had not known his father but nevertheless kept his memory with great respect. Some authors even go so far as to see this absence of a father as one of the reasons for the economist's liberal choices.

At the end of the eighteenth century, Bordeaux counted nearly 70,000 inhabitants and was the fourth or fifth city of the kingdom, ahead of Nantes and Toulouse, which was only the eighth city in France. However Bordeaux was also characterized by its very high rate of urban growth since at the time of the Revolution in 1794, the city was in third place, ahead of Lyon but behind Marseille, with 105,000 inhabitants.

Bordeaux was also the metropolis par excellence which gathered at its heart all the services of the state, the judicial and military powers of the largest French province in surface area. The province was about a third larger than the current administrative region, before the recent creation of "Nouvelle Aquitaine", which occupies about the same area. In the 1760s, it included the generalities of Montauban, which extended all the way to the Rouergue, thus to the borders of the Massif Central, as well as that of Auch, which adjoins the frontier with Spain on its southern border and whose eastern limit was the Garonne river. In many respects the city of Bordeaux could compete with Toulouse for the title of second French city not because of its population or its history but because of its power of attraction, its economic and commercial dynamism, and its wealth both ancient and potential.

It possessed many advantages, such as year-round access to the Atlantic Ocean at the flow of a tide. It also had a large hinterland made up of the whole of Gascony, because rivers flowed naturally towards its port which thus made it possible to control exports from the towns situated on the banks of the Garonne, the Lot and its vineyards, the Tarn and its textile industry, the Agout, even the Dordogne, although more difficult of access, to mention only the most navigable.

Similarly, the Languedoc Canal, which had linked Toulouse to Sète since the end of the eighteenth century, seemed to be favourable to the development of the city of Bordeaux, since its large commercial sector was increasingly turning towards the Atlantic. The wines of the Montpellier region and in particular the long-maturing sweet wines which were very appreciated in all the north of Europe transited, in spite of very high taxes, through Bordeaux. Despite the trans-shipment of cargo required in Toulouse, the canal was considered preferable to rounding the Iberian peninsula by ship, since navigation in the Mediterranean was made more and more dangerous by the presence of Barbaresque corsairs and other Ottoman pirates who took over from the English in the role of aggressors of ships under the French flag.

But more than its geographical position on the road from Paris to Spain, France's safest ally in the eighteenth century, what struck any traveller as he approached the city was its extraordinary dynamism and growth.

As has been indicated, Adam Smith and his young student did not leave any written testimony of their visit and their arrival in Bordeaux. Fortunately, twenty years after the arrival of our travellers, the English economist and essayist Arthur Young gives us a detailed description in the years 1787–1789. Young (1741–1820), after inheriting his father's estate, began to improve farming practices with mixed success. On the strength of his experience, he undertook trips throughout Great Britain and then France from 1787 onwards in order to compare agricultural methods and draw lessons from them. Although historians do not unanimously agree to the accuracy of his observations, he is a leading observer of the rural economy and his data collection is an important step in the development of national auditing.

> The 25th—Pass through Barsac, famous also for its wines. They are now ploughing with oxen between the rows of the vines, the operation which gave Tull[1] the idea of horse-hoeing corn. Great population and country seats all the way. At Castres the country changes to an uninteresting flat. Arrive at Bordeaux, _through a continued village—30 miles. (Young 1793, p. 66)

Arthur Young approached Bordeaux by the same route that Smith had taken a few years earlier, so his description is particularly useful. He mentions country houses. These houses far from the city had long served as a refuge for the wealthy inhabitants of the port city fleeing the frequent epidemics of plague, whose last outbreak only dates back to the beginning of the eighteenth century. In addition, the Bordeaux region before the major drainage works of the nineteenth century remained a region of swamps along the "jalles", suitable for incubating all kinds of diseases; consequently the houses were grouped together along rare available spaces. Hence the view of these suburbs and these very long villages. This proved that the city was growing rapidly and that, like any city centre, it

[1]Arthur Young refers here to the English pioneer of agronomy; Jethro Tull (1674–1741) who recommended the use of horses instead of oxen for agriculture. It should be noted that the Bazas oxen are a much sought-after breed of cattle which today are certainly more used for beef. Boulaine and Legros, 1998, pp. 45–56.

extended largely outwards towards the surrounding villages, especially as the terrain was flat, as Young also points out. The fact is also interesting because he would have a diametrically opposite vision of Toulouse, describing it as an almost desert region from the outskirts of the city to the ramparts that still surrounded that city. After a pause, Young continued his approach to the city:

26th. Much as I had read and heard of the commerce, wealth, and magnificence of this city, they greatly sur passed my expectations. Paris did not answer at all, for it is not to be compared to London; but we must not name Liverpool in competition with Bourdeaux. The grand feature here, of which I had heard most, answers the least; I mea1l the quay, which is respectable only for length, and its quantity of business, neither of which, to the eye of a stranger, is of much consequence, if devoid of beauty. The row of houses is regular, but without either magnificence or beauty. It is a dirty, sloping, muddy shore; parts without pavement, incumbered with filth and stones; barges lie here for loading and unloading the ships, which cannot approach to what should be a quay. Here is all the dirt and disagreeable circumstances of trade, without the order, arrangement, and magnificence of a quay. Barcelona is unique in this respect. (Young, p. 67)

Already by this simple extract from this travel journal we can see all that will bring Smith closer to the city. A certain contrast, a commercial dynamism, a city on a river, a port, so many points of difference with Toulouse. The ochre stone, the principal construction material in Bordeaux, is reminiscent of Paris or Barcelona, but also of the large English cities which had been influenced in their building by the architecture of Normandy and the use of "Caen stone". It could not, however, link Bordeaux to the city of London because the latter, although showing a certain similarity, was much larger. In London both sides of the river were used, while in Bordeaux the width of the Garonne made the crossing difficult. There was still no bridge over the Garonne at this time and crossings were difficult depending on winds and tidal currents; thus the road to Paris began or ended with a river crossing which was often delicate. Young continues:

The theatre, built about ten or twelve years ago, is by far the most magnificent in France. ..., The establishment of actors, actresses, singers, dancers, orchestra, &c. speak the wealth and luxury of the place...The mode of living that takes place here among merchants is highly luxurious. Their houses and establishments are on expensive scales. Great entertainments, and many served on plate: high play is a much worse thing. (Young 1793, p. 68)

All these details seem to indicate that the city was experiencing great development and that the money was flowing in, the complete opposite of the atony of Toulouse that the unfortunate Smith had experienced for four months. Bordeaux was thus experiencing not only significant demographic growth towards the end of the modern period, but also a period, a "golden era", which would be that of its maximum expansion.

The port of Bordeaux, known as the "Port of the Moon" because of its shape, became the main port on the Atlantic and even grew to equal Marseille. If wine (from Bordeaux but also from the whole of the southwest) now represented only 30% of its traffic, it was not because of a drop in activity but only because of the increase in other forms of traffic.

The end of the Seven Years' War led to the resumption and specialization of trade with those Caribbean islands that remained under the sovereignty of the King of France (Martinique, Guadeloupe, but also Haiti, part of Santo Domingo, on which many Gascons settled in often unprofitable plantations).

It is estimated that nine-tenths of the sugar, coffee, and indigo that landed at the Port of the Moon were re-exported to destinations in Northern Europe: Germany, Russia, Baltic, England, and Scotland.

But Bordeaux could also provide products that ensured a return freight and limited for a time the use of a purely triangular trade. There were two types of production: on the one hand consumer goods, sheets, and woollens from the Languedoc and the Pyrenees, and on the other hand weapons and metal tools which had become the speciality of the Dordogne, where many small mills occupied the riverbanks.

It was not yet a question of referring to an "invisible hand" of the market, but more to a very specific river along which wealth slowly flowed with the current towards the port city, creating surplus value.

The other products exported by Bordeaux were wheat and other cereals which transited from the plains of the Languedoc by the canal, then along the Garonne before finding, at times of full harvest a possible outlet in Scotland or in Northern Europe where the often delicate climatic conditions make their production more unreliable.

One of the other characteristics of the port of Bordeaux is that it became a slave trade port relatively late. First of all, the slave trade was difficult for economic reasons, as the journey of Bordeaux ships along the coast of the African continent was often dangerous. Moreover, the Bordeaux merchants themselves had to import the required goods, as the wine and agricultural production of the Bordelais were not counterparts that were appreciated by slave traders in Africa, because of their religion. Some also mention sociological or even moral reasons. Among the Bordeaux ship-owners, Montesquieu, the Baron de Segondat (1689–1755), who was the president of the Parlement of Bordeaux from 1716 to 1722, a hereditary office he held from his wealthy family, left writings which used irony to express his opposition to this type of source of wealth. Often the strongest denunciation took the form of the irony present in his *L'esprit des Lois*, (*the Spirit of the Laws*), his most famous essay which appeared in 1748. However, towards the end of the modern period, the slave trade experienced a rapid expansion that can be traced back to the 1760s. There can be many explanations. At the sociological level, Montesquieu disappeared in 1755 and there is information about him confirming that despite his denunciations of slavery, he was himself one of its promoter through his financial participation in the Compagnie des Indes.

Furthermore, the slave trade took an important turn towards the end of the seventeenth century. The Kingdoms of the south were experiencing their first financial difficulties, those of the north were beginning to question the value of this trade which offended all the precepts they advocated and sought to promote. This trade became more accessible to certain Bordeaux traders who had no moral sense. During the years leading up to the Revolution, it even became a trade that was relatively flourishing, involving not only the islands under royal control but also colonies such as Brazil, still under Portuguese domination, which could receive men and women, who would have to live as slaves, indirectly from the Kingdom of France.

Traders and traffickers in Bordeaux at the end of this century would behave like true capitalists, using capital from previous generations to organize a commerce in labour that was considered by many as the true source and origin of modern capitalism, by capturing the surplus value of millions of workers who no longer even owned their own bodies.

For Adam Smith, this flourishing trade must have come as a novelty. The port of Glasgow was never a transit port for slaves, this dangerous and ugly trade which had been the monopoly of the Royal Africa Company, operating out of London. Following the loss of the company's monopoly in 1689, Bristol and Liverpool merchants became increasingly involved in the trade. By the late seventeenth century, one out of every four ships that left Liverpool harbour was a slave trading ship.

However, beyond this brief presentation of the city of Bordeaux and the living conditions that Smith encountered there, he came to the city essentially to meet and introduce the young duke to personalities useful for his future life. If he was a little disappointed when he arrived in

Toulouse, he seems to have had high hopes, in his letter to Hume, of the Governor of Guyenne, his second in command, and his Intendant.

4.2 Marshal Richelieu

The governor of the province of Guyenne was an extraordinary character. An atypical aristocrat at the end of this modern period. His uniqueness was not so much in his duties, his fortune, or his creative genius, although he possessed all these attributes, but in the way he exercised them. He was both a man of action who always sought to be as close as possible to events and a great intellectual, member of the French Academy and great friend of the Philosophes amongst whom the most celebrated was Voltaire. While many governors of royal provinces led a lavish lifestyle at the court of Versailles, he chose to reside in Bordeaux. Residing in the provinces did not cut him off from the court but forced him to make frequent trips to the capital to be close to royal power. More than anyone during this century he seems to have assimilated a quality that would become indispensable in the following years: considering France not as a country but as a territory. Being close to each and everyone and understanding that the map is not the territory.

This man was the Marshal of Richelieu (1696–1788) whose complete surname allows a better glimpse of his complex personality: Marshal François Armand de Vignerot du Plessis, Duc de Fronsac, then Duke de Richelieu (in 1715), Prince de Mortagne, Marquis de Pont Courlay, Prince de Cosnac, Baron de Barbezieux, Baron de Coze, Baron de Saugeon. Unless one is fully versed in the genealogy of the Ancien Régime or in the study of aristocratic families, explaining the origin of all these glorious titles is problematic. From his great-great-uncle, the great minister of Louis XIII and symbol of absolute power, as he liked to conceive it, he derived the first name, thus demonstrating that from his birth, he was the heir of the glorious and ambitious family which had remained ever since well placed at court, which meant that the future marshal had Louis XIV himself for godfather. His title as Duke of Fronsac as well as the more modest title of Baron of Barbezieux also linked him to the province of Guyenne, which he would endeavour to direct, as Voltaire indicated in a letter, as "his little kingdom". The title of Marshal, he owed only to his own merits, as it had been acquired on the battle field, but his titles were many, if we are to believe Voltaire:

> It is always to the first gentleman of the room, the great master of games and pleasures, that I have the honour to address myself, I write to him in favour of Patrat, whom I believe very useful to the theatre that my hero wants to establish. For a long time, Your Excellency, I have been looking for a way to send you a collection containing the Laws of Minos and several small works, in prose and verse, which are rather curious. I would ask you for a small place for this book in your library. [...]
> We are going to play the *Lois de Minos* in Lyon; the show will be very beautiful, but the actors are very mediocre. I expect that the play will be better performed in your capital of Guyenne. I will not go to see show in Lyon: the consequences of my illness do not allow me to do so; but when it comes to obeying your orders, I will find wings and I will fly. (Voltaire at Ferney, 5 May 1773)

In order to better understand how the governor managed to keep his post for half a century (first seventeen years in the Languedoc, then thirty three years in Guyenne) and managed to live like a monarch, it is important to note how this well-born character also became indispensable.

He was first and foremost a soldier in the field. Although the period required a regiment and rank to be bought and traded, under the control of Royal Power, this did not prevent exceptional soldiers, from time to time, from emerging. Such was the case with Marshal de Richelieu, who took part in all the military campaigns of the century. He may have begun his career in Versailles as one of Louis XV's most assiduous courtiers, but he would also make himself useful. In Versailles, where he had apartments, as the King's private aide de camp, in the north wing of the palace, he also led a courtly and social life and became known for his female conquests, which seemed to be numerous. His reputation testifies to many gallant adventures with princesses who frequented the court, but he also seems to have had the favours of the various royal mistresses, some even going as far as to affirm that he presented them, at least with regards to his favourites, to the King.

But these qualities did not stop at the charms pertaining to a great soldier. He was also a fine scholar, a spectator and an organizer of royal pleasures. It was the Duke of Richelieu who organized in Versailles during the 1740s and 1750s, with immense success, the shows and dinners of the brilliant society gathered around Louis XV. He was also a member of the Académie Française, an Academy which, it should be remembered, had been created by his great-great-uncle. Not that this gave him any advantage, although it is clear that it did not harm his career. From those years on, he became friends with his contemporary Voltaire. Their correspondence, written in a tone of deep friendship, involved more than 300 exchanges of letters.

Before taking sides in the Calas affair, Voltaire turned to the Duke of Richelieu to ask for his opinion and the ins and outs of the procedure. But between a Duke who liked to travel, particularly around the Mediterranean, and a hermit who liked to keep to his room in his château in the Pays de Gex, meetings would be infrequent.

However, it has been mentioned that the Duke of Richelieu was a great soldier, thus it is worth considering what his exploits were. As an aide de camp to the King, he took part on May 11, 1745, in the battle of Fontenoy between France and England and its allies, under the orders of the Maréchal de Saxe. Thanks to a clever manoeuvre of which de Saxe was the originator, the battle turned very quickly in favour of the French. According to Jacques Levron, Louis XV turned to him and said: "I will never forget the service you have just rendered me."

Voltaire, the lifelong friend, wrote in an epistle the day after the battle:

> Richelieu, who flies where'er the hosts engage,
> Valiant with knowledge, and with ardor sage;
> Favorite of Love, by Mars to combat taught,
> By wisdom's goddess to express each thought;
> He calls your bands; his soul, discerning, knows
> From whence your enemy's success arose.
> Depending on your valor Richelieu flies.
> And shows where you may win the victor's prize.
> (Voltaire 1859 [1745])

Coming from Voltaire, this eulogy is quite surprising. It is true that in many studies Voltaire is always represented as the author of acid and crude criticism. The philosopher and man of letters however also knew how to handle a compliment, using the same lack of restraint as in his witticisms.

Although celebrated in Paris, the Duke of Richelieu wanted to conduct a completely different battle. Indeed, at the head of an army he conquered Dunkirk and taking advantage of the English defeat, he wanted to operate a landing directly on the coast of England. It must be said that the Catholic Stuart claimant has already landed in Scotland some time previously and that despite the weakness of his troops and the small amount of armament given to him by France, he had already managed to build an army that had known victory; indeed his troops were heading for London. Since the treaty of union in 1707, the Highlands and the bellicose barons of the north no longer had a leader. As keen as ever when it came to fighting, the Scots took up arms and a column was formed, taking back cities and castles, without risking their lives in the capital, Edinburgh. The column was marching towards the centre of England. It was this army that Marshal Richelieu wished to join up with, or more exactly he wanted to catch what remained of the English army between two fires.

Richelieu's brilliant idea did not meet with approval because in Versailles decisions did not follow through and the Ministry of the Navy did not wish to commit its ships. This point is a constant in the history of the French navy over the centuries. France had frequently had a navy superior on paper to the English navy, but conservative management has always led to its preferring the calmer waters of ports and naval parades to the high seas. In late winter 1746, in February, Richelieu had to give up, since he was unlikely to get the ships essential to his expedition. The end was already written and has been mentioned earlier. The Scottish column was routed in central England and the Battle of Culloden, South of Inverness, on April 1, 1746, put an almost final end to the Stuarts' hopes that Scotland would once again become an ally of France.

During the period of peace that followed, Richelieu became an administrator in the service of the King of France. In 1738 he became lieutenant-general of the Languedoc and it seemed to him that "this place [...] is the most beautiful that the king has to give in this genre, if it were as stable as governments are" (quoted by Ravel-Cordonnier, p. 218). But it was in Bordeaux that he gave his full measure. Richelieu was not obsessed with the court and liked to stay more and more in his province. In 1758, he confided that he had "spent his life on the main roads and twenty years outside Paris and the court". He describes in his memoirs the coach he had built for himself. It was a converted vehicle with a large bed and a suspension system that was said to make it comfortable. In winter, an ingenious heating system not only ensured a pleasant temperature inside, but also kept the aristocrat's lunch or evening meal warm. If Richelieu liked to have direct contact with the province, he also liked to dazzle, seduce, and in short "play the little king" as Voltaire, always quick to grasp a trait of character, so rightly noted.

Fate favoured this man who knew how to detach himself from the court while being in the right place at the right time. It was Richelieu who tackled Robert François Damien, the man who with a small knife attempted to stab Louis XV on January 5, 1757. His gesture was doomed to failure because in winter Versailles is an icy palace and people were dressed in many layers of clothing. However, because of the means used,[2] history will remember a trial reminiscent of another century. It was a barbaric killing unworthy of a reader of Beccaria. This incident would bring King Louis XV and his illustrious courtier together once again. However, a new war loomed on the horizon, the Seven Years' War, and once again the Duke of Richelieu would cover himself with glory.

The Seven Years' War was, as has already been mentioned, a war that can be considered as the First World War. Indeed this war would oppose two coalitions gathered around France or England on almost all continents. The navy would therefore play an important, not to say capital, role.

Richelieu intended to be at the centre of events, and, given his age, wanted to see strategic action. Because of his knowledge of the Languedoc and therefore of the Mediterranean coast, he was appointed, following the intervention of Father Bernis and Madame de Pompadour (to whom he did not seem indifferent), commander in chief of the land and naval forces of the Mediterranean coast.

The French lacked a point of support on that sea, and trade threatened to be disrupted for France to the benefit of the English who had controlled the rock of Gibraltar for some time. Following also the advice of Bernis, a native of Toulouse and friend of Voltaire and, at the time, Minister of Foreign Affairs before his disgrace, he decided on an expedition to the Balearic Islands and in particular its most important point of support, the port of Mahon located on the island of Menorca, the most eastern and most developed island of the Catalan archipelago.

Thanks to his experience in Dunkirk, the port where he had prepared the expedition to join Charles Edward Stuart but had to wait in vain for the arrival of the navy, with a certain vision as organizer and master of such projects, he took charge of the whole expedition, ensuring its financing and a sufficient naval presence. The squadron set sail in the spring of 1756 and Fort Mahon was captured in July of the same year. It is indisputable that this is not only an unprecedented personal success but also probably one of the greatest feats of arms of the war and, in a way, of the French navy throughout its long history. This capture of Fort Mahon would also have important consequences during the negotiation of the Treaty of Paris

[2] Damien was torn apart by four horses, after many hideous tortures, and his torso burnt at the stake.

in 1763, in which Lord Hertford and David Hume would participate, since the capture of Menorca would make France, if not England's equal, at least a negotiating power.

For the Duke of Richelieu, this capture was the most glorious moment of his life.

Thus when, in 1755, he became governor of the province of Guyenne, replacing the Comte d'Eu, a prince of the royal house, who exercised the same function in neighbouring Languedoc, he arrived in Bordeaux as an almost royal hero.

This is certainly how this new governor was described, with some emphasis:

> He arrived by way of Blaye where boats[3] which the city of Bordeaux had had richly decorated, led him to the port. When he appeared all the ships, both foreign and French, fired their guns and the Château Trompette answered: a military band preceded his ship; and when he arrived at the Place Royale, he found a triumphal arch where the Parlement came to receive him and greet him. Then he rode his horse through the whole town, followed by the nobility of the province and his beautifully dressed household who were also on horseback and went to the cathedral, where the archbishop and clergy came to meet him. After the "Te Deum", he was taken back in the same order to the Hôtel du Gouvernement that the city had had prepared. never had a Governor had been so magnificent. he was King in Bordeaux. Preceded by a large guard, whose captain was a very good gentleman, he did not neglect any opportunity to appear with brilliance. (Faur 1792, p. 209)

But the celebrations continued and the Duke in turn offered a number of festivities to his new constituents or, to stay in the same tone as the chronicle, to his "subjects".

> A few days after his arrival, he gave a supper with four hundred place settings in his garden, where the most beautiful women were gathered along with the nobility and the legal profession. In return he was offered a very large masked ball in the city, where someone in a mask presented him with the following sonnet:

[3] The first bridge over the Garonne dates from the Napoleonic period. The Emperor wanted to be able to send troops quickly to Spain and the passage through Bordeaux and Bayonne would always be preferred to the road through Catalonia which was much longer and more difficult.

Though under that disguise,
You can know me easily
By my soul's feelings alone:
If I fear you, I am English,
If I love you, I'm French,
If I love you, I'm a woman.
(Richelieu 1889, p. 238)

But the Duke of Richelieu did not content himself with appearances and fully participated in the administration of the territories of Guyenne. From 1758 onwards, he went there every year for six months and even stayed there ten consecutive months in 1765 and 1766. Not only did he exercise real power in Guyenne as he had previously in Languedoc, but he retained an influence on the Languedoc through his networks: in 1765, Beauvau, his successor, asked him for his support with Bastard, the president of the Parliament of Toulouse, while he also strengthened his networks by supporting the promotion of Languedociens. By influencing the choice of intendants, whom he did not want to be too active in their provinces, he manoeuvred to restrict local royal administration and keep for himself the reality of power.

This is the personage Smith and his student met in July 1764. Given his importance, we better understand the care Adam Smith took to get letters of recommendation from the highest levels of the court, in order to be well received.

Of course our travellers helped in this by the very astute and Catholic Abbé Colbert de Castle-Hill, presented themselves to him as Scots, a quality which they would put forward in the whole of France. Smith and his pupil were, consequently, opportunely provided with a letter of introduction, written by Choiseul[4] at the instance of Lord Townshend and the Ambassador of England in France, Lord Hertford, to the Duke of Richelieu to indicate to him all the importance that this last has at the level of the history of Scotland, always allied.

[4] The Duc de Choiseul was a French military officer, diplomat and statesman. Between 1758 and 1761, and 1766 and 1770, he was Foreign Minister of France and had a strong influence on France's global strategy throughout the period. From 1761 to 1766, his cousin César Gabriel de Choiseul, duc de Praslin, was minister for foreign affairs, but Choiseul continued to control the policy of France until 1770, and during this period held most of the other important offices of State.

Even if the Buccleuch family's choice of alliance and collaboration with England from that time on, as the period of progress that was beginning suggests, the family nonetheless remained one of the original clans of the Caledonian nation's aristocracy. The young Duke was also a descendant of the Stuarts and consequently of King Henry IV of France, who remained, in Bordeaux and Guyenne—to which is attached the generality of Auch and Pau, his native town—even more than elsewhere a much admired character.

However, and this is an anecdote that deserves to be mentioned, the Duke of Choiseul in his writing was wrong. He called Smith 'Robinson' in the letter of introduction. The latter seems to be surprised enough, not to say offended, but the error probably comes Choiseul being distracted at the time of writing.

Indeed, a play by Favart, first in Paris, then in the provinces, had enjoyed a certain fame. It is a very pleasant comedy whose action describes the presence of an Englishman in Bordeaux, a young aristocrat who stays in France and whose valet's name is Robinson.

This unpretentious play was a topical work since the English had truly flocked to France since the end of the Seven Years' War and Favart feared that through contact with them a certain corruption of morals would occur, but the play is also, in its unfolding, an ode to reconciliation between the two peoples.

If Smith does not refer to it, it is because he sees himself playing a rather unpleasant role if he is thought to resemble Robinson. The latter plays the valet and therefore is often impertinent, as in the comedies of Pierre Auguste Caron de Beaumarchais, who will soon become more famous and relegate Favart's work to the background. The offense may seem even greater to Smith as Robinson is often formulated as a simpleton sidekick, which was not Smith's position with regards to the Duke, but which may have seemed ambiguous to some Frenchmen unfamiliar with the customs in practice on the Grand Tour. Smith, and here is one of the handicaps incurred during his journey, was often in an in-between role, in an aristocratic world where he was only the preceptor, although maybe a prestigious role in the eyes of some, to a discreet aristocrat whose name opened doors through his links to the crown of France.

It is highly probable that Smith and his young student saw the play which, after being released in Paris, was performed the following year in Bordeaux in 1764. It must be said that the Duke of Richelieu sponsored much animation in Bordeaux and that the theatrical life of the city was at that time very rich, equal to Paris if one believes Voltaire's comments. Although the current Grand Théâtre was still only a project, there were many theatres. Our three visitors attended a different show every evening, including Sundays. Theatre performances were provided either by visiting troupes or by a troupe that had fled Toulouse following the crisis with the Parlement and the lack of security in the city and which was now in permanent residence in Bordeaux.

Voltaire, who maintained an ongoing correspondence with the governor of Guyenne, indicated in a letter in the summer of 1764 that the season of pleasures was particularly brilliant that year. This seems perfect for Smith who was coming out of a long abstinence due to the localized and unexpected circumstances he met in Toulouse.

> Ferney, September 21, 1764,
>
> The parties that my hero gave in his kingdom of Aquitaine rang out in our deserts. He always supports the honour of France, in peace as in war. Certainly we have an obligation to him but we do not imitate him in any way. I don't know if he's accompanying Mme. D'Egmont to Italy. We'd like to give him some new play from Ferney's puppet theater. That's all we can offer him unless we have some relatives of Mme. Ménage to introduce him to. Our Genevan women are not worthy of him. what an attractive life you lead, Monseigneur le Gouverneur de Guyenne. While your substitute[5] just applies leeches to his arse and gets his testicles framed. My miserable health prevents me from going to see him. I do not leave Ferney, and I will leave it only for you; I have renounced an itinerant and noisy life. For if you are young, I am old,[6] and I spare what little time I have left. (Voltaire 1856, t. 1, p. 328)

With his meeting with the Duke of Richelieu and the presentation of the young Henry who accompanied him, Adam Smith had just completed an important mission, his first success, as it were. Lord Townshend had recommended that Smith introduce the young student to people who, in his own words, had gone from being "politicians to statesmen".

[5] This is the Duke of Lorges (1714–1826), another hero of the Battle of Fontenoy for whom Smith asked Richelieu for a letter of recommendation.

[6] The age differences are not as great as Voltaire seems to indicate since in 1764, Voltaire was 70 years old, which was already an advanced age, but he lived until the age of 84. The Marshal-duke was then 68 years old, he lived until the venerable age of 94.

But as we have seen, it was not possible for him to meet such characters for a fairly simple reason: at that time in Toulouse, the city did not boast anyone of the stature of the Duke of Richelieu.

In Toulouse, Smith and the young Scott were certainly rapidly able to meet Loménie de Brienne on his return from Paris and Montpellier. But Loménie was only a young archbishop, thirty-seven years old, for whom Toulouse was the first post of any real importance. Marshal Richelieu, on the contrary, was a man who, if he still had a future ahead of him, was already haloed with his past military glory. He had become, beyond his duties as an administrator, a true statesman. Loménie, on the other hand, was a man who aspired to deal in politics; he would become a statesman and a man of government only some fifteen years later, a few months before the Revolution, which he would not survive either politically or physically.

In Bordeaux, thanks to the meeting with the Duke of Richelieu, Smith fulfilled his first and main mission, in addition to his role as a teacher, that of introducing his student to men of quality. More than a simple encounter, Smith wanted to become a close friend of the Duke and his father in law. It is true that Richelieu's role could also appear to be a solution for the Scottish nation: "First gentleman of the King's House, the Marshal-duke of Richelieu is the archetype of those courtiers who drew their power in the provinces from royal favour, and, at court, from their weight in the distribution of provincial charges" (Ravel-Cordonnier 2009, p. 218).

In "Pays d'élection", provinces that did not have assemblies, the roles of governor and intendant were much more important than in "Pays d'Etats" which did. They necessarily had a role in politics, of representation of public affairs, which had to manifest itself in a form other than authoritarianism, that often led to revolt.

The intendant Louis-Urbain-Aubert de Tourny (1695–1760) left behind many achievements in Bordeaux. Before coming there, he was for thirteen years intendant of the Limousin, a position which seems very formative since Turgot would occupy it in his turn. It must be said that being an intendant in a Pays d'Election and therefore having greater powers than elsewhere, in the poorest region of France, could allow initiatives to be taken.

It is also notable that the intendants, if they were from the north of the country and if they started a career in the South of the Kingdom, were likely to continue to pursue it in these regions. Specialization or desire for a certain quality of life, probably a bit of both. It should also be noted that the career of these high servants, true ancestors of the civil servants in our current prefectural administration, ended in the vast majority of cases in the capital or nearby.

Smith's comments in a paragraph of the *Wealth of Nations* specify his observations on the city he visited: the city's fortune was the consequence of the legislation put in place on wines, but also of the infrastructure developed around communication routes, such as the canal built in the last century by Riquet, a Languedocian concerned with the common good.

> Bourdeaux is in the same manner the entrecote of the wines which grow upon the banks of the Garonne, and of the rivers which run into it, one of the richest wine countries in the world, and which seems to produce the wine fittest for exportation, or best suited to the taste of foreign nations. Such advantageous situations necessarily attract a great capital by the great employment which they afford it; and the employment of this capital is the cause of the industry of those two cities. (WN, II.iii, p.336)

Smith's visit to Bordeaux marked his first success in this atypical Grand Tour. For the first time he achieved a precise objective, that of meeting a great man, a statesman who could represent a model for the Duke.

Charles Townshend himself envisioned for him, in some of his writings, a kind of career "à la Richelieu", retiring to his wife's lands and becoming somehow King in a small kingdom, as Voltaire affectionately said.

Smith, in a letter to his friend Hume, reveals his good humour, proof of his first successes, by formulas of gratitude which contrast greatly with his previous letter with its sad tone. Finally France was opening up to him and he could make new acquaintances. The philosopher and teacher, probably by mimicry, is beginning to be more cordial. There is no doubt that the influence of the Duke of Richelieu, a rather exceptional figure, had a lot to do with it. For his part, Guyenne's governor perhaps retained some nostalgia for his attempt to land in Scotland, the only major failure of his rich and, in his own eyes on-going, career.

> I take this opportunity of Mr Cook's going to Paris to return to you, and throw'you, to the Ambassador, my very sincere and hearty thanks for the very honourable manner in which he was so good as to mention me to the Duke of Richelieu in the letter of recommendation which you sent us. There was indeed one small mistake in it. He called me Robinson instead of Smith. I took upon me to correct this mistake myself before the Duke delivered the letter. We were all treated by the Marechal with the utmost Politeness and

> attention, particularly the Duke whom he distinguished in a very proper manner. The intendant was not at Bordeaux, but we shall soon have an opportunity of delivering his letter as we propose to return that Place *in order to meet my Lords Brother*. (Letter # 83 to Hume, 21 October 1764)

Moreover in his letter Smith showed he was well aware of all that the city of Bordeaux could bring him in his research on public finances, but in a way more directly connected to the continuation of the trip. Among the letters of recommendation sought by Smith was one for Guy Louis de Durfort de Lorges (1714–1775). Richelieu's lieutenant, Guy Louis de Durfort de Lorges (1714–1775), was absent for a reason that Voltaire himself reveals to us in a letter in which, always with verve, he shows us the relations between Richelieu and Lorges and himself:

> 31 August 1764, at Ferney.
>
> I experienced considerable alarm these past days, Monseigneur, for your commander of Guyenne. I sent from my bed from which I hardly leave, news of the brilliant health that Tronchin[7] had promised him, he had just received his sacraments and made his will; here is the reason for this sudden operation.
>
> Tronchin condemned him to eat only vegetables, carrots and beans cooked in water. Sir said, the Duc de Lorges, I cannot digest your gallimaufry, it makes me swell at the front and the back, and he had himself punctured at the front; his wind has increased in fury, but the sacraments have calmed him down a little so that it is now safe. Mr. the Duke of Randan, his brother, and the Duc de Trémoille arrived with twenty officers: Mme. Denis[8] absolutely wants play a joke on them. I will receive my sacraments also so that I have a valid reason not to make the trip at seventy and ten years. (Voltaire 1832)

[7] Théodore Tronchin (1709–1781) was the most "serious" French or Swiss doctor of the time. Unlike others who only practiced medicine, he was based in Geneva and journeyed around the world. He travelled to and studied in Cambridge, Leiden, Amsterdam. He contributed to articles in the Encyclopédie and is known to have been one of the doctors of the poor, which in the doctor is always a source of questioning. He was as the doctor of the perpetually ill Voltaire. Tronchin also played an important role in the smallpox inoculation debate. This debate immediately found its place in the social arena: does individual behaviour influence the well-being of all? This is a debate that would lead to utilitarianism.

[8] Madame Denis was Voltaire's niece, she was also at that time the person who ran his household and who is considered to have been his mistress during their young years.

If de Lorges was not in Bordeaux it was because he was ill or probably simply on a diet according to Voltaire's indication. He doesn't seem to worry too much about the Duke's health, but as usual as a lonely old man, he worries about his own.

Intendant Charles Robert Boutin, known as Boutin de La Coulommière, was a great French official and financier of the eighteenth century (1722—died after year IV). One only has to go through the positions he held to understand Smith's interest in him, to the point of embarking on a second visit to Bordeaux. Boutin de La Coulommière was successively deputy public prosecutor of the Parlement of Paris (1741), Councillor to the first chamber of petitions (February 5, 1743), master of petitions (February 17, 1749), president of the Grand Council (April 19, 1754), commissioner of the king to the Compagnie des Indes (1756); he was intendant of Bordeaux in 1758 and remained so until 1766. He was mainly a protégé of Turgot who made him Intendant des Finances before he was called, after various adventures, to the Royal Finance Council from 1777 to 1787.

The intendant would certainly be back in Bordeaux for Smith's second stay in the city, so before their departure from Bordeaux and knowing their destination, two additional remarks can be made that help illustrate and understand the traveller's next step.

Bordeaux was a city of exchanges and spectacle, but it was also a city where gambling was omnipresent at the time.

In a port city the presence of gambling in sailors' circles is no surprise, its presence at all levels of society is more so, can even shock. It must be said that the century is one of games, which are all the more practiced that although their rules are well established, any research associated with probabilities is still in its infancy, even in the field of insurance.

Gaming was quite logical in garrison towns, although barracks did not yet exist and in times of peace, troops went from town to town, or from port to port. In popular circles, games were played in the street, but also in drinking establishments.

It was impossible for a traveller to pass through Bordeaux without noting the extent of the phenomenon. Jean François Marmontel (1723–1799), a French man of letters who would meet Smith a few months later while in Paris, describes in his memoirs his time in Bordeaux during the same years while he was on his way to the city of Montauban:

> Even though there were people in this town of spirit and generosity I enjoyed their trade less than I would have liked. following a fatal game of dice, whose fury blackened their minds and absorbed their souls, I had the sorrow every day to see someone sorry for the loss he had made. They seemed to eat and dine together only to cut each other's throats when they came away from the table; and this bitter greed, mixed with enjoyment and social affections, was for me something monstrous. (Marmontel & Barrière 1846, p. 268)

Indeed, beyond the working classes, gaming had won over the whole of society in the city. The governor of the city, the imperious Richelieu, was not the most moderate of the players. He was often the first to make bold bets in the aristocratic salons where "trictrac", the aristocratic version of the more vulgar backgammon, was played along with other games and where billiard tables flourished. In short, the city had fun and can be described by some as a being dedicated to pleasure under Richelieu's rule. He even went so far as to imagine the setting up of a huge gaming establishment which would have been created on the banks of the Garonne, near the Château Trompette, in the form of a joint stock company in which he would have taken the majority of the capital. This establishment would have been in the image of the casinos which, in the following century, would be exiled, with a very bourgeois wisdom, mainly to holiday resorts. Thus the rich could ruin themselves in private, without tempting proletarians who were destined to manufacturing jobs.

We do not know what effect this gambling debauchery in a commercial town had on Smith. It can be imagined that as a prudent man whose feelings must always remain under the control of reason, he energetically warned the young Duke against the spiral of debt.

It must be said that their budget did not allow them to participate a great deal in gambling. However, there remained the threat of any debt of honour which his family, still in Scotland, would have been obliged to discharge. From this point of view, it seems Smith's success was total since the Duke was never ready to risk large sums in hazardous schemes. The only time he took a chance was the Ayr Bank scandal, which almost brought him to ruin. It was a Scottish bank, Douglas, Heron & Company, which was based in Ayr and operated from 1769 to 1772. The bank had been incorporated as a company in which the 131 partners undertook, indefinitely and jointly and severally, to pay the company's debts from their personal assets. The partners were large landowners so that the bank initially attracted many customers reassured by the guarantees offered. But the banking crisis of 1772 was fatal to it. Heavily in debt and unable to repay its notes to panicked customers, the bank had to close its doors on June 25, 1772. The central bank's role as lender of last resort was not yet defined, and neither the Bank of England nor the Bank of Scotland wanted to save the Ayr Bank, leading to the collapse of many of the partners. The amount of the debts for which the Bank of England sued the Duke of Buccleuch himself amounted to 300,000 pounds. Smith had to seek a solution from Parliament and the Bank of England, which finally granted very long-term loans to pay off the debts, an operation that lasted until the 1830s.

Smith waited until the scandal had subsided before publishing the *Wealth of Nations* in which he showed himself emollient towards the Ayr Bank:

> In the midst of this clamour and distress, a new bank was established in Scotland for the express purpose of relieving the distress of the country. The design was generous; but the execution was imprudent, and the nature and causes of the distress which it meant to relieve, were not, perhaps, well understood. This bank was more liberal than any other had ever been, both in granting cash accounts, and in discounting bills of exchange. With regard to the latter, it seems to have made scarce any distinction between real and circulating bills, but to have discounted all equally. It was the avowed principle of this bank to advance, upon any reasonable security, the whole capital which was to be employed in those improvements of which the returns are the most slow and distant, such as the improvements of land. To promote such improvements was even said to be the chief of the publick spirited purposes for which it was instituted. By its liberality in granting cash accounts, and in discounting bills of exchange, it, no doubt, issued great quantities of its bank-notes. But those bank-notes being, the greater part of them, over and above what the circulation of the country could easily absorb and employ, returned upon it, in order to be exchanged for gold and silver, as fast as they were issued. (WN, II.ii, 313)

Smith's solution of very long-term bonds saved the reputation of the Duke who became Governor of the Royal Bank of Scotland in 1774. As for Smith, if the episode did not change his support for the freedom of establishment of banks, the hostility he showed towards joint-stock companies can better be understood because of the carefree behaviour of directors which economists call agency problem; but Smith in the same passage saw the distant consequences of the financialization of capitalism via joint-stock companies and he thus wrote:

> This total exemption from trouble and from risk, beyond a limited sum, encourages many people to become adventurers in joint stock companies, who would, upon no account, hazard their fortunes in any private copartnery. Such companies, therefore, commonly draw to themselves much greater stocks than any private copartnery can boast of. (WN, V, ii, p. 741)

4.3 Bordeaux Meetings, Montesquieu, and Colonel Barré

During the summer of 1764, Smith and the Duke had many reasons to go to Bordeaux in addition to honouring Choiseul's recommendation to Richelieu. Firstly Bordeaux was the city of Montesquieu and all his life he was challenged by Montesquieu's thoughts on government. Bordeaux is also a convenient entry point by sea from the British Isles to Guyenne and the Languedoc, and served for many Huguenots as an exit port after the revocation of the Edict of Nantes. Also, without being able to exactly date the meetings, a raft of elements in epistolary exchanges between Smith, Hume, and various correspondents indicate that our travellers met there with Montesquieu's son Jean-Baptiste a contributor to *The Spirit of the Laws*, who was passionate about natural sciences and also about Bagnères-de-Bigorre, and also met with Colonel Barré, who was to accompany them in part of their peregrinations.

4.3.1 Baron Secondat de Montesquieu between Bordeaux and Bagnères-de-Bigorre

In Bordeaux, Smith's curiosity must have been piqued by the presence in the city of the Montesquieu family. Smith knew of course that the great thinker had died, he already had written of his death in a letter to the readers of the *Edinburgh Review* written and published in 1756 and he was challenged during his whole life with the philosophy of the Bordelais. Thus during the year 1760 he had Lord Shelburne's son read Montesquieu at least one hour a day and again on March 11, 1790, an anonymous correspondent of the *National Gazette* reported the following information:

> It is claimed that the famous Mr. Smith, so well known for his treatise on the causes of the wealth of nations, is preparing and is going to print a critical examination of *the Spirit of the laws*; it is the result of several years of reflection, and we know enough what we have a right to expect from a mind like that of Mr. Smith. This book will be a landmark in the history of politics and philosophy; at least that is the judgment of educated people who know fragments of it, of which they speak only with the most auspicious enthusiasm.

Unfortunately, a few months later Smith disappeared after having thrown on to the fire the last iteration of his criticism of Montesquieu. Indeed, his admiration for Montesquieu, quoted explicitly about fifty times in the *WN*, did not prevent him from asserting his own originality:

> Mr. Locke, Mr. Law, and Mr. Montesquieu, as well as many other writers, seem to have imagined that the increase of the quantity of gold and silver, in consequence of the discovery of the Spanish West Indies, was the real cause of the lowering of the rate of interest through the greater part of Europe ° Those metals, they say, having become of less value themselves, the use of any particular portion of them necessarily became of less value too, and consequently the price which could be paid for it. This notion, which at first sight seems so plausible, has been so fully exposed by Mr. Hume, that it is, perhaps, unnecessary to say anything more about it. The following very short and plain argument, however, may serve to explain more distinctly the fallacy which seems to have misled those gentlemen. (WN, II.iv, p. 354)

To explain his thinking on money which anticipates both the classical theory of currency neutrality and Say's law, Smith first tackled the influx of precious metals into Europe following the conquest of the Americas, disrupting the world economy. But, using a second line of argument, he turns to Hume who has imagined a famous thought experiment:

> For suppose, that, by miracle, every man in Great Britain should have five pounds slipt into his pocket in one night; this would much more than double the whole money that is at present in the kingdom; yet there would not next day, nor for some time, be any more lenders, nor any variation in the interest. And were there nothing but landlords and peasants in the state, this money, however abundant, could never gather into sums; and would only serve to encrease the prices of every thing, without any farther consequence. The prodigal landlord dissipates it, as fast as he receives it; and the beggarly peasant has no means, nor view, nor ambition of obtaining above a bare livelihood. The overplus of borrowers above that of lenders continuing still

> the same, there will follow no reduction of interest. That depends upon another principle; and must proceed from an encrease of industry and frugality, of arts and commerce. (Hume 1760 [1752], p. 69)

Hume's answer lies in the famous quantitative money theory: doubling the quantity of money will double prices and "real" ratios will remain unchanged. Yet the detail of Hume's analysis is less categorical and he admits that a temporary effect of the transition from the old to the new prices may exist. Hume, who gives money a symbolic and quantitative role, criticizes the financial relationships that can result from a credit-based society. Smith's positions were to diverge significantly from Hume's on both the role of banks and the neutrality of money. Hume is not, for all that, the precursor of the contemporary monetarists even if some of them could claim it to be so.

Smith was undoubtedly an admirer of Montesquieu and it was therefore logical that he sought to get to know his family. Montesquieu had an only son who inherited his offices and titles. Baron Jean-Baptiste de Secondat was born on February 10, 1716, so was a few years older than Smith. He had a brilliant mind, and his father wanted him to pursue a career in the judiciary or in the army, as is mentioned in the first lines of his *Thoughts*:

> [5] My son, you have enough good fortune not to have to either blush or swell with pride because of your birth. My birth is proportionate to my fortune in such a way that I would be disturbed if one or the other were greater. You will be a man of the robe or the sword. Since you will be responsible for your status, it is up to you to choose. In the robe, you will find more independence and freedom; in the sword camp, grander hopes. (Montesquieu-Clark 2012, Thought Nr 5)

One year after the birth of his son, in 1717, Montesquieu acquired for the first time an address in Paris where his stays became longer and longer, despite the fact that as a parlementaire he was supposed to reside in Bordeaux. He freed himself from this obligation once success came with the publication of the *Persian Letters* and his entry into the French Academy. This Parisian attraction explains why he placed his son at the age of 8 at the Collège Louis-le-Grand then at the Collège d'Harcourt under the special supervision of Abbé Quesnel while he undertook his three-year tour of Europe (1758–1761) which took him to the great European capitals, notably London where he was initiated into Freemasonry. Montesquieu's father arranged for him a very comfortable union with a young wife from a very old Bordeaux family. On July 7, 1726, for a 5200 livres annuity, he provisionally yielded his charge to the advocate-general Jean-Baptiste d'Albessard, reserving nonetheless for himself the possibility that he or his son could assume the office again at any time (François Cadilhon 2008). Thus when he was younger than the twenty one years old required, Jean-Baptiste was received into the Parlement of Bordeaux. But Jean-Baptiste was more concerned with scientific progress than with legal proceedings, and at the end of the 1740s, the father and the son sold their offices and recovered enough to protect themselves from money concerns and devote themselves to their preferred activities, the Sciences of Man for the father who associated his son with the preparation of *the Spirit of the laws*, and the Sciences of Nature for the son. Very quickly the son's research, helped by some good fortune, earned him an international notoriety. One year after his marriage, he had gone on holiday in the Pyrenees, but passing by Dax, he had made various observations, either to study the nature of the warm waters there or to measure the depth of the abyss from which they came out, which at the time was thought unfathomable. He succeeded in achieving this measurement and reported back to the Academy. According to his biographer:

> The following year, the son of Montesquieu returned to the Pyrenees, and made, in July 1743, an ascent of the Pic du Midi, to carry out some barometric experiments there. The famous Englishman, Mr. Fahrenheit, had argued that the gravity of the atmosphere exerts a considerable influence on the degree of heat at which water boils; Lemonnier's experiments had confirmed this theory. Mr. de Secondat, wanting to ensure himself of the fact, climbed the Pic du Midi, equipped with the necessary instruments, and he obtained the same result. (Delpit 1888, p. 39)

A later paper entitled *Observations sur les fossiles des environs de Bagnères et de Barège et sur les eaux minérales de Bagnères* which he presented to the Académie was published in England before the French edition since it appeared in the *Philosophical Transactions* on January 1, 1744, as Remarks on stones of a regular figure found near Bagneres in Gascony: with other observations, communicated by Monsieur Secondat de Montesquieu, of the Academy of Sciences of Bordeaux, in a letter to Martin Folkes. The latter (1690–1754) was an English antique dealer, numismatist, mathematician, and astronomer. His mathematical work earned him admission to the Royal Society at the age of 23. In 1723, Newton, who was president of the Society, made him a vice-president and, upon his death, Folkes postulated to be his successor. He became president in 1741 and was elected the following year to the French Académie des Sciences. Perhaps Montesquieu's father knew him since he was assistant to the Grand Master of the Grand Lodge of England in 1724–1725 shortly before Montesquieu, during his trip to London, was initiated.

Folkes, beyond his Newtonian reputation, had another claim on Smith's interest. His fascination for currencies led him to publish a *Table of English Silver Coins* which allowed Smith perhaps for the first time to present the distinction which is so familiar to us today between real and nominal values, as the title of Chap. 5 of Book I of the *WN* clearly indicates: "The real price and nominal price of goods or their price in labour and their price in money."

Montesquieu had been very impressed by the scientific work of his son whom he considered more gifted for the sciences than himself, to the point of asking for his help for the finishing touches of the *Spirit of the laws*; he also no doubt counted on him to publish his complete works (cf. Letter from Montesquieu to the Abbé of Guasco, February 10, 1745). This cooperation between father and son cannot have escaped an observer as attentive to French current events as Smith and even less David Hume, who between 1749 and 1750 edited a translation of *the Spirit of the Laws* in Edinburgh, for which he exchanged a series of letters with the author so as to include modifications to the work.

J.-B. Secondat ticked one further box with regards to Smith and the Duke: wine constituted an important source of income for Montesquieu and Jean-Baptiste devoted a great deal of interest to the nascent science of agronomy. Towards the end of his life, after his meeting with and the passage of Adam Smith, he turned to economics, the so-called human sciences. Beyond all the new techniques he sought to implement, he was at the origin of the creation of the Guyenne Agricultural Society. Whereas in Scotland these learned societies were very successful, they were blocked in Bordeaux by a ruling of the Parlement.

Although Secondat travelled little in his youth despite his father's opportunities and multiple invitations, he maintained throughout his life a sustained correspondence with the various academies of Europe, including the Royal Academy of London of which he became a correspondent. In addition he also corresponded with the Academies of Toulouse and

Montpellier. Their exchanges focused on observations, mainly astronomical. This is how he came into contact with the members of the Toulouse Academies who, from that time on, through the trio formed by D'Arquier, Riquet de Bonrepos, and Garipuy, specialized in observing the heavens.

Thus, Secondat shared the second part of his life between his domain in Bordeaux and the town of Bagnères-de-Bigorre in which he lived throughout the summer season. He climbed the Pic du Midi several times, carrying out experiments there, recreating Mariotte's experiments on the compressibility of gases. Some may see him as the first scientist at the origin of the Pic de Bigorre Observatory.

4.3.2 A Huguenot Between France, Great Britain and the United States

In Bordeaux, by chance or as a prepared encounter, Smith found the man who has gone down in history as "Colonel Barré". His journey is a true adventure novel, rooted in the changing world and a veritable founding myth of the American nation, which has many legends and heroic stories. Isaac Barré was the son of Pierre Barré, and his wife Marie-Madeleine Roboteau. She came from a Protestant family, some of whom had already emigrated before the revocation of the Edict of Nantes to Ireland. After this event, Mary Madeleine and her sister joined their uncle in the extraordinary circumstances imposed by the persecutions inflicted by the Catholic authorities. Shortly afterwards Pierre Barré, who had also left La Rochelle in the 1720s, married Marie-Madeleine; they had their first son Isaac in 1726. Pierre Barré's rise to wealth made him a notability in Dublin in a few decades.

The young Barré, after studying at Trinity College Dublin, joined the English army. He was to make a name for himself during the Seven Years' War. He took part in the amphibious raid on Rochefort in September 1757 under the command of General Wolfe, whom he followed in 1758 to North America as Adjutant-General. He participated in the siege of Quebec in 1759, when the English commander, General Wolfe, lost his life on September 15 during the assault on the Plains of Abraham. The British command then returned to Colonel George Townshend (1724–1807) who gathered the surrender of French troops on September 18. George Townshend was the brother of Charles Townshend, who a few years later would become the instigator and funder of Smith and the Duke's trip.

It is striking to see how events unfold here in a very small world, for the rest of Colonel Barré's life would bring him even closer to Smith and Hume. Indeed, Barré had been wounded during the siege of Quebec, and facial injuries left him scarred. He returned to Europe in September 1760 and in 1761 was commissioned to recruit an infantry regiment in Ireland. In December 1761, under Lord Shelburne, he entered the House of Commons where he did not go unnoticed. Walpole describes the strong impression he received of the contrast between "his face marked by a ball lodged in his cheek which gives a wild glow to his eye" and a "very classical and eloquent diction with a determined audacity as if he were accustomed to holding harangues in these places". He was soon to make a famous use of this eloquence during the discussion of stamp duty in February 1765 by sharply upbraiding Charles Townshend, who defended this duty imposed on North American settlers in exchange for the support they received from the British army. Townshend condescendingly referred to the colonies as "children raised by us, fed by our indulgence, protected by our weapons". Barré rose up against these assertions by taking up Townshend's words: "Raised by your care? No! Your oppression transplanted them to America. Fed by your indulgence? They grew up while you neglected them. Protected by your weapons? They nobly took up arms to defend you." Barré ended his intervention by greeting the settlers as the "Sons of Freedom", a denomination that remains attached to those settlers determined to fight against English domination, for the freedom of the future United States. This decided support for the settlers earned Barré the recognition of the Americans who named several cities after him.

In Bordeaux in 1764, Barré was already no stranger to Smith. Indeed Lord Shelburne, Barré's patron, had entrusted the education of his son Thomas Fitzmaurice from 1759 to 1761 to Smith, with whom he resided. In addition, David Hume had participated with the future historian Adam Ferguson and the future General Clerk, another protégé of Lord Shelburne, in a failed raid by English forces on Lorient in 1746 (see Ferguson Campbell Mossner 1960). There was thus an Irish-Scottish connection of liberal minds and it should be mentioned that Barré was the Governor of Stirling fortress, forty kilometres from Glasgow, from April to December 1763. There is evidence of this relationship between Barré and Smith in a letter from David Hume to Smith sent from Paris in July 1763 in which he asked him to transmit a message to Barré (Hume and Greig 1932, p. 391). A year later, Hume wrote from Compiègne to Barré to express his regret at not having met him in Paris. On August 3, 1764, Barré wrote to Hume from Rochefort asking for his help in an inheritance affair (cf. Burton 1849). His father had a younger brother, Jean, who died intestate in 1760, and his fortune, valued at £10,000 (approximately two million Euros in 2016), was divided between nephews and nieces with nothing going back to their emigrated uncle. Unfortunately for him, in the eighteenth century religious affiliation played its part in questions of inheritance and as a consequence of the Edict of Nantes, there was no question of a Protestant inheriting from a Catholic, a situation which should not have surprised Abbé Colbert since a symmetrical rule in Scotland would prevent his uncle Abbé Alexandre Colbert from taking over the family estate.

Having become aware of the complexity of the situation, Isaac Barré wrote to Hume on September 4 that he was in Toulouse with Smith and a paragraph in his letter shows the familiarity between the four men: "Smith agrees with me that you have been softened by the delights of a French court and that you no longer write with this nervous style which makes you remarkable under more northern skies" (ibidem.). This presence of Smith in Toulouse on September 4th is the result of a temporary return between trips around Toulouse whose main stopover, an incursion into nascent thermalism, follows.

4.4 Taking the Waters at Bagnères de Bigorre

In order to meet Montesquieu's son, there was certainly no shortage of intermediaries available, whether in Great Britain, Bordeaux, or Toulouse, and the most propitious place was still Bagnères-de-Bigorre. In the summer months, all the best societies of Bordeaux and Toulouse took the road to the Pyrenees, including the great animator of the city's festivals, the Maréchal-gouverneur Richelieu himself.

Visitors had previously come to the south of France to study its customs and habits, the Pyrenees being a popular destination since Daniel Defoe's famous account of the struggle against a bear that picaresquely closes Robinson Crusoe's adventures. In some ways, these regions seemed as wild as the Highlands. This sojourn, this expedition, could only be a pleasant experience, while the presence of so many aristocrats also held the promise that the stay would make it possible to enjoy a number of interesting encounters.

Of course, once again we have no detailed account from Smith of his route through the landscape of the Landes which was then totally different from the one travellers see nowadays.

Smith and his pupil probably contemplated a landscape closer to that which can be seen on the Scottish moors than that of the great forest of contemporary Gascony. The travellers left in the very first days of August, also fleeing the heat of a city which, although at the edge of a large river, suffered from the unhygienic conditions of the time. The miasmas spread through the narrow streets, making everyone fear epidemics of these fevers whose origins were unknown but whose harmful and fatal consequences terrified the populations, disarmed before these plagues.

4.4.1 Pyreneism and Thermalism in Bagnères-de-Bigorre

After these few weeks spent in Bordeaux, the travellers resumed their journey and arrived in the valley of the Adour and the small thermal town of Bagnères-de-Bigorre. Since his departure from Glasgow in December 1763, more than six months previously, this period opened a new phase in Smith's peregrinations. For the first time, visitors were staying at a resort. They found themselves in a semi-rural setting, and no longer in a large city, apparently far from the places of power that constituted the purpose of the trip, but in a small town in the Pyrenees, in the middle of a nature that was there for the admiration of people taking the waters and visitors—including English people who already went there for the quality of the air and water, but also to enjoy the flora.

Finally, more obviously than before, travellers found themselves in a city that proudly displayed its distant Roman origin. From the city of wine, the most famous in France at that time, they came to the city which was the symbol of water. This transition owed nothing to any desire for abstinence, although Smith had condemned excesses all his life and celebrated measured behaviour:

> In the command of those appetites of the body consists that virtue which is properly called temperance. To restrain them within those bounds, which regard to health and fortune prescribes, is the part of prudence. But to confine them within those limits, which grace, which propriety… (Smith, TMS, I.ii. I.4, p. 28)

Since the Roman period, Bagnères had continued to attract powerful people concerned about their health. The Bigerion people, the local Celts under Roman occupation, with their help founded the town of *Vicus Aquencis*, the "city of waters".

From this first foundation, dating from 28 B.C., date the first thermal baths, some remains of which still exist: a Roman stone altar, which today decorates the great thermal baths of the city on which can be read: "To the divine person of Augustus, Secundus, son of Sembedo raised this altar in the name of the inhabitants of the Bourg des Eaux and in his own."

Throughout the Middle Ages, the city was called "Balnéria". The word, which is transformed in French into "Bagnères", gives its name to the city from the Renaissance onwards.

The city was attached to the small province of Bigorre, a Pays d'Etats, of which it became the capital. The Estates of Bigorre met every two years in the city of Lourdes during the quiet winter period. In the skein of the structures of the Ancien Régime, Bigorre was part of the généralité of Auch while for finances it was attached to the Cour des Aides of Montauban. It may be noted that due to the short duration of his stay, Adam Smith may not have attended any assembly sessions since these took place outside the tourist season for obvious economic reasons.

The complexity of this administrative organization was not without advantages for a resort town like Bagnères. Indeed many important people could come to stay there during the summer and from considerable distances, without the possibility of their position being declared vacant. Such was the case, for example, of Anne-François-Victor le Tonnelier de Breteuil, Bishop of Montauban from 1763 to 1790, who for purely political reasons (he disagreed with certain administrators, including from 1782 to 1790 with the Abbé Colbert, by then Bishop of Rodez) chose diplomatic exile each year in Bagnères in order not to attend the Estates of Haute-Guyenne while still remaining within the territory of his post.

Until the seventeenth century, the city did not experience any significant development. It is true that the region suffered both from its proximity to Spain, so often in conflict with France, and from its distance from the major urban centres, Toulouse, Bordeaux, and Paris. It was also affected by a bad reputation as a consequence of numerous earthquakes which seem to have been more frequent and to have caused greater damage during these years than nowadays.

The awakening of the city owed much to the "Grand Colbert". Spain, following the installation of the Bourbons on the throne of Spain, became an unconditional ally of France and the Spanish Princes were prone to go to the small town on the northern slope of the massif to escape the heat of the peninsula, while enjoying the social life and the advantages of thermalism for their health.

Thus, following the publication by La Guthère of *Du Bon usage des eaux de Bagnères [On the Good use of the Bagnères waters]* in 1659, an attraction for this type of cure developed rapidly in wealthy circles. The author of the scientific book was not totally disinterested because he had financial interests in the city, where he owned a house with a thermal spring. La Guthère was also Guy-Crescent Fagon's adviser, who became King Louis XIV's doctor in 1663, which reinforced Bagnères' success (Merat & Lens 1829, p. 526).

Thus, throughout the "great century", the city underwent significant development, mainly based on the quality of the people who came from Versailles to stay there and engage in a new activity: taking the waters. The Grand Colbert, for his part, charged Pierre-Paul Riquet, whom he had grown to appreciate during the construction of the Languedoc Canal, with a mission to prospect for mineral waters throughout the Languedoc in order to determine their therapeutic virtues.

Throughout the century, the most famous visitors would follow one another in the Adour valley. According to Jean-Michel Sanchez, Louis-Auguste de Bourbon (1670–1736), the legitimate son of Louis XIV, was accompanied by Madame de Maintenon, Madame de Montespan, the Duchess of Picquigny, daughter of Colbert, later the Duke and Duchess of Biron, as well as many other personalities from outside the region.

The small mountain town had become in less than a century a destination in which not only the nobles and aristocrats of the Bordeaux region but also those of Toulouse met. The Riquet families became regular holidaymakers, as did people from the court of King Louis XV and foreign courts like those of nearby Spain. Laurence Sterne's stay also proves that the resort was already known in England. The altitude and coolness of the mountains do not seem to have attracted those suffering from tuberculosis if the disease was too advanced to hope for a cure or a remission. Another English writer, Henry Swinburne (1743–1803), ten years after Smith's visit pens a vision of romanticism which was only then emerging:

> All the meadows, even on the declivities of the mountains, are watered by small cuts from the springs or rivers, and produce annually two crops of hay, the first extremely abundant: the fields in the plain admit of a third mowing in October. Bagnères contains about three thousand inhabitants; they subsist comfortably upon their paternal inheritances and the money they amass from the annual visits of strangers who resort hither to drink or bathe in its waters. It is surrounded with old walls, and is tolerably built, but the streets

> are narrow and crooked; the quantity of water that runs through them render the town cool and pleasant in summer, but in winter it is exceedingly cold in account of the vicinity of the mountains, and the heavy falls of snow; that remain several months upon he ground. It has no buildings of any note. The Adour is here a fierce torrent; its waters are white like those of an mountain streams proceeding from snows; thy are diverted at several places from their natural course, and conveyed in canals across the plain, and through the town, where they are employed in numberless useful operations. (Swinburne 1787, pp. 301–302)

The roads made it possible to reach Bagnères in approximately two weeks from Paris, in greater comfort each day thanks to the permanent improvement at this time of the forms of transport available. Since a stay was likely to last several months, the temptation was great to undertake a trip which was considered quite exotic and invigorating.

One might think that, like Michel de Montaigne from Bordeaux in his *Journal de mon Voyage en Italie*, the main purpose of the journey was to cure and therefore care for the body through the use of thermal springs. This was true in many cases, but the way patients were treated should be highlighted here. There was no central facility with identified springs, but a very large number of independent facilities all offering different therapy. Jean-Baptiste de Secondat counted more than fifty of them in his work on thermal medicine, from the Source de l'Hôpital to the spring known as the Queen's spring which owed its name to Jeanne d'Albret, the mother of King Henry IV, via the baths of Lavedan or the spring of the Hospices des Capucins (Secondat, 1750).

Each "source" was owned and operated by an owner/operator. Although specialist doctors and scientific chemists published a few documents in their respective academies on the composition of mineral salts in springs, they could not yet at this period give a therapeutic evaluation of their virtues.

The first doctor who really made it possible to classify the springs and thus provoke the rise not of so much thermal spas but of thermal medicine was indeed a doctor from Bagnères-de-Bigorre whose work was contemporary with Smith's stay. His name was Théophile de Bordeu (1722–1776). This scientist and doctor was the first inspector of the thermal waters of the Auch generality then was the doctor of Madame du Barry, at Versailles, and became a friend of Diderot's during his travels and stays in Paris. At this time, he was one of the doctors who sought new ideas in science in general and in scientific experiments to overcome the diseases and long-lasting pathologies from which most of his patients suffered.

But before the appearance of a true science of thermal medicine, the city of Bagnères could appear to the visitor as a vast market of well-being without any particular organization or specific hygiene control. Each spring in the small valley had its own spa. The buildings could even be very modest, a few baths separated by a palisade of boards or even a single large collective pool, but could also be more luxurious, some establishments even offering marble baths (fortunately marble or granite quarries were not far away). Of course each bath was charged according to a perfectly free rate. Given the lack of therapeutic information and a wide range of baths, it was not uncommon for foreigners to try several springs and to rely either on the reputation of the place or on the rates charged in their choice of one or other of the establishments.

There is no doubt that this market had caught the attention of the Scottish economist because Smith's visit to Bagnères-de-Bigorre corresponded above all to his desire to assuage his curiosity and make discoveries. None of the travellers suffered from a particular pathology or disease worthy of treatment. Smith, the oldest of the three, was only forty-one years old, and he had never reported any medical problem in any of his letters.

So what to do in this charming little town if you didn't come here to enjoy the benefits of its thermal waters and thus relieve an ailment whether chronic or occasional?

As the spas would demonstrate perfectly in the following years, the cure was accompanied by a period of rest. To entrust one's health to water, to soak one's body in water, to immerse oneself in a hot liquid was, however, unconventional for the time. Bathing also meant entering into communion with nature and thus was a new experience for that century. In the middle of the eighteenth century, ways of thinking changed, nature and the environment, long considered as man's enemies, gradually became his allies, to the point of entrusting them with one's health and thus one's essential vital functions. Nature played a decisive part and was considered the nourishing breast that would provide a source of progress, since it was here that the world's first riches resided. This change in attitude was noticeable among the most famous of the thinkers defending this new vision, Jean-Jacques Rousseau (1712–1778), mainly in a work that has become symbolic: *Rêveries du promeneur solitaire*.[9] Rousseau, during this month of August 1764, maintained an epistolary friendship with David Hume, which reached its climax a few months later and ended up in a famous quarrel in which Adam Smith was involved, just as he returned from the Languedoc.

Furthermore, one of the purposes of stays in spas was also the "promenade". The promenade was then an institution and had its rules, its uses, its places, and its codes. Going for a walk created a place for sociability par excellence, all participants were equal, everyone greeted everyone else. In a holiday town and in particular in a spa town, no one was at home. No aristocrat, whether from Toulouse, Bordeaux or the court of Versailles, owned a property in the city. Everyone, all aristocrats, resided either in a hotel or in an inn, or with the locals who rented out rooms or small apartments. It was not until the creation of the Grand Thermes or the Thermes du Salut, which brought together several springs, that accommodation was organized, a century later, around the "cure" and for the therapeutic comfort of patients.

Smith, who had complained in his previous letters about the limits his accommodation imposed on him when it came to receiving and paying visits, was now on a perfectly equal footing with the people he was to meet. Housing was no longer in the valley, a criterion of social discrimination, and everyone shared the summer comforts that were always a little precarious in holiday resorts. Exchanges were thus made easier. For the travellers, the small resort in the Pyrenees finally became a place of shared sociability and bolstered by this new situation, they could thus very easily form relations with all the people in residence in the city.

But beyond the simple promenade, other places of sociability existed as a concession to the century. It has already been mentioned that gambling, games of chance, and the emotions they brought had appeared in all sectors of society.

The rumours run faster when society is limited, at most a few hundred people taking the waters, as the place was small and they had nothing else to do but the three activities that have been mentioned and which punctuated the day, treatments in the morning, the afternoon walk, games in the evening. There was not yet a central establishment such as a single casino allowing a unique type of gaming, but rather several independent competing establishments. A first central establishment would be created a few

[9] [*Reveries of the Solitary Walker*]

years later in 1775, the Vaux-Hall. The name is a generic term that refers to the first establishment that bore this name and which was originally founded (in 1661) in London in Kennington Gardens, South of the Thames.

The revival of this name both in Bordeaux and Bagnères tends to prove that England had a lead in the domain entertainment or that one wished to attract new British tourists to these new establishments. Conviviality could also take the form of small concerts of chamber music or harmony thanks to small ensembles performing classical music. Haydn (1732–1809) or his predecessor Telemann (1681–1767), Bach (1685–1750), and his descendants, but also the very Toulousain André Campra (1660–1744), were composers regularly played by small ensembles, such as could be encountered in improvised music salons.

As a final possible place for sociability, excursions in the Pyrenean valley were undertaken. The upper Adour valley and the Bastan valley were particularly suitable for exploring nature. The average altitude guaranteed walking in the most favourable climatic conditions and the use of mules, numerous in this rural setting, offered relative comfort to the less hardy. So it was not rare that to fight boredom, later to become famous in the form of "spleen" a symbol of romanticism in the next century, longer hikes of several days, almost adventures for urbanites, were organized. The ascent of the first slopes of the Pic du Midi or the ascent of the Col du Tourmalet to Barèges allowed the more adventurous and the more specialized to enrich the long evenings of their holidays with their adventure stories, which probably grew heroic as the feelings of danger got further and further away.

The three travellers found themselves for the first time since the beginning of their stay in a favourable situation to make profitable encounters and reinforce their networks of acquaintances and thus approach men and women of quality, which remained one of Smith's missions.

The people who frequented the hotels, baths, and gaming tables of the city were all men of property, mostly aristocrats whose social status allowed them to lead, for at least a few days each year, a perfectly idle life. They came from the two neighbouring provinces for the most part, if the cities of Toulouse and Bordeaux are included in the local framework.

Some, however, such as the Prince of Monaco or the Count of Caraman, came from further afield, from the courts of Spain or Versailles, and undoubtedly constituted the centre of local society life. Abbé Colbert seems to have taken advantage of this period to get to know the ecclesiastics of the province better. The Abbé would show himself all his life a courteous man of great curiosity and, it must be said, quite typical of the portrait of the Vicars General of Loménie made by Aldégier, exploiting every possible advantage on the road to obtain a see, as the duchess of Fitz-James perfidiously suggested about another of Loménie's vicars.

4.4.2 *Bagnères-de-Bigorre in the Literature of the Time*

The benefits of Bagnères had made it a very popular place not only for the polite society of Toulouse and Bordeaux but also of all Europe if we believe *La coquette dupée par un religieux b***. et par un marquis*, a short story published in 1774 in a collection with an even more evocative title, *La Gazette de Cythère*, or *Avantures galantes et récentes*, sold in the main cities of Europe. The passages devoted to Bagnères open with a general remark on the Languedoc:

> In general, the French would be wrong & especially those who live in the southern provinces of France, if they were accused of godlessness and irreligion towards the goddess of Cythera [Aphrodite goddess of love and sexuality]. It has no people more subject to its laws nor more attached to its cult than the Languedocians; in all times, in all ages, this province has provided heroes and heroines who rightly reaped the most glorious laurels in the field of love and who make an immortal name for themselves in the most remote posterity...; their names are written for the most part in the registers of the court of the Parlement of Toulouse, which transmits them from one generation to another, and if we needed outdated facts or anecdotes of gallantry whose date was not fresh we would find an ample collection in the collection of 'causes célèbres' in this genre.

With such a disposition, it is not surprising that the portrait made of Bagnères insists on depicting, besides the thermalism, the other advantages of the city:

> The mineral waters of Bagnères have long been famous for their virtue. Not only do the French experience its beneficial effects, but their health-giving effect extends to all the peoples of Europe who come here every year, as much to seek to remedy the real ailments they experience, as to enjoy the amusements and pleasures in which they indulge without reserve and without constraint. Bagnères in the season can compete for taste, abundance, wealth and luxury with Paris, all proportions kept, and it is certainly much

above this Capital, for the delights of life in whatever sense one understands it; assistance from French people, of all ranks, ages and sexes, and that of foreigners, makes the stay all the more delightful, and attracts there, more for pleasure than for need, all those who, being able to afford the expense, want to devote three months to their pleasure, and spend them in the most brilliant company. The journey to Bagnères has been in 'de bon ton' in France for a very long time it is the only fashion that is constantly encouraged there [...].

The young Duke, on the other hand, seemed to have established ties with Bagnères on his own account. He was about to celebrate his eighteenth birthday and according to Colbert, he was "very well made in himself". He was Scottish, which gave him the exoticism necessary for seduction. He was also rich and has a famous name. In addition, when he reached majority, he would become the head of the house of Buccleuch, so it is hardly surprising that he attracted attention. This was particularly the case for the Baroness de Spens, who shortly after the days spent in Bagnères sent him a letter which the Duke would bring back to Scotland and keep carefully; while we deplore the lack of documents making it possible to reconstruct Smith and the Duke's journey.

Saint Sever October 20, 1764

A Milord

My lord the Duke of Buccleugh

Truly, my lord, you quickly forget absent people! I flattered myself that I would find a little more memory among the English, but I realize that they differ from the French only by their words; you had promised to send me, as soon as you were at Christmas, a letter of recommendation for your aunt, in favor of my cousins. I waited vainly for the effect of this promise, you probably have not thought about it any more; but this delay is not an irreparable evil, my lord, if you have the kindness to write your letter and to send it to me I would then be in time to address it to Paris to those ladies who are likely to stay there five or six days, I hope my lord, that you will subscribe to this arrangement otherwise, you will understand that I would be entitled to say that one must thus count even less on the English than on the French; As I do not know, milord, the length of time you have stayed at Noë and even more, where you have been since leaving this place, I address my letter to the abbé Colbert and I look to him to have it delivered to you where you will be: I'm not moving from here yet.

I am occupied here by a building project, in any case I almost drowned since I had the honor to see you; I fell in the gave [Gascon word for torrent], which is a very fast river, it looks almost like a miracle that I did not remain in there, it is thanks to M. de L'Etang that I was rescued. This accident left me in a lot of fear, but fortunately did not disturb my health which is always very good, I would be very comfortable to learn that yours continues to be too, I have the honor to be very perfectly, milord, your very humble and very obedient servant.

Labarrere d'espens

Please give my best regards, I beg you, to Mr. Chmit, I hope he will remember to send me his book. How is the Baron, are his eyes dry now? give him a little word of consolation from me.[10]

The Spens family is, by chance, a very old Scottish family that had been settled for a few centuries in a town in the Landes, Saint-Sever, where they owned a considerable agricultural estate while lodging in the dark and medieval local château. Saint-Sever is on the Adour River, the same waterway that flows through Bagnères, making the 140 km journey easy and direct for people residing in this agricultural plain, at the time very wealthy.

The Spens family had been sent to France in 1450 by the Stuart King James II of Scotland in the middle of the Hundred Years' War to help the French in their struggle against the English occupier. It was then a question of limiting their presence to Guyenne rather than yet reconquering the territory for the benefit of the King of France. Since 1295, in fact, the Kingdoms of France and Scotland had sealed an alliance in which each undertook to support the other against the Kingdom of England. Over the centuries and the vicissitudes of relations between the three countries, the political and strategic content of the Franco-Scottish alliance had become blunted, but:

> it remained a kind of affection nourished by memories of the past (like the Auld Alliance), sometimes confining to myth. In this important and lasting sense, cultural exchanges between France and Scotland have been continuous, but they reached their peak in the Enlightenment. (Dawson and Morère 2004, p. 13)

King Louis XI of France (1423–1483) had granted the Spens family letters of naturalization in 1474, which were registered on August 15, 1475, in Paris. Patrick de Spens[11] is described by the King as the "first man

[10] French original: NAS GD22 with permission from the Duke of Buccleuch and Queensberry, KT.

[11] http://www.spens.info/genealogie.php.

of arms of France" after having killed in a skirmish one of the enemies of the King of France, Duke Charles the Bold of Burgundy. Later King Charles VIII (1470–1498), perhaps in recognition, made the Spens' motto his own: "If God is for us, who shall be against us?"

Very quickly the Spens family, through the play of marriages, took root in France in the province of Guyenne. As early as the sixteenth century, they formed the French branch of the Spens, thereafter known as Spens d'Estignols. There also still remained a branch of the family in Scotland which remained a powerful feudal family of the Highlands.

The young woman the Duke was seeing in Bagnères came from a family with many soldiers. Her father Jean-Baptiste Cazenave de Labarrère (1705–died 1775 in Dax) was a musketeer for three years, officer in Martinique (1748–1753), then on the island of Grenada (1753–1754), finally in Guadeloupe (1754–1757) where he was appointed but did not go. He returned to France in 1753 because of ill health and, a future family tradition, he took the waters at Barèges. For services rendered he obtained the cross of Saint-Louis in 1754. Finally he became provost of the maréchaussée of Auch and the Béarn in 1763, an office he passed on to his son Jean-Gabriel who ended up guillotined on April 12, 1794.

Jean-Baptiste Cazenave de Labarrère married, perhaps in 1740, in Martinique, Claire Françoise de Francesqui, born on February 25, 1719, in Fort-de-France (Martinique) and who died on 19 pluviôse year VI in Saint-Sever, daughter of Antoine and Marie-Anne Girardin de Champmeslé, settlers in Martinique.

Françoise had brothers, one of whom, Jean-Gabriel, "prévot de maréchaussée" in Auch, perished on the scaffold in Dax during the Revolution at the end of a mission, a good example of an enlightened nobleman, rallied to the Revolution in 1789 and finally crushed by the Terror. This brother gives us an additional indication of the networking of the elites at the end of the Ancien Régime: he was indeed the nominated prosecutor of Paul-Marie-Arnaud de Lavie, Knight, and Count of Belhade and other places, son of a "président à mortier" of the Parlement of Bordeaux whose contribution to political economy will be examined later. For her part, the letter-writer, perhaps born herself in Martinique, married Joseph, baron de Spens d'Estignol, in 1759. Her husband was born in Saint-Sever in 1729. He was captain commander of the Auvergne regiment which had been heavily engaged during the Seven Years' War on the fronts of Germany and the Netherlands, and thus remained very far from the Château d'Onnès. It seems that the husband's removal had reinforced the role of the baroness who “is making a building”. The young Duke had promised a recommendation to his aunt in Paris for Mme. de Spens’ cousins.

It is not so easy to determine the person for whom the Duke had promised a recommendation, according to the information contained in the letter. Indeed, the Duke’s father was an only child but his mother Caroline Campbell (1717–1794) had at least three sisters: Lady Elizabeth (born around 1720), Anne, and Mary (1727–1811), the youngest. Elizabeth had married James Stuart Mackenzie (1719–1800) who had been ambassador to Turin before being entrusted with Scottish affairs, despite his desire to represent England in France or Spain. Walpole celebrated the attractiveness of Ann, Countess of Stafford, whose beauty can be judged from her portraits in the British Museum, but of all the Campbell girls, it seems to be the last one that is being referred to, because Lady Mary Coke was to lead a rather tumultuous life and take centre stage during the reign of George III, welcoming the Duke and Smith to London. Her letters and diary are an inexhaustible source of gossip about the social élite of the Georgian era and it is she who is at the origin of an anecdote that has definitively made Smith pass for the most distracted man on earth:

> While L(ad)y George was with me Sir Gilbert Elliot came in; they talk’d of “Mr. Smith, the gentleman that went abroad with the Duke of Buccleugh, & many things in his praise, but added he was the most absent man that ever was. Ly George gave us an instance that made me laugh. Mr. Darner, She said, made him a visit the other morning as he was going to breakfast, & falling into discourse, Mr Smith took a piece of bread and butter, which after he had rolled round and round he put into the teapot and poured the water upon it. Sometime after he poured it into a cup, & when he had tasted it he said it was the worst tea he had ever mett with. Mr. Damer told him he did not in the least doubt of it, for that he had made it of the bread and butter he had been rolling around his fingers.” (Lady Coke, Vol.1, p. 141)

Lady Coke’s proximity to the Duke and her travels across the continent suggest that she was the person in question. It is possible that the cousins intended to go to London or that Lady Coke was soon to go to Paris, although she did not finally visit Europe until the 1770s (Fig. 4.1).

Is it possible to deduce, as the letter has been kept safe, that the Baroness caused some emotions in the Duke or his guardian that she does not fail to mention in her letter? Or Baron Secondat de Montesquieu whose eyes

Fig. 4.1 Portrait of Lady Mary Coke by Thomas Bardwell of Bungay. (Source: Buccleuch Living Heritage Trust)

are the subject of a somewhat ambiguous allusion at the end of the letter? In any case, the speed with which she remarried just over a year after the death of Baron de Spens, with another soldier, seems to indicate that she was an attractive person. Very skilfully she had the letter transmitted by Abbé Colbert since she did not know at what stages of their journey the Duke and Smith were. After Bagnères, the Duke has stayed with Smith and Abbé Colbert in the lands of their new friend Count Louis-Pantaléon de Noé (1728–1816), another of these eighteenth century personalities, like his father, whose life took place on both sides of the Atlantic.

4.4.3 *The Comte de Noë*

The letter of the baroness tells us that in their journey towards their second stay in the city of Bordeaux, the travellers stopped in the magnificent chateau of Isle-de-Noé. Louis-Pantaléon, Count of Noé, spent his entire childhood in the Caribbean. He was the heir, through his mother, of several plantations belonging to the Bréda family. He was a great slave owner in the part of Santo Domingo called Haiti, in the region known today as Cap-Haïtien (previously Cap aux Français). After a happy childhood on the slave plantation, he was sent to France to receive an education worthy of his rank. Then Count Louis-Pantaléon chose to begin his life with a military career and he had fought the English in the war that had just ended. He distinguished himself in particular in battles that took place on European territory, and not on the seas as one would think for a man from the overseas colonies.

It is certain that the count had, through his life to that point, a vision of the world probably more global than that of an aristocrat of the Languedoc who never left his province. Jean-Louis Donnadieu in his book tells us that his career has just undergone a turn that would inflect his future life:

> The Battle of Minden (1 August 1759) was a turning point in his military life. During this confrontation lost by the French troops, he was very seriously wounded by a shot to the right arm. His horse is killed under him. Would the fall have contributed to further aggravate the injury that just burned his arm? What is certain is that the rider remains "crippled"; however, his military papers do not specify the seriousness of the after-effects if not the handicap from which he will suffer from now on. (Donnadieu 2009, p. 58)

After a very long convalescence, the Comte de Noë returned for good to his native island, Haiti, during the second half of 1769, where he would lead a great career as a colonist. It is on his plantation that a coachman named Toussaint Louverture worked. There would exist between the two a complicity which would begin with the liberation of the slaves and would culminate in a letter which was at the origin of the work of Jean-Louis Donnadieu. This very detailed letter shows the complexity of the relations which may have existed between the various protagonists of the colonial drama which was slavery, denounced on numerous occasions by Adam Smith for its economic inefficiency. This letter is also an illustration of the moral questions that a man like the Comte de Noë was able to formulate during his stays in Europe and his long conversations with the men of quality he met there, among whom can of course be included Adam Smith as well as the Baron de Secondat.

Jean-Louis Donnadieu is not precise about the sojourns of the Count between Paris, Bordeaux, and Noé from the end of the Seven Years' War until his return to his plantations in the first quarter of 1769. However his presence in Bagnères is probable since on the one hand the count was present in Guyenne during these precise months and on the other hand his injury was completely compatible with care with mineral water and hot mud in Bagnères-de-Bigorre or even in the nearby resort of Barèges which had possessed for years a thermal establishment specially intended for wounded soldiers.

Thanks to the letter from the Baroness of Spens addressed to the Duke at the Chateau de Noë, we know that his stop there followed the meeting in the spa town. Thus one can imagine the long conversations between Smith and the Comte de Noë on the islands and the colonial system, conversations in which the Baron de Secondat willingly joined. The Baron's passion during these years indeed related to agriculture, new ploughing techniques as well as the first agricultural tools born under the hammer of the blacksmiths of the villages and the steel mills of the Dordogne or the Landes. The Baron de Secondat was also passionate about the new more effective breeding establishments that were being born throughout southern France, under the constraint of epizootic diseases that were decimating traditional forms of production. In Gascony, but also in the Languedoc, the success of maize is well known: this new cereal had been introduced a few years previously and contributed to feeding not only poultry but also people. Maize residue also provided excellent fuel and quality straw for mattress filling. However, from a mind turned towards nature and the agricultural world, the thinking of the baron would turn more and more towards the economic and political questions which resulted directly from these concerns. The presence of the Riquet family in Bagnères-de-Bigorre can also be noted, as indicated in the Abbé Colbert's correspondence.

The stay in Bagnères-de-Bigorre can appear at first as a simple tourist visit in a city where a climate of leisure, idleness, and rest reigned. For the travellers the passage to Bagnères marked a turning point. Before this trip to Bagnères, Smith had had difficulty getting to know the people he had the mission of meeting and getting the Duke to meet, but thanks to this stay in a town where, in a way, the holiday season favoured meetings, he was able to build up a first network of acquaintances. This network was all the more important as it included some of the most important people in the Languedoc and Guyenne. Jean-Baptiste de Secondat, the Riquet family, the Count of Noé, the Prince of Monaco, the Baroness de Spens have been discussed and probably there were other important figures not mentioned in the various letters to hand.

But nothing beats Smith's direct testimony. In his letter of October 21, 1764, he comments succinctly but very positively on his stay.

> Our expedition to Bordeaux, and another we have made since to Bagneres, has made a great change upon the Duke. He begins now to familiarize himself to French company and I flatter myself I shall spend the rest of the Time we are to live together, not only in Peace and contentment but in gayety and amusement. (Letter # 83 to Hume 21 October 1764)

4.5 Discoveries During Summer Wanderings

The letter from Colonel Barré to David Hume tells us that Smith and Abbé Colbert returned to Toulouse on September 4, 1764, while a letter from Smith at the end of October mentions the forthcoming departure for Montpellier. Did Smith stay in Toulouse in September? Nothing is less certain because he mentioned a second visit to Bordeaux and it is more than likely that he returned there during the period of the wine harvest when all the big owners would be present to supervise the harvesting of the grapes. It is a strong possibility since the travellers were happy to spend several days in a post chaise to meet the people who seemed important to them. However, among the various missions that Townshend entrusted to Smith, there was the question of public deficits and finances in France. So far Smith has not been able to gather first-hand information on this subject. As was indicated, during his first stay in Bordeaux, Smith was not able to speak with the intendant of the province who had been recommended to him by the British Embassy, and even directly by the ambassador himself.

The Duke of Lorgnes, Guy Michel de Durfort (1704–1773), as has been mentioned, had been delayed in Geneva by illness, with Voltaire's famous doctor, Tronchin, in attendance. During the summer, the intendant, after a regime that Voltaire claimed was severe, returned to his post in the capital of Guyenne. Thus, following this recovery, Smith would have been able to come and talk with him and inform himself about the French situation.

It was in all likelihood in Bordeaux that Smith was able to make decisive progress in his search for information on France's public debt, so interesting to his sponsor, who was struggling with the same difficulties following the Seven Years' War, under an incredible set of circumstances that must now be mentioned.

The "pays d'élection", like the Guyenne, were subject to the personal *taille* [The taille was a direct land tax on the French peasantry and non-nobles in Ancien Régime France. The tax was imposed on each household and was based on how much land it held.] and to all ordinary royal taxes shared out by the intendant. In contrast, "the pays d'états" (like the Languedoc) retained the right to consent to the tax (and to distribute it as they wished) and to maintain particular civil servants.

Smith was well aware that in the case of a "pays d'élection" the role of collector belonged uniquely to the intendant who was charged, with the assistance of the Parlement as well as the Courts des Aides of the audit and the appropriate collection of funds, bound for the central government. If the Parlement merely registered the royal ordnances and desires, the intendant was in charge of coordinating the organization of the various forms of taxation.

While the Parlement generally registered tax proposals without too much debate, the increase in taxes in recent months was not without its problems. In general, the taxation system was designed to prevent the "parlementaires", the vast majority of whom were nobles attached to certain privileges, from voting on taxes that directly affected them through their individual economic interests.

The proposal to introduce a tax of one-twentieth on all income (the "vingtième") was the main cause, as has been mentioned, of the revolt of the Toulouse Parlement. The Parlement of Bordeaux, which represented the interests of an exporting region and was favourable to free trade, would take advantage of Article V of the Letters Patent of July 12 to put forward reform proposals based on an examination of the situation and an evaluation of France's public debt in:

A "Mémoire" is a communication addressed to an absolutist sovereign. If the memorandum is too critical or if the subject of the memorandum touches on delicate subjects such as religious practice or the person of the King, it is often, at least initially, anonymous. The brief deals with a specific subject, generally quite limited and which must be stated in its title. It leads to a proposal submitted to the monarch. There are also mémoires which evoke points of doctrine and serve to state a position with regard to currents of thought.

Most historians who have studied France's financial situation and its tax system have underlined its complexity, which frightened even the most important economists or ministers of this period. In any case, this is what Jacques Necker, the Minister of Finance of Louis XVI, speaking of indirect taxes, declared twenty years later:

> We are really frightened when we go deeper into[their] study, when we discover their number and diversity: so this legislation is so confused, that hardly one or two men per generation come to understand their complexity completely [...]. The multitude of particular cases, the accumulation of regulations, the confusion of principles, all this old context finally formed of so many knots, presented the idea of an immense undertaking, every time one wanted to proceed to a reform through their detailed study. (Necker (1821[1784], p. 538)

Indeed, indirect taxes were numerous and diverse and affected a large number of everyday consumer goods, but also all transport, via tolls, whenever goods took to the roads or left the places of production. The main difference with the contemporary period concerns the determination of the total amount of taxes and their collection. The amount of tax to be paid was fixed arbitrarily by the King. Consequently, the sums had to be collected from a certain number of taxpayers according to obscure distribution systems that did not always accord well with fiscal justice. As Smith would explain in his writings, it was often a matter of long historical developments and traditions that originated from the feudal past of the provinces and the royal domain.

However, there was a second type of tax, more modern, which was similar to the direct taxes that we know today. The royal civil services fixed in this case a percentage of deduction on incomes or on the estimated value of an inheritance. This method of calculation was a guarantee of justice for the taxpayer who knew what to expect. However, this form of tax had a major disadvantage for the central services, which had only a very imprecise knowledge of incomes and fortunes, so that they could only anticipate the amount that would be collected in a very approximate way.

The social homogeneity of the Parlements is essential to understanding their reaction to royal power. Thus in the area of taxation, "opposition to tax increases had been the Parlement's most constant activity during the last thirty years of its existence… There is no doubt that despite everything that tended to reduce the tax burden on them, parlementaires considered themselves, and the province as a whole, to be overtaxed" (Doyle 1967. p. 365). It is a major explanation for the real openness of the Bordeaux Parlement to the society it represented.

The introduction of this type of tax must therefore be accompanied by complex means of collection and involve forecasting tools that the royal services were not equipped with. The low success rate of the second type of tax, which can be perceived however as fairer, was due to the weakness of the statistical apparatus, that the tax services would from this period seek to reinforce by the experimental implementation in Languedoc and Quercy of a single and modern land register.

In this year 1764, the management of the enormous debts that France and England were burdened with was a very essential question, because speculation on the ability of each state to reduce its debt was absolutely essential, debt management being linked to a country's military capacity and the possibility of ensuring national security.

Smith would benefit from an incredible combination of circumstances which would put in his hands an amazing document which he brought back to Britain, the *Memoir on the Liberation of the State and the Relief of the People, presented by the Parlement of Bordeaux, as a consequence of the declaration of November 1763 & Article V. of the Letters Patent of 12 July 1764*. The document appeared in various catalogues of the French National Library without any indication as to authorship (see, e.g., Department of Printed Matter 1855) as the identity of the author had not been revealed. To avoid losing the precious document, Smith had it bound, taking care to write an index with the author's name. Unfortunately, it was only in the 1930s that James Bonar systematically catalogued Smith's library for the first time, but a reading error (Baculan instead of Bacalan) further delayed by half a century the rapprochement between the 1764 memoir and its author. Finally, the renewed interest in the public finances of the period of the Enlightenment logically lead José Félix to conclude that the memorandum came from Isaac de Bacalan, a young councillor to the Bordeaux Parlement, torn between his hometown and Paris where he was spotted by the Comptroller General of Finance, L'Averdy, then the Minister of Finance. This author's untimely death caused him to fall into oblivion, before a Bordeaux economist became interested in him at the beginning of the twentieth century, and the authorship of the 1764 memoir was finally returned to him at the beginning of the twenty-first century.

In July 1764, he had just written a memorandum responding to the appeal contained in the letters patent of July 12 issued by King Louis XV, which stated in Article V:

> In the event that our Courts deem it necessary to propose some provisional operations to us, they may, without waiting for the aforementioned briefs to be drawn up, send us their observations on this subject, so that we may be so provided as to advise well.

Bacalan belonged to a Protestant family from Sauveterre-de-Guyenne, a "bastide" built by the English during the Hundred Years' War in the Bordeaux region. The family supplied many members of the Parlements during the seventeenth and eighteenth centuries to the city of Bordeaux. They owned a huge estate on the banks of the Garonne below the Château Trompette in Bordeaux. The development of this district in the eighteenth century by a Dutch engineer, who drained the marshes, led to the creation of a district dedicated to shipbuilding. The area still bears the name of the MP's family and is located close by the docks running alongside the Garonne.

The *Mémoire* opens with a long question that may appear still current:

> One cannot help but recognize these two truths: the first, that the people pay too much tax; the second, that it is not feasible to reduce the king's income. And first of all it is certain that the peoples pay too much taxation: indeed, if we do not reduce the enormous weight of the tributes that make agriculture languish, discourage industry, oppress trade, we will soon see the exhaustion of these three main sources of the nation's wealth.
>
> If it is true, as it is assured, that they are barely sufficient for ordinary and indispensable expenses, how will it be possible, by reducing them, to make our colonies flourish, to expand our trade, to revive the arts, culture and population? Above all, how can we manage to repay the State's debts, which, according to moderate calculations, amount to two billion four hundred million, and produce one hundred and twenty million in interest? Now it is no less important to pay off the national debt rapidly than to reduce taxes: for it has been shown that the enormity of the interests it produces is the greatest *obstacle to the* restoration of the prosperity of the kingdom because it has been shown that, of two nations almost equal in wealth and industry, the one which has most liberated its income will increase its power the most.

It is certain that this question corresponded entirely with Smith's concerns and with those of Charles Townshend, who was seeking information on France's finances. This brief had the merit of clarity, even if some aspects of it may have made it appear much too reductive. If, as Necker stated, only one or two people in France were capable of understanding public finances, it was difficult for a young councillor to the Bordeaux Parlement to give an exhaustive account of them in a few pages. The memorandum had the merit of providing a first method for calculating the amounts of taxes paid by the subjects of the Kingdom of France. This summary method would be taken up by Adam Smith as an example in the *Wealth of Nations*. In the same vein, the memorandum also showed how to calculate the wealth produced in the country, which also answered a question that Smith had been asking himself since the first version of his draft of the *Opulence of Nations* was written. Moreover, this brief from Bordeaux immediately shows a very liberal orientation. The drafting seems to have been entrusted to large-scale merchants whose only or principal interest would be to see their colonial affairs grow in a world free from all constraints. The solutions envisaged were radical and may surprise, according to the introductory statements, as shown in the conclusion which is reproduced here. But it should also be noted that in addition to the state, which must be reduced to the bare minimum, the people to be taxed were the ones who mainly lived on the money they had lent to the state. Individual interests must be ignored in favour of the interest of all, since the interest of all is to have a debt-free country that will thus be more powerful. The memorandum, when read at the end of the first decade of the twenty-first century, at a time when Europe is going through a new sovereign debt crisis, is very much in fashion since its conclusion remains the major question that still seems to be posed to the peoples of the old continent.

> To this objection two answers: I°. The evils of the State are pressing, agriculture, the arts and trade groan under the weight of taxes; they cannot be relieved too soon: the national debt is immense, the interests are exorbitant, the payment of these interests crushes the nation; the State cannot be liberated too soon. Jealous neighbours are watching you and it is to be feared that they have made peace only to prepare for war. One cannot too soon put oneself in a state of defense yet the great work of reformation will necessarily go slowly it is doubtful that it will suffice to cure all our ills, as we have proved. What fatal insensitivity would then make us swing to execute a

> plan, which at the same time provides the prompt liberation of the State, the prompt relief of peoples?
>
> We add, and this is the second, that assuming that the reform of the finances was prompt and sufficient to our needs, we should nonetheless tax unearned incomes to relieve the burden on other forms of revenue? If we remember what was said in the first part of this brief; if we listen to the wishes of all enlightened citizens who have written about politics, if we consider all the evils that dividends on the state produce; we will be forced to agree that we must tax unearned revenues, not only like other goods, but even beyond: justice wants it, the public good demands it, the interest of good morals orders it, sixteen million citizens claim it. To fight such obvious maxims is to sacrifice one's homeland to a vile self-interest. Such feelings never penetrated the august sanctuary of the laws. To forget oneself, to sacrifice oneself for the people, such is the prerogative of the magistrates. Those most interested in pension immunity will be even more jealous to seek the extinction of this barbaric privilege. One can hardly believe that among the large number of rentiers who display their pomp in the capital, there are men who are traitorous enough towards their homelands, reckless enough, to raise their voices against such a fair and useful project. When the light is spread, when the nation is enlightened, personal interest is hidden, blushes and falls silent.

The text, fully in the spirit of the Enlightenment, calls for collective intelligence and affirms the condemnation of the unearned "rentes". According to Joël Félix, the solution recommended corresponds to the projects of L'Averdy who provided perhaps the inspiration for it. What better experiment than a young advisor from Bordeaux belonging to a large parlementaire family testing the response given to this proposal by the rentiers themselves? It must have been quite pleasant for the Comptroller General to see the son and son-in-law of "présidents au mortier" travelling through France in order to diffuse this memorandum which proposed to tax the income of annuitants.

Smith does not seem to have been insensitive when reading this. The evidence is twofold. On the one hand, he brought back in his three trunks of documents a copy of the article, in its printed form, which, until the end of his life, appeared prominently in his library alongside very rare works on economics and finance and what is more, he inscribed in his own hand the author's name on an index of the documents that he had bound together.

Furthermore, he quotes it in the *Wealth of Nations*:

> In France a much greater proportion of the publick debts consists in annuities for lives than in England. According to a memoir presented by the parliament of Bourdeaux to the king in 1764, the whole publick debt of France is estimated at twenty-four hundred millions of livres; of which the capital for which annuities for lives had been granted, is supposed to amount to three hundred millions, the eighth-part of the whole publick debt. The annuities themselves are computed to amount to thirty millions a year, the fourth part of one hundred and twenty millions, the supposed interest of that whole debt. These estimations, I know very well, are not exact, but having been presented by so very respectable a body as approximations to the truth, they may, I apprehend, be considered as such. It is not the different degrees of anxiety [4x5] in the two governments of France and England for the liberation of the publick revenue, which occasions this difference in their respective modes of borrowing. It arises altogether from the different views and interests of the lenders. (WN, V.ill, p. 918)

The quote focuses on the second part of the brief. Smith uses it to estimate the value of the "rentes" paid out in France. An annotation in the margin seems to indicate that he did not fully approve of the calculation, but this critical annotation may relate to a calculation error as well as to the method. By returning to the author, it may be possible to infer the content of his exchanges with Smith, exchanges that are highly plausible. Indeed, if there is no absolute certainty that Bacalan personally submitted his brief to Smith, the hypothesis of a meeting can be based on knowledge of the identity of the author of the brief and the coincidence of dates of Smith's stay in Bordeaux. Finally it is also possible that Smith heard about the brief in Bagnères through another connection. Indeed, as has been indicated, Françoise de Spens' brother was the representative at the assemblies of the nobility of Paul-Marie-Arnaud de Lavie, Isaac de Bacalan's brother-in-law. In any case, the documents exhumed by Joël Félix from the French National Archives give substance to the hypothesis of a meeting because it provides a precise timetable for the preparation and distribution of the brief:

> Mr. de L'Averdy suggested to Mr. de Bacalan that he undertake the trip to Paris, to communicate to him the particular knowledge that he could have of the province of Guyenne. He spoke for the King, Mr. de Bacalan obeyed. Thus from March 1764 until September, he was employed in negotiations and all kinds of work. Obliged to return to Bordeaux at this time which is that of our grape harvests, he was charged to travel to Burgundy, Dauphiné,

> Provence and Languedoc, to try to persuade the Parlements of Dijon, Grenoble, Aix, Toulouse and Bordeaux 1) with the recording of the precious edict, which was going to appear, of the freeing of the grain trade, 2) to ask the King for taxation on the rentiers, applicable to the debts of the State. Mr. de Bacalan succeeded beyond even what we had hoped. (Félix 1999, p. 142)

It is thus very likely that Smith, who returned to Bordeaux in September, was able to meet Bacalan who was also there, even if it cannot be completely excluded that it was during his stopover in Toulouse to meet the parlementaires that Bacalan was able to meet Smith, who had many relations in this milieu. In any case, the economic ideas of de Bacalan, who died early at thirty three, could only suit Smith. Alfred Sauvaire Jourdan, who at the beginning of the twentieth century devoted several publications to this "forgotten figure" of French economic thought during the Enlightenment, summarized his work as follows:

> Two of his writings, however, are worthy of the greatest interest: 1—First, *the Philosophical Paradoxes concerning the Freedom of Trade Among Nations* (1764), in which he defends the total and absolute freedom of trade in an eminently modern perspective, refusing mercantilism and adopting a generous view of the harmony of the interests of the nations of the world; 2—Secondly, *Observations made by M. de Bacalan, intendant du commerce, in his journey from Picardie, Artois, Haynaut and Flanders, in 1768*, where our author distills a vigorous criticism of corporations, regulations and the permanent intrusion of the law into economic affairs. (A. Sauvaire-Jourdan 1904)

Sauvaire-Jourdan had not pierced the anonymity of the document but Bacalan's work, which he published, left no doubt: the Bordeaux economist would have been of great interest to the Glasgow economist.

Thanks to these summer talks, Smith fulfilled part of the mission entrusted by the British Finance Minister and brought back a number of valuable documents and ideas from the city of Bordeaux where he met the very liberal bourgeoisie, consisting essentially of traders turned towards the open seas.

According to the letter sent to Hume on October 21, it is likely that the travellers returned to Bordeaux again in early November.

Before leaving the Atlantic port, the travellers took charge of Hew, the younger brother of the Duke, who had arrived from England via the port of Caen. The young aristocrat who was three years younger than his brother did not travel alone, of course, but in the company of Mr. Cook, Townshend's trusted man. Smith and his two students would return to the Lower Languedoc. Here Smith gives his impression of Bordeaux he visited in the Summer of 1764, close to England in multiple ways and which remained a crucial element for understanding his stay in France, and also Rouen then a great merchant port:

> If you except Rouen and Bourdeaux, there is little trade or industry in any of the parliament towns of France; and the inferior ranks of people, being chiefly maintained by the expence of the members of the courts of justice, and of those who come to plead before them, are in general idle and poor. The great trade of Rouen and Bourdeaux seems to be altogether the effect of their situation. Rouen is necessarily the entrepôt of almost all the goods which are brought either from foreign countries, or from the maritime provinces of France, for the consumption of the great city of Paris. [...] In the other parliament towns of France, very little more capital seems to be employed than what is necessary for supplying their own consumption; that is, little more than the smallest capital which can be employed in them. (WN, II.iii, 335)

4.6 To Montpellier on the Languedoc Canal

In mid-October 1764, the Scottish travellers, now three with the arrival of Hew, took the road to the Languedoc and their main town of residence, Toulouse. According to information from his correspondence, it is probable that Abbé Colbert returned to Toulouse at the very beginning of October, required by his archbishop who wished to entrust him with some missions, with a view to preparing the annual meeting of the Estates of Languedoc which they would all attend.

The return journey followed a route that Arthur Young describes a few years later. The climatic conditions were probably quite different and the climate less contrasted than during the fierce summer storms, but the contrast with Bordeaux is no less important and deserves to be recalled in the context of an eighteenth century journey.

While the housing around the city of Bordeaux spread out far from the centre, the city of Toulouse was on the contrary concentrated within its old walls, which were still intact, although totally unused, when Smith was there. Actually Toulouse did not enjoy much growth during the eighteenth century, whereas Bordeaux and its port benefited fully from the colonial trade and attracted many inhabitants to increasingly distant suburbs.

> The 13th. Pass Grisolles/where are well built cottages without glass, and some with no other light than the door, Dine at Pompinion at the Grand Soleil, an uncommonly good inn, where Capt. Plampin, who accompanied us thus far, took his leave. Here we had a violent storm of thunder and lightning, with rain much heavier I thought than I had known in England; but, when we set out for Toulouze, I was immediately convinced that such a violent shower had never fallen in that kingdom; for the destruction it had poured on the noble scene of cultivation, which but a moment before was smiling with exuberance, was terrible to behold. All now one scene of distress: the finest crops of wheat beaten so fiat to the ground, that I question whether they can ever rise again; other fields so inundated, that we were actually in doubt whether we were looking on what was lately land or always water. The ditches had been filled rapidly with mud, had overflowed the road, and swept dirt and gravel over the crops. Cross one of the finest plains of wheat that is any where to be seen; the storm, therefore, was fortunately partial. Pass St. Jorry; a noble road, but not better than in Limosin. It is a desert to the very gates; meet not more persons than if it were 100 miles from any town. (Young 1909, pp. 32–33)

The presence of Smith in Toulouse, mentioned since September 4 by Colonel Barré, is confirmed by a letter from Smith himself of October 21, 1764. On this very day he reported very succinctly about the summer stays he had just experienced. A change in the tone of his letter can be observed, by comparing it to his letters of the spring of 1764. A certain weariness can be detected and, why not, a certain nostalgia for his homeland and for a well-regulated Scottish life; nonetheless the October letter is full of enthusiasm. This seems quite logical since Smith and his pupil(s), thanks mainly to their stay in Bagnères, had made contact with the great aristocratic families of southern France.

From now on, they would be received on an equal footing in the intellectual circles of the city. In short, Smith and the Duke socialized relatively quickly and from this moment onwards would not live the life of travellers but that of two people inserted into the social life of the town, sharing the daily life and residences of the Toulouse bourgeoisie and its aristocrats. Smith and his pupils were still present in Toulouse on November 14, 1764. This is evidenced by the note he wrote to the Duke of Buccleuch, proof of the delivery of the sum of 125 pounds sterling which corresponded to his quarterly pension, part of an annual amount of 500 pounds sterling. Although comparisons of purchasing power between countries and periods are difficult to make, one can get an idea of the amount of these travel allowances from the conversion rates in the Channel Islands, where both the pound sterling and the livre tournois were in circulation. Thus in the eighteenth century, before the depreciation of the French currency during the Revolution, the pound sterling was worth 14.20 livres tournois. The £500 allocated to Smith for his annual expenses therefore corresponded to about 7000 Livres tournois. The discussions of the 1765 assembly of bishops on the "portion congrue" provide an element of comparison. In the eighteenth century, the priests of parishes did not directly receive the tithe collected by the church, which paid them a share to cover the normal expenses of a parish priest. This amounted to 300 Livres tournois in 1765. Certainly the "portion congrue" became, over time, an expression synonymous with poverty but with 7000 livres no doubt that Smith had the means to ensure a comfortable standard of living.

This new stay of a few weeks in Toulouse was devoted to the updating of the accounts, reading mail which had not followed during the trips as well as to the drafting of answers, and the rapid acclimatization of Hew, the Duke's younger brother.

But events are rushing on for Smith. If in Guyenne, they lived happy days in a "pays d'élection", they would find in the Languedoc a "pays d'état". To respect Townshend's wishes, Smith and his pupil had to become better acquainted with the political mores of this type of administration in the Languedoc. This can be deduced from the letter quoted, which details at length the experience which needed to be acquired regarding the administration of the Estates. What could be better than debates to garner a certain vision of political life, even if it was not on the French field that fate should call the Duke? Smith, always curious about public life and having to educate the Duke in the various forms of organization of a province of the Kingdom of France, could therefore not miss this important annual event.

The meeting of the Estates opened on November 29, 1764, in the town hall of Montpellier. They would close on January 7, 1765. Smith, his pupil, and his younger brother would attend all the sessions, even if some did not seem to be of major interest to them. It was a deliberate choice, made at the beginning of their journey and that nothing would alter afterwards.

The travellers decided, this time, to take the canal boat that provided transport for almost all travellers to the Estates. This mode of transport was most comfortable, and it made it possible to reach in four days from Toulouse the city of Agde, which was the closest to Montpellier, to their final destination. Staging points were organized for rest and dinner in inns especially dedicated to their wellbeing.

In 1764, when Smith and his students began their journey by this method, commercial navigation on the canal had already been open for almost a century. The inaugural voyage began on May 19, 1681, in the presence of members of the Parlement and Pierre de Riquet's two sons. The inaugural procession consisted of twenty-three standard size boats carrying goods from Toulouse to the Beaucaire fair. It was, at the time, the most important fair of the South of France, at the junction of multiple communication routes and different provinces. It is probable that the date of the inauguration and the method of its execution were chosen for this highly symbolic aspect.

Several indications suggest that the Languedoc canal was one of the reasons behind Toulouse's choice for the first part of this Grand Tour. Smith had certainly noted the dithyrambic presentation in the article "artificial channel" in the *Encyclopédie* of "this monument [...] comparable to all the great endeavours attempted by the Romans" while the article on "Languedoc" traced the history of this construction:

> It was in 1664 that Mr Colbert, who wanted to prepare sources of prosperity from afar, had the bold project of joining the two seas by the Languedoc canal promoted. This enterprise, already conceived in Charlemagne's time, if we are to believe some authors, was certainly considered under Francis I. From then on it was proposed to build a 14 league canal from Toulouse to Narbonne, from where one would have sailed by the river Aude, to the Mediterranean. Henry IV and his minister thought about it even more seriously, and found the thing possible, after a mature examination; but the glory was reserved for the reign of Louis XIV. Moreover the execution of the project was much more considerable than the project put forward by Mr. de Sully, since this channel was given 60 leagues in length, in order to promote the circulation of a greater quantity of food. The work lasted 16 years; it was begun in 1664, and completed in 1680, two or three years before Mr. Colbert's death; it is the most glorious monument of his ministry, by its utility, by its grandeur, and by its difficulties.

The *Encyclopédie* refers in a large number of articles to Bernard Forest de Bélidor (1698–1761), a French military engineer whose *Architecture Hydraulique, ou l'Art de conduire, d'élever et de ménager les eaux pour les différens besoins de la vie*, was authoritative, while his treatise *La Science des ingénieurs dans la conduite des travaux de fortification et d'architecture civile* (1729), extending Vauban's work, might have interested Smith for his developments on the establishment of estimates, where one can find an initial reflection on the scientific organization of work and the amount of work as a measure of values. Anyway, that book was in his library.

The canal that all Europe and Turkey wanted to see was a technical gamble, won thanks to the revolutionary processes employed for its construction. Most of the engineering structures along the 241 kilometres between Toulouse and Sète proved to be up to their expectations, even if maintenance was often heavy for the operators. The bet of having such a long canal, fed by one almost single source, in a universe where water was scarce, finally paid off.

The 63 metres of difference in altitude was resolved thanks to twenty-six locks operating on the Atlantic side, as well as the most delicate part, the one that was most subject to water supply issues, the Mediterranean side, which could boast seventy-three locks covering a difference in height of 189 metres. This was the most impressive feat and achievement in the eyes of a Scot who knew the specificities of his country and all the advantage that would result from such infrastructures.

In the busiest years of its construction, the building site counted more than 12,000 workers. It should be made clear here that these were workers who were employed and paid for their work and not peasants still subjected to forced labour as was the case for roads until the Revolution. Since then, however, the structure had undergone improvements and modifications, often major, in response to changes in traffic and technical developments.

Along the canal, Smith was also able to admire some 328 engineering structures, the number of which was equalled only by their complexity or ingenious design. There are too many to describe, but to understand the mechanism, one can refer to descriptive texts which accompany the plans. Although highly questionable on many aspects, the descriptive and non-scientific work *Canal royal du Languedoc* makes it possible to realize, thanks to a generous iconography, the quality and the architectural technicality of the various engineering features and structures none of which present the same characteristics (see Mukerji 2009).

The canal is indeed a typical example of a complex hydraulic system, invented by an engineer and modified by a technician like Vauban. It could only function over the centuries thanks to its regulation by people who could control the water supply through simple and coordinated mechanisms. This simple regulation became complex in its coordination and over the years, the construction of new engineering structures that allowed its control would become necessary.

From Toulouse to Sète, Smith, if he took the time, was able to admire the 126 bridges that permitted a continuity of traffic, but also the transport of local produce, or the 53 aqueducts that allowed a regular water supply management.

Finally Smith and the Duke certainly admired the seven canal bridges whose unique technique allowed it to cross rivers and offered travellers a unique view on nature.

But even more than the engineering structures and unique architecture of the canal, its slow layout is majestic. It seems to meander in the long Languedoc plain espousing the slightest ground contours. Although a means of rapid transportation in the eighteenth century, the canal seems to take its time, all along its route. What also struck Smith was the animation that could be seen all along the canal in the cities it crossed. This is certainly a difficult aspect to understand for a contemporary visitor, but the canal at that time was the main vector of trade and consequently of wealth creation. Along this extraordinary private property which extended for 187 kilometres, the Riquet family, or to be quite exact, the lords of Bonrepos, had the right to give justice on the canal estate. They were also free to set charges and taxes on goods using the transport route. Privileges that they constantly had to defend and that gave rise to multiple court cases, including against royal authority, which was also forced to pay a tax.

Commercial life on the canal was thus important, often passing far from the city centres for a simple topographical reason, or sometimes more political, a city having refused during the construction to be connected to the new traffic route. However, over the years, other towns or cities initially excluded from the traffic intervened with Pierre-Paul Riquet and in return for a financial contribution obtained a modification of the route of the canal. This was, for example, the case for Castelnaudary where the consuls of the city, noting that the route of the canal planned by Pierre Paul-Riquet ignored what was then only a large village, made contact with him. The city financed the modification of the route, which as a result would be less close to the ideal drainage line and would require some additional engineering structures.

But elected officials sometimes went even further. Having taken a first step, they became the canal's most fervent supporters. Castelnaudary would thus create an important basin which would become the largest inland port on the canal. The architecture of the city would be completely modified, as was the case for Carcassonne.

Once again Smith did not leave us any account of his journey across the Languedoc aboard the canal barges, but J. de La Lande can be referred to here: he tells us that

> Navigation on the canal is pleasant & convenient: it is a continuous garden. a post boat leaves every day, which goes, in four days, from Agde to Toulouse. We spend the nights in Sommail, in Trèbes, near Carcassonne, and in Castelnaudary, and we only pay 6 pounds for the four days.
>
> The only disadvantage is to change boats twenty-five times, to avoid passing through double, triple or quadruple locks, which would delay passengers too much, but the passage through the locks at Fonserane, near Béziers, is especially inconvenient at certain times; but there are transport carriages for passengers who do not want to go on foot. (de La Lande 1775, p. 90)

By way of illustration and to compensate for the absence of a travel diary, Father Labat's diary can be drawn on again: he undertook the same journey a few years before the Duke and his party.

> I left Toulouse on Tuesday 23 March (1706) to go to Béziers by canal. Nothing compares to this convenience. I will not describe this magnificent work, enough other people have done it before me. It is certainly the most beautiful, most convenient and best executed thing you can imagine in the world. The canals which cut Holland and the Netherlands have nothing approaching it, since it was not a question of digging ditches in a low and united ground, but of making the construction go up over the mountains, and make them go down as quietly as they had been made to go up, to make boats pass along with the water which carries them over, and under rivers which would spoil it by the sediment which they would bring, if they entered there; to pass through a considerable mountain that has been dug, so that the canal occupies the middle, and that leaves a track on each side for the convenience of horses and foot people, in a word to overcome nature by the force of art. (Labat 1730, t.2, p. 16)

The journey continued, and the Father gives us some technical details on how to travel:

> On the banks of this canal, there are well-built and well-stocked hotels where one must dine or sleep, with chapels where there is always a priest ready to begin mass when there is an obligation to hear it, as soon as the boat arrives. There's usually pretty good company in these boats. There is no shortage of thieves, and if you are not on your guard, it is rare not to lose something there. (Ibidem., p. 18)

These trips were always the object of social events that would federate for a few days a micro-society, which had in common only the desire to reach without hindrance their final destination. As proof, as soon as the destination was reached, people dispersed and no longer spoke to each other, the journey over, society dissolved:

> A lady of quality who was in my boat approached a woman who appeared to be a good bourgeoise, very well dressed, who had a small basket beside her, covered with a white towel. This lady, even more curious than the animals of her species, did not fail to inform herself of the journey of the person who was with her and finally asked to know what she was carrying in her first basket.
>
> This woman answered as best she could all the questions the lady asked her, but she always skilfully avoided uncovering her basket. This resistance increased the lady's curiosity and she pressed the woman so hard as to the basket that she was forced to say she would let her see it at dinner. having got to that moment, the woman wanted to escape because she was leaving the canal and the boat there, but there was no such chance. The lady summoned her to keep her word and uncovered the basket herself, but what a surprise, when she found that it was filled with ropes all ready to put around the necks of a few thieves, that the husband of the woman in question was going to hang in a nearby town. (Ibidem., p. 18)

Father Labat's travel account is quite representative of this kind of literature. The details of everyday life don't count. It does not describe the many economic activities on the banks. For the people of the time, only their fellow men matter. The many proletarians who are busy searching for, pulling and pushing goods and raw materials do not seem to belong to the same world. They are outside the micro-society and are therefore excluded from the field of vision (Fig. 4.2).

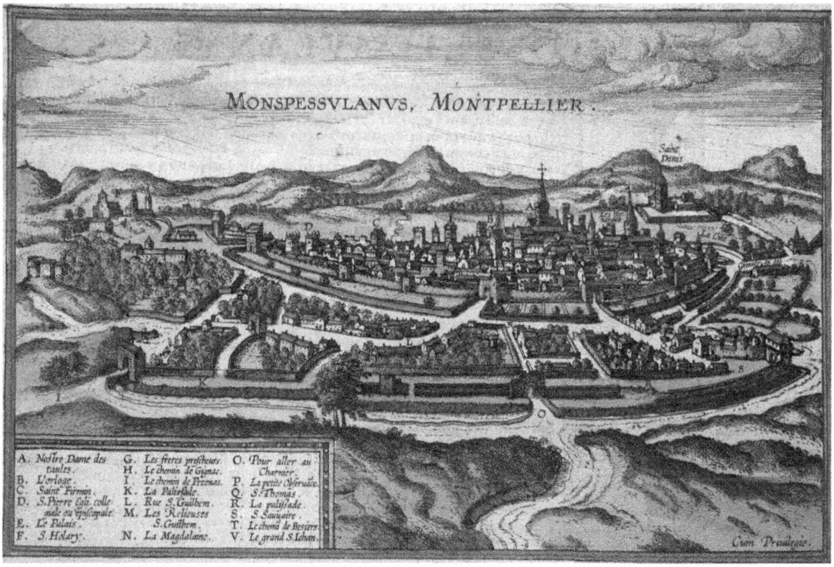

Fig. 4.2 Boats on the Canal (Voies navigables de France, archives des canaux du Midi (ACM-FA721-01))

Mrs. Cradock is more observant and on May 21, 1785, she notes in Béziers "with surprise that, in [her] hotel, all the maids are barefoot, the mistress of the dwelling alone is shod: it is, it seems, the custom of the country", and especially keeps a rather mixed remembrance of the following night:

> The dinner at the table d'hôte was excellent and well served. We were about thirty at the table, and, as it is fashionable to travel by water in this season, almost all the passengers belonged to high society; most were going to Toulouse to attend the Fête-Dieu, one of the biggest festivals of the year. The hotel was so full that Mr. Cradock had to share his room with seven other gentlemen. I shared mine with my maid and the poultry, for I will never forget the abundance and diversity of dirt accumulated in this room. Finally, we were so devoured by all kinds of insects, that at three o'clock I left this disgusting nest, and went for a walk and breathed the fresh air until six o'clock. (Cradock and Delphin-Balleyguier 1896, pp. 168–169)

Scientific observation illustrating the simple passage from an agriculture adapted to an Atlantic climate to that of a Mediterranean climate seems reserved for explorers or more attentive travellers such as Charles-Marie de La Condamine or Arthur Young a few years later.

However, each journey was the subject of an anecdote, a slight tale that could be understood by all, placing itself in the limelight with an element of wit in a story that was often dull. This type of literary or more exactly epistolary process is also frequently used by Abbé Colbert as in his letter to the Duke (and his tutor) in the autumn of 1766. This worthy Abbé, while keeping to the great seriousness expected of his function, relates the same type of stories where fun is had with the slightest fact that disturbs the micro-society that is formed in any closed place that concentrates travellers. The anecdote then acts as a catalyst to find out and determine who is part of this temporary society and who, for various reasons, is excluded as we can see in the letter of Abbé Colbert whose introduction we quoted before (p. XXX & p. XXX).

> I was from Lyon to Avignon by the Rhône, our boat ran a great danger near a mill; in Avignon I got embarked in a coach whose wheels were supposed to roll us but more properly make us feel as being broken on the wheels[12] my fellow travellers were a Jew and a Capuchin named Father Evangelist, sick, dirty, bearded, stinking and foolish; However good a Catholic I am, in that moment I renounced my religion and became the most fearless Huguenot, I cursed St. Francis the patron saint of the stinking father, I gave him and all his order to the great devil Lucifer and I wished that there were no more religions where Capuchins were allowed. Despite my imprecations I suffered no less from the smell and heat, but finally I arrived in Montpellier, where I saw Mr. Ré who asked about your news in Greek verses. (Letter dated 09/18/1766)

In Abbé Colbert's letters, the anecdotes underline his mastery of discourse but they also show us that Colbert was very close to his Scottish visitors, he shared many experiences with them and was deliberately familiar. There was no need for long circumvolutions, the anecdote by its real

[12] Colbert in French plays word as the coach is called "roulante" (for rolling wheels) and he suggests that it should be called "rouante" (breaking wheels). The pun is underlined by the Abbé who seems to want to increase the emphasis of his good word or make himself surer of his good understanding by a young aristocrat who certainly speaks French but does not yet master all its subtleties.

side, taking into account the lived fact, is enough on its own to evoke shared memories. It acts in the narrative as a discursive metaphor of the experience lived in common. Abbé Colbert injects a great dose of humour and even displays it against the Catholic Church on which he depends and which welcomed him. It is probably also a private correspondence between friends who have established trust. He certainly knows Adam Smith's religious ideas and wants to show that he is capable of looking outside any confessional blinders. The last sentence, no doubt equally caustic, indicates that Smith and his pupil also met a certain Mr Ré during their stay in Montpellier, but this scholar versed in Greek literature has not been identified, unless the Greek verses are only a joke here.

Among the many goods that circulated along the waterway, there was one that more specifically drew Smith's attention. It was a local product: wine. The wine that can usually be described as "ordinaire" travelled only as far as Toulouse. Coming from the Languedoc vineyards, it was exchanged, along the route in particular, at the ports of Somail or Castelnaudary for wheat or other cereals. Thus the testimony of this canal trader, Pierre Fayet, seventeen years old, who wrote in a letter[13]:

> For 90 years my father and his grandfather have lived only through the Languedoc canal. My grandfather was a young contractor on the canal while it was still under construction.

Another peculiarity that Smith notes is the very particular way in which the canal was operated by its owners. Ownership of the canal was controlled by the heirs of the Riquet family who were direct descendants of the founder and main contractor, Pierre-Paul.

At the time of Smith's stay, the ownership but also the management of the canal were the responsibility of the two branches of the family, Bonrepos and Caraman, heirs of the original entrepreneur. Over the years, they had not without difficulty maintained the estate attributed by the King and by the "Grand Colbert" to the canal builder, Pierre-Paul Riquet (born at an unknown date between 1604 and 1609 in Béziers, died on October 1, 1680, in Toulouse). Already during Pierre-Paul's lifetime, his eldest son Mathias (1638–1714), Baron de Bonrepos, Count of Caraman, and President of the Parlement of Toulouse, assisted his father and upon

[13]Archives Privées du Canal du Languedoc, Toulouse "Commerce des Grains de 1657 à 1784" (Grain trade from 1657 to 1784).

his death he inherited two thirds of the shares and assumed responsibility for the completion of the works. Mathias married three times and he had a son from his second marriage to Madeleine de Broglie, Victor Pierre François, Lord of Albiac (1698–1760), and from the third, Jean-Gabriel, who was Attorney General in the Parlement of Toulouse, the same person who pronounced the indictment against the Jesuits and against Calas. He held one third of the shares in the canal but his position was strategic since the Parlement of Toulouse was competent in all appeals concerning the conflicts relating to the canal: he resided in Toulouse, he was prosecutor general at the Parlement of Toulouse and as owner of the fief he also had the right of justice all along the 235 kilometres of the canal.

The builder had a younger son named after his father, Pierre-Paul (1646–1730). A soldier, he finished his career as lieutenant-general of the King's armies and he did not seem interested in the canal. Pierre-Paul II had inherited one third of the shares of the canal. He had also regained the title of Comte de Caraman. When he died childless, the title went to his oldest nephew, Victor-Pierre, who had inherited two thirds of the canal from his father.

Smith has just met him in Bagnères-de-Bigorre during his holiday. He was undoubtedly impressed by an exceptional career. His military career began as a "black" musketeer at thirteen, then as a cavalry captain at sixteen he took part in the battle of Fontenoy. On May 11, 1745, he narrowly escaped death, when a bullet lodged in the saddle of his horse. At the age of eighteen, he was appointed colonel of dragoons, then campaigned in Flanders during the Seven Years' War as a brigadier before finishing as "maréchal de camp" (major general). His military career did not prevent him from taking a close interest in the management of the canal. Passionate about horticulture, he was naturally concerned about the issue of plantations along the canal on the "terriers" (twenty metre strips on either side of the canal belonging to the Riquet family) which would ensure substantial income for the Riquet family.

The conditions under which the canal operated fascinated an attentive observer like Smith, curious about the role of law in the development of Western societies during the transition from feudal to capitalist society, and the legal uncertainties that this transition created.

The construction of the canal had been financed essentially by the King and the Estates of the Languedoc, but at the time when the King accepted the handing over of the canal (March 16, 1685), the two brothers were in a very difficult financial situation. Not only had their father incurred more than two million livres of debt, but it was clear that additional improvements were needed to make the management of the canal profitable. To complicate the situation, a question concerning the status of the canal was the subject of a legal dispute. The original title document to the canal stated:

> By his edict of October 1666 and by his letters patent of the 7th of the same month and the same year, duly registered, King Louis XIV created and erected the Canal-royal de communication des Deux Mers, with its banks and diversion channels, in a fief immediately under the jurisdiction of the Crown, with the right of high, medium and low justice in all its extent, over forty leagues of Languedoc, which make about fifty common leagues in the vicinity of Paris. Justice is administered there by a first judge-chatellan, six senior lieutenants, and six judicial prosecutors. The appeal of the sentences of this jurisdiction goes directly to the Grand'Chambre of the Parlement of Toulouse. The owners of the canal have the right to build a castle with crenellated towers, to place there the headquarters of their justice. The owner and his heirs and successors must enjoy it in full ownership, incommutably and in perpetuity, without this effect ever being deemed to be state property, nor subject to redemption, since the king did not possess it, and the construction, as well as the incommutable ownership, the two being inseparable: this is the first condition of the enterprise, as King Louis XIV declared by the edict of 7 October 1666.

During medieval and modern times, the fiefdom refers to a property or real estate income originally entrusted as payment for a service. This feudal conception was opposed by an economic conception of general well-being clearly set out during the meeting of the Languedoc Estates held in Béziers in 1665, according to which "this region that the sun and light make prosperous lacks the means of transport which would restore trade, bring back prosperity to the factories, promote the production of its fruits and allow for receiving them easily from neighbouring provinces or foreign countries" (quoted in Maistre 1998, pp. 132–133). The compromise solution was to entrust the canal as a feudal possession to Riquet and his descendants in perpetuity, the State reserving only the right to fix tolls and also certain supervision rights so as to guarantee efficient management and conservation of the facilities.

When Louis XIV died in 1715, some jurists noted that a gift from the sovereign could not be perpetual but that it had to stop when the sovereign died. The heirs replied that at the time the fief had been granted (1666), the canal did not exist and that property that did not exist could not be considered as belonging to the royal domain. At the time of Smith's voyage, the matter had just been settled for the benefit of Riquet's descendants. Adam Smith probably did not lack topics of conversation with the descendants of Riquet, uncle and nephew that he met.

The management of the commercial services was the object of all the attentions as to its quality. The boats were the property of "owners" (independent contractors) who owned one or more boats. Some specialized in passenger transportation, others, more numerous, were dedicated to freight transportation. The managers were very attentive to the quality of the transport and, strengthened by their monopoly, in the first decades of the exploitation of the canal were to be very attentive in their concern regarding the qualities of boat owners. All boat owners had to respect a code of "boatmaster's good conduct". The rules of conduct of the owners were, for example, dependent on the schedules of the lock operators, who were direct employees of the Riquet family. The regulations also set some rules to make navigation less dangerous. Although it seems rather strange, after eight decades of exploitation, some passages remained very dangerous in the eighteenth century because the overall layout was not perfect. Particularly during flood periods, delicate stretches existed near rivers.

But more than the administrative and regulatory side, the boatmaster had to be open and available for the control of goods as well as for the payment of taxes and duties. These rights were fairly detailed and demonstrated a desire for justice:

- A so-called *droit de voiture* was paid when each boat was rented and was fixed by the canal administration.
- A toll (rather reduced) of five "sous" at the opening of each lock whatever the load of the boat.
- Finally, a toll was levied on all goods, commodities, and other things seen on the canal.

Of course, for the sake of justice, the rates were not adjusted for each customer but were displayed so that all users, including ordinary travellers, were aware of the taxation method in force:

> Article 42: The tariffs shall be printed on a placard and posted in the most visible place of the ports and collection offices. They will essentially contain the ratio of weight to volume of all objects whose weight could be easily verified and found only by measurement.

> Article 43: All loads may be checked not only at the office of departure and arrival but also at all collection offices and other intermediate points where loading and unloading may take place.

The travellers were therefore witnesses to this intense traffic where the boatmen possessed perfect control of their working tools. If they were independent and therefore owners of the boats, they were chosen because of their human quality of probity and competence. It is therefore not surprising that the first quotation concerning the canal in Book V of the *Wealth of Nations* is an extract that concerns not the financial and economic aspect of the canal but its technical and physical aspect, in line with Belidor's work. Smith writes:

> The strength of a bridge must be suited to the number and weight of the carriages, which are likely to pass over it. The depth and the supply of water for a navigable canal must be proportioned to the number and tunnage of the lighters, which are likely to carry goods upon it; the extent of a harbour to the number of the shipping which are likely to take shelter in it. (WN, V.i.d, p. 724)

References

Boulaine, Jean & Legros Jean-Paul. 1998, *D'Olivier de Serres à René Dumont. Portraits d'agronomes*. Paris: Tec & Doc Lavoisier. pp. 45–56.

Burton, John Hill. 1849. *Letters of eminent persons, addressed to David Hume*. Edinburgh: W. Blackwood and Sons.

Cadilhon, F. (2008), *Jean-Baptiste de Secondat de Montesquieu: au nom du père*. Bordeaux: Presses universitaires de Bordeaux.

Ferguson, Adam, Campbell Mossner, Ernest. 1960. Of the Principle of Moral Estimation: A Discourse between David Hume, Robert Clerk, and Adam Smith": An Unpublished MS by Adam Ferguson. *Journal of the History of Ideas*, Vol. 21, No. 2 (Apr.–June), pp. 222–232.

Coke, Mary Campbell & James Archibald Home. 1889. *The letters and journals of Lady Mary Coke*. Edinburgh: David Douglas.

Cradock, Anna Francesca, & O Delphin-Balleyguier. 1896. *Journal de Mme Cradock: voyage en France (1783–1786)*. Paris: Perrin.

Dawson, Deidre & Pierre Morère. 2004. *Scotland and France in the Enlightenment*. Lewisburg [Pa.]: Bucknell Univ. Press [u.a.].

Delpit, Jules. 1888. *Le fils de Montesquieu*. Bordeaux: P. Chollet.

Doyle, William. 1967. *The parlement of Bordeaux and the end of the old regime: 1771–1790*. Thesis PhD, University of Oxford.

Donnadieu, Jean-Louis. 2009. *Un grand seigneur et ses esclaves: le comte de Noé entre Antilles et Gascogne, 1728–1816*. Toulouse: Presses universitaires du Mirail.

Faur, Louis François. 1792. *Vie privée du maréchal de Richelieu, contenant ses amours et intrigues et tout ce qui a rapport aux divers rôles qu'a joués cet homme célèbre pendant plus de quatre-vingt ans*, tome II, Paris: Buisson.

Félix, José. 1999. *Finances et politique au siècle des Lumières: le ministère L'Averdy, 1763–1768*. Paris: Comité pour l'histoire économique et financière de la France.

Ferguson, Adam & Ernest Campbell Mossner. 1960. "Of the Principle of Moral Estimation: A Discourse between David Hume, Robert Clerk, and Adam Smith": An Unpublished MS *Journal of the History of Ideas*, Vol. 21, No. 2 (Apr.–June). pp. 222–232.

Hume, David. 1760 [1752], *Essays and treatises on several subjects*, Vol. II. London: Millar.

Hume, David & John Young Thomson Greig. 1932. *Letters*. Oxford: Clarendon Press.

La Lande de, Jérôme. 1774–1775. Lettre sur le canal de Languedoc, *Le journal des sçavans*, janvier, pp. 18–29, février, pp. 85–93.

Labat, Jean-Baptiste. 1730. V*oyages du P. Labat, … en Espagne et en Italie*. Tome premier [-VIII], Paris: Delespine.

Maistre, André. 1998. *Le Canal des deux-mers: canal royal du Languedoc, 1666–1810*. Toulouse: Privat.

Marmontel, Jean-François & François Barrière. 1846. *Mémoires de Marmontel*. Paris: Firmin Didot frères.

Merat François Victor, Adrien & Jacques Lens (de). 1829. *Universel de Matière Médicale et de thérapeutique générale*. Paris: Éditions Baillère.

Montesquieu Charles de Secondat. 2012. *My thoughts* (*Mes pensées* translated by Henry C. Clark). Indianapolis, Indiana: Liberty Fund.

Mukerji, Chandra. 2009. *Impossible engineering: technology and territoriality on the Canal du Midi*. Princeton Univ. Press.

Necker, Jacques. 1821. *Œuvres complètes*, t. IV: *De l'administration des finances de la France* (1784). Paris: Treuttel & Würtz.

Ravel-Cordonnier, Agnès, Les courtisans, le Roi et le gouvernement du pays: noblesse aulique et décentralisation dans la France du XVIIIe siècle in Legay Marie-Laure & Roger, Baury. 2009. *L'invention de la décentralisation: noblesse et pouvoirs intermédiaires en France et en Europe, XVIIe-XIXe siècle*. Villeneuve d'Ascq: Presses universitaires du Septentrion. pp. 205–28.

Richelieu, Louis-François-Armand de Vignerot Du Plessis (duc de), *Mémoires du maréchal duc de Richelieu, avec avant-propos et notes par m. Fs. Barrière*. Paris: Firmin-Didot. 1889.

Sauvaire-Jourdan, François. 1904. Un économiste bordelais du XVIIIe siècle: Isaac de Bacalan *Revue philomathique de Bordeaux et du Sud-Ouest*, septième année, no. 12, 1er décembre, pp. 529–540.

Secondat, Jean-Baptiste. 1750. *Observations de physique et d'histoire naturelle sur les eaux minérales de Dax, de Bagnères et de Barèges, sur l'influence de l'air dans la chaleur des liqueurs bouillantes, et dans leur congélation....* Paris: Huart et Moreau fils.

Swinburne, Henri. 1787. *Travels through Spain, in the years 1775 and 1776.* London: Printed by J. Davis.

Voltaire. 1832. *Oeuvres complètes. Correspondance générale*, tome VIII. Paris: Librairie de Fortic.

Voltaire. 1856. *Lettres inédites de Voltaire recueillies par M. de Cayrol.* T. 1. Paris: Didier.

Voltaire. 1859 [1745]. *The Henriade; with the Battle of Fontenoy [...] from the French of M. de Voltaire; with notes of all the commentators.* New York: Derby & Jackson.

Young, Arthur, and Matilda Betham-Edwards. 1909. *Arthur Young's Travels in France during the years 1787, 1788, 1789.* London: Bell.

CHAPTER 5

The Languedoc Estates and the End of the Stay

After four days of navigation on the canal and shortly before the opening of the Languedoc Estates, Smith, the Duke of Buccleuch, his brother, and the Abbé Colbert arrived in Montpellier around November 20, 1764. This town was a rather traditional stage in the Grand Tours which led the British elites on their search for Roman grandeur. From Sète to Montpellier, travellers also reached the Mediterranean, along which England was beginning to establish itself at the same time as the Austrian and Russian empires. But distant geopolitical stakes undoubtedly held their attention less than the functioning of a deliberative assembly which attempted, despite competing interests, to elaborate an economic policy. These economic concerns and the triumph of free trade were also sensitive topics during the second year of their stay in Toulouse, a city which had been won over to physiocratic ideas (Fig. 5.1).

5.1 Montpellier and the Meeting of the Languedoc Estates

Montpellier was the third largest city, after Toulouse and Bordeaux, in which Smith stayed. However, his sojourn was in rather exceptional circumstances as the regular attendance of an assembly transformed the city of Montpellier for a few weeks. But beyond the object of this new stay, a visit to Montpellier was also clearly the discovery of the Mediterranean world for a man who had poured over Latin and Greek texts all his life.

A. Alcouffe, P. Massot-Bordenave, *Adam Smith in Toulouse and Occitania*, https://doi.org/10.1007/978-3-030-46578-0_5

Fig. 5.1 Montpellier on the Map of Cassini (eighteenth century). (Source: Archives Municipales Montpellier [18172658])

The city of Agde in particular, on the canal, began as a Greek trading post, a dependency of the city of Marseilles, and although distant from the Greek world both in time and in space, this would be the only direct contact between that vanished society of antiquity and the Scottish traveller. It would be the same for the city of Montpellier and that of Nîmes for the ruins of the Roman and Gallo-Roman world that the latter preserves. It is certain that this episode in the stay, even if it does not seem to raise any particular emotion in the very meagre correspondence of the economist, was one of the criteria in planning the trip and Smith's visit to the Languedoc Estates.

To verify this, it is worth referring to the readings that Smith had suggested to the young Duke as early as 1759. They included numerous texts by authors from the great Latin world born around this *Mare Nostrum*, on whose coast our travellers would be staying. It is more surprising, however, that Smith did not seek to explore the Mediterranean world more, as was generally the case with the Grand Tours which often included a visit to Italy. On the contrary, it was planned that the Tour would end with a visit to the Netherlands and Germany. Everything happened as if Smith had sensed the shift of the Mediterranean world economy towards the Atlantic world, described by Fernand Braudel (1979, p. 144).

The description of the city of Montpellier, such as Smith could have imagined and read about before leaving for his journey, and of which he could have kept a memory—since this work is the only account of a voyage in France which appears in the library of Kirkcaldy—is provided to us once again by Piganiol de la Force, who provided a picturesque description of the South of France:

> Montpellier, in Latin *Mons Puellarum*, is situated on a hill, the river Lez watering its foot. This city was built after Charlemagne had Maguelonne demolished, because it served as a refuge for the Saracens. The bishopric and the inhabitants were transferred to Soustancion, which was the capital of a county of the same name; but the air was so unhealthy that they decided to abandon it. They also decided to build a new city on a mountain which was a mile away, resulting in the origin of the city of Montpellier. It is believed that they were determined to choose this land by the holiness of two girls who had lived there in a kind of hermitage, and that this is what influenced the name of the town of *Mons Puellarum*.
>
> Montpellier was one of the most beautiful cities of the kingdom, although its streets were sometimes describes as irregular (mal percée) and its situation was both high and low. It had seven gates and a fairly large number of churches. Houses made little show on the outside, but were clean on the inside. The house belonging to the Président des Plans was beautiful, convenient, and provided some of the best accommodation in the whole city. The Princes of France resided there in 1701, during their stay in Montpellier. The cathedral church was sacred to Saint Peter. It was a fairly large building, with only one nave, without aisles. In the choir there were three paintings from the life of Saint Peter, the middle of which was by Sébastien Bourdon.[1]

[1] Sébastien Bourdon (1616–1671) is a painter from Montpellier whose talent first led him to Rome and then to Paris where he died.

King Louis XIII, at the head of an army, besieged this city, which had been occupied by the Calvinists in 1623, and having made himself its master after a long resistance, had a citadel built there which commanded the city and the countryside. Its shape was a perfect square, composed of four bastions. Around it there was a ditch full of water, which featured three half-moon fortifications of earth. The ditches of these half moons were dry, because they were higher than the body of the square. The whole citadel was surrounded by a covered path and glacis.

This city was the see of a bishop, had a Chambers of Accounts, a 'cour des aides',[2] a finance bureau and a Présidial.[3] La Canourgue was a terrace where one could walk in the evening. The Peyron was a promenade out of town. It was one of the most beautiful squares of the kingdom by its situation and by the sights that could be viewed from all sides, as well over the sea, the Pyrenees, and the neighbouring mountains. A bronze equestrian statue of Louis XIV, made by Coysevox, added to the charm of the square. The city gate through which one went to this promenade was a triumphal arch built at much expense, accompanied by four perfectly beautiful bas-reliefs. As one exited through this arch, one could see the King's Garden on one's right. It was built in 1598 at the request of André de Laurens,[4] Chancellor of the Faculty of Medicine, and at the time principal doctor to King Henry IV. This garden was very well maintained, and had six large main driveways, some of which formed an amphitheatre. Those of medicinal plants were raised and covered with stone. There were channels from place to place, and taps to provide water for them.

The people of Montpellier are human, love society and foreigners. The women are beautiful, and it is hard to understand how one city can produce so many beautiful people. (Piganiol 1740, t.2, pp. 51–55)

[2] The "cour des aides" (or in eighteenth century spelling cour des aydes) were sovereign courts in Ancien Régime France, primarily concerned with customs, but also other matters of public finance. They exercised some control over certain excise taxes and octroi duties, which were regarded as of a different nature from the taille, the gabelle, and the general imposts of the kingdom.

[3] The Présidial was a judicial tribunal of the French Ancien Régime, set up in January 1551 (Old Style) by Henry II of France and suppressed by a decree of the National Assembly in 1790.

[4] André de Laurens (1558–1609) is a French scientist from Arles. He naturally studied medicine at the University of Montpellier, which for centuries was the best medical university in France (at least in the south of the kingdom). He was also the doctor of Catherine de Medici, then quite logically that of King Henry IV of France. He died in 1609 in Paris. He was particularly interested in melancholy, a disease that will develop more and more as life becomes more industrial and normalized.

This was a rather flattering description of the town, but it must be noted that the city of Montpellier had just undergone an important period of development thanks to the trade it was developing with neighbouring countries. This was a trade which was based on agricultural production but also grew owing to the textile industry ever present in the Bas-Languedoc, from Nîmes to Carcassonne. The city also possessed a very particular industry of which it had a quasi-monopoly of manufacture: the colour green. Today called "copper acetate" or in popular language "verdigris", verdet is the result of a chemical transformation described in an article in the *Encyclopédie*. It is used as a colouring matter but also in the field of medicine, in which case it is a virulent poison. This industry was exporting strongly since the majority of the production (around 15,000 quintals (48.95 kg) in 1777) was dispatched via the Languedoc canal, then the port of Bordeaux towards the United Provinces, and Northern Germany. This industry gave rise to a real chemical industry whose most famous representative was Jean-Antoine Chaptal (1756–1832). Chaptal would be at the centre of the origin of the collaboration between producers and academics, as he would contribute significantly to creating a real, practical link between industry and research in France.

The first industrial production that enriched the Montpellier region was the production of wool blankets and fabrics that were traditionally exported to the Levant, but also to Spain and the French colonies.

If it was the regional economy that explained the wealth of the city, it was further reflected in the architecture of the town thanks to the statesman Smith had just met in Bordeaux, the current governor of Guyenne, who was the governor of the province of Languedoc from 1755 to 1762. The interest that the Duke of Richelieu had for the South of France and its Mediterranean façade has already been pointed out. A man of entertainment and pleasure, he had greatly transformed the city of Montpellier. It is to him that we owe the numerous promenades and terraces of the city, but also the modern Théatre de la Comédie which was subsequently able to offer all types of plays and music concerts to the society of the town. If the city presented all the advantages of an average size, it was classified, with a population of 35,000, as the eleventh city of France in 1750 (by comparison, Toulouse, with 45,000 inhabitants, occupied the eighth rank after Paris, Lyon, Marseille, Rouen, Lille, Bordeaux, Nantes and Versailles).

However, if one were to refer to the quality of public and collective facilities, the city of Montpellier corresponded more to a real metropolis, known throughout Europe, than to a simple provincial city. This celebrity was due to the influence of its university and more precisely its medical faculty.

Montpellier, a metropolis, was also in the centre of the Languedoc province, which at that time still included the Vivarais and the Gévaudan, two large regions that form the southern part of the Massif Central. They were directly accessible from the city. Communications, particularly with Paris and Versailles, were also facilitated by the proximity of the Rhône valley.

As has been seen, the east-west communication route was the Languedoc canal, which put Toulouse about four days away. It was doubled by a road as good as the period could devise.

As a result of these changes in infrastructure since 1737, the Languedoc Estates ceased to be held alternately in the other cities of the province, in order to settle permanently in Montpellier. They adopted the principle of an annual session, which was a good indicator of their importance in the province as well as the part played by the people in determining their living environment.

France, as has been mentioned, was divided into two major types of provinces: Pays d'Etat and Pays d'Election. The rise of absolutism since the century of Louis XIV tended to encroach upon the prerogatives of the Estates as there were only four large provinces in which the Etats still played an important role: Brittany, Burgundy, Artois, and Languedoc.

The neighbouring province of Provence, although it did have the status of a Pays d'Etat, organized its meetings in an increasingly irregular manner, which certainly hindered what can be called an "embryo of democracy". This "democratic" life was often rather a formality, but the Languedoc was somewhat of an exception, both in terms of the periodicity of the assemblies' meetings and the Estates' involvement in economic life. This fully justified Smith's decision to attend the 1764 session, for it must be remembered that Charles Townshend gave him not only the role of "bearleader" but also that of observer, in order to understand how France dealt with the serious problem of public debt in Europe as well as the way in which it organized its economy in this period of industrial revolution. This last question had cyclical aspects, as France had just lost its colonies in North America, which the textile industry of the province of

Languedoc had found to be until then an important outlet for all fabrics and wool of average or poor quality.

> Taken as a whole, small draperies were therefore developing well. While the growth of the domestic market had played an undeniable role in this dynamism, the appeal of foreign markets—Spain and its colonies in particular—had been equally decisive. The manufacturers of large draperies had almost succeeded in being concentrated solely on the market of the Echelles du Levant (the ports of the Levant) so much had this proved promising. But for almost all small draperies, the Spanish market with its colonial dependencies was of considerable interest. As for the North American colonies, particularly Canada, they also offered a major outlet for the fabrics of Castrais or the generality of Montauban. Finally, the Italian, Swiss and, to a lesser extent, Northern European markets also played a significant role. (Minovez 2012, pp. 74–76)

The question is far from anecdotal, since, the textile industries were at the forefront of the industrial revolution and the theory of international trade, as Isaac de Bacalan began to elaborate it, deliberately took as a privileged illustration, specialization in cloth as opposed to specialization in wine production, several decades before David Ricardo.

5.1.1 The Estates of Languedoc, the Embryo of Legislative Power

If it was in Montpellier that the Languedoc Estates had met annually for nearly thirty years, when Smith attended, they were not a recent creation but the result of a long historical process.

In his *Historical essay on the Estates General of the Languedoc*, which complements Dom Joseph Vaissette's *Histoire du Languedoc*, Baron Trouvé dates the first edition of the Languedoc Estates General to 1351, when, during the Hundred Years' War, King Philip VI turned to his kingdom in search of funding. It was already a matter of finding financial resources for the State. In the centuries that followed, the Estates lost their importance as the central government developed a tax system to be implemented throughout the kingdom. The role of the Estates would then be above all to introduce a minimum of justice or equity in the methods of calculating levies.

Its main role would therefore be to collect taxes and vote for the "don gratuit", the "free donation" which would soon be set at a fixed amount of three million livres. The Estates retained the task of distributing the tax as fairly as possible between the various territories according to the wealth they produced, hence the demand for a plethora of briefs and formulas of calculation which very often failed, from the lack of statistical tools and mathematical rules subscribed to by all.

The Estates General of the Languedoc were made up of the three orders that were also found in the Estates General of France, namely the nobility, the clergy, and what was called the Third Estate. The Estates included three kinds of deputies, depending on whether their tax constituencies belonged to a "seigneurie", ecclesiastical, secular, or other. This last category was constituted by the cities that possessed the privilege of criminal jurisdiction contrary to what Abbé Sieyès affirmed in his famous pamphlet *What Is the Third Estate*? the deputies did not represent the members of their order, that is those of the nobility the nobles, those of the clergy the clergymen and the deputies of the Third Estate the commoners, but all the population of their constituencies. From this characteristic of representation flowed another: the vote was nominative, thus allowing a greater freedom in the discussions. However, as there was no vote discipline by order, there was always the possibility of achieving majorities on each debated subject. The assembly was governed by internal regulations that had been amended and modified over the centuries (Fig. 5.2).

In 1764, the assembly had twenty-three representatives of the nobility. Deputies came from every city in the province. Depending on the size of the city, the number of representatives could vary, and thus Toulouse had three representatives at the assembly while a city like Castres had only one. The number of clergymen present and having the right to deliberate and vote was fixed at the same number. In the case of the clergy, there was no election or co-optation since each diocese was represented by its bishop.

As the bishoprics did not coincide exactly with the towns, in some cases, as in the case of the bishopric of Rieux in the Pyrenean foothills, now disappeared, no deputy from the nobility came to echo the bishop's voice. Finally, in the interests of justice, the Third Estate was represented by forty-six deputies (their number was equal to the sum of the other two orders). Here again the distribution was as fair as possible, but it also reflected the weight of ancient history and traditions that evolved only slowly. The clergy was represented by the three archbishops and twenty bishops of the province. The nobility was also represented by twenty-three barons. The forty-six representatives of the Third Estate were generally wealthy property owners, rich merchants, or municipal magistrates. In the

Fig. 5.2 Fonds Ancely—A Estampes 1-Assemblée Général (sic) des Etats du Languedoc. (Source: Bibliothèque municipale de Toulouse)

end, some rural areas were better "represented" than cities like Toulouse or Montpellier, both of which had only two members from the Third Estate. The territorial repartition was modelled on the ecclesiastical institution, which thus was decisive for obtaining the total of ninety-two deputies. The twenty-three bishops or archbishops were matched by twenty-three representatives of the aristocracy, and balanced by forty-six delegates of the Third Estate.

Of course, the status of delegate of the Third Estate was not entrusted to a person from the lower social classes, but generally reserved for wealthy proprietors, rich merchants, members of the so-called idle classes, or the nobilité de robe who had already held important positions within the municipal authorities of their respective cities.

Smith arrived in Montpellier at the end of November 1764, although there is no certain evidence of the date of his arrival. It is more than likely that he was present on the day of the inauguration which took place on

November 29, 1764. His presence did not go unnoticed in the small British colony in Montpellier. Thus we find in the *Memoirs* of John Horne Tooke the following passage:

> Upon his arrival in Montpelier (sic), Mr. Horne and his young friend visited all the quality people [genteel company] of this city, both French and English. Among the latter was the late Duke of Buccleugh, accompanied by the famous Doctor Adam Smith, the author of the *Wealth of Nations*, his tutor. (Horne, t.1, p. 75)

Horne's notation draws attention to social relations in the eighteenth century and prosaically to Smith and the Duke's accommodation during the meeting of the Estates. The *Gentleman's Magazine* of April 1786 thus gives advice on the subject to the British travelling in France:

> First of all, there is no fully equipped accommodation in Paris or elsewhere in France. There are of course furnished hotels and furnished rooms, but nothing that corresponds to what one finds in London as "ready-furnished lodgings". A single person and even less a family cannot hope to find housing of this type. Secondly, staying with a family of quality is impossible. The meaning of the word "genteel" varies with the rank of the people. But what we mean is that no person in France will agree to house a person who has the same rank in Great Britain as that person has in France. A person of a lower rank in France will still only with difficulty accept, and only with a view to reaching a higher level, to house a person of a rank much higher than his own.
>
> Thirdly, it is very extremely difficult to associate with people of quality. By "genteel company" (personne de qualité), we mean in France the company of rich or at least very comfortable people, from a reputable family and who have visited many places in the world. For this type of company, we speak of "good company".

There was no doubt that this was a barrier to finding suitable accommodation, but at the end of 1764, due to contacts made with the Parlement of Toulouse, the archbishopric and the academies, a solution had been found that enabled travellers to find these quality French and British people then staying in Montpellier.

As one account of the time tells us, the Languedoc Estates were not ostentatious:

All these moderations and the like are strictly possible; but, isn't there some pomp needed in the assembly of a great province? Is there not some form of external show that would make an impression on the people and satisfy them in their representatives? Do we want an assembly to observe in details of this kind the same kind of economies as an individual? The latter finds a benefit in the management of the smallest matters; an assembly finds some in the overall arrangements, which, although more costly in appearance, are in reality less expensive, because they are less prone to error.

There is certainly no magnificence in the very ordinary hall in which the Estates held their sessions; there is no magnificence in the way it is decorated; there is no magnificence in their external ceremonies, which are limited to a solemn procession three days after the opening; They will therefore say with confidence that they see no suitable and worthwhile reduction on any item of this expenditure and they will add that, although everything has been increased since the year in which these expenses were fixed by a decree of the council, they are not in fact increased; so that if they had been excessive (which is difficult to suppose, remembering the circumstances of that time) the passage of time would have corrected this, and economy alone would have prevented the increase that the other objects of expenditure would have experienced. (Baron Trouvé 1818, pp. 534–535)

The seriousness and rigour with which the Estates operated were probably deliberate. They would have had to show themselves as working without luxury or ostentation, which would have seemed inappropriate in a place where the different classes of society were mixed, where the purpose was not to feast or to take pleasure, but to work for the general interest.

However, it is likely that the Estates did not have the physical facilities for working in great comfort because they had to appear in no case to be an alternative to royal or ecclesiastical power.

A ScoTMSan cannot have been be indifferent to this sobriety, since he would have been used to a certain rigour, coming from a city where the façades of buildings lacked ostentation. In seeking to oppose Mandeville, he almost regretted an excess of sobriety since a certain luxury could prove useful for society:

If the love of magnificence, the taste for elegant arts and the perfectioning of human life, for anything pleasant in terms of clothing, furniture, crew, architecture, sculpture, painting and music is to be considered as luxury, sensuality and ostentation, even in those whose situation allows them to indulge in these passions without inconvenience, then it is certain that luxury, sensuality and ostentation are public advantages. For without the qualities on which Dr. Mandeville finds it convenient to cast the opprobrium of such names, the refined arts would find no encouragement and would languish for want of employment. (Smith, *TMS*, VI, II, 4, pp. 411–417)

It is the great fallacy of Dr. Mandeville's book to represent every passion as wholly vicious, which is so in any degree and in any direction. It is thus that he treats everything as vanity which has any reference, either to what are, or to what ought to be the sentiments of others: and it is by means of this sophistry, that he establishes his favourite conclusion, that private vices are public benefits. If the love of magnificence, a taste for the elegant arts and improvements of human life, for whatever is agreeable in dress, ? furniture, or equipage, for architecture, statuary, painting, and music, is to be regarded as luxury, sensuality, and ostentation, even in those whose situation allows, without any inconvenience, the indulgence of those passions, it is certain that luxury, sensuality, and ostentation are public benefits: since without the qualities upon which he thinks proper to bestow such opprobrious names, the arts of refinement could never find encouragement, and must languish for want of employment. (Smith, TMS, VII.ii. 4. 12, p. 313)

However, the King ensured that the Estates were only a place of assembly and not one of power, a simple place of discussion of which he intended to keep control. Only the King could summon the Estates. Only the King was able to set the agenda, only he (through his legal representative, the governor general of the province) appointed the chairman of commissions. The Estates were not permanent and were not allowed to sit for more than forty days under penalty of complete annulment.

Thus, on November 29, 1764, the Languedoc Estates opened in the large hall of the town hall of Montpellier. The Estates convened by the King were placed under the institutional presidency of the archbishop of Narbonne, Arthur Richard Dillon, a prelate of quality and experience. According to the portrait drawn by historian L. Dutil, it is clear that he corresponded well to the kind of contacts Townshend had recommended:

Descended from Irish peers, trained at Saint-Sulpice and the Sorbonne, he was Bishop of Evreux at 32, Archbishop of Toulouse at 37, and obtained five years later, in 1763, the primatial siege of Narbonne. Because of his archiepiscopal function, he was entitled to chair the Estates of Languedoc, which some translated as viceroy of Languedoc. More and more in the limelight during the periodic assemblies of the clergy of France, he finally became their president in 1785 and thus occupied the highest position that a clergyman could dream of in the kingdom. (Dutil 1941)

The Estates brought together a future minister (Loménie de Brienne), a future president of the clergy assemblies (Arthur R. Dillon), and the future president of the Haute-Guyenne Assembly (Abbé Colbert).

The King was represented by Louis-Charles de Bourbon, Comte d' Eu, who made the journey from his Normandy lands to Montpellier. Also present were the very dynamic Intendant Jean-Emmanuel de Guignard, Vicomte de Saint-Priest (1714–1785), who died in office, and his son Marie-Joseph de Guignard (1733–1794), who, in the year 1764, was associated with the office of Intendant of his father, then rose to the prestigious post of Councillor of State. Marie-Joseph de Guignard remained Intendant until the revolutionary period, of which he was one of the victims, a consequence not only of his convictions but also of his function. The Saint-Priest family was originally from the Dauphiné and did not have any particular ties with the southern provinces. It is an example of an ambitious family that took advantage of its proximity to Royal Power and its multiple networks to promote its position and social advancement. The intendant also had a second son, François-Emmanuel de Guignard, who had just been appointed, thanks to Choiseul, ambassador to Portugal, a country which had been undergoing reconstruction since the great Lisbon earthquake and which required great commercial expertise. Conscious that he owed his position a great deal more to his uncle, the abbé de Barral, than to his own skills, he wrote in his memoirs:

> I was in my twenty-eighth year and was very happy at that age to begin such a mission in my diplomatic career. I had no particular knowledge of this kind other than a background in history and geography and I have seen from my experience that it is almost all that is needed in terms of preliminary studies, diplomacy, politics, being nothing other than the correct application of judgment about people and circumstances; the rest is routine. (Saint-Priest, p. 80)

François-Emmanuel Saint-Priest would distinguish himself greatly in this field, developing trade in particular between the Languedoc and Portugal. Perhaps at Smith's invitation or initiative, he made a trip to England in 1767 that led him to meet Prime Minister Pitt, then Lord Privy Seal, as well as Prime Minister, and thus in the House of Lords as Lord Chatham. On the other hand, he never met Charles Townshend, his trip coming a few weeks after the latter's death. In his memoirs, he shares an anecdote that relativizes but also sheds light on intellectual and academic practices:

> My travelling companion Phipps absolutely wanted to accompany us, which gave us great pleasure. English youth are almost always on the move. Phipps was all the better for this trip as he had been a student at Oxford University. The rector was one of his friends and he thought of bringing him to my house to tell me that the university was willing to give me the doctor's hat. It is a proposal that it sometimes offers to foreigners to whom it wants to do honour. The Duke of Nivernois had been received in this capacity four or five years earlier and I gave in to this offer. I chose law school like him. My concern was having a Latin speech to make, but I was assured that the Duke had composed one in that language that no one had understood, not being pronounced in the English way. I was happy to imitate him, being not sure of my school latin. This ceremony consisted only in dressing me in a red robe and covering me with a square hat while going to the university where I heard, without understanding it, a speech in my praise. Then I sat on the doctors' bench and came home in the same suit. It cost me a dozen guineas of rights, gifts and other small expenses. At that time one could be made doctor in most provincial universities at cheaper prices. (Ibidem., p. 96)

This was the kind of character Smith frequented. It is likely, however, that he did not share this type of narrative, where humour and mutual incomprehension concerning questions of institutional differences are conflated. As his career demonstrates, Smith had a completely different view of university life and the seriousness of learning in a noble institution, even if he sometimes regretted that the teachings were not always at the level they should be.

The very first days of the Estates were devoted to inaugural speeches which, unfortunately, were not recorded in the minutes, available from the Archives de la Haute-Garonne.[5] The speeches consist of a long statement of the obligations of the Estates and a general agenda of work to be carried out before the end of the session. Following the introductory speeches, the Estates focused, always within an administrative framework, on the members who had joined the assembly for the first time. Councillors served six-year terms, but were renewed on a voluntary basis or following the death or possible resignation of their predecessors. In this year 1764,

[5] AD 31, C Series, Proceedings of Parliament, C2407.

no new member of quality was presented and only the routine of formal registration came under this heading.

Finally, after a few days, the Estates officially requested the reception of the King's Commissioners who, as soon as they appeared, communicated the main request, the main reason for holding the assembly. This was obviously the area that seemed most important for the Kingdom, the adoption, immediately and without discussion of the "don gratuit".

The Estates were not consulted on a possible contribution to the national tax burden. The "free donation" was a fixed amount of three million livres in 1764; the tax was then distributed among the various territorial subdivisions according to a system which was the subject of constant negotiations.

But beyond "free donations", Estates could also decide to make extraordinary donations. This was the case during the 1761 meeting of the Estates when, under the impetus and at the request of the Archbishop of Narbonne, Arthur Dillon, Choiseul's personal friend, the Estates decided on a free donation aiming to offer to His Majesty a ship of the line of seventy four guns and to give it in this way to the rest of France:

> This represents a signal of what subjects truly worthy of the best of masters can and must do. There is no good Frenchman who does not feel motivated by the desire to sacrifice everything to contribute to the efforts of the King and a wise and enlightened minister in order to restore the French navy.[6]

If the Estates could agree to do this, that is offer the King additional sums, the opposite, the suspension of taxes, was a more delicate notion.

Thus during the Estates, "dons gratuits" do not cause problems, the second major tax of this decade, the subscription to the "vingtième" will have to be voted without any discussion. And the Estate register says:

> But we will make the king the strongest representations to obtain the reliefs without which the impotence of the indebted would put an obstacle as real as legitimate to the effects of the good will of the Estates.

[6]AD 34, Montpellier, C 7530, 160–161. The ship, started in 1764 and launched in 1766 will take the name of *Languedoc*. It also had a very brilliant career during the American War of Independence under the colours of Admiral d'Estaing, who commanded the squadron. The ship participated under various names in France's multiple battles against Great Britain during the American Revolution and up to the siege of Toulon, in which the young Bonaparte participated, in 1793.

The question of taxation was thus quickly debated, once the main taxes had been voted—it must be said that the situation in the Languedoc compared to the other provinces of France was exemplary—and Smith must have been impressed by such efficiency. The Estates then seem to be making modest criticisms of the sums earmarked for militias and other military troops. Criticisms which, in view of the way they were reported, seem rather conventional and do not call into question the well-oiled functioning of this very amiable assembly.

After a few days of interruption devoted to various processions, masses, and other festivities, work resumed. It is important to understand that this assembly of quality people in a city such as Montpellier represented an opportunity to organize balls and shows to which parlementaires and their companions were regularly invited.

The young Scott, who seemed to appreciate worldly distractions as much as his teacher, who enjoyed honours, were both under the guidance of their guide Abbé Colbert, himself present in the train of the Archbishop of Toulouse, Loménie de Brienne, and included onto the limited guest list for these festivities.

After the distractions, the work quickly resumed around the issue of a dispute. In 1764, it was an argument over the ownership of the banks of the Rhône. This type of challenge was recurrent at the Estates. It was important to know where the boundaries of the province were. In order to ensure its legitimacy vis-à-vis the outside world, it was not surprising to see this assembly examining the question. The question of territorial limits, more than a hundred years old, was brought up back to the fore in 1764 because work needed to be carried out to make the great river perfectly navigable and to ensure a link with the Royal Languedoc canal. Thus the double ownership of the land, if it generally presented disadvantages, would, this year, be useful in order to share costs with the neighbouring province, Provence.

This was the introduction of the next phase of the Estates, which studied in a very thorough and precise way the infrastructures that were necessary for the economic and human development of the province. Initially, the Estates noted the completion of the bridge over the Ardèche which made it easier to communicate with the north of the province, then called the Vivarais, which remained for a long time one of the most remote and isolated parts of the Kingdom. The report indicates that the bridge was built for 380,000 livres taken from the Estates' budget. On this subject, the rapporteur added: "This bridge made up of five large arches of ten toises in diameter and built with beautiful cut stones is one of the most beautiful structures in the province."

After the assembly formally acknowledged the work done, they reviewed and voted budgets for the construction of new structures. In particular, the construction of two bridges, one in wood in Cazères, the other in masonry in Carbonne. These two towns were close and the bridges would connect the Couserans (a Pyrenean valley heavily populated at that time) with the rest of the province and the neighbouring Guyenne and, beyond, towards the county of Foix.

The assembly also voted and approved the expenses incurred for the development of the post road at the level of the Minimes district, namely the northern entrance of the city of Toulouse, entrance which Smith and the Duke used and which Arthur Young would describe during his passage a few years later.

It must be said that the routes of communication were throughout France, at the end of the eighteenth century, the object of much attention. The work of Intendant Turgot in the Limousin is noteworthy, because he made it a sort of laboratory of his ideas; it was the establishment of the Royal School of the "Ponts-et-Chaussées" (focused on roads and bridges) that was created by Daniel-Charles Trudaine (Intendant of Finance, 1703–1769) in 1747 that was at the origin of this transformation of the country.

In 1764, this school, which quickly became a celebrated institution, created a real "corps d'état". It was overseen by Jean-Rodolphe Perronet, who would be one of the main contributors to Diderot's *Encyclopédie*. In particular, he would collaborate with Deleyre in the writing of the article on the fly, which would be used as an illustration by Adam Smith during his brilliant demonstration on the benefits of the division of labour. This new paradigm, by its extension to the market and to free and perfect competition, is one of the foundations of contemporary economics.

If Léon Dutil is to be believed, in his book on the economic condition of the Languedoc, which quotes Arthur Young, a British traveller himself:

> 'I know nothing as remarkable for the traveller as the roads of Languedoc' and further on he declares that he has crossed an incredible number of magnificent bridges and superb roads. These compliments are good to record, but you have to see their value by trying to get a clear picture of the means of communication that our province had to offer. The roads on which the post relays are established constitute the first class and are now the

> responsibility of the province as a body; they must be 36 feet between the ditches. Sometimes at the request of the government or for considerations of major utility the Estates also take on some important roads such as the road to the Auvergne via the Vivarais, or others in the Gévaudan. The second class includes the coach roads and the routes connecting the Episcopal cities with the post roads or between them; their width must be 30 feet; they are entrusted to the care of the 'sénéchaussées'[7] Next came the paths connecting two parts of a diocese, under state supervision: their width was 24 feet. Finally the fourth class consisted of the roads connecting the communities to each other and to the previous roads; 21 feet wide, they remained the communities expense, which needed the authority of the Intendant to act. (Dutil 1911, pp. 653–655)

At this point in the recording of the 1764 Estates, it is worth looking at what Smith was to write a few years later on transport infrastructure, land-use planning terms, and on roads in particular. His argumentation, the line of his analysis, and his object of study do not, that is clear, relate to the detail of what he heard during his long days in November in the town hall of Montpellier. However he synthesizes the arguments exchanged and above all he reveals the source on which he relied when he mentions the term "Intendant".

While its purpose in Book V of the *Wealth of Nations*, but also in this paragraph, is intended to be general, what could be more universal in Europe of the eighteenth century than roads, bridges, even canals for an economist and universalist? However, he wrote the term "intendant", which is a term unique to France; the only true such he had met were the Intendants de Saint-Priest, father and son. Turgot can be excluded, whom he met in a completely different setting and not as part of his duties. Smith's comment merely reiterates some simple logic about the need for a state to promote development factors. Without stating it clearly, it indicates that choices must be made with an adequate level of vision. If the vision is too distant, at the level of Royal Power, the infrastructure may not

[7] Before the French Revolution, the sénéchaussées were administrative, financial, and judicial districts supervised by a sénéchal. They had been created during the thirteenth century in the County of Toulouse. From the sixteenth century onwards their competences were diminishing as other divisions were created. Among the multiple divisions utilized for various purposes by the kings' administrators, généralités emerged gradually from the fourteenth to sixteenth centuries. Initially fiscal, their role steadily increased to become by the late seventeenth century—under the authority of an intendant (reporting to the Controller-General of Finances)—the very framework of royal administration and centralization.

be adapted to the real needs of a province or small nation. If each city, or in the case of some Mediterranean countries, city-states, is entrusted with the task of building and maintaining the structures, the risks of disagreements are numerous.

Smith is therefore, as with his famous metaphor of the impartial spectator, in search of the right observations, the right distance, the right authority to make administrative and management decisions. The model he met in the Languedoc Estates seemed close to ideal. His commentary is in fact only an account of the debates he attended. From a detailed debate, anecdotal and perfect, fit to enthuse a man of property, Smith draws a systemic analysis applicable to all countries or nations in the world.

> That the erection and maintenance of the publick works which facilitate the commerce of any country, such as good roads, bridges, navigable canals, harbours, must require very different degrees of expence in the different periods of society, is evident without any proof.
>
> The expence of making and maintaining the publick roads of any country must evidently increase with the annual produce of the land and labour of that country, or with the quantity and weight of the goods which it becomes necessary to fetch and carry upon those roads. The strength of a bridge must be suited to the number and weight of the carriages, which are likely to pass over it. The depth and the supply of water for a navigable canal must be proportioned to the number and tunnage of the lighters, which are likely to carry goods upon it; the extent of a harbour to the number of the shipping which are likely to take shelter in it.
>
> 2 It does not seem necessary that the expence of those publick works should be defrayed from that publick revenue, as it is commonly called, of which the collection and application bisbin most countries assigned to the executive power. The greater part of such publiek works may easily be so managed, as to afford a particular revenue sufficient for defraying their own expence, without bringing any burden upon the general revenue of the society.
>
> 3 A highway, a bridge, a navigable canal, for example, may in most cases be both made and maintained by a small toll upon the carriages which make use of them: a harbour, by a moderate port-duty upon the tunnage of the shipping which load or unload in it. The coinage, another institution for facilitating commerce, in many countries, not only defrays its own expence, but affords a small revenue or seignorage to the sovereign.
>
> 2 The post-office, another institution for the same purpose, over and above defraying its own expence, affords in almost all countries a very considerable revenue to the sovereign. 3 4 When the carriages which pass over

> a highway or a bridge, and the lighters which sail upon a navigable canal, pay toll in proportion to their weight or their tunnage, they pay for the maintenance of those publick works exactly in proportion to the Cwearand tear_ which they occasion of them. It seems scarce possible to invent a more equitable way of mainmining such works. 4 This tax or toll too, though it is advanced by the carrier, is finally paid by the consumer, to whom it must always be charged in the price of the goods. As the expence of carriage, however, is very much reduced by means of such publick works, the goods, notwithstanding the toll, come cheaper to the consumer than they could otherwise have done; their price not being so much raised by the toll, as it is lowered by the cheapness of the carriage. The person who finally pays this tax, therefore, gains by the application, more than he loses by the payment of it. His payment is exactly in proportion to his gain. It is in reality no more than a part of that gain which he is obliged to _',’e up in order to get the rest. It seems impossible to imagine a more equitable method of raising a tax.
>
> 5 When the toll upon carriages of luxury, upon coaches, post-chaises, &c. is made somewhat higher in proportion to their weight, than upon carriages of necessary use, such as carts, waggons, &c. the indolence and vanity of the rich is made to contribute in a very easy manner to the relief of the poor, by rendering cheaper the transportation of heavy goods to all the different parts of the country.
>
> 6 When high roads, bridges, canals, &c. are in this manner made and supported by the commerce which is carried on by means of them, they can be made only where that commerce requires them, and consequently where it is proper to make them. Their expence too, their grandeur and magnificence, must be suited to what that commerce can afford to pay. They must be made consequently as it is proper to make them. A magnificent high road cannot be made through a desert country where there is little or no commerce, or merely because it happens to lead to the country villa of the intendant of the province, or to that of some great lord to whom the intendant finds it convenient to make his court. A great bridge cannot be thrown over a river at a place where nobody passes, or merely to embellish the view from the windows of a neighbouring palace: things which sometimes happen, in countries where works of this kind are carried on by any other revenue than that which they themselves are capable of affording. (WN, V.i.d, p. 725)

Before moving on to the level of financial resources needed to finance the maintenance and construction of infrastructure, as Adam Smith rightly points out, there is a small anecdote, dealt with during the Estates which should be cited to show to what extent the travellers rubbed shoulders with the popular history of France.

In December 1764, the Estates in their deliberation voted: "A gratification of 2000 livres, promised to the person who will destroy a ferocious beast which has appeared for some time in the Gévaudan and devoured several people there and spread the greatest consternation."

The Estates thus seized on a news item which marked the end of the reign of Louis XV. It should be noted, however, that beyond the anecdote, the phenomenon continued from 1764 to 1767 and cost the lives of at least eighty-three people and perhaps sixteen more. These facts still remain unexplained, but could be based on the harshness and length of the winter of 1764; Smith will note in writing that the climate of southern France has nothing to envy that of northern Scotland. These facts also remain in the collective French memory due to not only to the ancestral fear of the wolf but also echoing the feeling of abandonment of the weakest and most exposed populations of the country. Thus the episode of the Beast of the Gévaudan, which is one of the most remote regions of the Vivarais, serves as a symbol. Symbol of the rupture of a certain ancestral "social contract" where the King by divine right had to bring prompt and immediate assistance to his subjects.

Proof of the change of era, or change of paradigm as an economist might say, the Languedoc Estates, which showed in this a total lack of solidarity, had recourse to the most individualistic of solutions by offering a simple bounty to the hunter who could kill the beast.

Adam Smith never mentions this fact, which he must consider anecdotal.

Smith may have seen in the offering of a reward an illustration of the alignment of individual interests with the collective well-being: after all, the wolf hunter who receives the bounty will contribute to the common good by eliminating the beast. But the beast was not unique and it was the organization of a full hunt that would stop predators causing more harm.

5.1.2 Budgets of the Estates

Once all expenses had been taken into account, costs that the Estates wished to cover either for the creation of infrastructures (roads, creation of new side canals, development of the port of Sète) or for maintenance works (certain maintenance works on the Languedoc canal, dredging of the port of Sète, and the banks of the Rhône) but also miscellaneous expenses such as those entailed by the Vivarais events, the assembly considered how to raise income.

Although the Estates' deliberations were more complex than the summary account that can be given of them here, the total budget and the way it was established can be analysed.

In 1764 the total revenue from taxes amounted to 9,714,245 livres and expenditure to 9,819,950 livres which, the statements note, left a deficit of 100,685 livres. Admittedly, the deficit was less than 1%, but the Estates did not have sovereignty over monetary policy and therefore the deficit could only be offset by borrowing or raising taxes.

Fortunately the economic situation improved at the end of the Seven Years' War, allowing the repayment of various loans, as can be seen in the deferred expenses in the accounts. Thus the Estates declared:

> The statement of the sums to be repaid by lottery on 7 loans is (was?) established and is (was) made by the province both on the King's account and for itself. The debt which had been "initially" of 43 million (the secretary does not specify a date) was in 1764 reduced to 29 million.

Yet the Estates were prepared to borrow, tempted as they were by the system of borrowing in the form of lotteries, which Lucien Febvre calls "financial curiosities". This form of financial resources was indeed very curious and perhaps even hazardous. Borrowing in the form of lotteries was certainly very profitable but presented significant risks. As these were not "pari mutuel"[8] the amount involved, if misjudged, could at any time put the borrower in difficulty. On the other hand too much caution or too much complexity led to a lack of transparency in the organization of the lottery, leading the bettors to turn away from a good deal. Beyond these simple lotteries and sometimes confused with them, other "original financial techniques" could be used.

These were called "tontine" loans. A subscriber group was divided into age classes (generally from 0 to 70 years, i.e. classes from 0 to 7, 7 to 14, 14 to 21... 63 to 70) and each subscriber paid a fixed sum to the borrower. Every year the borrower paid out interest which was generally 5% per year.

On the death of the penultimate representative of the age bracket, the last survivor received a capital amount. This general system was subject to

[8] Pari Mutuel or mutual betting is a betting system in which all bets of a particular type are placed together in a pool; taxes and the "house-take" or "vigorish" are deducted, and payoff odds are calculated by sharing the pool among all winning bets. In some countries it is known as the Tote after the totalizator, which calculates and displays bets already made.

multiple variations, including in particular a draw in the form of a lottery which allowed the early repayment of the capital to certain subscribers who, in this case, recovered their capital with a possible premium. This double hazard offered a certain lack of transparency which made it possible to have numerous subscribers attracted by an immediate profit, the annuity of 5% and the hope of surviving the others and thus, to acquire in old age a substantial amount. The drawing of lots allowed the borrower to repay his debt more quickly and avoided the lender having to gamble on the length of his life while having the enjoyment of his annuity. By the time Smith attended the Estates, this financing process was no longer in great favour in England while it was still flourishing in France.

David Weir, in his comparison of the place of tontines in Great Britain and France at the end of the Ancien Régime, concludes:

> Britain offered tontines at market rates of return and found the demand to be low. The French government's greater success at raising money on tontine loans in the eighteenth century can be attributed mainly to the high level of interest rates offered, especially for older nominees. If French investors had any cultural preference for life contingent loans, the government did not take advantage of it. The tontine's reputation in France as an onerous form of borrowing for the state was therefore deserved. Public recognition of this fact by the government led to abandonment of tontines and eventually to partial repudiation of tontine obligations. It did not lead to a rationalization of public debt, because the life annuities offered in replacement were, at a flat 10 percent interest rate, just as onerous. (Weir 1989, p. 124)

Smith in the *WN* mentions this type of financing, proof of his great interest in this kind of practice which he probably found original and ultimately more ethical than simple life insurance, because it encouraged a citizen to lead as healthy a life as possible and to move away from vices that could lead to a rapid death. In passing, it is worth mentioning that he perpetrated a small error that can only be attributed to his partial vision of Europe. It may have been during the Languedoc Estates that he examined the various means of raising income, but the tontine was by no means a French invention but was imported by Cardinal Mazarin in 1652, who asked a Neapolitan banker in exile in France, Lorenzo Tonti, to set up an original financing system.

Lottery loans and tontines are certainly the most original methods that the future economist was able to examine during the 1764 session of the

Languedoc Estates. Smith was probably not very impressed by the innovative aspect of the financial statements; at most he may have been able to detect skilful manoeuvres.

5.1.3 *An Industrial Policy for the Languedoc*

Once the finances and budget seemed set for the coming year, the statements move on to what might be termed "other business". The only report of the debates was transcribed during the meetings by a secretary who recorded the discussions while making a quick summary in the moment or more probably in the evening or between two meetings. If the testimony is first hand, it is however a transcription including its shortcomings and emphases. Thus this part is the least structured because it is highly variable according to the sessions and the process of osmosis which always occurs in a group gathered during several weeks to work on a subject of common interest. The comments which describe the last days of work are a little more messy even if they are, for Smith, of the greatest interest, because they are often points of detail but reveal questions of importance often hidden behind banal comments.

Report on factories presented to the Languedoc Estates:

> It was made in 1764: Mahoux cloth, 475 pieces; Londrins first[9] 560 p; Londrins second 555 p; Sayes of Venice, 95 p; in all 65 920 pieces, 9 370 pieces more than in 1763, and more than twice what was made in 1760. We can only be saddened to see in the reports of the provincial inspector and the guards of the main manufacturers, that the infidelity of many led them to depart from the regulations, either by reducing the width of the sheets, or by using in their composition bad wools and in their dyes bad ingredients, to such an extent that it was only possible to get rid of them at a very low price in the Levant, they remain accumulated and unsold in Marseilles, from where will result, the interruption in the work of the factory, which will reduce to the most horrible misery a multitude of workers who have no other occupation, and cause an even greater evil by the discrediting of the sheets of France among the Orientals who will soon be revolted by having to deal with the traders of France and will give a just preference to those nations from which we had managed to remove almost the trade.

[9] LONDRINS, s. m. pl. (Com.): wool sheets made in France and sent to the Levant. There are two types, distinguished by epithets of first and second according to quality.

Here Smith was confronted by a corporatist economic way of thinking that rejected competition. In this type of organization, the manufacturers, as indicated, were strongly supervised by an organization that in the case of cloth manufacturers originated with the state. Controls were strict, but some did not follow established rules and sought to put inferior quality products on the market.

In this case the greed of some damaged everyone's reputation. The culprits, far from having a long-term vision of the development of the local economy, chose the option of immediate profit, increasing apprehension about long-term prospects. These discussions could only comfort Smith in his idea of the harmfulness of State interventions in the economy:

> That this mercantile system was not very favourable to the income of the masses of the people, to the annual product of the land and the work of the country, is what I have tried to show in the fourth book of this work. It does not appear that it was more favourable to the sovereign's income, at least as regards that part of the income which depends on customs duties. (*WN*. Book II, Chapter V)

The Languedoc Estates were also sensitive to the international context and its associated vicissitudes.

> 9000 pounds payable in two years are granted to the diocese of Castres which wants to try to make bayettes,[10] whereas the woollen fabrics and hosiery factory which was the only resource of the inhabitants is almost entirely wasted by the loss of Canada where it was the main consumption. (Report of the Estates of Languedoc)

It should be remembered that by the Treaty of Paris of 1763, France definitively lost Canada, a protected market. How then would the French manufacturers who supplied these regions with their wool production ensure their redeployment? In particular, would they implement innovative business techniques? Some experts, during the Estates of 1764, which provided many lessons, contributed by their reports and presentations to reinforcing Smith's free trade doctrine, based on comparative advantages.

> Mr. Lamarteloy's report in which he exposes the disadvantages that result from the ordinary use of raising silkworms in places that have little

[10] Fine white, black, or brown wool cloth.

> communication with the outside air, which makes them unhealthy, harms the product of silk and is contrary to the health of those who are used to raise silkworms so to make known the vices of the old method, last spring he had built an open-air workshop three floors long by six wide. (Report of the Estates of Languedoc)

Adam Smith thus understood the many techniques that specialists in the field used and developed to enable the Languedoc to develop silkworm cultivation. Despite all the efforts deployed during more than a century, quality remained unsatisfactory. This lack of quality was not the consequence of a lack of application or work, but a climatic problem which made the breeding of silkworm very complex and not very compatible with the proximity of the Mediterranean and its variations in climate, its frequent and particularly unpredictable humidity.

As the quality of the fibre was not as expected, it was impossible and useless to provide the industry with the most modern means of production, because it was difficult to manufacture a quality product from raw material of poor quality. As a silk historian in Languedoc recounts, this local activity could never equal such places of production, however close, as Lyon or northern Italy, not to mention of course the Asian productions whose trade always enjoyed a world-wide reputation. This is a perfect illustration of Smith's famous theory of absolute benefits in international trade. It should however be noted that he would demonstrate the validity of his reasoning by using another example, probably more persuasive than the too technical one of sericulture.

> The fibre processing process required sophisticated technical means, such as Bolognese mills, the existence of which local spinners were not aware of for a very long time. On the eve of the Revolution, the driving force of Nîmes silk mills was still man and it was also the case in many mills in the Cévennes. What weapons could good will or local initiatives use against the capital and decisions of the great silk cities? And in particular Lyon? Technically, the gamble was audacious, but it required a regional metropolis, a decision-making centre that was able to coordinate, by means of solid capitalist measures, isolated attempts and generate others. These structures, if they existed, were not sufficiently developed. On the commercial and political level, the struggle was not even unequal, it simply did not exist. Any attempt to do so came up against Italian hegemony and Lyon's domination. (Lise Teisseyre-Sallmann 1995, p. 138)

However, the Estates kept to their agenda. Their deliberations now focused on the textile industry in general. One of the roles of the assembly, as has just been seen, was to try to promote the quality of the Royal Label by all means, essentially financial:

> [...] It is granted..: 5 000 livres in the country of Gévaudan which will employ them to introduce in the principal places of manufacture of the wheels and the reels (the sieur Holker, inspector general of manufactures, came to the Languedoc with the wishes of the Estates, having noticed that the wool of Gévaudan is very good, but that it was very imperfectly spun), and also to change certain parts of the looms, in order to give the "chalons or escots"[11] of the country the width of the English chalons and thus to make their commerce easier in Turkey, and in Spain and Portugal. To the Sieur Colon de Mende, to give him the means to imitate perfectly the Malbrougs[12] and the other English fabrics by importing from England two heat presses with plates and cartons.
>
> The observations made by Mr. Holker in the course of his travels in different dioceses of the province will be printed in order to multiply both herds and pastures in the mountains. (AD 34 C 4673—Holker file)

It is certain that John Holker's visit to the Languedoc did take place. He came to the province at the invitation of the Estates as well as various industrialists from the Cévennes. In particular, it was noted in a letter that this invitation was essentially at the initiative of, among others, Mr Colson, a particularly active industrialist of English origin. Holker arrived in the Languedoc in April 1764 and visited the various sheet, wool, and silk factories during the months of his stay.

After each of his visits he gave a very precise account in which he described not only the machines used, which represented the productive capital of the factory, but also the productive processes. He also noted carefully the different operations that were carried out through the work of people assigned to unique and individual tasks.

This type of observation is one of the specificities of the time. Holker's descriptions are very close to those which can be found in the articles of the *Encyclopédie* whose last volumes were still to appear in 1764. Whether

[11] Format of wool sheets to make clothes for religious orders in convents or monasteries, or work aprons.

[12] This is the deformation of Marlborough (in Wiltshire) in the form Malbrought then Malbrougs which are wool fabrics of English origin in general quality.

one considers the article on brass, the anonymous one on wool mills or the one that will serve as a model in the *Wealth of Nations* for Smith's first demonstration on the importance of work, the famous article on the pin and pin makers, all these descriptions have the common purpose of describing industrial work in detail and especially the advantages of the division of labour. At a time when it is still operating on a limited scale, it is celebrated. Perhaps some already thought that work and not land was the source of human wealth. It was not until Smith's publication and demonstration, however, that the world became convinced of this and made it a general principle.

Holker attended the Languedoc Estates to bring his expertise. It must be said that John Holker (the father, at first) is a very singular character. John Holker was born in the north of England in 1719 where he began an honest career as a businessman and entrepreneur in the then booming textile industry in England.

It was at the age of twenty-six that his life changed. The column led by Bonnie Prince Charlie, who led a brief incursion into England, was stationed in the city of Stretford, near Manchester. Strong in his Catholic convictions and always eager for adventure, the young merchant joined the rash and foolhardy Prince. He was captured by the English, his compatriots during the retreat of the column and led to the Tower of London, where while waiting for his imminent hanging he managed to get away, despite the prison's reputation for being escape-proof. Nothing tied him to England anymore, so he quickly moved to France, the country he chose by default.

He then stayed at the small court of Saint-Germain-en-Laye near Paris where he found a safer haven with the Young Pretender, who had also escaped the clutches of the British. John Holker was from the beginning of his career an adventurer of the eighteenth century. He would be considered as a spy after his escape by the English, especially since the Seven Years' War was still to come. Charles Trudaine, then head of the "Bureau du Commerce" in France, sought to use his skills. He began a brilliant industrial career in the textile industry, which led him to own an important cotton sheet factory in Rouen in Normandy.

As relations with England improved, John Holker, who would hold the very official position of Royal Factory Inspector, would become a transmitter of knowledge between France and England, enabling the two industries to share each other's technical discoveries in order to compete fairly in a single market, the world at large.

Holker's actions in this sense could not go unnoticed by Smith, especially since the British were not legion in Montpellier and we know from Horne Tooke's memoirs that they had the opportunity to meet in the "good company" of Montpellier. Did Charles Townshend not recommend meeting remarkable men? Was Holker not the very model of the talented entrepreneur who succeeded with equal ease on both sides of the Channel?

If Smith did not choose to illustrate his presentation on the division of labour by describing a cloth factory, this was probably due to the complexity of the description and the difficulty for a broad readership of understanding the productive process. It may also be that Smith was also aware that working in textile factories had disadvantages of dullness and alienation of labour and child labour that would not allow him to present his arguments so easily. The pin factory could easily be presented in the corporate world, as it was different from a complex manufacturing process.

However, what we do know for certain is that Smith was very interested in the productive processes described by Holker since he brought back or more probably had sent by Abbé Colbert a printed copy of the transcriptions of visits, the paper version of which was printed at the request and expense of the Estates during the first half of 1765.

The Holkers, father and then son, pursued a long career as industrialists and technical advisors to the French public authorities. John Holker's son, also John Holker, specialized more in travelling and exploring the world. After the French Revolution, he emigrated to the newly united States where he became a member of Congress and then Consul of France to the young American nation.

As far as the Estates of 1764 were concerned, their work ended with the examination of agricultural questions of little interest, which would be submitted to the deliberations of the members still assembled in January 1765. It seems that the small group of "Toulousains" celebrated Christmas and the New Year among the representatives:

> A bonus of 1000 livres to Mr. Serres, surveyor, author of a method approved by the Montpellier Academy of Sciences, which is likely to cadastral surveying more accurate and more prompt and puts it within reach of any kind of person by means of the triangulation tables that he has set up. The usefulness of Serres' work being unambiguous, it is deliberated that it will be made public by having it printed.

In their latest meetings, the Estates were very much in favour of modern methods for drawing up a cadastre. Thus in the "généralité" of Montauban innovative techniques would also be often used in the development of this administrative tool.

The "Cadastre", or land registry, as a tool for revealing and measuring wealth, played an important role in Smith's reasoning in the *WN*.

> Some states, instead of the simple and obvious expedient of a register of leases, have had recourse to the laborious and expensive one of an actual survey and valuation of all the lands in the country. They have suspected, probably, that the lessor and lessee, in order to defraud the publick revenue, might combine to conceal the real terms of the lease. Doomsday-book seems to have been the result of a very accurate survey of this kind. (WN, V.ii.c, p. 834)

If it can be considered that the cadastre is the tool or the set of techniques that allows everyone to know and recognize private property in a secure, certain, and indisputable manner, the cadastre is also an essential element of a system based on private property. For Adam Smith, private property also seems to be the first condition that will lead to the exploitation of workers. This realistic vision of social classes is clearly discernible in the following passage:

> But this original state of things, in which the labourer enjoyed the whole produce of his own labour, could not last beyond the first introduction of the appropriation of land and the accumulation of stock. It was at an end, therefore, long before the most considerable improvements were made in the productive powers of labour, and it would be to no purpose to trace farther what might have been its effects upon the recompence or wages of labour. As soon as land becomes private property, the landlord demands a share of almost all the produce which the labourer can either raise, or collect from it. His rent makes the first deduction from the produce of the labour which is employed upon land. (WN, I.viii, p. 83)

Finally, the Estates concluded their work on agricultural matters by evoking the rather curious demand that a representative made for his city:

> Rejection of a request from the community of Clermont-Lodève which would have liked to establish a duty on wine of 18 pounds on the muid[13] in favour of the hospital, on the grounds that the Estates always had great attention to allowing only modest taxes on wine.

The Estates in this case were opposed to a local wine tax. Here again, one can only surmise that this refusal must have pleased Smith. He was a fierce opponent of the multiplication of local taxes which hindered the creation of a market, favour particularisms while remaining an obstacle to foreign trade. If exceptions multiply, the collective interest disappears before the welter of private interests that distort the prices of goods. Adam Smith tells us:

> Through the greater part of a country in which a tax of this kind is established, nothing can be produced for distant sale. The produce of every part of the country must be proportioned to the consumption of the neighbourhood. (WN, V.ii.k, p. 899)

More than trade, moreover, the Estates seemed to consider that it was also a real obstacle to production. In this sense they took a much more liberal path than Smith.

It seems that on this precise point, Adam Smith does not give his intellectual agreement to the decision of the Estates. Perhaps he already perceived in deciding thus the lobbying of producers and retailers who wanted to promote their particular interests over the imperatives of public health, which recommended temperance.

> The taxes upon ale, wine, and spirituous liquors, which are advanced by the dealers, are finally paid by the different consumers exactly in proportion to their respective consumption. But if the tax was to be paid by purchasing a licence to drink those liquors, the sober would, in proportion to his consumption, be taxed much more heavily than the drunken consumer. A family which exercised great hospitality would be taxed much more lightly than one who entertained fewer guests. (WN, V.ii.k, p. 877)

Finally, to close the deliberations, in particular the deliberations on agricultural issues, the Estates considered the allocation of subsidies for wheat production. The argument put forward by the Estates is also very

[13] The Montpellier muid is a volume measurement that corresponds to about 700 litres.

interesting. It was by no means a direct subsidy to production but the establishment of an infrastructure to allow greater freedom of transport. Road improvements should enable production to reach the city of Toulouse or at least the main communication route for all agricultural production: the Languedoc canal.

The Estates attributed to transport infrastructures a major role as market regulator, not as a financial regulator that controlled prices, but as a regulator that reduced, according to the logic of free trade, all the difficulties that hindered access to a given market. Although not expressed directly in the short report, the goal was to lower the price of wheat for the good of all:

> To give an outlet to the grain trade, the sale of which is the only resource one has to raise taxes; the Diocese of Toulouse is authorized to borrow 400,000 pounds which will be used strictly to repair the roads from Toulouse to Revel by Caraman and from Toulouse to Lavaur by Verfeil whose estimate amounts for the first road to 230,000 livres and for the second to 106,000 livres, The diocese of Toulouse is authorized to borrow 20,000 books for the construction of the Auterive road.

On this precise point, Adam Smith will only note the certain backwardness of France compared to England during this period as regards freedom of trade:

> This freedom of interior commerce, the effect of the uniformity of the system of taxation, is perhaps one of the principal causes of the prosperity of Great Britain; every great country being necessarily the best and most extensive market for the greater part of the productions of its own industry. If the same freedom, in consequence of the same uniformity, could be extended to Ireland and the plantations, both the grandeur of the state and the prosperity of every part of the empire, would probably be still greater than at present.
>
> In France, the different revenue laws which take place in the different provinces, require a multitude of revenue officers to surround, not only the frontiers of the kingdom, but those of almost each particular province, in order either to prevent the importation of certain goods, or to subject it to the payment of certain duties, to the no small interruption of the interior commerce of the country. (WN, V.ii.k, p. 900)

Smith's criticisms were unfair because the period when he stayed in France was precisely that of the reforms that were beginning to affect the Kingdom. In the province of Languedoc mainly, but also in France as a whole, the question of trade in cereals and particularly wheat was a major issue, the occasion for many written proposals and many decisions by the central authorities.

When Smith attended the Estates, he found himself in France during a very particular period when the wheat trade had become, since the royal edict of May 25, 1763, totally free. Free as far as production was concerned, but also free to be sold and exported according to the different outlets available. It was certain that in this very particular sense France appeared much more liberal than England, even for a professor from Glasgow who knew the British Corn Laws and their constraints, whereas as these two articles prove, France had established statutes on this point that were absolutely liberal.

> ARTICLE ONE: Let us allow all our subjects, of whatever quality and condition they may be, even the nobles and privileged, to do, as they see fit, in the interior of the kingdom, the trade of grains, to sell and buy them, even to store them, without them being, for reason of this commerce, disturbed nor constrained to any formality.
>
> IT IS ALLOWED THAT: our subjects may transport freely from one province of the kingdom to another any kind of grain and food, without being obliged to make any declaration, nor to obtain any authorisation or permission. Let us make very express inhibitions and forbid all our officers and those of the lords, from demanding any formalities, under whatever pretext it may be.

It is not surprising, therefore, following his French experience, that one of Smith's favourite subjects in the *Wealth of Nations* was the wheat trade, all the more so since many French authors who were interested in economics made it a subject in their writings. Among them are Claude Jacques Hébert (1700–1775), the most famous representative of the physiocrats, François Quesnay (1695–1774), Abbé Nicolas Baudeau (1730–1792), and Smith's future friends, Pierre Samuel Dupont de Nemours (1739–1817) and Anne Robert Turgot. The issue of the wheat trade discussed during the Languedoc Estates was thus promised to a long career in which the role of the Toulouse Parlement would not be negligible.

5.2 End of the Languedoc Estates and Return to Toulouse

As prescribed by the internal regulations, the Estates ended in the first days of January, a few days before their deadline. After some Te Deum masses which were intended to protect the various representatives from evil and disease during the year to come, the delegates to the Estates retired to their respective places of residence until their next meeting, planned to take place in Montpellier around the month of November 1765. Smith did not intend to attend and would already be away from the province at their next meeting.

Adam Smith, along with the Duke and his brother Hew took the road to Toulouse and arrived in their apartments around January 20, 1765, after more than six months of adventures and experiences which had led them on many of the roads of Guyenne and the Languedoc. Smith had already fulfilled most of his contract with Charles Townshend, the initiator of the voyage. The Duke's Grand Tour was as much about studying French political institutions and the French economy as it was about entertainment and discovering the world of French aristocracy.

His return to Toulouse plunged him back into a known world where the splendours of the Estates were no longer appropriate. However, the second part of his stay in Toulouse began under much better auspices than the first, because Smith now had relationships, almost friends, and at least knew how to make new ones.

The diarist Pierre Barthès points out in his writings that Toulouse suffered from much more immediate problems than the political questions which had occupied the travellers during the past months:

> The city and its surroundings are being flooded with a crowd of unconfessed vagabond rascals who under the precious pretext of asking for alms, interfere in the houses in broad daylight and at the fall of night put a gun to people's throats, especially the shy ones from whom they always tear some things. The capitouls, with their ordinary wisdom, wishing to stop the course of such recklessness and unbridled license, issued an ordinance enjoining all the hosts and innkeepers of this city to inform themselves every evening exactly of the name of the homeland and of the duties of persons who would come to stay with them, and pass on the information to the decision-makers of the districts to make a faithful report of it to the consistory under penalty of a large fine and have ordered the patrols to circulate all night and to ruthlessly without distinction beat up all those who after

> eight o'clock in the evening would be in the streets without carrying lights with them and to lead them immediately to prison to account there for their conduct.
>
> Who will not welcome, along with sensible people and lovers of rest and public tranquility, that such a wise and well thought-out ordinance should be in force, so long as the city of Toulouse will stand, without departing from any of its articles. However, alas, it suffered the fate of many other regulations that had preceded it and that had been made for the same reason, it perished in the cradle and for the price of having been made public by its proclamation and the affliction it generated in all the streets we only learned that the regulation had been decided. (Barthès, *Lost Hours*, February 1765)

Smith is now in charge of two teenagers since Mr. Cook, Charles Townshend's trusted man, during one of the many trips he made to France on behalf of his master, accompanied Hew Scott to his older brother. As a result, the time devoted to teaching by Smith was increased, since the very younger man needed more individual lessons, leaving less room for leisure, writing, but also for boredom for his regular teacher.

It should be noted that the second half of 1764 was divided between trips and stays in Toulouse so that it is likely that it was the same accommodation, very inexpensive, near the current Jardin des Plantes, which was kept throughout the stay in Toulouse. The conditions were now much better: Smith suffered during the first months of his stay in Toulouse from a major difficulty in getting to know the important people of the city, but this was no longer the case now. The multiple journeys, the long stays in places of conviviality made Smith a true bourgeois of the South of France. His French has also improved considerably, to the point that he would be talking to his Parisian interlocutors who regularly remarked upon it, in a French rather coloured by a Southern accent. His French may also have been interlaced with some Occitan expressions. Occitan must have been all the easier and more familiar to Smith's ear since Latin was quite familiar to him. His Scottish origin also predisposed him to multilingualism.

Thus during his second stay which would last nearly ten months the conditions were completely different from those they had experienced during his first visit. We can also say that in the city of Toulouse, the climate of relations between the inhabitants, but also towards foreigners, had improved and calmed down.

The struggle against the envoy of the King, the Duke of Fitz-James, which had led the city to live in an atmosphere close to insurrection, was now in the past. The Parlement, following the royal decisions, had got back to work, trials were once again taking place and the spice money, indispensable in this city which lived at the rhythm of its justice, was circulating again, perhaps even more easily as it was necessary to make up for a certain delay in past procedures.

During these few years, French economic life experienced a certain upheaval, of which the liberalization edict on wheat may appear to have been an immediate cause since it avoided price cuts that were always harmful to producers.

The other great affair which for a few months had really poisoned relations, between the Toulousains themselves, and the Toulousains with the rest of the Kingdom had finally come to a conclusion which had far from unanimous support: the Calas affair. Toulousains, at least the most "enlightened" among them, were relieved that this burden no longer weighed on their shoulders: their city had appeared to be more turned towards the prejudices of the past than towards the Enlightenment of the future.

The very long letter from Abbé Colbert (from which we have already quoted passages p. XXX) written after the departure from Toulouse while the Grand Tour continued through Ferney and Paris demonstrates us the familiarity between the travellers and their Scottish guide:

> Finally I arrived in Montpellier, where I saw Mr. Ré who asked about your news in Greek verses, I answered him in Erse that you had the[theine[14]]. I also found Colonel Ross[15] there not doing very well [...]
>
> And you, Adam Smith, Glascow Philosopher, high-broad Ladys hero and idol, what are you doing, my dear friend? How do you govern the Duchess of Anville and Mad. de Boufflers, where your heart is always in love with Madame Nicol and with the attractions as apparent as hidden of this lady of Fife that you loved.
>
> Could I hear from you, my lord? If you do not want to write yourself because you are lazy or because you scribbled like a cat or what is worse, like a Duke, If Adam Smith does not want to write to me for the same reasons, If the honourable milord also keeps silent at least tell someone in your house

[14] Abbé Colbert introduced here a Gaelic word teine or theine meaning « fire ».

[15] http://www.historyofparliamentonline.org/volume/1754-1790/member/ross-charles-1729-97.

to ask me something on your part, I am responsible for knowing if you went to stay in Paris this winter or if you went to run the world, I promised to inform myself. […]

Would you like to hear the news from Toulouse? the Parlement has disbanded and everyone has returned home to the countryside. We see only Princes and Princesses who profit by coming to the waters, the English in Bagnères were extremely galant towards Mad. de Monaco, Barré is in Bagnères also, he wanted to pay court to this princess but she found him *withered*[16] or too aged..; The rest of the Irish clergy prays to God for your conversion, The French abbés who are people of good sense embarrass themselves very little whether you are a Saint or damned; they believe you to be with the devil, so stay there, it is your business; I am like them.

Doctor Quin presents you his best wishes and Mr Caraman wishes very much to be recalled to the memory of Mr Smith, He goes this winter in Paris, if you are there I will give him a letter of recommendation for you.

Farewell, my lord, remember the last words I said to you when I left and that my mother had recently written to me in a letter, my son, she said to me, if you did not fear God be at least afraid of the Syph. Send me a word, my lord, in English, French or prose and be persuaded of my tender friendship and respect.

Le Grand Vicaire Ecossais,

Done in Congregation on September 18, 1766[17]

Four years later, Abbé Colbert continued the chronicle of Toulouse:

Toulouse, 17 June 1770

My Lord Duke,

[…]

The Toulouse Parlement is as you left it, except that a new first president has come to replace Mr Bastard. He is as tormented as was his predecessor although a perfectly honest man, and very eloquent. Mr Rafin is his antagonist, Mr de Bonrepos his friend. The others are divided, each according to his taste or interests; but all believe they have an interest in having no leader and that business should go according to their whim and not according to fixed invariable principles. […]

I like good order and honest people that's why I'm strong for the first president.

[16] In English in the original.
[17] National Archives of Scotland, Call Number: GD224/2040/62/3.

> Abbé McCarthy[18] often asks me about you and Mr. Smith; The Marquis and Marquise de Mirepoix have asked me to remind you of them.[19]

These letters from Abbé Colbert to the Duke of Buccleuch refer to people met in Toulouse and illuminate the intellectual and social environment in which the two travellers evolved. Since the large Toulouse families were linked by a recurrent endogamy, it is clear that at the end of the Toulouse stay in 1765, Smith and his pupil were no longer in the conditions of social isolation from which they had suffered in spring 1764; they became appreciated guests on the banks of the Garonne. Count Jean-Pantaléon de Noé, for example, was the close relative of a Bonrepos, who entrusted him with delicate missions of a private nature, as attested by a letter dated March 29, 1765, in which the owner of the canal, having purchased a diamond of a very reasonable size from a Parisian jeweller, proof of his relative fortune, asked his relative the Marquis de Noé to pay the sum of money corresponding to the value of the stone. The sum seemed too large to be entrusted to ordinary mail.

Abbé Colbert's letters also refer to a certain Madame Nicole. This allusion was misinterpreted, notably by the biographer John Rae, but in the Toulouse context, the allusion is clear: Abbé Colbert refers to Madame Nicol, the wife of Capitoul Nicol. He was the most Anglophile and the most faithful to the King that one can imagine. It was in fact Capitoul Nicol who welcomed the Duke of Fitz-James to his Mont Blanc estate, in the present Croix Daurade district. It was around his estate that the events leading up to the Parlement's crisis in 1763 took place. One can add to this the fact that Nicol was one of the people who did not harass Calas, but rather took his defence; he is one Toulousain touched very early by the spirit of the Enlightenment. The estate, located a few kilometres from the city centre, offered Smith, thanks to the quality of its environment, an incomparable place for relaxation and leisure.

During his second stay, Smith also grew closer to the Riquet family, of the Bonrepos branch, represented by Jean-Gabriel-Amable de Riquet-Bonrepos, the grandson of the builder Pierre-Paul, but also of Victor Maurice Riquet-Caraman, great-grandson of Pierre-Paul and nephew of

[18] Father McCarthy belongs to the Irish College and Seminary in Toulouse. He was also Laurence Sterne's guide.

[19] Letter to the Young Duke, 17 June 1770, National Archives of Scotland, GD 224/30/11/6

the prosecutor of the Parlement of Toulouse, who were also joint owners and regular operators of the Canal du Languedoc.

If Smith, as has been said, was impressed by the work, considering both the importance of the architecture and the economic underpinnings, he was also impressed by the regularity of operation of this tool for the development of trade and the relative liberalization of traffic that it allowed:

> The canal of Languedoc cost the king of France and the province upwards of thirteen millions of livres, which (at twenty-eight livres the mark of silver, the value of French money in the end of the last century) amounted to upwards of nine hundred thousand pounds sterling. When that great work was finished, the most likely method, it was found, of keeping it in constant repair was to make a present of the tolls to Riquet the engineer, who planned and conducted the work. Those tolls constitute at present a very large estate to the different branches of the family of that gentleman, who have, therefore, a great interest to keep the work in constant repair. But had those toils been put under the management of commissioners, who had no such interest, they might perhaps have been dissipated in ornamental and unnecessary expences, while the most essential parts of the work were allowed to go to ruin. (WN, V.i.d p.726)

It can be noted first of all that Smith accepts once again the estimate of the cost of the canal found in the article "Languedoc" of the *Encyclopédie*:

> This canal cost about thirteen million of that time, which can be estimated at twenty-five million today, which were paid partly by the King and partly by the province of Languedoc. (Diderot et al. 1765, p. 274)

However, unlike the *Encyclopédie*, Smith refrains from discounting the sum and uses a conversion rate between livres tournois and pounds sterling which did not convince the Abbé Blavet who corrected the exchange rate to 950,000 pounds sterling, contrary to Blanqui's translation which has generally been used in citations here. With regard to the French translations of the two books, it has already been indicated that Abbé Morellet had begun a translation of the *WN* while he was enjoying the hospitality of Loménie de Brienne. A first anonymous translation was published in 1778 and that of Abbé Jean-Louis Blavet was first published as a serial in the *Journal de l'agriculture, du commerce, des arts et des finances* in 1779 and 1780, then published as a book in 1781, then reprinted several times in 1786, 1788, and 1800–1801 (revised and corrected edition). Translators in the eighteenth century took into account the sensitivity of the French authorities (hence certain cuts) and of their readers and did not hesitate to insert remarks such as "let us not forget that it is an Englishman who speaks" (Faccarello and Steiner 2002). This first complete and signed translation from the translator of the *WN* was transmitted to Smith by a common relationship. Smith's letter of thanks deserves to be quoted in full because it does justice to the author's alleged difficulties in French:

> Edinburgh, 23 July 1782
> Sir, my respectable friend, Mr Lumsden, did me the honour of handing me your letter with your excellent translation of my book in my last stay in London, where I was so busy with various matters, that I did not have the time or the leisure to thank you for the great favour, as well as for the honour you did me. I am charmed by this translation and you have done me the greatest service that can be rendered to an author, by making my book known to the nation of Europe whose taste and judgment I consider the most. I was very pleased with your translation of my first book; but I am even more pleased with the way you translated it. I can tell you, without flattery, that wherever I looked at it (since I left London only a few days ago, I still haven't had time to read it in its entirety), I found it, in every respect, perfectly equal to the original. A few days after I left London, I received a letter from a gentleman in Bordeaux. His name is Count Nortl and he is an infantry colonel in the service of France. He asks me that he has translated my book into French and that he intends to come to Scotland to submit his translation to my judgment before publishing it. I will write him in the next letter that I am so satisfied with yours, and that I personally have so much obligation to you, that I cannot encourage or favour any other. (Letter #218)[20]

Like the translation of the *TMS* by Eidous, the translation of the *WN* had been criticized in particular by Morellet, and Smith himself accompanied his compliments with some reservations, but with regard to the passage devoted to the Languedoc canal, it is more precise than that of Blanqui which is generally used. The compliment towards the person who transmitted the book to him should also be noted: Andrew Lumsden was Bonnie Prince Charlie's former private secretary, a Jacobite from an Episcopal family who participated in the 1745 insurrection before following the Young Pretender to Paris and Rome. He finally abandoned the

[20] The original is in French (Glasgow edition).

Prince in the 1770s to return to Britain, obtaining the King's pardon and returning to Edinburgh where he became a member of the Royal Society.

To go back to Smith's observations and Blavet's initiative in increasing the estimate of the cost of building the canal, it is unfortunate that we have, from the great economist who devoted Book II of the *WN* to questions of monetary depreciation, only a conversion based on the amount of money without any discounting. But Smith uses the example of the canal not to deal with money but to discuss what would be classed today as the theory of incentives, dear to the Toulouse School of Economics. The main reason for approving the solution adopted for the Languedoc Canal was his mistrust of the agency relationship ("management of commissioners" in English). Blavet renders the idea by speaking of administration by "clerks", that is according to the Dictionnaire de l'Académie, "one who is charged by another with some job, some function for which he must account", a term which in the eighteenth century, the dictionary adds, was used only among secretaries of State, or in Finance. Blanqui refers to it as "governed by commissioners". The term civil servant is perhaps the most appropriate today. For Smith, "if a canal is entrusted to officials, they might be less vigilant in maintaining it" because their remuneration would not depend on its navigability. This is not strictly speaking a mistrust of the role of the State but simply a problem of alignment of stakeholders' interests. Moreover a little further on in the same passage of Book V of the *WN*, Smith disapproves of the concession of roads to private interests because, unlike a canal, the lack of maintenance of a road does not prevent its use.

The *Encyclopédie* presents Pierre Paul Riquet as the "entrepreneur" behind the canal, probably the largest construction project of the eighteenth century. It is therefore tempting to reread Smith's two books by linking his conception of the contractor more closely to the time he spent with the canal managers. For the *TMS*, it is of course the additions in the last editions which will draw attention, as has been the case previously for the remarks on Calas. New developments regarding the entrepreneur can also be found in Part VI, The Character of Virtue, which complements the latest edition of the *TMS*. The Smithian studies of recent decades identify "three human types of behaviour described in the *TMS* that lead to distinguish three sorts of characters, which refer to three figures of entrepreneurs" (Leloup 2002, p. 76). Thus, "as early as Chap. 1 of part IV, of the *TMS*", the son of the poor man appears a frugal man who spends his life accumulating capital; then, in part VI, in an addendum to the last edition of 1790, the prudent man who guarantees the enrichment of the nation is revealed, while finally, still in the *TMS*, we get acquainted with the character of the ambitious man who will become, in the *WN*, the project maker, taking the lead in chimeric projects" (ibidem.). In Toulouse, Smith met two "entrepreneurs", embodying the two branches of the builder's family who were frequently praised in the *Encyclopédie*. Of course, this is not a variant of the "Chinese portrait", where a string of questions, such as "if I were an animal, a book, and so on," and their answers reveal the special features of a person, but some similitudes can be found between the entrepreneurs met in Toulouse and the characters portrayed by Smith. Thus Pierre-Paul Riquet, who was not an engineer but a collector of gabelles (salt taxes); he was rich, but this wealth was rather recent when he tries to convince Colbert, he can lead the construction of the canal, and this wealth was also a little suspect (Mukerji 2009). In addition, completing the construction of the canal and the improvements that would make it economically useful would mean incurring considerable debt.

Although it is not an absolute measure of wealth which is the characteristic of the characters defined by Smith, there are however many similarities between Pierre-Paul Riquet and the "son of the poor man":

> The poor man's son, whom heaven in its anger has visited with ambition, when he begins to look around him, admires the condition of the rich. He finds the cottage of his father too small for his accommodation, and fancies he should be lodged more at his ease in a palace. [....] He thinks if he had attained all these, he would sit still contentedly, and be quiet, enjoying himself in the thought of the happiness and tranquillity of his situation. He is enchanted with the distant idea of this felicity. It appears in his fancy like the life of some superior rank of beings, and, in order to arrive at it, he devotes himself for ever to the pursuit of wealth and greatness. (Smith, TMS, IV. 1.7, p. 181)

One may wonder whether it is not also appropriate to apply to him the disillusioned judgment that Smith reserves for the project maker in the *WN*. The latter, under the influence of his passions, is mistaken about the amount of expected profits he may expect. He is convinced, for example, that his far-reaching project will lead to a large profit and yet:

> The projectors, no doubt, had in their golden dreams the most distinct vision of this great profit. Upon their awaking, however, either at the end of their projects, or when they were no longer [467] able to carry them on,

> they very seldom, I believe, had the good fortune to find it*. (*WN*, [II. ii, p. 310)

Can the Comte de Caraman be placed in this category? During Smith's visit, Victor de Riquet, Count of Caraman, was prey to the "madness of the mulberry tree". The mulberry plantations which were to separate the canal lands from adjacent properties were to provide income for the owners and the state, by producing raw materials, in the shape of mulberry leaves, which were then lacking for silkworm production. But it was also a question of providing additional income to the lockkeepers and thus making them more attentive to their responsibilities. The project did not measure up to expectations and after a few years it was abandoned. The fertile imagination of the Count also led him to imagine a project to have the canal bought by the Languedoc Estates, thanks to a lottery which would compensate the owners. Perhaps he was considering reinvesting the money in other areas. Again these strategies did not receive Smith's approval: in the *WN*, since shortly afterwards he condemns lotteries:

> It seldom happens, however, that great fortunes are made even in great towns by any one regular, established, and well-known branch of business, but in consequence of a long life of industry, frugality, and attention. Sudden fortunes, indeed, are sometimes made in such places by what is called the trade of speculation. The speculative merchant exercises no one regular, established, or well-known branch of business. He is a corn merchant this year, and a wine merchant the next, and a sugar, tobacco, or tea merchant the year after. He enters into every trade when he foresees that it is likely to be more than commonly profitable, and he quits it when he foresees that its profits are likely to return to the level of other trades_ His profits and losses, therefore, can bear no regular proportion to those of any one established and wellknown branch of business. A bold adventurer may sometimes acquire a considerable fortune by two or three successful speculations; but he is just as likely to lose one by two or three unsuccessful ones. (WN, I.x.b, p. 13I)

Unlike this "audacious" figure, in the part added at the same time as the notes on the Calas trial, the figure of the "ideal entrepreneur" emerges in which one can perceive certain traits, good or bad, of Riquet de Bonrepos. He is a wise man, a prudent man who should seek tranquillity and must flee the artifices and splendours of worldly life:

> In the bottom of his heart he would prefer the undisturbed enjoyment of secure tranquillity, not only to all the vain splendour of successful ambition, but to the real and solid glory of performing the greatest and most magnanimous actions. (Smith, TMS, VI.i. 13, p. 2016)

As noted by S. Leloup, the entrepreneur emanates “a certain coldness or a lack of sensitivity” but he must also favour “the judgment of the man inside and not that of the man outside” (Leloup 2002, p. 77). The Bonrepos Estate, as presented by Smith to his students, corresponds well to the modest residence, permitting a comfortable but frugal lifestyle as well as a virtuous division between consumer goods and accumulated capital.

In 1765 in Toulouse, the income from the canal was almost at its maximum and gave the Riquet family a certain ease. Most of the wealthy families of Toulouse at the end of the eighteenth century divided their time between their hotels in the town centre, often close to the Parlement, and their country domains located in the hilly countryside of Toulouse. Jean-Gabriel Amable de Riquet was no exception. He also had a brilliant career in the Toulouse Parlement and, in 1737, married Catherine de Maupeou, from a family of jurists still famous in modern French history for their attempt to reform the Parlements, which took place after Smith’s stay.

The castle of Bonrepos became, following various developments which took place there, a place for both holidaying and display for the family. The family gladly acted as hosts for people passing through the city. Moreover, like many Toulouse noblemen of the time, Bonrepos was passionate about astronomy, he was aware of the latest techniques for exploring the universe through optical glasses. In this he joined his colleagues at the Academy, of which he himself was a member, Garipuy or Darquier de Pellepoix.

In this year and spring of 1765, Adam Smith and his noble companions were among the visitors received at the château by the great canal manager. The philosopher could thus observe, in addition to indulging a passion for astronomy that he shared, the relative modesty of the place. He could also probably admire an ingenious system of canals, in fact a set of model locks and diversion bays which was used, it seems, for the design and validation of the first building works on the canal. As described in the *TMS*, the Bonrepos estate corresponded well to the modest dwelling, and to the comfortable but frugal lifestyle of the wise entrepreneur. The simple country life of the castle of Bonrepos was certainly of great importance in forming the young Duke of Buccleuch's personality. Indeed, on his return to England and then to Scotland, the latter led a rather secluded life, far from the judgment of people from the outside and more turned towards the judgment of his inner man. The Duke did not exactly lead a secluded life but that of a prudent entrepreneur especially in the field of mines, lead mines in Scotland and coal mines in the Midlands. A further proof of this is that, back in Scotland, after becoming independent at his majority and the death of his stepfather Charles Townshend in 1767 following a disease as sudden as unexpected, the young Duke invested a large part of his fortune in the construction of canals not only in Scotland but also in England. But he was also tempted a few years after his return from Toulouse by the creation of the bank of Ayr, a speculative enterprise. This was the cause of great alarm, for he did not follow the purely "Toulouse" model of the wise and prudent entrepreneur, but joined what Adam Smith himself called the "project makers". Ambitious men who prefer external judgments to internal virtue. The result of this adventure, although beyond the strict framework of this book, was the resounding bankruptcy of the Bank of Ayr. The group of entrepreneurs, having preferred to invest the money collected, intended for long-term investments, in very short-term investments presenting important commercial risks, quickly found themselves short of cash. To exonerate the Duke from his responsibility in this financial adventure which had become quite classic in the world of speculative capital, Adam Smith used the argument of the "poor information" that the Duke had received and his ignorance of all the real speculative mechanics put in place by his partners, the moneymakers.

This point is not just anecdotal, since it allows a better understanding of the almost filial relationship that was born between a philosopher and an aristocrat on the banks of the Garonne. This relationship which lasted until Smith's death went far beyond the simple relationship of a disciple to his master. Indeed for the Duke, who had lost his father when he was young and who lost his stepfather when he was twenty-one years old, Adam Smith, himself childless, was a tutelary figure. The Duke, who was very much affected both materially and personally, renounced public life for a few months and owed his salvation only to the arguments devised by Adam Smith, which served to bail him out.

5.3 Toulouse Academy

In addition to the elites of the city of Toulouse, Smith frequented in this year 1765 the "Académie des Sciences, Inscriptions et Belles-Lettres", a showcase for society in the town. It was the city's flagship institution. It may have emerged from the previous "Société des Sciences", which itself was inspired by an Academy of Floral Games whose foundation dated back to 1323, but it remained nonetheless much more independent from power than all those which preceded it.

> Recorded by the Parlement on July 13, 1746, read solemnly in the inaugural session, the letters establishing a Royal Academy of Sciences Inscriptions and Belles-Lettres in Toulouse, the statutes and the list of academicians attached thereto were inscribed at the head of its registers. The statutes would confer a form novel in many respects compared to that of the former Society of Sciences.

It is more than likely that Smith, with his new acquaintances, not only frequented the meetings which were generally held on Thursday of each week, but that he also frequented the library of the institution even if, as we shall see, it was quite sparsely stocked for a man accustomed to visiting the library of the Edinburgh jurists or even the Poker Club, which already at the time gathered together the documents and publications of the whole of the very rich and eclectic English press.

Documentary proof was sought initially in the registers of the meetings for the year 1765. The records do not mention the presence of Adam Smith. However, by looking in more detail, it can be seen that there is only mention of visitors known to the assembly or of people who will join it in the near future, or who intervene during the presentation of briefs. However, the register often contains the additional indication "(...)" at the end of the list, which suggests certain other persons attended the debates by invitation. As there were no calls for interventions from the attendance, these people were present, but without taking part. This situation suited Smith, whose French was not yet perfect.

The description given by the Toulouse historian Michel Taillefer, specialist of the institution, also paints a picture which brings Smith closer to the assembly. Smith was a man who always remained modest in his behaviour, but who nonetheless was also a man of distinction who felt more at ease in a framework with strict norms than in the Parisian salons hosted by the salonnières, where a joyful disorder always reigned. If his intelligence and therefore his ability to adapt and listen worked wonders there, it was nonetheless a transition period for him. In Toulouse, a provincial city where life was somewhat monotonous and boring, fashionable salons were not yet available. The life of the Academy presented the modest pomp of scientific knowledge shared by men concerned with improving the techniques and economic conditions of the province:

> The general inventories of 1774 and 1793 provide numerous indications on the layout of the rooms devoted to academic exercises. The writer's desk contained a cabinet containing registers and archives, and the seals of the academy with its press; this seal had been made in 1746 by the engraver Simonin Ainé who also engraved the stamp of the company in 1751. Illuminated by a crystal chandelier and heated by an iron stove, the ordinary assembly hall was furnished with several tables covered with green carpets, armchairs and cane chairs. There is also a book cabinet, a second clock by Julien Le Roy[21] offered in 1748 by the Count of Caraman, a bell clock [...], physics instruments and some antiques. The walls, covered with Indian tapestry, were decorated with an etching by François Parmasse sent by Titon du Tillet in 1751, engravings on glass made by Jean Pierre de Puymaurin, silk or satin theses (not sure what a 'thèse' is in this context) dedicated to the company, and portraits of some of its members, Samedies, the Count of Caraman by Rivaltz,[22] Saint-Amand by Despax,[23] President Puivert, Mgr de Brienne by Fauré as well as the Abbé Héliot by Roque.
>
> Finally, the public meeting room, which was accessed by a monumental staircase and whose windows opened onto the two courtyards, was 54 feet long and 27 feet wide, furnished with chairs and benches, it was decorated with a bust of Fermat, a full size portrait of Louis XV in coronation robes by

[21] Julien Le Roy (1686–1759) was more than a watchmaker, he was a true scientist who restated some of Newton's theories. He was one of the artisans and creators of French haute horlogerie, greatly improving watchmaking techniques and partly catching up with the English, notably Graham. Julien Le Roy was the watchmaker for Louis XV and also arranged the installation of flat clocks with Lepaute.

[22] Antoine Rivaltz (1667–1735) was, essentially, the painter of the modern period of the city of Toulouse for whom he created many paintings and the great staircase of the Capitole. Rivaltz was a world-renowned artist who studied for many years in Rome before returning to his native city for his career.

[23] Jean-Baptiste Despax (1710–1773) was the son-in-law and disciple of Rivaltz, but his painting did not match that of his master.

> Roques after Varloo[24] and a life-size bust of Louis XVI set on a Pyrenean white marble stand, rendered in Carrara marble by François Lucas.[25] The room was sometimes lent to individuals who requested it; the opening of the Royal School of Surgery, whose amphitheatre was not finished, took place there on October 4, 1762. It offered the public events of the academy a prestigious setting which undoubtedly favoured its success. (Taillefer 1975, p. 220)

Nevertheless, the Academy was an important place of exchange for Smith now that he was well known to the principal Toulousains. Among them were the President of the Academy in 1763 none other than the Archbishop of Narbonne who presided over the Estates of 1764 in the presence of Smith and who had just left his post in Toulouse, Archbishop Dillon.

In 1764, the presidency was attributed to Count Victor-Maurice de Riquet-Caraman who was Jean-Amable Riquet de Bonrepos's cousin and who shared his time between Paris and Toulouse where he was very generous towards his Academy, perhaps with the aim of another even more prestigious election in Paris. That same year, the Baron Nicolas de Puymaurin, a rich industrialist from Toulouse who had made his fortune in drapery by establishing a cloth factory on his land in Carbonne, a town in the Pyrenees, became vice-president. Curiously enough, his fortune made him a great collector who encouraged and gathered a collection of works by the artists just mentioned, Antoine Rivalz and Jean-Baptiste Despax. He exhibited his collections in a private mansion which he had just acquired and which currently happens to be the Academy's headquarters. A new example of the benevolent entrepreneur for Smith and his two students, a person who devoted his fortune to the arts and not to ostentation, even if the two can go hand in hand.

Finally, in 1765, the president was Archbishop Charles-Étienne Loménie de Brienne, who continued his brilliant career, since it led him to the prestigious Académie Française in June 1770. It must be said that he was often in Paris, as has been mentioned, where he shone, among other

[24] François Lucas (1736–1813) was a sculptor born in Toulouse, who was considered the official successor of his teacher Pierre Rivalz as regards the interior design of chateaux and other sumptuous places in the city of Toulouse.

[25] It is probably Charles Amédée Philippe Van Loo (1719–1795) who was a French painter of the Enlightenment period. He spent much time in Italy, in Rome, and Turin. He continued his career in Paris where he became a professor at the École des Beaux-arts.

places, in the salons of Madame du Deffand and Mademoiselle de Lespinasse, with his two lifelong friends, Turgot and the Abbé Morellet whom Smith would soon meet.

In the same year 1765, the Academy also had a man of quality as vice president. This was François Garipuy from Toulouse (1711–1782). Garipuy was, as has been said, the creator of the Toulouse observatory. If he was a lawyer by training and profession, it was above all mathematics and scientific calculations that fascinated him. Thus he was the very type of scientist who put his passion at the service of science. He became inspector and director of public works in Carcassonne. Thus he would be led to draw up the plans of the Royal Canal of Languedoc with documents of a splendid precision, in which engineer's talents are displayed more than those of a lawyer.

Finally, passionate about this great work that was the canal, he bought a large property featuring many ponds and went to the Netherlands to study how to drain his land. He brought back some processes, but had to admit that a Toulouse man already had hydraulic machines of equal if not superior quality. One is reminded of the great mills of the Bazacle which so impressed Smith by their size.

Beyond the sessions, Adam Smith, as a good teacher, was also interested in the library of the Academy. It was, however, quite rare at the end of the eighteenth century to have large public libraries. Although books themselves were not rare, they were still confined to private libraries such as, for example, that of the Riquet family, of which an inventory[26] survives (in the absence of the library itself) or that of a Loménie de Brienne.

According to Michel Taillefer, the library of the Academy was made up of a few diverse but constantly growing works.

> The Toulouse company never had a well-defined policy in this field, nor even a librarian in post. The library therefore consisted of books randomly collected from acquisitions and donations, the latter being the most numerous by far. Its spending was limited to the purchase of a few books on astronomy (1750), botany (1758) and numismatics, collections from the Académie des Sciences, the Académie des Inscriptions and the Académie de Chirurgie de Paris, as well as subscriptions to the Journal des Savants and the Journal de Physique. It received free of charge the Gazette du

[26] The Riquet library inventory contains 1173 books AD 31- Riquet Background4 J.

> Commerce[27] and the Journal Encyclopédique[28] that Pierre-Rousseau sent there as a tribute that he believed he owed to a body that cultivated science and literature in his homeland. (Taillefer 1975, pp. 304–306)

In the absence of a large amount of reading material, however, Smith perhaps made contact for the first time with physiocratic thought. Indeed the courses that Smith gave before his departure from Glasgow, and in particular the last readings or conferences as they are reported, focused more and more on subjects close to the economic thinking of the future, on topics such as work or the circulation of money. Nevertheless, these later writings do not address the predominance of agriculture, nor the general economic picture that are the main themes of the "sect". Thus the long hours of reading on this new form of thinking must have influenced Smith in forming his opinion. All the more so since the documents he would have read or listened to are not as innovative in economic matters as the Parisian journal received by the Academy, the *Journal Encyclopédique*. The intellectual quality of the documents presented during these years in Toulouse was very uneven. If the submissions and observations presented by the group of astronomers present in the assembly were of good standing, it was not the same for others. The subjects were not very varied. They revolved around experiments in chemistry and mineral exploration. The most interesting of them dealt with Pyrenean explorations and metal discoveries. These texts gave birth to a mining and processing industry in many Pyrenean valleys, profoundly modifying the sociology of the inhabitants by the violent emergence of development in its most capitalist form. Finally, other documents submitted, also numerous, dealt more or less happily with the implementation of new agricultural processes and the improvement of production and cropping methods. More than Smith, it is the Duke, the largest landowner in Scotland, who would be able to

[27] *The Gazette du commerce* was a newspaper published twice a week. It appeared from January 1763 to 1783. It was the first newspaper that can be described as "economic" from the content of its articles. It would quickly become the official journal of the physiocrats, from the first issues, and through the participation of Dupont. The vast majority of articles were devoted either to agriculture and its improvement or to price calculations. The examples used in price calculations were almost invariably wheat and other maize or millet but also wheat from Turkey.

[28] It should be remembered that the *Edinburgh Gazette was* intended to be like the *Journal Encyclopédique*. This journal was the first on the continent to make a very positive criticism of the *Theory of Moral Sentiments* as early as 1760, helping to make Smith known in France and at the origin of the first translation of this work.

profit from these long hours of listening by transforming his family estate and making his training bear fruit.

5.4 And Toulouse Converted to Physiocracy

As has been pointed out, the Seven Years' War played a crucial role in the survival of the French monarchy and primarily in its survival economically. In 1759, Henri Bertin, born in Périgueux in 1720, lawyer, intendant of the Roussillon, of Lyon, then lieutenant-general of police of Paris accepted the office of controller-general of finances in 1759 on the grounds that France was then at war and that finances were easier in times of war since all expedients were then allowed. He left his post in December 1763, once peace had returned, to occupy a Secretariat of State whose multiple responsibilities made it an early and productive Ministry for Recovery. Bertin was one of the architects of an agricultural renaissance and it was under his leadership that the provincial intendants created fourteen provincial agricultural societies. While he was still Comptroller General of Finance, on May 27, 1763, under the influence of Vincent de Gournay (the Intendant of Commerce, who died in 1759) and Quesnay, he authorised the free movement of "grains, flours and vegetables throughout the Kingdom". Selling and purchasing operations were made more or less free. On July 19, 1764, a royal edict removed all obstacles to the grain and flour trade, with the exception of Paris and its hinterland. In addition, export and import were partially allowed. The preamble to the edict, written in part by Dupont de Nemours, who was then working with Turgot, is a true physiocratic profession of faith (see Charbit and Virmani 2002).

This victory of economic liberalism was variously welcomed by the Parlements responsible for registering the edict. Toulouse's Parlement stood out thanks to the letter it sent to the King to ask that the liberalization in process be further increased. The Parlement sent a letter of congratulations on August 11, 1764, in which it was written:

> We have seen more than once ploughmen, oppressed by the weight of the foodstuffs that the ban on exporting accumulated in their granaries, murmuring about the abundance of crops, blaming the earth for its fertility, and, in the powerlessness to pay their taxes and provide for the needs that money can satisfy, invoking scarcity to find in the misfortune of their fellow citizens the resource that arbitrary acts had taken away from them abroad. We have seen stealthy and clandestine permissions to export wheat, bought with credit or corruption, causing the most blatant and heinous abuses. (Le Trosne 1765)

Thus the Parlement criticized the negative effects of protectionism by relying on what economists call King's Law, according to which insufficient or excess supply produces on markets for agricultural products, whose demand is relatively stable, price variations that are much greater than the observed volume variations. A supply shortage causes prices to skyrocket, an excess of supply causes a significant price drop. Gregory King (1648–1712) was one of the first great economic statisticians of the modern world. His approach was continued by Charles Davenant (1656–1714) who formulated the relationship between price and quantity as follows: "We observe that a reduction of the harvest by one tenth is enough for the price to increase by three tenths." Smith quotes King twice and Davenant once, which is not surprising since the latter was rather mercantilist and Smith was not used to quoting authors whose ideas he did not share.

This position of August 1764 in favour of the freedom of agricultural trade was to become a constant of the interventions of the Parlement of Toulouse. It is all the more remarkable because "these truths and those derived from them were then clear and obvious only to seven or eight studious men", according to the judgment of Dupont de Nemours (1768, p. V).

> A host of prejudices based on an ignorant and barbaric policy, filled almost all heads. It was almost universally believed that a nation could raise its greatness only on the ruin of neighbouring nations: one fought, as we do today, with great blows of taxes, exclusions and prohibition; but what was worse, people believed they were acting positively, instead of starting to suspect, as now, that the evil of others does not cure ours, and that it could on the contrary aggravate it. (Ibidem., p. VI)

This early conversion of the Toulouse Parlement to physiocratic ideas is even more evident in the letter it addressed to the King in December 1768 "to thank him for the edict which allows the export of grains, and to ask him for the conservation of this law". It invokes the economic realities of the province, which it describes as follows:

> Most of the Languedoc, Sire, and the part of Guyenne that is entrusted to us, usually produce more grains than are needed for their consumption. The superfluous grains are necessarily, in these regions, the main, and almost the

only, object of trade. Is export prevented? Your Majesty sees the infallible consequence: more commerce, more traffic, more money.

The Parlement cites England as an example in support of its request:

The evidence of reasoning, the fatal and so long-tested consequences of prohibitions, the happy experience of a neighbouring nation, and now ours, all speak in favour of this beneficial policy, whose maintenance and continuation we urge.

And to conclude the Parlement pays a vibrant tribute to the physiocrats:

What presumption is still added to the strength of evidence, when we see the thousand times repeated praise given to this propitious law by these virtuous and enlightened citizens who, in recent years, have spread so much light on this important matter; who, full of zeal for their prince and for their country, dedicate their talents and their vigils to dispel destructive prejudices, to remove all doubts, all obstacles; to make the truths most useful for your glory triumph, Sire, for your power, and for the happiness of your subjects. (Ibidem.)

The Parlement tirelessly returned to the attack, as in 1770 in a ruling concerning the freedom of the grain trade transcribed on the records of the Parlement of June 13, 1770. The judgment in fact takes up the argument of the Attorney General Riquet de Bonrepos, who denounces the "prohibitive precautions[which] far from ensuring abundance in countries which fear lacking the species necessary for their consumption, on the contrary accelerate and ensure the scarcity which one would have liked to avoid". Riquet has no doubt about the cure: the only way to avoid famine is to facilitate the free movement of grains from one country to another, "and to remove any obstacles that might delay or cool the action of the trader".

This adherence by the Attorney General to physiocratic ideas is perhaps not unrelated to his interests as owner of the Languedoc Canal, who has everything to gain from the development of grain and wine exports to the northern provinces. In any case, *Les Ephémérides* reports prominently the decisions of the Parlement of Toulouse and even takes up the cause of the owner of the canal, attacked by Simon-Nicholas Henri Linguet (1736–1794).[29] Linguet had published in 1769 a work on navigable canals in which he questioned the usefulness of the Languedoc canal and its management, entrusted to the descendants of Riquet (Fig. 5.3).

After a few barbs launched against Corneille, guilty of having celebrated "the junction of the two seas executed under Louis XIV", Linguet attacked the "canal now all silted up which passes near Béziers". But it is especially in comparison with the royal canal of China that he writes:

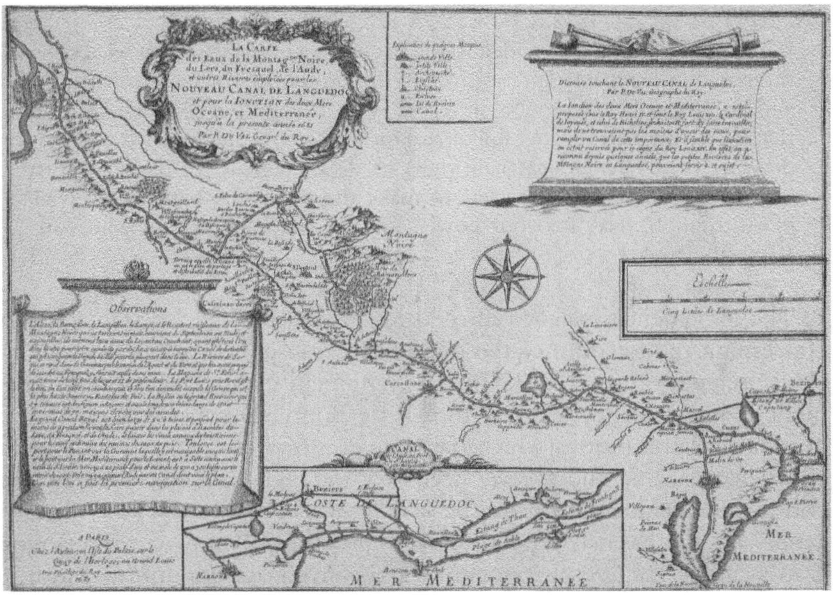

Fig. 5.3 Map of the Canal de Languedoc between Toulouse and Sète highlighting the water supply. (Source: Pierre Duval—Ville de Toulouse, Archives municipales, 20Fi167)

[29] Simon Nicolas Henri Linguet, a famous lawyer, had a stormy career. Expelled from the bar, feared polemicist, ardent and tireless journalist, refugee in Switzerland, Holland, England, Brussels, imprisoned for two years in the Bastille, resident at the court of Emperor Joseph of Austria, defender of the black population of Santo Domingo in the Constituent Assembly, he published more than fifty works and founded the Annales politiques, civiles et judiciaires (1777) (Source: https://sites.google.com/site/lavieremoise/biographies-remoises/biographies-remoises).

> What a difference between this miserable little canal of the Languedoc, of which we have made so much noise, and this prodigious royal canal, of which the missionaries who travelled it have given us the description! One is hidden in a corner of the Kingdom where it was built, and is used there only for the communication of two provinces, the other crosses the center of the empire over a length of two hundred leagues. It ends up in the capital: it enriches or relieves the most distant parts by the various branches that it throws there. The French take pride in one that is small, tight, shallow, already degraded and almost unusable, loaded with taxes, customs, which do not provide benefits to the state; all it did was make the entrepreneur rich. (Linguet 1769, pp. 42–43)

And after having pondered on whether the work was of real interest he added that Riquet's company would not have succeeded "if its protectors had not known how to interest the vanity of Louis XIV in the success of this company. It was the brilliance of the work, far more than its utility, that made it be adopted and succeed" (Ibidem., p. 75).

The Earl of Caraman certainly spoke out against his assertions. Linguet developed his criticism in a polemical piece, in which he attacked all those who had criticized his previous work. As far as the canal was concerned, he was concerned about the tolls set by a private operator who took into account only his own interest:

> I said that the canal was loaded with taxes and customs of all kinds. I did not mean by this revolving taxes for the benefit of the King, but tolls inconvenient to the navigators and ruinous for the trade. It does not matter to the person who pays which hand receives; all it is doing is costing him his money, and I have named 'customs fees' or 'taxes' all the operations whose purpose is to wrest money from him. However, the toll that is paid on the canal, so much per quintal (48.95 kg) of goods, is certainly of this kind. The tax on each lock opening is probably the same. Finally, everything that forms the income of the canal is the fruit of a tax, of a customs charge, since it is not a voluntary offering, but a tribute fixed by a tariff and payable under the authority. It seems that the Estates of the Languedoc have been hit, since they have considered acquiring ownership of their canal. If it were in their hands, they would undoubtedly rid it of these embarrassing obstacles: they would sacrifice their income for the public benefit, which individuals could not do, and it only be expected of them if they are awarded compensation commensurate with the harm they would receive from such a sacrifice. (Linguet 1770, p. 140)

Linguet's criticism is not lacking in relevance: if looked at from a modern perspective on the economy, we could say that the canal represents an example of externalities. The opening of markets through the canal provides multiple benefits to the province's economy beyond the revenues generated by the operators and the surpluses of the merchants who transport their goods through the canal. It is therefore logical that the monopoly price charged by operators reduces social welfare which could be increased by lower prices and higher traffic. This is clearly what the Estates had in mind in their attempt to purchase the channel by means of a lottery (see Cotte 2003).

But Linguet was firing on all cylinders and, relying on his visit to the canal in 1763–1764, therefore a year before Smith, he sustained his criticism of its poor state of maintenance with quite a bit of bad faith, for the Count of Caraman had documents delivered to him establishing the good maintenance of the canal in the 1760s; Linguet saw in it however proof that he had been ignored earlier. Linguet undoubtedly exaggerates and the canal cannot have been in such a bad state since the post boat between Toulouse and Agde was the usual conveyance for visitors of repute to Toulouse. It was the case of the Count of Provence (future Louis XVIII), for whom the Count of Caraman organized in June 1777 a sumptuous voyage on the canal, or of the Emperor of Austria Joseph II who was keen at the end of the same month to "see the various curious parts of this famous canal which joins the two seas. The idea is unique and the execution really worth seeing and admiring." For this he followed the route from Toulouse to Agde and Cette (Sète). He retained the idea that "The Languedoc is a superb province which possesses a really pleasant culture" (letter from Joseph II to his brother Leopold on July 3, 1777). As in the same letter Joseph II was very critical of the French navy, whose crews he pitied because of the "continuous damage that occurred to their ships", the sincerity of the compliments addressed to the canal can be relied on. But the most interesting thing, it seems, is the way *Les Epémérides* flew to the rescue of the canal. It must be said that the question of tolls was very debated and Dupont de Nemours had published a book on the issue.

Dupont de Nemours gave a lengthy account of Linguet's book and vigorously defended the Canal du Languedoc, obviously using information on the canal's development and maintenance received from the Count of Caraman, who was expressly mentioned (Dupont de Nemours 1768). Linguet did not admit defeat and answered Dupont de Nemours in a letter addressed in principle to the Count of Caraman but aimed at economists. Finally, Dupont wanted to have the last word in his account of Linguet's letters, published in 1770 in *Les Ephémérides*, where he ironizes about Linguet's errors.

Les Ephémérides of 1771 were to host a final exchange between the Count of Caraman and Dupont about the canal in which different systems of appropriation and management of the canal are examined. The question was thorny because if Pierre-Paul Riquet had played a great role in the construction, including financially, there was no doubt that the King and the Estates of the Languedoc had also contributed financially, so that the evaluation of the compensation which the descendants of Riquet could claim was not self-evident and it is not surprising that, in a period when economic calculations were the object of much attention, both the Count of Caraman and Dupont sought to measure the amount of the revenues of the canal and their effects on the economy of the Languedoc. Mirabeau wrote that "calculations are to economics what bones are to the human body. Without the calculations, [economics] would still be an indeterminate science, confused and open to error and prejudice everywhere" (Mirabeau, p. XX).

Dupont had made himself known as early as 1763 by publishing *The Wealth of the State*, so it is quite possible that he had been in contact with the Count of Caraman since that time. Dupont de Nemours was still defending the Riquet family during the Revolution if we believe the *Voyage à Rennes-le-Château*:

> When the ownership of the canal[30] by Caraman's family was challenged, the witty Mr. Dupont de Nemours wrote about this discussion: "Mr. Marragon proposes to break the contract determined a century ago, to the very noble advantage of the nation, to cover Riquet with glory and to ruin his family. He suggests you send the father to the Pantheon and the children to the hospital. (Labouisse Rochefort 1832, p. 173)

But the triumph of physiocracy was not limited to eminent personalities like the two branches of the Riquet family. In 1770, it was the Académie des Jeux Floraux that crowned an *Ode à l'économie politique* written by a lawyer in the Parlement, Guillaume Martel, which won him not only the

[30] In 1797, the deputy of the Aude, Marragon proposed the forfeiture of the Riquets' property, because of their emigration. He wanted the Canal du Languedoc transferred to the Republic.

prize for this category, but also meant he was "choisi comme mainteneur".[31] Born in Toulouse in 1731, Martel studied at the Collège de l'Esquille and followed a career at the bar. His poetic work seems to have been quite thin and he is not known for "economic works" except for the notes with which he accompanied his verses. He must have felt that economics was not necessarily very familiar to the "mainteneurs" of the Academy, for he accompanied his verses with an introduction in which he gave a presentation of economics which he characterized by the harmonization of interests:

> Although this *Ode* does not need notes to be heard, nevertheless the author believed that he should put before the eyes of the reader the first principles of economic science, a science which is nothing other than the evidence of natural law whose light leads men by the knowledge and consideration of their own respective interests, rights and duties to contribute to the universal good.

The notes themselves constitute a brief presentation of the most remarkable material and works, in his opinion: *La Physiocratie, or the natural constitution of the government most advantageous to mankind*, by the famous François Quesnay [1767/1768]; *La Philosophie rurale*, by M. de Mirabeau (1763), *L'Ordre naturel et essentiel des sociétés politiques* (1767) by M. de La Rivière; *Mémoire sur les effets de l'impôt indirect* de St Peravi. Undoubtedly Martel was well aware of the main members of the "sect of economists" and his entire *Ode* is intended to celebrate free trade.

Is it possible to go further and deduce from this convergence of Parlement, Estates of the Languedoc, and the Académie des Jeux Floraux during the 1760s that political economy had made many followers there? That it was the subject of discussions beyond economic considerations on harvests and food shortages and the free movement of foodstuffs? It is tempting to answer in the affirmative insofar as the *Ode* contains, beyond a celebration of "laisser faire, laisser passer", considerations on what will be called three decades later the "law of outlets" by the great French classical economist, Jean-Baptiste Say. In his *Treaty of Political Economy* of 1803 (Book I, Chapter XV) he maintains that production provides the means by which products are purchased. "We buy only with what we have

[31] "mainteneur" was the title given to the academicians members of the "Académie des Jeux floraux".

produced" (this idea is often expressed in the history of economic thought by a "shock formula"), "supply creates its own demand" (which is not literally in Say), and its corollary "money is only an instrument that facilitates trade. It is used for this in the same way as posters and notice sheets which, in a large city, bring together people who are concerned with doing business together" (Say 1803, pp. 152–153).

Among the "mainteneurs" who granted this distinction to Martel, and immediately welcomed him, we find a large number of parlementaires and jurists but also Cardinal Dillon and Archbishop Loménie de Brienne, so that the scope (eminence?) of the distinction granted to Martel should not be underestimated: it is really the Parlement and the Estates which voted for the ideas of economists.

The Ode did not go unnoticed by Pierre Rousseau, always attentive to Toulouse productions, who published large extracts, including notes. Another French expatriate, in his case in Germany, Nicolas Paradis de Tavannes, did the same thing in his newspaper published in Frankfurt, the length of title of which is inversely proportional to its durability (*Les Fastes du goût or Les Nouveautés du jour. Weekly sheet, which contains succinctly the details concerning in general the siences[sic], arts, industry, fashions, more particularly philosophy, mathematics, mechanics, history, criticism, morality, poetry, painting, sculpture, engraving, architecture, music, dance, economy, agriculture, finance, shows, and variations in clothing: all mixed with anecdotes, predictions, short poems, and witty comments*). Naturally *Les Ephémérides* hastened to rejoice in this success and reproduced most of the *Ode*.

5.5 Getting Ready for Departure

But it seems Smith was getting impatient. Indeed, he considered that the learning about provincial life was now achieved. As has been indicated, he adhered to the moral contract between Duke and tutor by staying in Toulouse during the apprenticeship phase.

On April 22, 1765, Lord Townshend, from his office as Chancellor of the Exchequer, responded favourably to Smith's request, probably penned by the Duke, to set out for his new destination. The relationship between Smith and the Duke, who was about to reach adulthood a few months later, was not simply that of tutor to student, for it was the Duke's fortune that financed the journey and it was he who managed the travel funds, as one can see from reading the receipts Smith gave the Duke in exchange for his allowance. Smith seems to have had a much more paternal role towards Hew, the young man who would face a tragic fate before the end of the journey.

Taking into account the delays in the mail (approximately three weeks between Toulouse and London) and imagining that the minister answered this request urgently, which is entirely possible, it can be surmised that as of the end of February Smith thought that his goal in Toulouse had been reached, that is to say only a few weeks after his return from the assembly of the Estates of Languedoc, new proof of the interest which he vouchsafed this institution. Smith wanted to wait until the end of the academic year so that the break would be clean, but on the other hand, he applied relatively early so as not to take the risk of having to spend another year in the Languedoc. He probably felt ready to discover Parisian life:

> London, 22th of April 1765. [...] In the next place, I am to acknowledge your extreme respect and confidence in leaving a point so agreeable to yourself to my final decision, for which further instance also of your good opinion I will make the most ample return I can to you, by conforming to your own plan and adding my wishes and advice upon the manner of exercising it.
>
> With respect to Tholouse, I consent to your leaving it when you please for the very reasons which you alleged, but when you settle at Paris, I must entreat you will still think the place of residence only changed and not your age, nor your plan of improvement, nor the propriety of continuing the same study and the same exercises.
>
> I have already desired Mr Guerchy to signify to the Ministry of France that you are removing to Paris. I have wrote to Lord Hertford and will write to Mr Hume. I wish you to fix upon a residence as near the best academy as you can, and at the same time as near to Lord Hertford that you may take your exercises early, without loss of time, and be with Lord Hartford as his business and your age admit.
>
> By Mr Hume's assistance you will have an easy access to men of letters, who in France are men of the world and are therefore the most useful society to you, who must be one and ought to be the other of these characters. The conversation of such men will familiarise subjects to you otherwise abstruse; it will give you the fruits without the labour of application; it will do more it will lead you to further application and insensibly form your mind to a preference of liberal men and a taste for elegant amusements. This habit once obtained, it is, believe me, my dear Lord, it is a security against every folly, every meanness, nay and every ennui in life.[...]
>
> If you go much into mixed company, as I suppose you will, let me warn you against any female attachment. Your rank and fortune will put women

> of subtle characters upon projects which you should not be the dupe of, for such connexions make a young man both ridiculous and unhappy. Gallantry is one thing, attachment is another; a young man should manifest spirit and decorum even in this part of his character, and preserve his minds entire and free in less as well as great things. (Letter from C. Townshend to the Duke, Ross 1974, 181–182)

While using the strong diplomatic language appropriate to his function, it remains quite clear that Townshend's authorization was indeed necessary in order to leave for Paris and thus continue the Grand Tour. The advice he gave is proof of his love for, and his ever renewed trust in, the young aristocrat. There seems to be no doubt that he wished to see him become a true statesman. To this effect, it almost seems that the latter should behave like a student of Smith's and like an "intern" for the English ambassador. David Hume's experience would allow him to enter Parisian salons. The minister thus admits to knowing the charming and affable side of the embassy secretary well, easily establishing contacts with the salonnières who provided the spice of life in Paris. He nevertheless did not admit to understanding much about all the philosophical subjects that were debated there. But he also conceded his poor knowledge of the city of Paris since he did not know where the main colleges and universities were located. His only desire was that the place of dwelling chosen be close to them, so he was well aware of the difference in size of the cities of Toulouse and the capital.

As has been mentioned, in recent months, life in Toulouse having become much more pleasant for Smith, the travellers were therefore not rushing to act following Townshend's agreement, a permission, and not an injunction. There was in any case during these few weeks a real change of attitude in Smith and his students, perhaps the celebrated Mrs Nicol, or more simply the invitations of Toulouse families including those from the Riquets. They now took part in a life full of invitations but also subject to the obligations that flowed from them. For example, one ought not to respond unfavourably to an invitation if one was at risk of offending one's friends or acquaintances. In any case, in August Smith was still in Toulouse and he wrote to his friend Hume:

> Toulouse, August 1765,
> My dear friend,

> Nothing has alarmed us more among all the latest extraordinary changes than Lord Hertford's departure from Paris and the appointment of Lord George Lennox[32] as Secretary of the British Embassy. Let me know immediately if you are leaving Paris yourself, and if an appropriate preparation has been made in your case. We propose to be ourselves in Paris at the beginning of November and it would be a great disappointment for the Duke of Buccleugh not to find you there.
>
> He has read almost all your work several times, and were it not for the salutary doctrine that I take care to inculcate in him, I fear he might risk adopting some of your wicked principles. You'll see he's improved a lot. (letter # 86)

In reality Lord Hertford had left Paris after two fruitful years at the embassy, however the appointment of his successor would only be known in France several months later, since it was only in November 1765 that the *Courrier D'Avignon* pointed out the hesitations surrounding his appointment.

In the letter quoted earlier, Smith indicates in fact that he intends to be in Paris in the first days of September, that is to leave Toulouse during the month of August, taking advantage of his return journey to make some stops, and perhaps he was even already thinking of a break in the Alps and a passage through Geneva. One can wonder about the arguments put forward vis-à-vis Hume. It was not in the name of their great friendship that he wanted to be present in Paris but so that Hume could comment on his essays, that the young aristocrats might have misunderstood. The pedagogical argument was not lacking in persuasiveness and an author is always flattered to be asked for explanations about his work, but just as Charles Townshend mentions in the previous letter, Smith certainly relied on Hume to introduce him to Parisian intellectuals.

Still not having left the delightful life available in Toulouse, its country resorts, its pleasant evenings, Hume's answer reached him at the end of September and left no doubt about the upheavals at the Paris Embassy that the changes in London would bring with them.

[32] John Charles Lennox (1735–1806) is better known as the Duke of Richmond; he was descended from a recognized son of King Charles II. He was ambassador in Paris and arrived in that city on November 11, 1765, and was presented to the King on the 17th of the same month.

From David Hume
Dear Smith
Paris, 5 [Sept.]1 1765
I regreat much I shall not see you. I have been looking for you every day these three Months. Your Satisfaction in your Pupil gives me equal Satisfaction. You must direct to me under the Title of Chargé des Affaires d'Angleterre de la Cour de France, without anything farther. I cannot by the Post enter into a Detail of our late strange Revolutions: But it is suspected, that the Accession of Mr Pit will be necessary to give Stability to the present Ministry. The Duke of Richmond coud not appoint me Secretary. He coud appoint none but his Brother, without affronting Sir Charles Bunbury, his Brother in law, who had been rejected by Lord Hertford. Yours most sincerely—David Hume. (Letter # 87)

David Hume's imminent anticipated departure would in fact be delayed, and he when he left he would take his new friend, Jean-Jacques Rousseau, for a brief and memorable English stay and the start of a quarrel that would long remain the height of literary bad faith. But this is another event of which Smith and his group knew nothing at that time. Convinced of Hume's having departed, Smith did not rush towards Paris and beyond the farewell visits of which there is no trace in the correspondence, for example in that of the Bonrepos, there remained however one last mission to accomplish.

5.5.1 *The Ramifications of the Douglas Case in France*

A very mysterious affair whose developments extended on both sides of the English Channel divided the Scottish aristocracy during the years 1760. This was the Douglas Case, which has already been mentioned. It was a simple question of succession, but it set French, Scottish, and English procedures against each other, while minds were still exercised by the Calas affair which was referred to, with positions reversed, by the defenders of the contested heir, whereas the plaintiffs were supported by authors of the Scottish Enlightenment. This matter was referred to Adam Smith before he left Scotland. In a letter dated September 13, 1763, David Hume informed Smith of his satisfaction with a new exhibit that had just been added to the submissions of the current trial. The situation was as follows: the trial of Archibald Stewart, born in Paris in 1748, Sir John Stewart (1687–1764), and Lady Jane Douglas (1698–1753) against the Duke of Hamilton. Lady Jane Douglas was the sister of Archibald Douglas, the first Duke of Douglas (1694–1761) from a line that had long oscillated between Jacobites and their adversaries. The Duke himself had sided with the Hanoverians in 1715 and fought alongside them. Later, his mind had become unreliable and he had killed one of his cousins in his castle, but given his rank he had not been judged and he had simply gone into exile in Holland to get himself forgotten somewhat. In 1745 his castle had been looted by the Jacobites. His younger sister, at twenty, had long been courted by Francis Scott, the second Duke of Buccleuch and the father of Smith's pupil. Several versions circulated regarding the reasons for the rupture. In one of them, it was a false break-up letter signed by the Duke of Buccleuch but written by the sister-in-law of the girl he was to marry shortly afterwards in April 1720 and who, to complicate the story, was also called Jane Douglas. In any case, the sequel would show that Jane was having trouble taking the plunge and getting married. Perhaps her brother's jealousy of her was a key to their sibling relations: hadn't the Duke killed a relative he was sheltering on the grounds that he had dishonoured his sister? Jane Douglas, who was financially dependent on her brother, refused many suitors in the following decades, until she fell in love with a penniless but very attractive nobleman, John Steuart of Grandtully. The youngest of a family of little nobility, he had ruined himself by speculating on Law's Mississippi Company and had entered the service of Charles XII of Sweden. After a turbulent courtship punctuated by a two-year breakup, Jane married her handsome colonel in 1746, without notifying her brother, whom she feared would oppose the match with all his might. She was forty-eight and the husband fifty-nine. Two years later, Lady Jane gave birth, according to her story, to very dissimilar "twins" Archibald and Soltho. Jane had long hidden her marriage from her brother, who disinherited her nephews when he learned of their existence. Despite her attempts, Lady Jane died in 1754 without being reconciled with her brother who had designated a collateral branch, the Hamilton family, as his heirs. Against all odds, her brother had finally married a cousin in 1758, Margaret Douglas de Maines (then Duchess of Douglas), but the couple had remained childless when the Duke died in 1761. The Duchess of Douglas had managed to convince her husband to rewrite his will and bequeathed her property to her nephew Archibald, who remained alone after Sholto's death (Fig. 5.4).

Upon the death of Lady Jane's brother, the Hamilton Branch, seeing the inheritance slipping away, sharpened its weapons and in 1762 registered a document listing charges against Lady Jane and reasons why

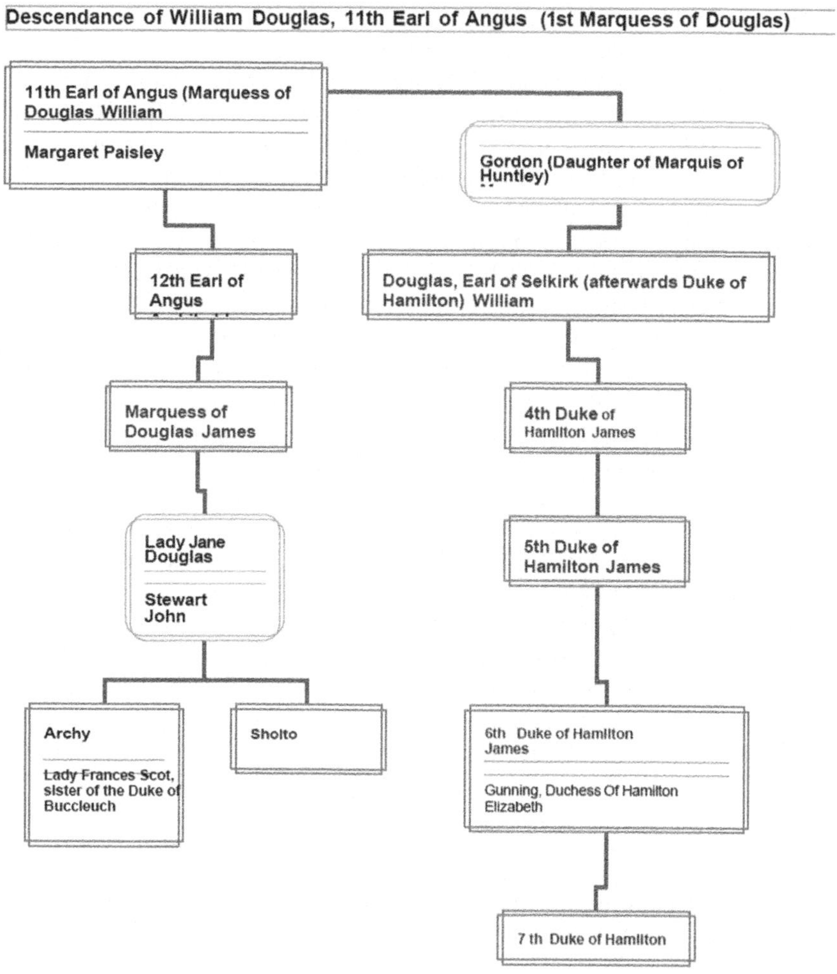

Fig. 5.4 Family tree of the Douglas cause

Archibald could not inherit. They contested Archibald's filiation on the basis of the age of the parents at his birth (they were sixty-two and fifty respectively). Although there were late births in the eighteenth century, the circumstances of the birth gave rise to suspicions of a subterfuge and the Scottish court ruled in favour of the plaintiffs in February 1767, however the House of Parliament reversed the decision in favour of the nephew two years later, in February 1769.

To understand how close this trial was to the Duke's family, it should be noted that his younger sister, Lady Frances Scott (1750–1817), married Archibald Douglas in 1783, allowing his fortune to remain in the clan. A form of undeclared endogamy that perpetuated the ancient clan formula. Seignelay Colbert de Castle-Hill had been "enlisted" by the Douglas clan's bloodhounds in their search for evidence of Lady Jane's pregnancy (De Le Torre, p. 124). Thus Smith's last known act in Toulouse was to solicit a testimony from the clergyman. In this testimony, which Smith took care to have registered before a Toulouse notary, the young abbé showed himself in favour of the Douglas family by indicating that nothing could call into question the natural presumptions.

Even if the opinions of Smith and the abbé on religion and its role in daily life will have been divergent throughout the Toulouse stay, one can judge this feeling in a letter: "The French abbés who are people of good sense embarrass themselves very little whether you are a saint or a damned person; they may believe you have gone to hell, but if you stay there, it is your business; I am like them."

This last act suggests that the two Scots whose paths would now separate nevertheless got along perfectly well. It is certain that Smith's influence was very important in the evolution of Colbert's thinking and one finds traces of this in his role at the head of the Haute-Guyenne Assembly.

On the other hand, the friendship between the two Scots did not change Smith's bad opinion of the Catholic religion.

> In the church of Rome, the industry and zeal of the inferior clergy is kept more alive by the powerful motive of self-interest, than perhaps in any established protestant church. The parochial clergy derive, many of them, a very considerable part of their subsistence from the voluntary oblations of the people; a source of revenue which confession gives them many opportunities of improving. The mendicant orders derive their whole subsistence from such oblations. It is with them, as with the hussars and light infantry of some armies; no plunder, no pay. The parochial clergy are like those teachers whose reward depends partly upon their salary, and partly upon the fees or honoraries which they get from their pupils, and these must always depend more or less upon their industry and reputation. The mendicant orders are like those teachers whose subsistence depends altogether upon their industry. They are obliged, therefore, to use every art which can animate the devotion of the common people. The establishment of the two great

mendicant orders of St. Dominick and St. Francis, it is observed by Machiavel, revived, in the thirteenth and fourteenth centuries, the languishing faith and devotion of the catholick church. In Roman catholick countries the spirit of devotion is supported altogether by the monks and by the poorer parochial clergy. The great dignitaries of the church, with all the accomplishments of gentlemen and men of the world, and sometimes with those of men of learning, are careful enough to maintain the necessary discipline over their inferiors, but seldom give themselves any trouble about the instruction of the people. (WN, V.i.g, p. 790)

The link between religious affiliation and literacy is still the subject of discussion, so Smith's judgment seems tainted by prejudice, but it is above all completely unfair to Loménie de Brienne who had spared no effort to develop elementary education, that of priests and that of young girls. But to return to the Douglas case, it shows once again that the protagonists are acting in a small world since Archibald was to marry Lady Frances Scott, the sister of the Duke. By early October 1765, Smith knew that David Hume, according to his information, had left Paris with Lord Hertford, the English ambassador. No one was expecting him in the capital and he could therefore take his time over the beginning of the second part of the journey.

Charles Townshend was perfectly satisfied with Smith's services and left to him certain initiatives on the organization of the rest of the stay. Smith then took the decision to leave Toulouse and go up not by the direct route through Limoges, nor by that of Bordeaux which he already knew, but to pass by Geneva where he hoped to greet one of his former students who had graduated in 1763 from the University of Glasgow, the young François-Louis Tronchin.

Beyond finding his former student, there was certainly also the desire to meet his family. The Tronchin family was one of the most influential families in Geneva. The father of the young François-Louis was Théodore Tronchin, a famous doctor who treated even better known patients, including the great Voltaire who resided at the Château de Ferney, a few leagues from the border. Thus with the relative comfort of a coach and horses, the small troop set off by a route that may well have taken them to Montpellier, Nîmes, Orange, Avignon, Montélimar, Vienna, Valence, Lyon, Meximieux, and Nantua. They thus left around October 10, 1765, by crossing the Rhône, they left the Languedoc never to return.

References

Braudel, Fernand. 1979. *Le temps du monde*. Paris: Gallimard.

Charbit, Yves & Arundhati Virmani. 2002. The Political Failure of an Economic Theory: Physiocracy, *Population*, Vol. 57, No. 6 (Nov. - Dec., 2002), pp. 855–883.

Cotte, Michel. 2003. *Le canal du Midi: merveille de l'Europe*. Paris: Belin-Herscher.

Diderot, Denis, et al. 1765. *Encyclopédie, ou Dictionnaire raisonné des sciences, des arts et des métiers, par une société de gens de lettres, Tome neuvieme, JU-MAM.*

Dupont de Nemours, Pierre. 1768. Avertissement in, *Éphémérides du citoyen, tome quatrième.*

Dutil, Léon. 1941. Un prélat d'Ancien Régime. Arthur-Richard Dillon, archevêque de Toulouse d'après des témoignages contemporains. In: *Annales du Midi: revue archéologique, historique et philologique de la France méridionale*, Tome 53, No. 209, pp. 51–77.

Dutil, Léon. 1911 *L'état économique du Languedoc à la fin de l'ancien régime (1750–1789)*. Paris: Hachette.

Faccarello, Gilbert & Philippe Steiner. 2002. *The diffusion of the Work of Adam Smith in the French Language: an Outline History*, Pickering & Chatte, pp. 2–10.

Graham, Henry Grey. 1901. *The Social Life of Scotland in the eighteenth century*. London: Adam & Charles Black.

Labouïsse-Rochefort, Auguste de. 1832. *Voyage à Rennes-les-bains*, avec des fac-simile. Paris: A. Désauges.

Leloup, Sandrine, 2002. Les entrepreneurs smithiens: le fils de l'homme pauvre, l'homme prudent et le faiseur de projets, *Cahiers d'économie Politique*, no. 42, pp. 75–87.

Le Trosne, Guillaume-François. 1765. *La Liberté du commerce des grains, toujours utile & jamais nuisible, par M. Le Trosne, avocat du roi au bailliage d'Orléans.* A Paris: [s.n.]. https://www.institutcoppet.org/liberte-commerce-grains-toujours-utile-jamais-nuisible/

Linguet, Simon-Nicolas-Henri, 1769. *Canaux navigables, ou développement des avantages qui résulteraient de l'éxécution de plusieurs projets en ce genre pour toute la France en général.* Amsterdam, [s.n.].

Linguet, Simon-Nicolas-Henri. 1770. *Lettres sur la théorie des loix civiles, &c. Ou l'on examine entr'autres choses s'il est bien vrai que les Anglois soient libres, & que les François doivent, ou imiter leurs opérations, ou porter envie à leur gouvernement.* A Amsterdam: [s.n.].

Martel, Philippe. 1979. Le XIIIe siècle: Ordre Chrétien et ordre monarchique, pp. 291–344, in *Histoire d'Occitanie*, sous la direction d'A. Armengaud, et R. Lafont. Paris: Hachette.

Minovez, Jean-Michel. 2012. *L'industrie invisible, Les draperies du Midi XVIIe-XXe siècles, Essai sur l'originalité d'une trajectoire*. Paris: Éditions du CNRS.

Mirabeau, Victor Riqueti (marquis de). 1763. *Philosophie rurale ou Économie générale et politiqu*had long hidden her marriage *e de l'agriculture*. Amsterdam: chez les Libraires associés.

Mukerji, Chandra. 2009. *Impossible engineering: technology and territoriality on the Canal du Midi*. Princeton: Princeton University Press.

Parlement de Toulouse. 1769. Lettre du Parlement de Toulouse, pour le remercier de l'édit qui permet l'exportation des grains, & lui demander la conservation de cette loi, in *Ephémérides*, tome quatrième, pp. 181–97.

Pélaquier, Elie, (Dir.), Atlas historique de la province de Languedoc, http://pierresvives.herault.fr/ressource/atlas-historique-de-la-province-de-languedoc-0 (01/07/2019).

Piganiol de la Force, Jean-Aymar. 1740. *Nouveau voyage de France*. Paris: T. Legras.

Richelieu, Louis-François-Armand de Vignerot Du Plessis (duc de). 1889. *Mémoires du maréchal duc de Richelieu, avec avant-propos et notes par m. Fs. Barrière*. Paris: Firmin-Didot.

Ross, Ian Simpson. 1974. Educating an Eighteenth-Century Duke, in Cant, Ronald Gordon & Barrow, Geoffrey Wallis Steuart, *The Scottish tradition essays in honour of Ronald Gordon Cant*. Edinburgh: Scottish Academic Press, 2001, pp. 178–197.

Say, Jean-Baptiste. 1803. *Traité d'économie politique ou Simple exposition*. Paris: Deterville.

Taillefer, Michel. 1975. *L'Académie des sciences, inscriptions et belles lettres au XVIIIe siècle*, PhD Toulouse.

Teisseyre-Sallmann, Line. 1995. *L'Industrie de la Soie en Bas Languedoc au XVII–XVIII° Siècles*. Paris: Éditions de l'École des Chartes.

Trouvé, Claude-Joseph. 1818. *Essai historique sur les Etats-Généraux de la province de Languedoc*. Paris: Firmin Didot.

Tooke, John Horne. 1813. *Memoirs of John Horne Tooke, interspersed with original documents* 1.1. London: Johnson.

Weir, David R. 1989. Tontines, Public Finance, and Revolution in France and England, 1688–1789, *The Journal of Economic History*, Vol. 49, No. 1 (Mar.), pp. 95–124.

Young, Arthur. 1793. *Travels during the years 1787, 1788 and 1789: undertaken more particularly with a view of ascertaining the cultivation, wealth, resources, and national prosperity, of the kingdom of France*. Dublin: Printed for R. Cross.

Conclusion

The pair of travellers had set off more than eighteen months previously, with a certain amount of comfort, on the roads of France. If Smith's goal was to improve his knowledge of the workings of the Kingdom of France, he had managed his affairs well, and his stay in Toulouse and more generally in Languedoc and Guyenne had proved very successful.

Following his first stay in Toulouse, he now understood the role of the capitouls and the power of municipal justice, and could also comprehend the functions of the Parlements of both city and province. Served by circumstances, he followed with interest the quarrel between the Duke of Fitz-James and the parlementaires. He understood the role in the Calas trial of the jurisdiction of Toulouse which had sent an elderly merchant to be tortured on a simple suspicion of murder, a decision based on the widespread representation in the Catholic population of the fanaticism attributed to Protestants, an interesting subject of reflection on the asymmetries of information.

Taking his explorations further, Adam Smith wanted to get to know French institutions. As a great theoretician of public life, he knew that for reasons linked to its history and the character of its populations, France presented diverse forms of organization. He then made sure he understood the two main modes of organization that regulated it: on the one hand, the organization of the Pays d'Etats, but also that of the so-called

A. Alcouffe, P. Massot-Bordenave, *Adam Smith in Toulouse and Occitania*, https://doi.org/10.1007/978-3-030-46578-0

Pays d'Election. To this end, he went to Bordeaux where he met the Duke of Richelieu who, as Voltaire put it, "acted like a small sovereign in his Kingdom".

Following these first explorations and after having discovered the Pyrenean resorts, the philosopher and his pupil went, towards the end of 1764, to the Languedoc Estates whose work they followed assiduously for more than two months.

Back in Toulouse, they met the most important families of the city. The main aim of these associations, which the Duke's father-in-law, the sponsor of the trip, ardently wished for, was to validate the knowledge acquired and to learn by example.

Through his improved practice of the French language and his good knowledge of customs and political institutions, the Duke was able to make new, albeit ephemeral, acquaintances. This apprenticeship was also a preparation for the remainder of the stay which was to continue in Paris.

His life in Toulouse was, in this sense, a period of intellectual preparation for his stay in Paris. If he chose Toulouse, it is because the city then possessed many assets: the second Parlement of France, situated in the centre of an important region, a university town, a merchant town, an industrial town, and a bourgeois town.

From Toulouse, Smith was easily able to radiate out because the city is ideally located along the Via Aquitania that runs between Narbonne and Bordeaux.

Political life, far from the French central government, was driven by many cases that had a national scope. The Calas affair was the perfect representation of this. The institutions, the organizations observed were diverse and multiple, the stock exchange, the society of the mills of Bazacle, the setting up of the cadastre, or the distribution of taxes by the Estates of Languedoc were all strong points which favourably impressed him.

But beyond that, Smith's main mission was educating a young Scottish aristocrat. As soon as he came of age, shortly after his return to the United Kingdom, the Duke became the sole manager of an immense agricultural estate. He may have been the largest landowner of the entire United Kingdom. It was therefore a question of educating a young landowner who needed to combine agricultural skills with economic knowledge and couldn't neglect the political role associated with land ownership.

On his return to Scotland, young Henry Scott, however, chose a life away from politics, preferring to develop his estate, with great success. His passion for agriculture was manifested in major improvements to his land.

A simple anecdote is enough to show the contribution made by his stay in Languedoc. In the absence of building stone, most of the cottages of the estate when he left were modest hovels of earth and various unsightly materials. On his return he set up a real construction programme in red or pink brick of large farms established following the Languedoc model. There are other equally significant examples derived from the journey: work to dry up the marshes, introduction of the cultivation of corn, wheat from India or Turkey according to the nomenclature of the time, on the difficult terrain of the Scottish Borders. On the other hand, he decided not to embrace a political career. Had he seen too much politics in France, did he think the period was unfavorable in view of changes in France?

As far as Smith was concerned, can one surmise that first part of his stay in France was capital for him? It is difficult to answer such a question because his correspondence from Languedoc is sparse and contains only very few personal notations. It is unlikely that a hypothetical travel diary, which generations of historians have searched for in vain, will be discovered. Certainly he took many notes of random encounters and adventures, which are scattered throughout his works following his return to his native land.

David Hume, Abbé Colbert, and Madame de Spens deplored the absence of letters from both teacher and student. Is this laziness or restraint? Smith was very concerned about the image he would leave of himself, and Charles Townshend warned against the effect on his reputation; it is understandable that a certain discretion had been required. It is certain, however, that events experienced during his journey served as illustrations both for the *Wealth of Nations* (*WN*) and for subsequent editions of *Theory of Moral Sentiments.*

However, Smith's desire was to present a clarified vision of society ruled by laws, such as those Newton found in the cosmos. While other travellers give a more or less vivid and pictorial account of their journey, he wished to remain in the heights of abstraction. Laurence Sterne who followed an almost identical itinerary to Smith's in the Languedoc gives an impressionist version of his very painful stay in Toulouse. Similarly, Arthur Young, who travelled throughout southern France a few years later, just before the French Revolution, gave us a detailed description. It is almost a manual of geography or economics, but also at times of ethnology.

For Smith, none of this, the *Wealth of Nations* is not a travel narrative, the few passages that refer to his experience are always drowned in a historical explanation or in a comparison with his country of origin. Unfortunately, the comparison is often unflattering for Languedoc or even for the France, but Smith's target readership is primarily in Great Britain.

No description of the Languedoc countryside, no interest in the inhabitants who populate the Pyrenean valleys, seen during stays in Bagnères-de-Bigorre. However, the latter are very typical and will elicit the multiple and questioning comments of a future economist such as Frédéric Le Play.

This discretion is in contrast to the much clearer judgements found on the Grand Tours in the *Wealth of Nations.*

> In England, it becomes every day more and more the custom to send young people to travel in foreign countries immediately upon their leaving school, and without sending them to any university. Our young people, it is said, generally return home much improved by their travels. A young man who goes abroad at seventeen or eighteen, and returns home at one and twenty, returns three or four years older than he was when he went abroad; and at that age it is very difficult not to improve a good deal in three or four years. In the course of his travels, he generally acquires some knowledge of one or two foreign languages; a knowledge, however, which is seldom sufficient to enable him either to speak or write them with propriety. In other respects he commonly returns home more conceited, more unprincipled, more dissipated, and more incapable of any serious application either to study or to business, then he could well have become in so short a time, had he lived at home.
>
> By travelling so very young, by spending in the most frivolous dissipation the most precious years of his life, at a distance from the inspection and controul of his parents and relations, every useful habit, which the earlier parts of his education might have had some tendency to form in him, instead of being rivetted and confirmed, is almost necessarily either weakened or effaced. Nothing but the discredit into which the universities are allowing themselves to fall, could ever have brought into repute so very absurd a practice as that of travelling at this early period of life• By sending his son abroad, a father delivers himself, at least for some time, from so disagreeable an object as that of a son unemployed, neglected, and going to ruin before his eyes. (*WN*, II, 774)

A firm statement from Smith, but does this condemnation also apply to his pupil and the Grand Tour he had organized for him? However, this is not the opinion of Charles Townshend, who closely monitored the evolution of his son-in-law throughout the journey, sent him regular advice for his studies, but also controlled the evolution of his work through the accounts that the Duke sent him and which unfortunately have not been found to date. Townshend's high praise shows that the Duke was a diligent student with a demanding teacher, as Smith used to be with his private students. We know indeed the programme of studies which he had specified for Thomas Fitzmaurice and of which he speaks at length in his correspondence with Fitzmaurice's father, Lord Shelburne.

The first winter that Thomas Fitzmaurice spent under Smith's supervision, he attended no less than six hours of classes daily, including two hours given by Smith, but Smith was often still chatting with his pupil alone for two more hours. To these eight hours of teaching, Thomas had to add "some personal reading every day and much more on Saturdays and Sundays when he has the most free time" (Letter # 29). In addition to the considerable workload imposed on his students, Smith was careful to establish a very close relationship with them, attaching as much importance to developing their character as to increasing their knowledge. The warmth of the subsequent exchanges between Thomas Fitzmaurice and his former teacher proves that this proximity was appreciated by his students.

Townshend, for his part, did not content himself with exchanges with Smith and his son-in-law in order to evaluate the benefits he derived from his Tour, but he gathered testimonies from acquaintances and third parties as he wrote to the Duke on October 16, 1766.

VIII

(London, 16 October 1766)

My very dear Lord,

Give me leave to begin my letter with expressing the real happiness which I feel upon your recovery: having suffer'd during your illness the utmost anxiety, which affection & esteem can create in the danger of a friend. It was some consolation in the midst of our solicitude, to receive from all orders of men, from strangers as well as acquaintance, at home & abroad, so universal a testimony to your conduct & character, and to find you established, as you are, in the judgment & respect of all men who have known or heard of you. I, who have known you from your earlier years, had no doubt of this, but it was a great satisfaction to see my prophecy proved & my opinion become general. You have now nothing to think of, but the care of your health, for you have secured the world, & added the best of characters to the most ample advantage of birth & fortune. (cf. Ross, pp. 195–196)

Townshend's subsequent activity as a large landowner confirms his satisfaction, although the Grand Tour came to a tragic end with Hew's death. Certainly his participation in the capital of Ayr Bank was unfortunate and forced Smith to conceive of an acrobatic bailout, but his management of his domains receives only praise from the historian Harry Bonnyman who devoted his thesis to him in 2004. The latter saw the management of the Buccleuch estate under the third Duke as an important example of "top-down improvement". Land ownership has played a decisive role in the transformation of agrarian organization and practice. The Duke saw much more in his lands than a purely economic entity. His strategy was not to maximize tenant farming in the short term, but rather to improve the estate in the long term, while expanding the moral, social, and political influence of the family (Bonnyman).

There is no doubt that Smith would have approved of the Duke's solicitude for his farmers. Thus Smith's condemnation of the Grand Tour did not reflect his and the Duke's experience, but no doubt what he had observed for other young nobles. Moreover the reasons which he put forward for the vogue of the Grand Tours are at the antipodes of Townshend's attitude, as Smith's concern towards his students had nothing to do with what was then practised in universities.

> Nothing but the discredit into which the universities are allowing themselves to fall, could ever have brought into repute so very absurd a practice as that of travelling at this early period of life. By sending his son abroad, a father delivers himself, at least for some time, from so disagreeable an object as that of a son unemployed, neglected, and going to ruin before his eyes. (WN, II, 774)

Finally, it was perhaps Smith the moralist who learned the most from his stay in Toulouse. This is what can be deduced from a letter to Hume, whose exact date is not known but the content of which suggests that it was written in late 1765 shortly before the departure from Toulouse. This was a reaction to Hume's announcement that Lord Hertford, the British ambassador, had just left Britain. Rather than following Lord Hertford to Ireland, Hume was seriously considering moving to Paris where he was celebrated and famous. Smith undertook to make him change his plans, using the following argument:

> Do not imagine that the great Princes and Ladies who want you to live with them make this proposal from real and sincere affection to you. They mean nothing but to gratify their own vanity by having an illustrious man in their house, and you would soon feel the want of that cordial and trusty affection which you enjoyed in the family of Lord and Lady Hertford, to whom I must beg to be remembered in the most dutiful and respectful manner. (Letter #88)

It can be presumed that these remarks apply to Smith's experiences and that he had not been fooled by the way he had been received by the aristocracy in Toulouse, Bordeaux or Montpellier.

References

Bonnyman, Brian. 2014. *The third Duke of Buccleuch and Adam Smith estate management and improvement in enlightenment Scotland*. Edinburgh: Edinburgh University Press.

Cant, Ronald Gordon & Barrow, Geoffrey Wallis Steuart. 2001. *The Scottish tradition essays in honour of Ronald Gordon Cant*. Edinburgh: Scottish Academic Press.

List of Unpublished Material

Letter from Abbé Colbert to David Hume, 4 March 1764. NLS MS 23154.34; RSE Hume Calendar Ref IV, 34;

Letter from Abbé Colbert to David Hume, 22 April 1764. NLS MS 23154.35; RSE Hume Calendar Ref IV, 35;

Letter from Abbé Colbert to David Hume, 28 February 1765. NLS MS 23154.36; RSE Hume Calendar Ref IV, 36.

Letter from Abbé Colbert to David Hume, 10 April 1765. NLS MS 23154.37; RSE Hume Calendar Ref IV, 37.

Letter from Abbé Colbert to the Young Duke, 18 September 1766, National Archives of Scotland, GD224/2040/62/3

Letter from Abbé Colbert to the Young Duke, 17 June 1770, National Archives of Scotland, GD 224/30/11/6

Letter from Madame de Spens to the Young Duke, 20 October 1764, National Archives of Scotland, NAS02023 GD22

A. Alcouffe, P. Massot-Bordenave, *Adam Smith in Toulouse and Occitania*, https://doi.org/10.1007/978-3-030-46578-0

Index[1]

[1] Note: Page numbers followed by 'n' refer to notes.

A. Alcouffe, P. Massot-Bordenave, *Adam Smith in Toulouse and Occitania*, https://doi.org/10.1007/978-3-030-46578-0

The manufacturer's authorised representative in the EU is Springer Nature Customer Service Centre GmbH, Europaplatz 3, 69115 Heidelberg, Germany. If you have any concerns regarding our products, please contact ProductSafety@springernature.com

Printed and bound by CPI Group (UK) Ltd, Croydon, CR0 4YY
30/09/2026
02225246-0002